Biocultural Approaches to the Emotions

Are emotions innate or learned? Are they the same everywhere, or culturally variable? Research on the emotions tends to be polarized between neo-Darwinian and culturalist perspectives. In this volume, biological and cultural anthropologists attempt to transcend the traditional oppositions, proposing various strategies for integrating biological and cultural approaches to the study of the emotions. They discuss a variety of fascinating ethnographic examples, covering topics that range from the effects of music to the relationships between emotion and respiration. The editor's introduction provides a lucid review of the state of the field.

Alexander Laban Hinton teaches in the Department of Anthropology at Rutgers University. He has done ethnographic research in Cambodia, specifically on the cultural origins of the Cambodian genocide, and has published a number of articles in scholarly journals.

Publications of the Society for Psychological Anthropology

Publications of the Society for Psychological Anthropology is a joint initiative of Cambridge University Press and the Society for Psychological Anthropology, a unit of the American Anthropological Association. The series has been established to publish books in psychological anthropology and related fields of cognitive anthropology, ethnopsychology, and cultural psychology. It includes works of original theory, empirical research, and edited collections that address current issues. The creation of this series reflects a renewed interest among culture theorists in ideas about the self, mind–body interaction, social cognition, mental models, processes of cultural acquisition, motivation and agency, gender. and emotions.

1 Roy G. D'Andrade and Claudia Strauss (eds.): *Human motives and cultural models*
2 Nancy Rosenberger (ed.): *Japanese sense of self*
3 Theodore Schwartz, Geoffrey M. White and Catherine A. Lutz (eds.): *New directions in psychological anthropology*
4 Barbara Diane Miller (ed.): *Sex and gender hierarchies*
5 Peter G. Stromberg: *Language and self-transformation*
6 Eleanor Hollenberg Chasdi (ed.): *Culture and human development*
7 Robert L. Winzeler: *Latah in Southeast Asia: the history and ethnography of a culture-bound syndrome*
8 John M. Ingham: *Psychological anthropology reconsidered*
9 Claudia Strauss and Naomi Quinn: *A cognitive theory of cultural meaning*

Biocultural approaches to the Emotions

Edited by

Alexander Laban Hinton

Department of Anthropology
Rutgers University

CAMBRIDGE
UNIVERSITY PRESS

PUBLISHED BY THE PRESS SYNDICATE FOR THE UNIVERSITY OF CAMBRIDGE
The Pitt Building, Trumpington Street, Cambridge, United Kingdom

CAMBRIDGE UNIVERSITY PRESS
The Edinburgh Building, Cambridge, CB2 2RU, UK
http://222.cup.cam.ac.uk
40 West 20th Street, New York, NY 10011-4211, USA
http://www.cup.org
10 Stamford Road, Oakleigh, Melbourne 3166, Australia

First published 1999

Printed in the United Kingdom at the University Press, Cambridge

Typeset in Times 10/12 pt [wv]

A catalogue record for this book is available from the British Library

Library of Congress cataloguing in publication data
Biocultural approaches to the emotions/edited by Alexander Laban Hinton.
p. cm. – (Publications of the Society for Psychological Anthropology)
ISBN 0 521 65211 1 (hardcover). – ISBN 0 521 65569 2 (pbk)
1. Ethnopsychology. 2. Emotions – Physiology. 3. Emotions – Social aspects. I. Hinton, Alexander Laban. II. Series.
GN502. B53 1999
155.8′2 – dc21 98-49769 CIP

ISBN 0 521 65211 1 hardback
ISBN 0 521 65569 2 paperback

Contents

Figures

Tables

Contributors

After receiving her Ph.D. in Anthropology at Columbia University, ESTE ARMSTRONG did her postdoc in Neuropathology at Albert Einstein College of Medicine. There she began using digital imaging techniques to clarify questions concerning the evolution of the human brain. She continued to work with those techniques at Louisiana State University Medical Center, at the Yakovlev Brain Collection (Armed Forces Institute of Pathology) and with Path-Info, a telepathology company. She is currently continuing her interest in the limbic system by working with an electronic security software development firm.

LEE BLONDER is an Associate Professor in the Department of Behavioral Science and the Stroke Program of the Sanders-Brown Center on Aging at the University of Kentucky. Her interests focus on brain mechanisms of emotion and communication and the behavioral effects of stroke.

JAMES S. CHISHOLM is an Associate Professor in the Department of Anatomy and Human Biology, University of Western Australia, Nedlands, WA. His research interests are at the intersection of psychological anthropology, human development, and evolutionary biology and ecology. His latest book, *Death, Hope, and Sex*, will be published next year by Cambridge University Press.

IAIN D. EDGEWATER formerly taught at Seattle University, and is a Ph.D. candidate in the Emory University Department of Anthropology. His primary academic interests are romantic relationships, urban northern Viet Nam, and applications of psychological anthropology in artificial intelligence research. He occasionally performs with Seattle area gamelans.

DAN FESSLER received his Ph.D. in Anthropology from the University of California, San Diego in 1995. He is assistant Professor of Anthropology at the University of California, Los Angeles.

ALEXANDER LABAN HINTON is an Assistant Professor in the Department of Sociology and Anthropology at Rutgers University, Newark, New Jersey. He conducted ethnographic fieldwork in Cambodia in 1994–5 and is currently completing a manuscript on the cultural origins of the Cambodian genocide. His articles have appeared in *American Anthropologist*, *Anthropology Today*, *American Ethnologist*, *The Journal of Asian Studies*, *Ethos*, and other journals.

CHARLES LAUGHLIN completed his Ph.D. at the University of Oregon in 1972 and is a Professor of Anthropology and Religion in the Department of Sociology and Anthropology, Carleton University, Ottawa K1S 5B6, Canada. He has done ethnographic fieldwork among the So of Northeastern Uganda, Tibetan lamas in Nepal, and the Navajo of the American Southwest. He is one of the co-founders of the school of neurobiological anthropology called ''biogenetic structuralism.''

MARGOT LYON is an anthropologist on the faculty of the Department of Archaeology and Anthropology of the Australian National University. Her recent work focuses primarily on the areas of emotion and social theory, and critical medical anthropology.

KEITH MCNEAL is a doctoral candidate in the Department of Anthropology at Emory University in Atlanta, Georgia. His interest in human emotion connects more broadly to primary concerns in psychological and psychoanalytic anthropology, ritual performance, and the cultural politics of religious self-transformation. He is currently conducting person-centered ethnographic research on race and ethnopsychiatry in Trinidad, West Indies. He has also completed coursework at the Emory Psychoanalytic Institute.

JASON THROOP is a graduate student in the Program for Psychocultural Studies and Medical Anthropology at the University of California, Los Angeles. His research has focused on exploring experiential, developmental, and transpersonal approaches to the study of emotions, self, and consciousness cross-culturally.

CAROL WORTHMAN is a biological anthropologist and human biologist who is Samuel Candler Dobbs Professor of Anthropology and Director of the Laboratory for Comparative Human Biology at Emory University. Her focus on the biocultural interface is reflected in comparative research on human development, reproductive ecology, and psychobiology in settings as diverse as inner city Atlanta, rural western North Carolina, northwestem Tibet, highland and coastal Papua New Guinea, and northwestern Botswana. Her further orientation to identification of determinants of differential well-being extends not only to physical but also to mental health.

Acknowledgments

This book has been in the making for quite some time, and I would like to acknowledge several individuals for their encouragement and help. Roy D'Andrade, who was the series editor for the PublicationS of the Society for Psychological Anthropology when this book was first submitted, expressed strong enthusiasm about it. His successor, Naomi Quinn, helped this book achieve its potential. I want to thank her for her insightful comments, efficiency, persistence, and energetic engagement. Similarly, the reviewers of the manuscript went beyond the call of duty in providing elaborate suggestions that greatly strengthened the volume and helped shape it into its current form. I also want to express my appreciation to Jessica Kuper and the editorial staff at Cambridge University Press for their commitment to and production of this volume. Ravensara Siobhán Travillian and Iain D. Edgewater diligently constructed the index. This book originated from a session that was sponsored by the Society for Psychological Anthropology at the 1993 American Anthropological Association meeting in Washington, DC. I would like to thank the contributors who showed patience during the time lag caused by my fieldwork in Cambodia and the long and thorough review process. Finally, I want to thank Nicole Cooley for her enthusiasm and help in making this book become a reality.

Introduction: Developing a biocultural approach to the emotions

Alexander Laban Hinton

> Biological scientists, and those whose interests center on natural selection and the evolution of species, tend to emphasize species universals in the emotion process, often to the exclusion of variability; in contrast, social scientists and those whose interests center on ontogenesis and learning tend to emphasize the role of society and culture in shaping the emotion process. How can we reconcile biological universals in emotion with sociocultural sources of variability? (Lazarus 1991:35)

> In fact, the habit of thinking about phylogeny and ontogeny as alternative processes whereby information enters the organism is the very frame on which our endless nature–nurture disputations are woven. Nativism and empiricism require each other as do warp and woof. What they share is the belief that information can preexist the processes that give rise to it. Yet information ''in the genes'' or ''in the environment'' is not biologically relevant until it participates in phenotypic processes. Once this happens, *it becomes meaningful in the organism only as it is constituted by its developmental system.* (Oyama 1985:13)

In the past few decades, academic interest in the emotions has undergone a dramatic resurgence in such fields as psychology, anthropology, biology, philosophy, history, women's studies, and sociology.[1] Unfortunately, debates over the emotions frequently lapse into nature/nurture dichotomies. On the one hand, universalists claim that the emotions are innate, biologically based states that are modified only slightly by culture. On the other hand, relativists claim that, while emotions may have a physiological basis, this biological component is insignificant when compared to the impact of cultural factors. This type of biology/culture opposition is firmly rooted in a Western intellectual tradition dating back to Aristotle's Four Causes and Cartesian Dualism (Bunge 1980; Oyama 1985). Thus, we find the study of the emotions dividing along the following axes (Lutz and White 1986; White 1993):

nature/nurture
universalism/relativism
materialism/idealism
positivism/interpretivism
individual/social
body/mind
reason/passion
rationalism/romanticism
biology/culture

Though most scholars will deny that they partake in these dualisms, related assumptions frequently seep into their work.

The essays in this volume seek to demonstrate ways in which it is possible to move beyond such "nature or nurture" dichotomies and develop approaches to the emotions that take account of both biological and cultural factors. Some of the authors propose theoretical innovations that accomplish this goal; others provide examples of how biocultural research on the emotions can proceed. This introduction is intended to situate these essays within the larger context of academic debates about the emotions. The first section describes four traditional approaches to the emotions. I then discuss some of the differences between the seemingly antithetical universalist and relativist perspectives on the emotions and assess the strengths and weaknesses of each stance. In the third part, I locate the essays in this book in relation to four theoretical approaches – biocultural synergy, embodiment, systems theory, and local biology – that make it possible for the different contributors to bridge the universalist/relativist, biology/culture, nature/nurture divides. I conclude by outlining seven steps researchers can take to develop a more integrated approach to the emotions.

Traditional approaches to the emotions

Although René Descartes (1649/1989) himself took a somewhat interactive stance toward the emotions, his separation of mind and body provided a dualistic model that served as the basis of much subsequent theorizing on subjects such as the emotions. At the turn of the twentieth century, for example, many scholars assumed that emotions were located in the body and conducted their research accordingly. While it is possible to divide up the genealogy of emotion theory in different ways, four influential traditions – evolutionary/ethological, physiological, psychodynamic, and cognitive – continue to influence scholars.[2] I will provide brief sketches of these traditions, though obviously I do not have space to pay adequate due to the complexities of each one.

Charles Darwin's (1872/1965) research on the emotional expressions of

Table 1 *Traditional approaches to the emotions*

Tradition	Seminal figure(s)	Theoretical emphasis on emotion
evolutionary/ethological	Darwin	adaptive responses, behavior
physiological	James, Cannon	bodily processes
psychodynamic	Freud	psychic conflict, unconscious
cognitive	Aristotle	conscious mental activity

humans and animals laid the foundation for the *evolutionary/ethological tradition.* From a Darwinian perspective, emotions are viewed as adaptive responses to recurrent environmental situations that are significant to an organism's well-being. On the one hand, the emotions prepare organisms to react to such events in ways that increase their chance for survival (e.g., attachment behaviors, the fight or flight response). On the other hand, emotions serve a communicative function by signaling intention to others. Darwin's research convinced him that emotional expressions are an index of biologically based and, at least initially, precognitive emotional states of mind. Ultimately, these states of mind are ''the direct result of the constitution of the nervous system, and have been from the first independent of the will'' (1872/1965:66).

A number of evolutionarily and ethologically oriented scholars have built upon Darwin's notion that the emotions are adaptive, psychobiological responses that can be observed from expression and behavior (e.g., Eibl-Eibesfeldt 1980; Ekman 1973, 1980, 1994; Izard 1971; Konner 1982; Lorenz 1966; Nesse 1990; Plutchik 1980, 1993; Tooby and Cosmides 1990). Drawing upon the work of Silvan Tompkins (1962, 1963), for example, Paul Ekman has conducted extensive research on human facial expression. He argues that, while culture and individual experience shape ''emblems,'' ''body manipulator actions,'' ''illustrators,'' ''display rules,'' coping strategies, and the appraisal process, emotions are nevertheless part of an evolved ''affect program'' that is ''set off'' in appropriate contexts (Ekman 1980). Ekman states, ''Innate factors play a role in accounting for both the characteristics shared by emotions and for those that distinguish one emotion from another. Emotions have evolved for their adaptive value in dealing with fundamental life tasks'' (Ekman 1994:17). To support this view, Ekman and his colleagues have gathered impressive evidence indicating that there are strong cross-cultural similarities in facial expression (Ekman 1973). As we shall see, despite his attempts to take cultural variation into account, Ekman's universalist leanings have made him a target for many constructionists.

While Darwin noted that the nervous system played an important role in generating emotion, William James and Walter Cannon were perhaps the two most seminal figures in establishing the *physiological tradition*. James (1884) argued that ''standard'' emotions arise from a person's perception of visceral disturbances: ''My thesis . . . is that the bodily changes follow directly the PERCEPTION of the exciting fact, and that our feeling of the same changes as they occur IS the emotion'' (1884:189–190). In other words, people feel sad because they cry; they don't cry because they are sad. Over thirty years later, Cannon (1927), drawing on his research on brain lesions and autonomic nervous system (ANS) impairment in animals, criticized James for overemphasizing the viscera. Instead, Cannon argued, the source of the emotions could be found in the brain in general, and in the thalamus in particular. Because the thalamus was ''not associated with cognitive consciousness,'' the discharge of thalamic neuronal impulses created the emotional ''sense of being seized, possessed, of being controlled by an outside force and made to act without weighing of the consequences'' (Cannon 1927:123–124). Despite this critique, it is crucial to recognize that James and Cannon share the assumption that emotions are located in the body. For scholars in the physiological tradition, the emotions can be understood best by examining biological processes.

The James–Cannon dispute has had ramifications both for theoretical debates and for research agendas within the physiological tradition.[3] On the one hand, ''neurophysiologists'' have followed Cannon in focusing their attention on the anatomical structures that underlie the emotions. James Papez (1937), for example, proposed that there exists an emotion circuit comprising the interconnections between the hypothalamus, anterior thalamus, cingulate gyrus, and hippocampus. As Keith McNeal describes in detail in his chapter (see also Armstrong and Laughlin and Throop, this volume), Paul MacLean (1949, 1973, 1993) named a modified version of the Papez circuit the ''limbic system,'' claiming that it was the primary anatomical system underlying the emotions. This concept guided much future research, though it has been critiqued in recent years (e.g., Armstrong and McNeal, this volume; LeDoux 1986). Nevertheless, limbic structures such as the amygdala have been shown to play a crucial role in the emotions (Aggleton and Mishkin 1986; Damasio 1994; LeDoux 1994, 1995). A great deal of neurophysiological research has followed Cannon (1927) and Kluver and Bucy (1937) in examining emotion processing in various brain areas by studying the effects of cortical lesions, tumors, strokes, and brain stimulation on animals and, when appropriate, on human beings (e.g., Damasio 1994; Davidson 1993; Heilman and Bowers 1990; Kolb and Taylor 1990; Heath 1986; Heller 1990; Kandel *et al.* 1991; Konner 1982; LeDoux 1986, 1995; Plutchik and Kellerman 1986; Pribram 1984; see also Blonder, this volume).

Other scholars in the physiological tradition, who are often referred to as ''psychophysiologists,'' have followed James in exploring the extent to which the emotions are differentiated by ANS activity. Much of this research has been centered around the "specificity debate," or whether or not various emotions can be distinguished by unique patterns of somatovisceral arousal (Cacioppo *et al.* 1993; Ekman and Davidson 1994; Papanicolaou 1989). On the one hand, many psychophysiologists often attempt to demonstrate specificity by comparing two or more emotions on the basis of such measures as: skin temperature, heart rate, respiration, finger temperature, skin conductance, facial temperature, blood pressure, body movement, and so on (e.g., Ax 1953; Funkenstein *et al.* 1954; Ekman *et al.* 1983; Levenson *et al.* 1990; Levenson *et al.* 1992; Zajonc *et al.* 1993). On the other side stand some psychophysiologists who argue that arousal is undifferentiated and, therefore, that emotion differentiation is primarily the result of cognitive appraisals (e.g., Mandler 1984; Schachter and Singer 1962). As we shall see, this latter perspective dovetails with the views of cultural reductionists.

Sigmund Freud is the founder of the *psychodynamic tradition*. Because Freud was primarily concerned with psychopathology, he tended to analyze particular emotions, especially anxiety, rather than developing a systematic theory of the emotions. Nevertheless, Freud made the key move of associating "affect" with dynamic unconscious processes. During the course of his research, Freud's ideas about the emotions passed through three phases (Rapaport 1953; see also Noy 1982). First, his "discharge theory" equated affect with an unconscious quantity of psychic energy or tension that gave rise to feelings as it increased, decreased, was displaced, and was discharged (Freud 1894/1962). In the second phase of his work on the emotions, Freud's "safety-valve" or "conflict theory" held that affect was one of the channels by which inhibited drive cathexes were released into consciousness and experienced as feelings (Freud 1900/1965, 1915/1957). And, third, Freud's "signal function theory" viewed affects as innate structures that were progressively "tamed" by the ego during development. Eventually, the mature ego became able to use affects as signals that provided it with information about the inner workings of the id, thus enabling the ego to respond accordingly (Freud 1923/1960, 1926/1959).

Despite lacking a comprehensive theory of the emotions, Freud's ideas about affect have stimulated a great deal of psychodynamically oriented work by ego psychologists (e.g., Fenichel 1945; Rapaport 1953), self-psychologists (e.g., Kohut 1977), psychoanalytic anthropologists (e.g., Lindholm 1982; Nuckolls 1996; Obeyesekere 1982; Paul 1990; Spiro 1984), and others (e.g., Marcuse 1962; Reich 1942; Sullivan 1953; see Greenberg 1993). Perhaps the most influential psychodynamic research on the emotions has been conducted by object relations theorists (e.g., Bowlby 1969, 1973; Chodorow 1978; Klein 1975; Kernberg 1982, 1990; Mahler 1968; Schore 1994; Winnicott 1965). These scholars have focused their attention on the role affect plays in mediating the relationship between the self and significant objects/others in the environment. In a recent formulation of this view, Otto Kernberg has argued that affects motivate and build upon a child's earliest experiences: "Affects link a series of undifferentiated self-object representations so that gradually a complex world of internalized object relations, some pleasurably tinged, others unpleasurably tinged, is constructed" (1982:907). Similarly, Noy (1982) has suggested that early development is highly contingent upon the ability of the caretakers to respond appropriately to a child's emotional signals. As a result of these object relations, a limited number of innate affect programs are gradually differentiated – physiologically, psychically, and conceptually – into more complex emotions (e.g., attachment into love, aggression into resentment and rage).

Finally, the origins of the *cognitive tradition* can be traced back to Aristotle's writings in the *Rhetoric*. While he acknowledged the existence of a physical component to the emotions, Aristotle placed primary importance upon cognitive beliefs and judgments. Thus, in order to analyze an emotion like anger, Aristotle states that "we must discover (1) what the state of mind of angry people is, (2) who the people are with whom they usually get angry, and (3) on what grounds they get angry with them . . . unless we know all three, we shall be unable to arouse anger in anyone" (Aristotle 1941:1380). Implicit within Aristotle's perspective is the view that the emotions are intentional acts (e.g., one becomes angry about something [external], such as being slighted), involve beliefs (e.g., one has a set of beliefs about honor and proper respect), are based upon evaluations (e.g., one becomes angry after making the judgment that one's honor has been slighted), implicate moral concerns (e.g., one becomes angry because of a violation of a code of honor), and are made within a social context (e.g., one becomes angry because a person of an inferior social station has made insulting remarks about one in front of one's peer group). This type of emphasis on conscious mental activity – intentionality, belief, evaluation, ethical judgment, and appraisal of the social context – is what differentiates a cognitive approach from the evolutionary/ethological, physiological, and/or psychodynamic traditions.

Although Aristotle's cognitively oriented ideas about the emotions influenced a number of subsequent philosophers (e.g., Spinoza 1677/1992; Hume 1739/1978; Brentano 1874/1971; Sartre 1939/1948; see Solomon 1993), not until the decline of radical behaviorism and the beginning of the cognitive revolution in the 1960s did work in the cognitive tradition greatly proliferate – so much so that there is now a journal entitled *Cognition & Emotion*. Contemporary research in the cognitive tradition is fairly diverse, as scholars have examined and debated such issues as: the extent to which arousal/feeling is involved in the emotions (Bedford 1962; Frijda 1986; Mandler 1984; Oatley and Johnson-Laird 1987; Perkins 1966; Schacter and Singer 1962), the role cognitive appraisal plays in emotion processing (Arnold 1960; Buck

1986; de Sousa 1987; Frijda 1986; Lazarus 1984, 1991; Lyons 1980; Smith and Ellsworth 1985; Zajonc 1984; see also McNeal, this volume), the structure of cognitive models of the emotions (Lakoff 1987; Kövecses 1990; Lutz 1988; Wierzbicka 1994), and the existence of "basic emotions" (Lutz 1988; Mesquita and Frijda 1992; Oatley and Johnson-Laird 1987; Russell 1991; Stein and Oatley 1992; Wierzbicka 1994). With regard to this last topic, the most radical school in the cognitive tradition is the "constructionists," a group that I will examine in the next section.

Biological and cultural reductionism

As noted at the beginning of this introduction, one of the most vexing and contentious debates in emotion theory revolves around the issue of the extent to which the emotions are universal or culturally relative. Many social constructionists, for instance, have sharply critiqued the essentialist, universalizing tendencies – that we might call "biological reductionism" – of the evolutionary/ethological, physiological, and psychodynamic traditions, which tend to be predicated upon the assumptions of Western folk psychology (e.g., Abu-Lughod and Lutz 1990; Geertz 1984; Gergen 1995; Lutz 1988; Lynch 1990a; Solomon 1984; White 1993; Wierzbicka 1994). Consider the following quotes:

> These powerful [thalamic] impulses originating in a region of the brain not associated with cognitive consciousness and arousing therefore in an obscure and unrelated manner the strong feelings of emotional excitement, explain the sense of being seized, possessed, of being controlled by an outside force and made to act without weighing of the consequences. (Cannon 1927:123–124)

> Because emotions can occur with a very rapid onset, through automatic appraisal, with little awareness, and with involuntary changes in expression and physiology (which I will describe), we often experience emotions as happening to us, not as chosen by us . . . I do not allow for nonbasic emotions. (Ekman 1994:17, 19)

For a constructionist (see Lynch 1990a:5), these passages reflect the Western folk psychological view that an emotion is passive (i.e., something "happening to us"), irrational (i.e., one is "seized, possessed, controlled by an outside force"), natural (i.e., adaptive responses rooted in "a region of the brain"), essential (i.e., a biological state or thing caused by "thalamic impulses" or "involuntary physiological changes"), subjectively felt (i.e., we have an introspective "sense" or "experience" of the emotion), and universal (i.e., since they are natural phenomena, emotions are "basic" – the same in all cultures). Constructionists value deconstructionism as a means of unpacking these underlying premises. Thus, Catherine Lutz (1988, 1990), drawing on Michel Foucault (1980), has argued that emotion discourse has political ramifications. In North America, women (and, sometimes, minority groups) are often associated with the emotional and therefore viewed as potentially irrational, antisocial, uncontrollable, and dangerous. This link leads to power inequalities, since it "legitimates the need for control . . . [and] vindicates the distinction between and hierarchy of men and women" (Lutz 1990:87). According to this perspective, women should remain in the controlled, private, passionate realm of the female domestic space, while men should work in the rational, public, male marketplace.

The social constructionist platform has been developed largely in contrast to such Western folk psychological views. According to constructionists, as opposed to being private, natural, essential things that are subjectively felt and universally experienced, emotions are cognitive appraisals that are made and acted upon within an interpersonal social context and on the basis of a culturally relative set of beliefs and values (e.g., Abu-Lughod 1986; Armon-Jones 1986; Averill 1980; Bedford 1962; Besnier 1995; Feld 1982; Geertz 1984; Grima 1992; Harré 1986; Lutz and Abu-Lughod 1990; Lynch 1990b; Mandler 1984; Markus and Kitayama 1994a; Myers 1986; Oatley 1993; Rosaldo 1980, 1984; Shweder 1994; Solomon 1984; White 1993; White and Kirkpatrick 1985; Wierzbicka 1994; Wikan 1990). To demonstrate this point, constructionists often focus on the distinct ways in which emotion terms are interpreted and used. Lutz (1988), for example, has argued that there is no English word which is equivalent to Ifaluk emotion terms like *song* (justifiable anger) and *fago* (compassion/love/sadness), and that only by examining the array of culture-specific meanings and contexts in which these words are embedded can one adequately comprehend them. *Fago* most often takes place in situations of neediness – when one encounters a person who is sick, dying, infantile, socially or physically uncomfortable, and/or without land, food, or kin. The emotion is interrelational (it references a link between two or more people), marks significant relationships (by a person's willingness to care for another), indexes hierarchical standing (by one's economic and social ability to *fago* another), involves a moral judgment (that another person is in need and should be helped), and initiates public action (helping another). Thus, while *fago* involves elements of what English speakers call "compassion, love, and sadness," none of these terms can adequately convey the meaning of the Ifaluk emotion. Lutz' perspective and opposition to biological reductionism is illustrated by the title of her ethnography, *Unnatural emotions: Everyday sentiments on a Micronesian atoll & their challenge to Western theory.*

How valid is the constructionist critique of the evolutionary/ethological, physiological, and psychodynamic traditions? On the one hand, constructionists have correctly pointed out that these approaches are often based upon Western folk psychology and fall into the trap of biological reductionism. By doing so, social constructionists have been able to move to the forefront a side of the emotions – their public, interpersonal, contextual, and cultural dimensions – that tended to be neglected by emotion theorists whose ideas were predicated on the aforementioned biases. Moreover, social constructionists have conducted valuable research enabling other scholars to make their theories more culturally sensitive. On the other hand, social constructionists have sometimes made their arguments against biological reductionists in an unnecessarily antagonistic and oversimplified manner (see Edgewater and Hinton, this volume). *To believe that the emotions have a partial physiological basis neither makes one a biological reductionist nor precludes taking cognitive and cultural factors into account.* In fact, ultimately very few people are total biological reductionists. While related assumptions sometimes slip into the work of scholars working in the evolutionary/ethological, physiological, and psychodynamic traditions, most of these individuals are open to exploring the cognitive dimensions of the emotions, particularly through the concept of sensory evaluation and processing (see McNeal, this volume). Some of them have developed complex, multifactorial theories that already take account of cognition and culture (e.g., Buck 1986; Changeux 1985; Damasio 1994; Fessler 1995; L. Hinton 1998; Konner 1982; Lazarus 1991; LeDoux 1994, 1995; Levy 1984; Noy 1982; Nuckolls 1996; Scherer 1984, 1994; Schore 1994; Worthman 1992; see also parts of Ekman and Davidson 1994). Even Paul Ekman, the frequent scapegoat of constructionists, has made a serious attempt to account for individual and cultural variation through his notions of "display rules," "emblems," "elicitors," "appraisal mechanisms," and so on. We find him acknowledging that "biology may only predispose the organism to acquire these associations [between facial movements and emotion] through common learning experiences" (1980:92) and that "there is considerable amplification and detailing through social learning" (1994:16). As opposed to simply attacking such scholars, constructionists should also note their qualifications, which provide a potential entrée for developing a more biocultural stance toward the emotions.

Finally, I should note that the constructionist approach also has its own pitfalls. First, the strongest form of constructionism makes essentialist assumptions of its own since it dismisses biology and maintains that "emotion is an irreducibly sociocultural product" (Armon-Jones 1986:37; see also Rosenberg 1990 and Hinton, this volume). This type of "cultural reductionism" is evident in statements such as the following:

> An emotion is not a feeling (or a set of feelings) but an *interpretation* . . . Anger is not just a physiological reaction *cum* sensation *plus* an interpretation, a cause and certain forms of behavior. It is *essentially* an interpretation . . . The strong version [of constructionism], which I support but am not arguing here, is that an understanding of the conceptual and learned appetitive functions of emotion is all that there is in identifying and distinguishing them from each other and from non-emotions . . . An

emotion is a system of concepts, beliefs, attitudes, and desires, virtually all of which are context-bound, historically developed, and culture specific. (Solomon 1984:248–249)

When constructionsts assert that the emotions are "about social life rather than internal states" (Abu-Lughod and Lutz 1990:1–2), they erroneously portray biology and culture as mutually exclusive and force themselves into an extreme position that denies any substantive role to the body in generating the emotions (Leavitt 1996; Lyon 1995; Perkins 1966). This position makes it difficult for scholars like Lutz (1988) to explain in a complex manner why emotions such as *fago* and *song* are often associated with bodily feeling (i.e., the Ifaluk notion of "our insides" [*niferash*]). The constructionists' anti-body bias is due both to their desire to critique biological reductionism and to their emphasis on language and discourse which, while important, ignores crucial non-verbal processes and behavior (Lyon 1995; Reddy 1997; Scherer 1994; see also Besnier 1990).

However, *cultural reductionism is neither a necessary entailment of taking a social constructionist stance nor entirely characteristic of most work in this tradition.* As Claire Armon-Jones (1986:38) has noted, a weaker version of constructionism exists which acknowledges that bodily feeling contributes to emotional experience. Even some of the scholars who espouse a strong version of constructionism sometimes make important, albeit brief, qualifications about their views: "the biological basis of human experience, including that termed emotional, is not denied here. Rather, the point has been to critique essentialism" (Lutz 1988:210); "emotional discourses . . . seem to have some affective content or effect . . . emotions are also framed in most contexts as experiences that involve the whole person, including the body" (Abu-Lughod and Lutz 1990:10, 12); and "Emotions, as moral appraisals, are grounded in the nature of our bodily selves, securing for them their bedrock commonsense character" (Lynch 1990a:14). Other constructionists provide a more explicit role for feeling in their models of emotion (e.g., Averill 1980; Desjarlais 1992; Edgewater, this volume; Heider 1991; Rosaldo 1980, 1984; Shweder 1994; Wierzbicka 1994). Michelle Rosaldo, for example, defines emotions as "thoughts somehow 'felt' in flushes, pulses, 'movements' of our livers, minds, hearts, stomachs, skin. They are *embodied* thoughts, thoughts seeped with the apprehension that 'I am involved' " (1984:143). As we shall see, such a conception of the emotions as self-implicating embodied thoughts provides an opening for the development of a biocultural approach.

Biocultural approaches to the emotions

Given that most scholars in the evolutionary/ethological, physiological, and psychodynamic traditions are willing to grant a role, sometimes an important

Table 2 *Biocultural approaches to the emotions*

Biocultural approach	Contributor	Theoretical emphasis on emotion
biocultural synergy	McNeal Armstrong Blonder	synergistic, co-constructing relationship/interaction between culture & biology
embodiment	Edgewater Lyon	interpenetration of physiological/ mental processes
systems theory	Hinton Laughlin & Throop	systemic relations, development, dialectical feedback between component dimensions of system
local biology	Worthman Fessler Chisholm	phenotypic development emergent and contingent on contextual/ cultural cues

one, to self-involving cognitive appraisals, and that many social constructionists acknowledge that bodily feeling is involved in the emotions, there is clearly a common ground upon which biological and cultural perspectives can meet. Obviously, it is perfectly legitimate for scholars to bracket another domain of analysis – assuming they acknowledge that they are doing so and do not deny the legitimacy of other approaches. The chapters in this volume, however, though varying in orientation, methods, and goals, all seek to move beyond "nature or nurture" dichotomies and examine this nexus between biology and culture, body and mind. At least four broad biocultural approaches to the emotions can be discerned in these essays: biocultural synergy, embodiment, systems theory, and local biology.[4]

Biocultural synergy.

Perhaps the most basic point scholars must recognize is that not only are biology and culture both crucial "ingredients" in phenotypic development, but they are also synergistically related (Gottlieb 1991; Laughlin *et al.* 1992; Oyama 1985; Plomin 1994; Plomin and Daniels 1987; Scarr and McCartney 1983). Therefore, words like "culturally/biologically predetermined," "innate," "nature," and "nurture" should be omitted from, or at least extremely well qualified in, our analyses. Changeux (1985), for example, has pointed out that while the general organizational features of the nervous system are preserved during development by a species-typical "genetic envelope" (i.e., one that establishes the properties and boundaries within which cell division, migration, and differentiation take place), this epigenetic process requires environmental cues to shape the form of synaptic connections. In other words, neural development is "experience expectant"

(Greenough *et al.* 1987) – the genetic envelope requires the environment to fill in the contents of the blank letter inside. Thus, even water fleas, which breed by parthenogenesis, produce genetically identical clones that are phenotypically different. "The number of cells and the major features of their connections do not vary, but there is a fluctuation, a 'graininess,' in the details of their branches and connections" (Changeux 1985:209). Biology and culture create what we might call a "mutual impress" in which each is transformed through its synergistic interactions with the other.

While all of the authors in this volume are committed to examining such biocultural synergy, some make it the focus of their chapters. Keith McNeal's chapter, "Affecting experience: Toward a biocultural model of human emotions," lays out a biocultural approach to the emotions that stresses biocultural synergy. Using a computer metaphor, McNeal notes that much of the confusion plaguing the study of the emotions has arisen because researchers choose to focus on different levels of analysis: psychobiologists tend to look at the "hardware" of the species-typical, neurophysiological processing of emotion, while constructionists analyze the culturally variable "software" of socially learned knowledge that mediates emotional appraisal. McNeal carefully describes contemporary neurophysiological, psychological, and cultural research on the emotions in order to establish the importance both of "taking biology seriously" and of "taking culture seriously." McNeal demonstrates that emotions have both universal and culturally variable components and that the conundrum of emotions can potentially be resolved if scholars recognize that the evaluation and experience of an emotion is always mediated by culture, but that the general features of cortical and subcortical emotional processing are panhuman. For McNeal, the emotions are synergistic phenomena since the emotional "hardware" always requires and is fundamentally "programmed"/shaped by the emotional "software" (i.e., culture, learning, experience) available within a particular socioecological *milieu.*

Este Armstrong's essay, "Making symbols meaningful: Human emotions and the limbic system," provides an example of the close dialectical relationship between culture and neurophysiology. Drawing on comparative research concerning the size of human and non-human primate brain structures, Armstrong points out that MacLean's model of the triune brain does not take account of the fact that the limbic system, like the cortex, expanded greatly during human brain evolution. This neural expansion, combined with a decrease of olfactory input into the emotion centers, facilitated a great increase in the interconnections between the cortex and the limbic system. As opposed to there being a distinct separation between the (cognitive/cultural) cortex and (emotional) limbic system activity, these two brain regions interact to produce emotion. In fact, the majority of information received by the limbic system has already been mediated by the brain systems responsible for symbolic meaning, thus allowing cultural rules and norms to shape emotional experience. Emotions are thus neither just ''internal states'' nor just ''cultural symbols,'' but phenomena that emerge from the synergistic interaction between biology and culture.

In her essay, ''Brain and emotion relations in culturally diverse populations,'' Lee Blonder notes the difficulties in examining the interrelationships between different levels of analysis. After reviewing the neuropsychological literature on verbal/non-verbal communication, mood, and arousal and illustrating some of the important ways in which the right hemisphere and the frontal lobes are implicated in generating the emotions, Blonder demonstrates that much of the research is hampered by ethnocentrism, methodological constraints, and insensitivity to cross-cultural variation. Likewise, ethnopsychological analyses have often been hampered by an erroneous assumption of language-emotion isomorphism (see also Laughlin and Throop, this volume, on this issue) and a general lack of sophistication about neurophysiology. While such obstacles foster the continued intransigence of nature–nurture, mind–body dualisms, scholars can begin to move beyond these dichotomies by examining the ways in which neurobiological factors interact with environmental inputs to produce phenomena like the emotions. Blonder suggests that one productive avenue of future biocultural research will be to conduct more in-depth studies of how cultural factors such as learning and memory impact upon the neuronal patterning associated with given emotions.

Embodiment. In the last twenty years, a number of scholars have critiqued the traditional biomedical view of the body as a fixed, material entity that is separate from mind. To escape this type of mind/body dualism, many of these researchers have proposed using various conceptions of ''embodiment'' (or roughly similar terms), an alternative notion that generally emphasizes the interpenetration of physiological and mental processes (Csordas 1994b; Featherstone *et al.* 1991; Lock 1993; Scheper-Hughes and Lock 1987; Strathern 1996). Sometimes the mind is portrayed as being infused by the body. In these accounts, the body may serve as a crucial metaphorical or metonymical basis for ''natural symbols'' (Douglas 1966, 1970; Needham 1973; V. Turner 1967) or cognitive and/or cultural models (Johnson 1987; Lakoff 1987; Shore 1996; Varela *et al.* 1991), as a ''social skin'' upon which self-identity is constructed (T. Turner 1980), and as a site at which power and control are exerted and upon which sociocultural norms and values are inscribed (Bourdieu 1977; Foucault 1977). Drawing on Marcel Mauss (1935/1973) and Maurice Merleau-Ponty (1946/1962), other scholars take a more phenomenological perspective on embodiment that sees the body as being infused with mind. Bodily perception, techniques/practices, anatomical parts, processes, and products provide the basis of ''being-in-the-world'' (Merleau-Ponty 1946/1962), the embodied grounding through which the world is experienced and understood (Csordas 1990, 1994a, 1994b; Lyon and Barbalet 1994). As indicated by the Rosaldo passage I quoted earlier, the emotions may be productively conceptualized as embodied since they simultaneously implicate body and mind (Lyon and Barbalet 1994; Scheper-Hughes and Lock 1987).

Several essays in this volume follow from this insight. For example, in her chapter entitled, ''Emotion and embodiment: The respiratory mediation of somatic and social processes,'' Margot Lyon argues that emotions are contextually embodied phenomena that have somatic, behavioral, interpretive, and communicative dimensions and that mediate an organism's relationship to its social environment. To demonstrate that emotions are embodied, Lyon examines how respiration, a bodily process central to emotion, is at once physiological and embedded in a social relational *milieu*. From her phenomenological perspective, Lyon views respiration, which is distinct in being under both autonomic and conscious control, as being part of the biocultural ''background of being'' out of which the emotions arise in given social situations. Human beings constantly breathe, but the pattern of their respiration – like that of facial expression, endocrine levels, and central and autonomic nervous system activity – varies depending on if a person is having a panic attack, fighting, meditating, singing, training, or engaging in a ritual activity. Respiratory patterns are an important part of the emotions generated in these social contexts. Overbreathing may therefore contribute to feelings of anxiety in a psychiatric ward or to emotional ecstasy in a religious ceremony. In order to adequately explain the emotions, Lyon argues, we must take account of how bodily processes like respiration are implicated in human interaction.

Iain Edgewater's essay, ''Music hath charms . . .: Fragments toward constructionist biocultural theory, with attention to the relationship of 'music' and 'emotion,''' examines the embodied relationship between music and emotional response. Edgewater describes contemporary neurophysiological research which supports the view that the emotions are generated in response to salient environmental stimuli. Other evidence suggests that music somehow ''hooks into'' this physiological capacity by creating a non-conscious ''suggestion of significance'' in individuals. Drawing on Foucault's (1977) notion of the ''microphysics of power,'' Edgewater's claims that this bodily capacity for musical processing is a potential site for the exertion of power, since the general arousal effect can be selectively exploited to strengthen and reproduce dominant cultural structures, ideologies, and practices. Thus, instrumental music played at a religious congregation may facilitate one's feeling of communion with God; rock music may promote a feeling of solidarity among left-wing radicals; a national anthem may contribute to patriotic feelings; and a television jingle may increase one's desire for ''sinfully delicious'' desserts. In such situations, the bodily effects of music enable people, groups, and/or institutions to exert power over others. Edgewater uses this argument about the biocultural aspects of music and emotion to indicate how a constructionist stance can be developed by using – not opposing – biological research.

Systems theory

Systems theorists (e.g., von Bertalanffy 1968; Bateson 1972; Oyama 1985) have argued that many phenomena can be productively examined as systems that are comprised of component parts, which are linked by bidirectional feedback loops. (Each of the component parts, in turn, may itself be analyzed as a system composed of its own elements – e.g., moving from an examination of the parts of the emotion system to an examination of the parts of the limbic system.) None of the components is sufficient to fully account for the emotion system. Unfortunately, researchers working on a given level of analysis sometimes assume their partial explanation is a complete one. The result is the type of ''intellectual metonymy'' (Hinton, this volume) that has frequently hampered the study of emotion: cultural reductionists claim that emotions can be understood best in terms of the cultural system; biological reductionists assert that evolutionary, psychodynamic, and/or physiological factors have by far the most explanatory weight. From a systems theory perspective, biology and culture are two distinct, yet highly interrelated components of a larger emotion system.

Some systems theorists have taken what might be called a ''componential approach'' to the emotions (e.g., Buck 1986; Frijda 1986; Lazarus 1991; Mesquita and Frijda 1992; Ortony and Turner 1990; Perkins 1966; Scherer 1984, 1994; Shweder 1993, 1994). These scholars examine the generation of the emotions at a given moment in time as a process composed of various components. Klaus Scherer (1994:297), for example, suggests that an emotion can be broken down into the following parts, each of which has an adaptive function: cognitive stimulus processing (evaluation of environment), neurophysiological processes (system regulation), motivation and behavior tendencies (preparation of action), motor expression (communication of intention), and subjective feeling states (reflection and monitoring). Such componential accounts often remain agnostic about the existence of ''basic emotions,'' claiming that one must first conduct extensive research on the universality or relativity of the component parts. Thus, Richard Shweder (1993, 1994) has argued that, in order to avoid the projection of a researcher's ethnocentric assumptions onto indigenous conceptions of emotions, scholars must ''decompose the emotions (and the languages of the emotions) into constituent narrative slots . . . environmental determinants, somatic phenomenology, affective phenomenology, self-appraisal, social appraisal, self-management strategy, and communication codes'' (1993:428). Synthesizing the work of such componentially oriented scholars, Batja Mesquita and Nico Frijda (1992) have proposed that the cultural similarity and difference of emotional experience be assessed using the following list of components: antecedent events, event coding, appraisal, physiological reaction patterns, action readiness, emotional behavior, and regulation.

While componential frameworks often note the importance of ontogeny, other systems theorists have been more explicitly concerned with taking a ''dynamic, developmental systems approach'' in which emotion systems are viewed as being transformed over time through the dialectical feedback of their component parts. The action of dialectical feedback has been illustrated in embryological development (Changeux 1985; Edelman 1989). Within the ''embryo system,'' cells undergo a process of epigenesis that is regulated by their environmental interactions. ''The rules of interaction are laid down by the exchanges of signals between cells and, more particularly, by the relationships between intercellular signaling and the position of the cell in the embryo. The genes of each embryonic cell no longer constitute independent units. The communication network established between the cells continuously coordinates their expression'' (Changeux 1985:192). In other words, ''place-dependent'' cellular interactions influence gene expression and vice versa (Edelman 1989). Whereas previously this epigenetic process was thought to be ''genetically determined,'' we can now see that dialectical feedback takes place (albeit sometimes within a highly constrained genetic envelope) all the way down to the level of the gene. ''The major theoretical point is that the genes are part of the developmental system in the same sense as other components (cells, tissue, organism), so genes must be susceptible to influence from other levels during the process of individual development'' (Gottlieb 1991:9).

The aforementioned insights regarding the reciprocal interaction taking place between the gene and the environment open up the possibility of reconceptualizing our understanding of biology and culture in a more radical fashion. To do so, the system must be viewed from a diachronic perspective (see Hinton, Laughlin and Throop, McNeal, and Worthman, this volume). As opposed to there being a pre-existing code which determines phenotypic outcome, the notion of ''developmental systems'' is predicated on the assumption that a variety of inputs interact to probabilistically influence phenotypic outcome (Campos *et al.* 1996; Fogel and Thelen 1987; Oyama 1985). At any given point in developmental time, the past history of these outcomes combines with contemporaneously existing (and synergistically related) inputs to produce the next contingent stage of phenotypic development. From this perspective, the notion of genotypic ''determinism'' loses meaning. Beginning at conception, genes interact with the environment to produce phenotypic outcomes that progressively change over time. These historically contingent developmental systems are constrained by genetic envelopes that are themselves sometimes being altered in this interactional process. ''What shapes species-typical characters is not formative powers but a developmental system, much of which is bequeathed to offspring by parents and/or arranged by the developing organism itself'' (Oyama 1985:123).[5]

Applying this perspective to emotion, Charles Laughlin and Jason Throop's essay, ''Emotion: A view from biogenetic structuralism,'' explains how the development of neural structures, or ''neurognosis,'' takes place through a process of ''entrainment'' (i.e., the interconnections of dendritic, axomic, synaptic, and endocrinological pathways) as neural networks are formed within the parameters of the genetic envelope. Laughlin and Throop argue that emotional experience arises from the simultaneous activation of given neural networks, a process that is now commonly known as ''parallel distributed processing'' (see also Armstrong and Blonder, this volume). Specifically, emotions are generated out of the complex interaction between neural networks linking the prefrontal cortex, the sensory and association cortex, and subcortical tissues (i.e., the limbic system, thalamus, hypothalamus, and hippocampus). Combining MacLean's model of the triune brain with Gellhorn's model of the ''ergotropic'' and ''trophotropic'' systems, Laughlin and Throop delineate six types of neurocognitive operations that, in part or in whole, contribute to what an individual and/or a culture (re)conceptualizes as an emotion in given contexts. Such situationally ''entrained'' neural networks are analogous to a dynamic, developmental emotion system. In addition to specifying the synchronic dimensions of the emotion system, biogenetic structuralism also takes account of the process by which given emotional systems – or ''neurognostic entrainments'' to use Laughlin and Throop's term – develop over ontogenetic time (i.e., as they are ''entrained'' and ''tuned'' in an increasingly regularized manner).

Similarly, in my essay in this volume, ''Outline of a bioculturally based, 'processual' approach to the emotions,'' I argue that scholars can productively examine the emotions in terms of the ''feedback'' between these different analytical levels of the hierarchically organized system. While lower levels serve in part as an underpinning for higher levels, the latter have emergent properties which preclude their being reduced to the former. Each level of organization operates in terms of the principles that are internally generated yet embody properties of the system as a whole. Thus, emotion can be likened to weather. Snow, for examplc, arises from an emergent ''coherence'' between wind velocity, temperature, humidity, and barometric pressure (Kagan 1978). Similarly, I argue that an emotion can be said to emerge from the dynamic systemic interaction between biological processes, environmental cues, and cognitive evaluations. Instead of reifying this emergent state, however, we must recognize that it may change through developmental time. I note that an attachment system emerges in children at an extremely young age (Bowlby 1969). While this contingent developmental system arises from the "coherence" of physiological processes, individual experience, and environmental factors at a given time, the system is likely to be transformed into qualitatively different manifestations (e.g., what we call "love" and the Japanese call *amae*) during ontogeny. To understand the developmental complexities of such phenomena, scholars need to focus on the discrete process(es) by which these phenomena are generated both synchronically and diachronically; in other words, researchers must look at the processual and emergent aspects of the dynamic, developmental system.[6]

Local biology

While overlapping somewhat with a dynamic, developmental systems perspective, the emerging literature on "local biology" (Lock 1993) is more focused on how specific physiological processes shape and are shaped by the given sociocultural milieu in which they are embedded. As opposed to being a predetermined and universal genotypic outcome, phenotypic development is viewed as emergent and as contingent on contextual cues, particularly during "sensitive periods" in which environmental variables may have a profound organizational impact upon ontogeny.

> These considerations have led many developmental biologists to emphasize the contingent, multivalent properties of ontogeny, expressed in current attention to alternative live-history strategies, evolutionarily stable strategies, epigenesis, prepared learning, and the view of physical development as a process of selective stabilization (rather than stabilizing selection) . . . Overall, the increasing emphasis in human biology is to *explain* patterns of human variation. (Worthman 1993:339)

Other research on local biology has looked at such varied topics as the cultural understandings and health consequences of menopause and aging (Lock 1993), the onset of puberty and adolescence (Worthman 1993), the adaptive value of phenotypic plasticity (Chisholm 1992, this volume), physical growth (Worthman 1993), the interface between child and culture within a specific "developmental niche" (Super and Harkness 1986), and the ways experience shapes the neuronal structure (Changeux 1985; Edelman 1989; Worthman 1992). With regard to the emotions, a local biology perspective would examine the "affective tuning" (Markus and Kitayama 1994b:348) between the body and its local environments (e.g., Fessler 1995).

In this volume, several contributors take a local biology approach to the emotions. Carol Worthman's essay, "Emotions: You can feel the difference," argues that emotional experience is generated by the indeterminant, co-constructing person–environment interactions that take place within specific social microenvironments. Thus, emotional phenomena such as depression, temperament, and hostility emerge from the non-linear, probabilistic interaction of sociocultural and physiological factors – a process Worthman refers to as "developmental indeterminacy." Using this local biology perspective, Worthman critiques embodiment theorists who portray the body as passive, neglect ontogeny, and fail to specify the proximate mechanisms underlying embodied phenomena such as the emotions. Drawing on both sociocultural and neurophysiological data, Worthman shows how the emotions function as dynamic transducers that mediate interactions between the body and the environment. Instead of being opposed to cognition, the emotions play an important role in preconscious information processing by directing attention, participating in memory and learning, and signifying meaning. Throughout such activity, culture does not just shape the body (i.e., the passive view of embodiment). Instead, human physiology and culture co-construct one another during ontogeny, a process Worthman calls "dual embodiment."

Daniel Fessler's chapter, "Toward an understanding of the universality of second order emotions," argues that, while always local phenomena, given emotions are nevertheless derived from evolved predispositions. Drawing on his ethnographic fieldwork with the Bengkulu of Sumatra, Fessler describes how two salient Bengkulu emotions, *malu* and *bangga*, embody an adaptive, panhuman "logic" that also underlies the English emotion terms "shame" and "pride." Thus, the Bengkulu experience *malu/bangga* when: (1) Ego violates/fulfills a norm; (2) Ego is aware of her or his failure/success; (3) an Other is also aware of Ego's failure/success; (4) Ego is aware of the Other's knowledge; (5) the Other displays toward Ego either (i) contempt/admiration or (ii) pity/envy – OR – Ego assumes that the Other experiences these feelings toward Ego; and (6) Ego experiences the aversive emotion of *malu* (shame) or the pleasurable emotion of *bangga* (pride). Since he has elsewhere described the culture-specific instantiations of these Bengkulu emotions (Fessler 1995), Fessler is here primarily concerned with speculating about the evolutionary origin of their aforementioned "logic." In particular, Fessler suggests that *malu* (shame) and *bangga* (pride) are inversely related emotions that evolved in response to selective pressures involving the negotiation of rank, competition for resources, and cooperation. He proposes a three stage model in which changes in the emotions occurred in response to both increases in cognitive capacity and the behavioral opportunities which these increases created.

James Chisholm's essay, "Steps to an evolutionary ecology of mind," also argues for a local biology approach to the emotions. Asserting that human nature is "essentially, biologically, and adaptively local," Chisholm claims that life-history theory provides a basis for making predictions about how emotion-laden action schemas are shaped by evolutionary ecology. With regard to attachment relations, for instance, Chisholm asserts that the mind embodies an evolved psychobiological mechanism, perhaps mediated by the amygdala, that enables infants to indirectly perceive environmental risk from the quality of their emotional relationship to caretakers. Based on this assessment of the local ecology, infants develop mental models of attachment that motivate them to pursue locally adaptive reproductive strategies in later life. The biocultural framework that Chisholm outlines thus suggests that the mind embodies many of these evolutionary mechanisms that ascertain environmental risks to fitness and, based upon this determination, activate emotionally motivating action schemas that increase fitness by optimizing reproductive trade-offs, favoring locally adaptive time preferences, and defending against ecological threats.

Conclusion: Seven steps toward developing a biocultural approach to the emotions

In conclusion, all of the chapters in this volume, while varying in approach and orientation, are committed to showing, in theory or in practice, how it is possible to develop a biocultural approach to the emotions. Given the often contentious debates about whether the emotions are ''universal or relative'' or ''biological or cultural,'' the book makes a significant contribution to emotion theory by providing explicit frameworks for moving beyond these tired ''nature or nurture'' arguments. In the remainder of this introduction, I would like to draw out some of the implications of developing a biocultural approach to the emotions that emerge in the volume. I should note that what follows reflects my own view – not necessarily that of the other contributors – that scholars can most productively develop biocultural frameworks (and avoid ''nature or nurture'' dichotomies) by taking a ''processual approach'' to the emotions that examines ''the discrete process(es) by which the emotions are generated both synchronically and diachronically'' (Hinton, this volume). What follows is a seven step plan for doing so.

(1) *Specify the elements of which the emotion is composed.* As indicated in Figure 1 (reproduced from Laughlin *et al.* 1992:45), an emotion system can be viewed as comprising several elements. The four boxes could be designated as culture, biology, social structure, and personal experience (Hinton, this volume; Shore 1993b) which together constitute the circular emotion *gestalt*. Obviously, many other possibilities exist, depending on a scholar's perspective. Componential approaches, for example, are explicitly focused on breaking down the emotions in this manner. Thus, in Figure 2 (reproduced from Buck [1986:297]), an emotion is portrayed as involving

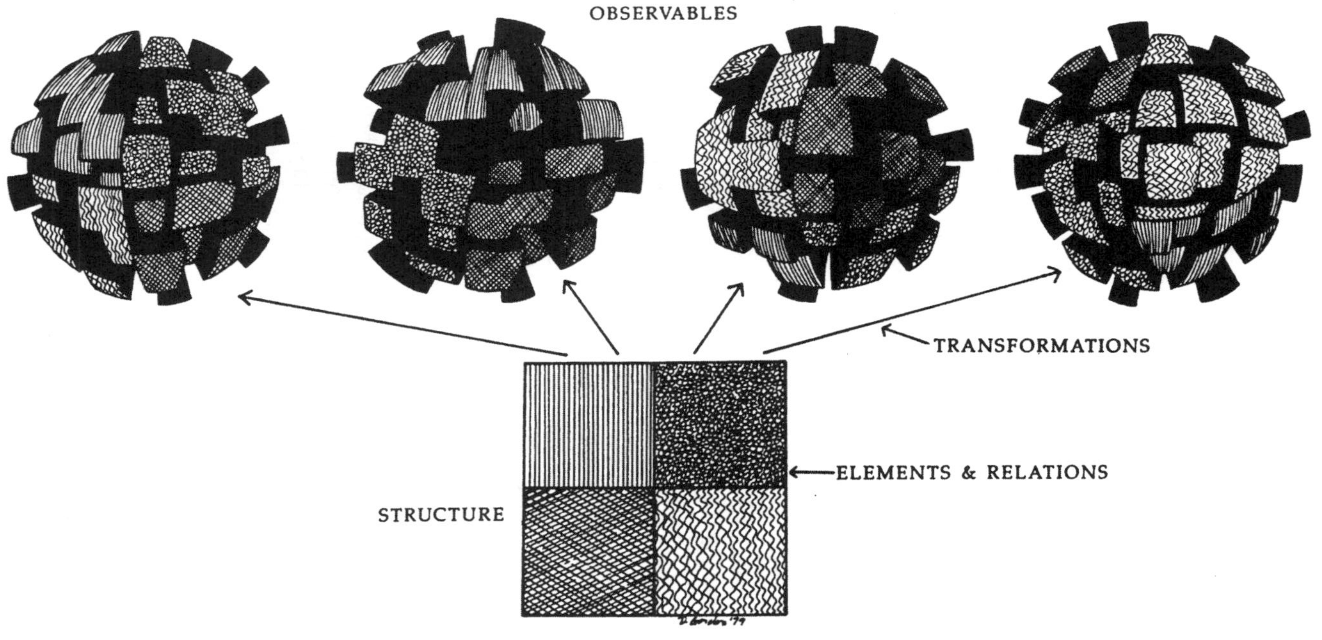

Figure 1. A synchronic structure. A single structure made up of elements and relations among elements produces various surface transformations that are the observables.
Drawings by Donna Gordon, from Laughlin *et al.* (1992).

cognitive/cultural processes, subjective experience, spontaneous expressive tendencies, and adaptive and homeostatic mechanisms. The point is for researchers to make their underlying assumptions about the emotion system explicit – both to themselves and others.

(2) *Specify how the elements in an emotion system function in an emotion event.* Having enumerated the elements in an emotion system, researchers should next specify how the elements together function to produce an emotion event. Figure 2 provides one example of the processes by which an emotion is generated. Within a given sociocultural frame (i.e., ''observed stimuli''), a self-implicating event occurs (''external affective stimulus'') which activates a number of cognitive/cultural and neurophysiological processes (''events within the organism'') that result in an individual's felt experience and sociorelational response (''observed responses''). Alternatively, an emotion event may be understood using Mesquita and Frijda's (1992) componential approach that examines antecedent events, event coding, appraisal, physiological reaction patterns, action readiness, emotional behavior, and regulation.

(3) *Specify the connections between the elements in the emotion system.* To understand the processes by which an emotion is generated, it is necessary to analyze the relationship between the components which constitute an emotion, or what systems theory refers to as ''feedback loops.'' In Figure 2, for example, the arrows both between ''relevant learning'' (i.e., culture and experience) and ''primes'' (i.e., the evolved neurophysiological mechanisms underlying the emotions) and between the ''cognitive system'' and ''relevant learning'' indicate a synergistic relationship between biology and culture. (See Shore [1993b] and Markus and Kitayama [1994b] for other diagrams that examine the relationship between various elements in the emotion system.) While the chapters in this volume focus largely on examining biocultural interconnections, some contributors have emphasized different dimensions of interaction. Thus, Lyon's chapter, like the work of other sociologists (e.g., Kemper 1987, 1990a; Lyon and Barbalet 1994; see also Kemper 1993 and Thoits 1989), explores the relation between social structure and physiology. Worthman and Chisholm, in turn, stress the importance of taking individual experience into account when developing a biocultural approach.

(4) *Specify how the emotion system develops diachronically.* After indicating the connections between the elements in an emotion system, one is able to examine the ways in which the emotions develop over time. Figure 2 and Figure 3 (reproduced from Laughlin *et al.* [1992:46]) provide a schematic representation of this process. In Figure 2, the arrow which connects ''cognitive system'' to ''relevant learning'' (which, in turn, is connected to ''primes'') indicates that, as an individual learns cultural norms and

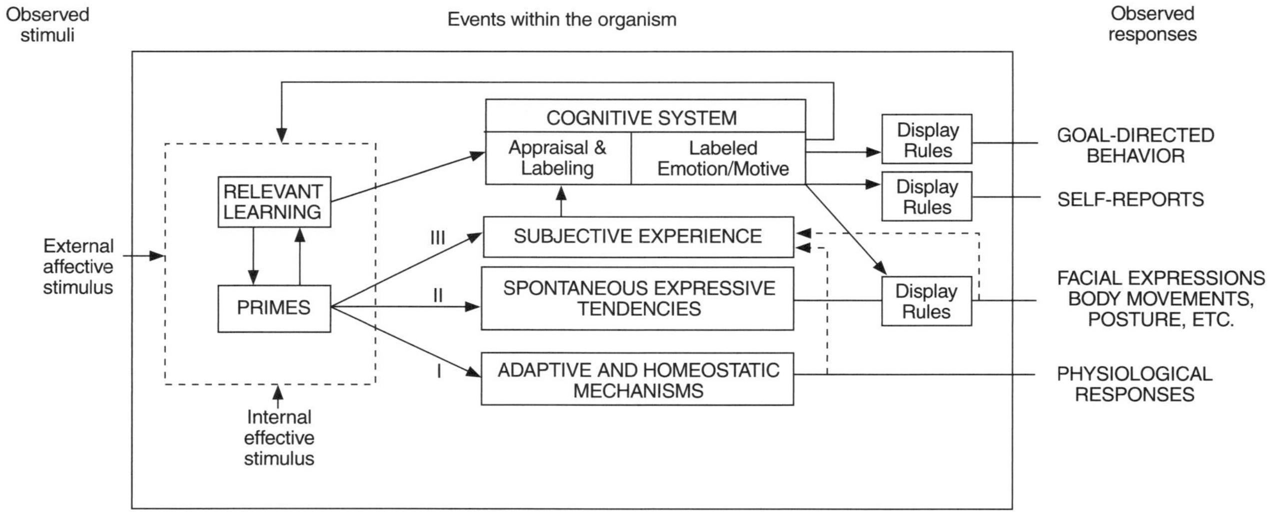

Figure 2. The interactions between the primes and the cognitive system
Source: From Buck 1984, reproduced by permission of The Guilford Press.

has personal experiences – including emotional ones – her or his emotions will change. Figure 3 shows how an emotion system existing at time^{1} is transformed by this environmental information to its instantiation at time^{2}; the emotion system existing at time^{2}, in turn, will be modified by other information into its time^{3} incarnation, and so on. The transformational periods which a researcher selects will, of course, depend upon her or his research agenda. A developmental psychologist may focus on the transformations that occur from birth through early childhood (e.g., Harris 1989, 1993; Lewis 1993). An anthropologist, in turn, may be concerned with mapping out the longer development of the emotion system – from early childhood to old age.

(5) *Specify potential sources of variation on the development of the emotion system.* An understanding of the diachronic dimension of the emotions enables scholars to see how the emotions are shaped into their culturally and individually distinct manifestations. For example, an emotion system may be influenced by such potential sources of variation as: learned cultural norms and values (e.g., information learned at home, at school, in the marketplace, in religious contexts), the social distribution of knowledge (e.g., differences due to gender, class, ethnicity, and local environment), social structure (e.g., kinship systems, hierarchy, and other social institutions), personal experience (e.g., the specific events, from ''normal'' to traumatic, that shape an individual's life-history), biological dispositions (e.g., a person's temperament and bodily constitution), and historical changes (e.g., macrolevel alterations in the way an emotion is conceived; see Stearns [1993]). An understanding of how and why the emotions vary can help researchers examine similarity and difference in a manner that avoids ''either-or'' dichotomies.

(6) *Specify the level(s) of analysis upon which research is being conducted.* While it is perfectly legitimate to conduct research on one level of analysis, researchers must recognize that they are doing so, maintain at least a rudimentary understanding of the larger emotion system in question, and acknowledge the legitimacy of other analytical domains. Many debates about the emotions begin because of intellectual metonymy – a scholar examining one dimension of an emotion system assumes that she or he can explain ''everything,'' thus using a partial explanation as a whole one. All of the aforementioned steps should help researchers to properly delimit the level(s) of analysis upon which they are conducting research (see Fessler 1996) and avoid falling prey to cultural or biological reductionism.

(7) *Remain open to radical possibilities.* No matter what level(s) of analysis research is being conducted upon, scholars should actively consider the possibility that their premises about the emotion system in question need to be substantially revised. The deconstructionist insights of cultural constructionism have illustrated that folk psychological assumptions frequently pervade work on the emotions. As I note in my essay, it is likely that disparate

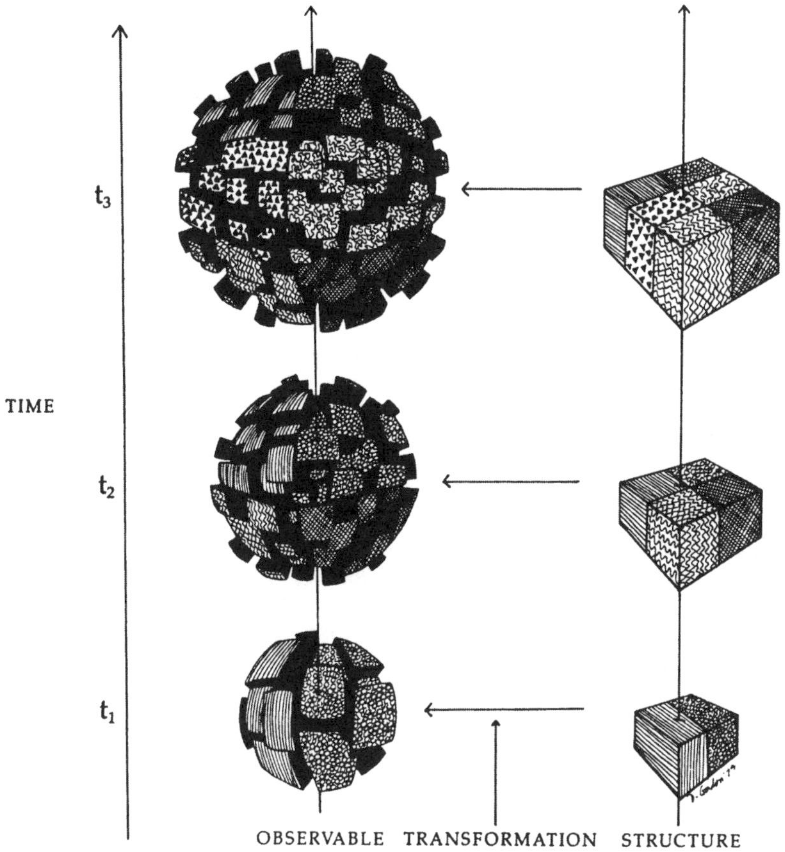

Figure 3. A diachronic structure. A structure develops through time and produces surface transformations that appear as maturing observables. Drawings by Donna Gordon, from Laughlin *et al.* (1991).

emotions are differentially constrained by physiology, thus making it necessary for scholars to examine the discrete processes by which each emotion is generated both synchronically and diachronically. Likewise, Shweder (1994) has suggested that the feelings that are "emotionalized" in one culture may be "somaticized" (or conceived as a form of bewitchment, sickness, or suffering) in another. If scholars keep their minds open to such radical possibilities, they may be able to help us rethink our understanding of the emotions. This book attempts to make a significant contribution to this reconceptualization by illustrating how one may develop syncretic, biocultural approaches to the emotions.

Acknowledgments

In addition to Naomi Quinn, Claudia Strauss, Dan Fessler, Ross Buck, Robert Paul, Charles Huckolls, Charles Laughlin and Roy D'Andrade, I would like to thank Bradd Shore, Owen Lynch, Ladson Hinton, Margot Lyon, Iain D. Edgewater, Keith McNeal, and Nicole Cooley for their helpful comments, and/or suggestions about this chapter. I am especially grateful to Carol Worthman who introduced me to biocultural anthropology.

NOTES

1. A list of the figures who have studied emotion prior to this period of resurgence reads like a history of philosophy: Aristotle, Descartes, Hume, Spinoza, Nietzsche, Darwin, James, Freud, Heidegger, Sartre, Ryle, and so on (see Calhoun and Solomon 1984 and Solomon 1994). The recent increase of interest in the emotions is due, in large part, to the decline of radical behaviorism, the beginning of the cognitive revolution, and the rise of a deconstructionist ethos. This interest in and controversy about the emotions is reflected by the large number of interdisciplinary conferences and edited volumes that have been devoted to the topic since the early 1980s – see, for example: Rorty (1980), Plutchik and Kellerman (1980, 1983, 1986, 1989, and 1990); Calhoun and Solomon (1984); Izard *et al.* (1984); Scherer and Ekman (1984); Shweder and LeVine (1984); Kleinman and Good (1985); White and Kirkpatrick (1985); Harré (1986); LeDoux and Hirst (1986); Kemper (1990b); Lutz and Abu-Lughod (1990); Lynch (1990b); Stein *et al.* (1990); Clark (1992); Stein and Oatley (1992); Lewis and Haviland (1993); Shore (1993a); Ekman and Davidson (1994); Goozen *et al.* (1994); Kitayama and Markus (1994); Marks and Ames (1995); Tangney and Fischer (1995); Kavanaugh *et al.* (1996); and Pfister and Schnog (1997).
2. My perspective on this theoretical genealogy is derived from a variety of sources including Calhoun and Solomon (1984), Hillman (1972), Lutz and White (1986), Lyons (1980), Lynch (1990a), and Plutchik (1980). I should also note that the four traditions described here are not mutually exclusive and, therefore, that some researchers I cite draw on a combination of these perspectives.
3. A third physiological tradition, upon which I do not focus because of the lack of research in this area, concerns the relationship between neuroendocrinology and emotion. For a review of some of the literature in this physiological sub-tradition, see Henry (1986), Panksepp (1993), Plutchik and Kellerman (1986), and Whybrow (1984). I should also note that my literature review does not discuss the Skinnerian *behavioral tradition*, which views emotions as "reflexes" and "operants" that can be analyzed in terms of observed behaviors (see Lyons 1980:17–17F.).
4. While I have placed each chapter within the categorical approach I feel it best exemplifies, I should note that several essays could be placed under alternative rubrics. Thus, all of the essays promote some form of biocultural synergy, and the Worthman chapter employs both local biology and an embodiment approach.
5. Since all of this is somewhat abstract, I will provide an example of a developmental system. One can, for instance, view physical growth in terms of an ongoing and historically determined set of inputs. The genetic envelope (usually) ensures a

course of ontogeny that takes the following course: the embryo becomes an infant; the infant, a child; the child, an adolescent; the adolescent, a young adult; the young adult, a middle-aged person; the middle-aged person, an elderly person. A person's physical size at each of these stages, however, is contingent on a progressive series of historical inputs. Thus, a Somalian child who suffers from prolonged and severe malnutrition caused by drought will probably not reach the height she or he would have achieved if she or he had been well fed (these effects are sometimes reversible to an extent). Alternatively, a person's weight will vary depending on lifestyle and diet, factors that are largely influenced by sociocultural norms.

6. Combining my processual approach with Laughlin and Throop's "biogenetic structuralism" and Richard Lazarus' (1991) notion of "core relational themes," we can define the emotions as *experiential process(es) that arise as "entrained" neuroendocrine networks are generated in given relational situations* – always noting that these systems are potentially subject to modification, or "reentrainment," over ontogenetic time. Extending this framework to specific emotions, such as shame and pride (see Fessler's chapter), we can view these emotions as *(un)pleasurably experienced "entrainments" of neuroendocrine activity that emerge when a person acts in such a way that her or his self-image is evaluated in a negative or positive manner by real or imagined others.*

References

Abu-Lughod, Lila. 1986. *Veiled sentiments: Honor and poetry in a Bedouin society.* Berkeley: University of California Press.

Abu-Lughod, Lila, and Catherine A. Lutz. 1990. Introduction: Emotion, discourse, and the politics of everyday life. In *Language and the politics of emotion*, ed. Catherine A. Lutz and Lila Abu-Lughod, 1–23. New York: Cambridge University Press.

Aggleton, John P., and Mortimer Mishkin. 1986. The amygdala: Sensory gateway to the emotions. In *Emotion: Theory, research, and experience, Volume 3: Biological foundations of emotion*, ed. Robert Plutchik and Henry Kellerman, 281–299. Orlando: Academic Press.

Aristotle. 1941. *The basic works of Aristotle*, ed. R. McKeon, trans. J. I. Beare. New York: Random House.

Armon-Jones, Claire. 1986. The thesis of constructionism. In *The social construction of emotions*, ed. Rom Harré, 32–56. Oxford: Basil Blackwell.

Arnold, Magda B. 1960. *Emotion and personality.* New York: Columbia University Press.

Averill, James R. 1980. A constructivist view of emotion. In *Emotion: Theory, research, and experience, Volume 1: Theories of emotion*, ed. Robert Plutchik and Henry Kellerman, 305–339. New York: Academic Press.

Ax, A. F. 1953. The physiological differentiation between fear and anger in humans. *Psychosomatic Medicine* 15:433–442.

Bateson, Gregory. 1972. *Steps to an ecology of mind.* New York: Ballantine.

Bedford, Errol. 1962. Emotions. In *The philosophy of mind*, ed. V. C. Chappell, 110–126. Englewood Cliffs, NJ: Prentice-Hall.

von Bertalanffy, Ludwig. 1968. *General systems theory.* New York: George Braziller.

Besnier, Niko. 1990. Language and affect. *Annual review of Anthropology* 19:419–451.

1995. *Literacy, emotion, and authority: Reading and writing on a Polynesian atoll.* New York: Cambridge University Press.

Bourdieu, Pierre. 1977. *Outline of a theory of practice.* New York: Cambridge University Press.

Bowlby, John. 1969. *Attachment and loss, Volume I, Attachment.* New York: Basic Books.

1973. *Attachment and loss, Volume II, Separation: Anxiety and anger.* New York: Basic Books.

Brentano, Franz C. 1971 [1874]. *Psychology from the empirical standpoint.* London: Routledge & Kegan Paul.

Buck, Ross. 1986. The psychology of emotion. In *Mind and brain: Dialogues in cognitive neuroscience*, ed. Joseph E. LeDoux and William Hirst, 275–299. New York: Cambridge University Press.

1984. *The communication of emotion.* New York: Guilford Press.

Bunge, Mario A. 1980. *The mind–body problem: A psychobiological approach.* Oxford: Pergamon.

Cacioppo, John T., David J. Klein, Gary G. Berntson, and Elaine Hatfield. 1993. The psychophysiology of emotion. In *Handbook of emotions*, eds. Michael Lewis and Jeannette M. Haviland, 119–142. New York: The Guilford Press.

Calhoun, Cheshire, and Robert C. Solomon, eds. 1984. *What is an emotion?: Classical readings in philosophical psychology.* New York: Oxford University Press.

Campos, Joseph J., Rosanne Kermoian, and David Witherington. 1996. An epigenetic perspective on emotional development. In *Emotion: Interdisciplinary perspectives*, ed. Robert Kavanaugh, Betty Zimmerberg, and Steven Fein, 119–138. Mahway, NJ: Lawrence Erlbaum.

Cannon, Walter B. 1927. The James–Lange theory of emotions: A critical examination and an alternative theory. *American Journal of Psychology* 39:106–124.

Changeux, Jean-Pierre. 1985. *Neuronal man: The biology of mind.* New York: Oxford University Press.

Chisholm, James S. 1992. Putting people in biology: Toward a synthesis of biological and psychological anthropology. In *New directions in psychological anthropology*, ed. Theodore Schwartz, Geoffrey M. White, and Catherine A. Lutz, 125–149. New York: Cambridge University Press.

Chodorow, Nancy. 1978. *The reproduction of mothering.* Berkeley: University of California Press.

Clark, Margaret S., ed. 1992. *Emotion.* London: Sage.

Csordas, Thomas J. 1990. Embodiment as a paradigm for anthropology. *Ethos* 18(1):5–47.

1994a. Introduction: The body as representation and being-in-the-world. In *Embodiment and experience: The existential ground of culture and self*, ed. Thomas J. Csordas, 1–24. New York: Cambridge University Press.

Csordas, Thomas J., ed. 1994b. *Embodiment and experience: The existential ground of culture and self.* New York: Cambridge University Press.

Damasio, Antonio R. 1994. *Descartes' error: Emotion, reason, and the human brain.* New York: Avon.

Darwin, Charles. 1965 [1872]. *The expression of the emotions in man and animals*. Chicago: University of Chicago Press.

Davidson, Richard J. 1993. The neuropsychology of emotion and affective style. In *Handbook of emotions*, ed. Michael Lewis and Jeannette M. Haviland, 143–154. New York: The Guilford Press.

Descartes, René. 1989 [1649]. *On the passions of the soul*. Trans. S. Voss. Indianapolis: Hackett.

Desjarlais, Robert R. 1992. *Body and emotion: The aesthetics of illness and healing in the Nepal Himalayas*. Philadelphia: University of Pennsylvania Press.

de Sousa, Ronald. 1987. *The rationality of emotion*. Cambridge: MIT Press.

Douglas, Mary. 1966. *Purity and danger: An analysis of the concepts of pollution and taboo*. London: Routledge & Kegan Paul.

1970. *Natural symbols: Explorations in cosmology*. London: Barrie & Jenkins.

Edelman, Gerald M. 1989. Topobiology. *Scientific American* May:76–88.

Eibl-Eibesfeldt, Irenaus. 1980. Strategies of social interaction. In *Emotion: Theory, research, and experience, Volume 1: Theories of emotion*, ed. Robert Plutchik and Henry Kellerman, 57–111. New York: Academic Press.

Ekman, Paul. 1980. Biological and cultural contributions to body and facial movements in the expression of emotions. In *Explaining emotions*, ed. Amélie O. Rorty, 73–101. Berkeley: University of California Press.

1994. All emotions are basic. In *The nature of emotion: Fundamental questions*, eds. Paul Ekman and Richard J. Davidson, 15–19. New York: Oxford University Press.

Ekman, Paul, ed. 1973. *Darwin and facial expression: A century of research in review*. New York: Academic Press.

Ekman, Paul, and Richard J. Davidson, eds. 1994. *The nature of emotion: Fundamental questions*. New York: Oxford University Press.

Ekman, Paul, Robert W. Levenson, and Wallace V. Friesen. 1983. Autonomic nervous system activity distinguishes among emotions. *Science* 221:1208–1210.

Featherstone, Mike, Mike Hepworth, and Bryan S. Turner, eds. 1991. *The body: Social process and cultural theory*. London: Sage.

Feld, Steven. 1982. *Sound and sentiment: Birds, weeping, poetics, and song in Kaluli expression*. Philadelphia: University of Pennsylvania Press.

Fenichel, O. 1945. *The psychoanalytic theory of neurosis*. New York: Norton.

Fessler, Daniel M. T. 1995. A small field with a lot of hornets: An exploration of shame, motivation, and social control. Ph.D. Dissertation. University of California, San Diego. Ann Arbor: University Microfilms.

1996. Anthropology in wonderland, or, the virtues of shifting levels and frames. *Anthropological Newsletter* 37(8):44, 42.

Fogel, Alan, and Esther Thelen. 1987. Development of early expressive and communicative action: Reinterpreting the evidence from a dynamic developmental systems perspective. *Developmental Psychology* 23(6):747–761.

Foucault, Michel. 1980. *The history of sexuality, Volume 1*. New York: Vintage.

1977. *Discipline & punish: The birth of the prison*. New York: Vintage.

Freud, Sigmund. 1962 [1894]. The neuro-psychosis of defense. In *The standard edition of the complete psychological works of Sigmund Freud*, trans. and ed. James Strachey, 3:43–61. London: Hogarth Press.

1965 [1900]. *The interpretation of dreams.* Trans. and ed. James Strachey. New York: Avon Books.

1957 [1915]. The unconscious. In *The standard edition of the complete psychological works of Sigmund Freud,* trans. and ed. James Strachey, 14:159–215. London: Hogarth Press.

1960 [1923]. *The ego and the id.* Trans. Joan Riviere. New York: W. W. Norton.

1959 [1926]. *Inhibitions, symptoms and anxiety.* Trans. Alix Strachey, Ed. James Strachey. New York: W. W. Norton.

Frijda, Nico H. 1986. *The emotions.* New York: Cambridge University Press.

Funkenstein, D. H., S. H. King, and M. Drollette. 1954. The direction of anger during a laboratory stress-inducting situation. *Psychosomatic Medicine* 16:404–413.

Geertz, Clifford. 1984. ''From the native's point of view'': On the nature of anthropological understanding. In *Culture theory: Essays on mind, self, and emotion,* ed. Richard A. Shweder and Robert A. LeVine, 123–136. New York: Cambridge University Press.

Gergen, Kenneth J. 1995. Metaphor and monophony in the 20th-century psychology of emotions. *History of the Human Sciences* 8(2):1–23.

Goozen, Stephanie H. M. van, Nanne E. Van de Poll, and Joseph A. Sergeant, eds. 1994. *Emotions: Essays on emotion theory.* Hillsdale, NJ: Lawrence Erlbaum.

Gottlieb, Gilbert. 1991. Experiential canalization of behavioral development: Theory. *Developmental Psychology* 27:4–13.

Greenberg, Leslie S. 1993. Emotion and change processes in psychotherapy. In *Handbook of emotions,* ed. Michael Lewis and Jeannette M. Haviland, 499–508. New York: Guilford Press.

Greenough, William T., James E. Black, and Christopher S. Wallace. 1987. Experience and brain development. *Child Development* 58(3):539–559.

Grima, Benedicte. 1992. *The performance of emotion among Paxtun women.* Austin: University of Texas Press.

Harré, Rom, ed. 1986. *The social construction of emotions.* Oxford: Basil Blackwell.

Harris, Paul L. 1989. *Children and emotion: The development of psychological understanding.* Oxford: Blackwell.

1993. Understanding emotion. In *Handbook of emotions,* ed. Michael Lewis and Jeannette M. Haviland, 237–246. New York: The Guilford Press.

Heath, Robert G. 1986. The neural substrate of emotion. In *Emotion: Theory, research, and experience, Volume 3: Biological foundations of emotion,* ed. Robert Plutchik and Henry Kellerman, 3–35. Orlando: Academic Press.

Heider, Karl G. 1991. *Landscapes of emotion: Three cultures of emotion in Indonesia.* New York: Cambridge University Press.

Heilman, Kenneth M., and Dawn Bowers. 1990. Neuropsychological studies of emotional changes induced by right and left hemispheric lesions. In *Psychological and biological approaches to emotion,* ed. Nancy L. Stein, Bennett Leventhal, and Tom Trabasso, 97–113. Hillsdale, NJ: Lawrence Erlbaum.

Heller, Wendy. 1990. The neuropsychology of emotion: Developmental patterns and implications for psychopathology. In *Psychological and biological approaches to emotion,* ed. Nancy L. Stein, Bennett Leventhal, and Tom Trabasso, 167–211. Hillsdale, NJ: Lawrence Erlbaum.

Henry, James P. 1986. Neuroendocrine patterns of emotional response. In *Emotion:*

Theory, research, and experience, Volume 3: Biological foundations of emotion. Robert Plutchik and Henry Kellerman, 37–60. Orlando: Academic Press.

Hillman, James. 1972. *Emotion: A comprehensive phenomenology of theories and their meanings for therapy*. Evanston, IL: Northwestern University Press.

Hinton, Alexander Laban. 1993 Prolegomenon to a processual approach to the emotions. *Ethos* 21(4):417–451 (reprinted in this volume).

Hinton, Ladson. 1998. Shame as a teacher: 'lowly wisdom' at the millennium. Paper presented at the International Congress for Analytical Psychology. August 28, Florence, Italy.

Hume, David. 1978 [1739]. *A treatise of human nature*. New York: Oxford University Press.

Izard, Carroll E. 1971. *The face of emotion*. New York: Appleton-Century-Crofts.

Izard, Carroll E., Jerome Kagan, and Robert B. Zajonc, eds. 1984. *Emotions, cognition, & behavior*. New York: Cambridge University Press.

James, William. 1884. What is an emotion? *Mind* 9:188–205.

Johnson, Mark. 1987. *The body in the mind: The bodily basis of meaning, imagination, and reason*. Chicago: University of Chicago Press.

Kagan, Jerome. 1978. On emotion and its development: A working paper. In *The development of affect*, ed. Michael Lewis and Leonard A. Rosenblum, 11–41. New York: Plenum Press.

Kandel, Eric R., James H. Schwartz, and Thomas M. Jessell. 1991. *Principles of neural science*. New York: Elsevier.

Kavanaugh, Robert, Betty Zimmerberg, and Steven Fein, eds. 1996. *Emotion: Interdisciplinary perspectives*. Mahway, NJ: Lawrence Erlbaum.

Kemper, Theodore D. 1987. How many emotions are there? Wedding the social and the autonomic components. *American Journal of Sociology* 93:263–289.

1990a. *Social structure and testosterone: Explorations of the socio-bio-social chain*. New Brunswick, NJ: Rutgers University Press.

1993. Sociological models in the explanation of emotions. In *Handbook of emotions*, ed. Michael Lewis and Jeannette M. Haviland, 41–51. New York: The Guilford Press.

Kemper, Theodore D., ed. 1990b. *Research agendas in the sociology of emotions*. Albany, NY: State University of New York Press.

Kernberg, Otto F. 1982. Self, ego, affects, and drives. *Journal of the American Psychoanalytic Association* 30(4):893–917.

1990. New perspectives in psychoanalytic affect theory. In *Emotion: Theory, research, and experience, Volume 5: Emotion, psychopathology, and psychotherapy*, ed. Robert Plutchik and Henry Kellerman, 115–131. San Diego: Academic Press.

Kitayama, Shinobu, and Hazel Rose Markus, eds. 1994. *Emotion and culture: Empirical studies of mutual influence*. Washington, DC: American Psychological Association.

Klein, Melanie. 1975. *Envy and gratitude and other works*. New York: Dell.

Kleinman, Arthur, and Byron Good, eds. 1985. *Culture and depression: Studies in the anthropology and cross-cultural psychiatry of affect and disorder*. Berkeley: University of California Press.

Kluver, H., and P. C. Bucy. 1937. ''Psychic blindness'' and other symptoms following bilateral temporal lobectomy in Rhesus monkeys. *American Journal of Physiology* 119:352–353.

Kohut, Heinz. 1977. *The restoration of self.* New York: International Universities Press.

Kolb, Bryan, and Laughlin Taylor. 1990. Neocortical substrates of emotional behavior. In *Psychological and biological approaches to emotion*, ed. Nancy L. Stein, Bennett Leventhal, and Tom Trabasso, 115–144. Hillsdale, NJ: Lawrence Erlbaum.

Konner, Melvin. 1982. *The tangled wing: Biological constraints on the human spirit.* New York: Holt, Rinehart, and Winston.

Kövecses, Zoltan. 1990. *Emotion concepts.* Berlin: Springer-Verlag.

Lakoff, George. 1987. *Women, fire, and dangerous things: What categories reveal about the mind.* Chicago: University of Chicago Press.

Laughlin, Charles D., John McManus Jr., and Eugene G. d'Aquili. 1992. *Brain, symbol & experience: Toward a neurophenomenology of human consciousness.* New York: Columbia University Press.

Lazarus, Richard S. 1984. On the primacy of cognition. *American Psychologist* 39(2):124–129.

1991. *Emotion & adaptation.* New York: Oxford University Press.

Leavitt, John. 1996. Meaning and feeling in the anthropology of emotions. *American Ethnologist* 23(3):514–539.

LeDoux, Joseph E. 1986. The neurobiology of emotion. In *Mind and brain: Dialogues in cognitive neuroscience*, ed. Joseph E. LeDoux and William Hirst, 301–354. New York: Cambridge University Press.

1994. Emotion, memory and the brain. *Scientific American* 270:50–56.

1995. Emotion: Clues from the brain. *Annual Review of Psychology* 46:209–235.

LeDoux, Joseph E., and William Hirst, eds. 1986. *Mind and brain: Dialogues in cognitive neuroscience.* New York: Cambridge University Press.

Levenson, Robert W., Paul Ekman, and Wallace V. Friesen. 1990. Voluntary facial action generates emotion-specific autonomic nervous system activity. *Psychophysiology* 27:363–384.

Levenson, Robert W., Paul Ekman, Karl Heider, and Wallace V. Friesen. 1992. Emotion and autonomic nervous system activity in the Minangkabau of West Sumatra. *Journal of Personality and Social Psychology* 62(6):972–988.

Levy, Robert I. 1984. Emotion, knowing, and culture. In *Culture theory: Essays on mind, self, and emotion*, ed. Richard A. Shweder and Robert A. LeVine, 214–237. New York: Cambridge University Press.

Lewis, Michael. 1993. The emergence of human emotions. In *Handbook of emotions*, ed. Michael Lewis and Jeannette M. Haviland, 223–235. New York: The Guilford Press.

Lewis, Michael, and Jeannette M. Haviland, eds. 1993. *Handbook of emotions.* New York: The Guilford Press.

Lindholm, Charles. 1982. *Generosity and jealousy: The Swat Pukhtun of Northern Pakistan.* New York: Columbia University Press.

Lock, Margaret. 1993. *Encounters with aging: Mythologies of menopause in Japan and North America.* Berkeley: University of California Press.

Lorenz, Konrad. 1966. *On aggression.* Trans. Marjorie Kerr Wilson. New York: Harcourt, Brace & World.

Lutz, Catherine A. 1988. *Unnatural emotions: Everyday sentiments on a Micronesian atoll & their challenge to Western theory*. Chicago: University of Chicago Press.

1990. Engendered emotion: Gender, power, and the rhetoric of emotional control in American discourse. In *Language and the politics of emotion*, ed. Catherine A. Lutz and Lila Abu-Lughod, 69–91. New York: Cambridge University Press.

Lutz, Catherine A., and Lila Abu-Lughod, eds. 1990. *Language and the politics of emotion*. New York: Cambridge University Press.

Lutz, Catherine, and Geoffrey M. White. 1986. The anthropology of emotions. *Annual Review of Anthropology* 15:405–436.

Lynch, Owen M. 1990a. The social construction of emotion. In *Divine passions: The social construction of emotion in India*, ed. Owen M. Lynch, 3–37. Berkeley: University of California Press.

Lynch, Owen M., ed. 1990b. *Divine passions: The social construction of emotion in India*. Berkeley: University of California Press.

Lyon, Margot L. 1995. Missing emotion: The limitations of cultural constructionism in the study of emotion. *Cultural Anthropology* 10(2):244–263.

Lyon, Margot L., and J. M. Barbalet. 1994. Society's body: Emotion and the ''somatization'' of social theory. In *Embodiment and experience: The existential ground of culture and self*, ed. Thomas J. Csordas, 48–66. New York: Cambridge University Press.

Lyons, William. 1980. *Emotions*. New York: Cambridge University Press.

MacLean, Paul D. 1949. Psychosomatic disease and the ''visceral brain'': Recent developments bearing on the Papez theory of emotion. *Psychosomatic Medicine* 11:338–353.

1973. *The triune concept of the brain and behavior*. Toronto: University of Toronto Press.

1993. Cerebral evolution of emotion. In *Handbook of emotions*, ed. Michael Lewis and Jeannette M. Haviland, 67–83. New York: The Guilford Press.

Mahler, Margaret S. 1968. *On human symbiosis and the vicissitudes of individuation*. New York: International Universities Press.

Mandler, George. 1984. *Mind and body: Psychology of emotion and stress*. Hillsdale, NJ: Lawrence Erlbaum.

Marcuse, Herbert. 1962. *Eros and civilization: A philosophical inquiry into Freud*. New York: Vintage Books.

Marks, Joel, and Roger T. Ames, eds. 1995. *Emotions in Asian thought: A dialogue in comparative philosophy*. Albany: State University of New York.

Markus, Hazel Rose, and Shinobu Kitayama. 1994a. The cultural construction of self and emotion: Implications for social behavior. In *Emotion and culture: Empirical studies of mutual influence*, ed. Shinobu Kitayama and Hazel Rose Markus, 89–130. Washington, DC: American Psychological Association.

1994b. The cultural shaping of emotion: A conceptual framework. In *Emotion and culture: Empirical studies of mutual influence*, ed. Shinobu Kitayama and Hazel Rose Markus, 339–351. Washington, DC: American Psychological Association.

Mauss, Marcel. 1973 [1935]. Techniques of the body. Trans. Ben Brewster. *Economy and Society* 2(1):70–88.

Merleau-Ponty, Maurice. 1962 [1946]. *The phenomenology of perception*. Trans. Colin Smith. London: Routledge & Kegan Paul.

Mesquita, Batja, and Nico H. Frijda. 1992. Cultural variations in emotions: A review. *Psychological Bulletin* 112(2):179–204.

Myers, Fred R. 1986. *Pintupi country, Pintupi self: Sentiment, place, and politics among Western Desert Aborigines*. Washington, DC: Smithsonian Institution Press.

Needham, Rodney, ed. 1973. *Right & left: Essays on dual symbolic classification*. Chicago: University of Chicago Press.

Nesse, Randolph M. 1990. Evolutionary explanations of emotions. *Human Nature* 1(3):261–289.

Noy, Pinchas. 1982. A revision of the psychoanalytic theory of affect. *The Annual of Psychoanalysis* 10:139–186.

Nuckolls, Charles W. 1996. *The cultural dialectics of knowledge and desire*. Madison: University of Wisconsin Press.

Oatley, Keith. 1993. Social construction in emotions. In *Handbook of emotions*, ed. Michael Lewis and Jeannette M. Haviland, 341–352. New York: The Guilford Press.

Oatley, Keith, and P.N. Johnson-Laird. 1987. Towards a cognitive theory of emotions. *Cognition and Emotion* 1(1):29–59.

Obeyesekere, Gananath. 1982. *The work of culture: Symbolic transformation in psychoanalysis and anthropology*. Chicago: University of Chicago Press.

Ortony, A., and T. J. Turner. 1990. What's basic about basic emotions? *Psychological Review* 97:315–331.

Oyama, Susan. 1985. *The ontogeny of information: Developmental systems and evolution*. New York: Cambridge University Press.

Panksepp, Jack. 1993. Neurochemical control of moods and emotions: amino acids to neuropeptides. In *Handbook of emotions*, eds. Michael Lewis and Jeannette M. Haviland, pp. 87–107. New York: The Guilford Press.

Papanicolaou, A. C. 1989. *Emotion: A reconsideration of the somatic theory*. New York: Gordon and Breach.

Papez, James W. 1937. A proposed mechanism of emotion. *Archives of Neurology and Psychiatry* 38:725–743.

Paul, Robert A. 1990. What does anybody want? Desire, purpose, and the acting subject in the study of culture. *Cultural Anthropology* 5(4):431–451.

Perkins, Moreland. 1966. Emotion and feeling. *Philosophical Review* 75(2):139–160.

Pfister, Joel, and Nancy Schnog, eds. 1997. *A cultural history of emotions in America*. New Haven: Yale University Press.

Plomin, Robert. 1994. *Genetics and experience: The interplay between nature and nurture*. Thousand Oaks, CA: Sage.

Plomin, Robert, and Denise Daniels. 1987. Why are children in the same family so different from one another? *The Behavioral and Brain Sciences* 10:1–60.

Plutchik, Robert. 1980. *Emotion: A psychoevolutionary synthesis*. New York: Harper and Row.

1993. Emotions and their vicissitudes: Emotions and psychopathology. In *Handbook of emotion*, ed. Michael Lewis and Jeannette M. Haviland, 53–66. New York: The Guilford Press.

Plutchik, Robert, and Henry Kellerman, eds. 1980. *Emotion: Theory, research, and experience, Volume 1: Theories of emotion*. New York: Academic Press.

1983. *Emotion: Theory, research, and experience, Volume 2: Emotions in early development*. New York: Academic Press.

1986. *Emotion: Theory, research, and experience, Volume 3: Biological foundations of emotion*. Orlando: Academic Press.

1989. *Emotion: Theory, research, and experience, Volume 4: The measurement of emotions*. San Diego: Academic Press.

1990. *Emotion: Theory, research, and experience, Volume 5: Emotion, psychopathology, and psychotherapy*. San Diego: Academic Press.

Pribram, Karl H. 1984. Emotion: a neurobehavioral analysis. In *Approaches to emotion*, ed. Klaus R. Scherer and Paul Ekman, 13–38. Hillsdale, NJ: Lawrence Erlbaum.

Rapaport, David. 1953. On the psycho-analytic theory of affects. *The International Journal of Psycho-analysis* 34:177–198.

Reddy, William M. 1997. Against constructionism: The historical ethnography of emotions. *Current Anthropology* 38(3):327–351.

Reich, Wilhelm. 1942. *The function of the organism*. New York: Orgone Press.

Rorty, Amélie Oksenberg, ed. 1980. *Explaining emotions*. Berkeley: University of California Press.

Rosaldo, Michelle Z. 1980. *Knowledge and passion: Ilongot notions of self and social life*. New York: Cambridge University Press.

1984. Toward an anthropology of self and feeling. In *Culture theory: Essays on mind, self, and emotion*, ed. Richard A. Shweder and Robert A. LeVine, 137–157. New York: Cambridge University Press.

Rosenberg, Daniel V. 1990. Language in the discourse of the emotions. In *Language and the politics of emotion*, ed. Catherine A. Lutz and Lila Abu-Lughod, 162–185. New York: Cambridge University Press.

Russell, James A. 1991. Culture and the categorization of emotions. *Psychological Bulletin* 110(3):426–450.

Sartre, Jean-Paul. 1948 [1939]. *The emotions: Sketch of a theory*, trans. B. Frechtman. New York: Philosophical Library.

Scarr, Sandra, and Kathleen McCartney. 1983. How people make their own environments: A theory of genotype–environment effects. *Child Development* 54:424–435.

Schachter, Stanley, and Jerome E. Singer. 1962. Cognitive, social, and physiological determinants of emotional state. *Psychological Review* 69(5):379–399.

Scheper-Hughes, Nancy, and Margaret M. Lock. 1987. The mindful body: A prolegomenon to future work in medical anthropology. *Medical Anthropology Quarterly* 1(1):6–41.

Scherer, Klaus R. 1984. On the nature and function of emotion: a component process approach. In *Approaches to emotion*, ed. Klaus R. Scherer and Paul Ekman, 293–317. Hillsdale, NJ: Lawrence Erlbaum.

1994. Toward a concept of "modal emotions." In *The nature of emotion: Fundamental questions*, ed. Paul Ekman and Richard J. Davidson, 25–31. New York: Oxford University Press.

Scherer, Klaus R., and Paul Ekman, eds. 1984. *Approaches to emotion*. Hillsdale, NJ: Lawrence Erlbaum.

Schore, Allan N. 1994. *Affect regulation and the origin of the self: The neurobiology of emotional development*. Hillsdale, NJ: Lawrence Erlbaum.

Shore, Bradd. 1993a. Emotion: Culture, psychology, biology – meeting report: Emory–Mellon Symposium. *Ethos* 21(3):357–363.

1993b. Feeling our way: Toward a bio-cultural model of emotion. Paper presented at the Emory–Mellon Symposium, "The emotions: Culture, psychology, biology." Calloway Gardens, GA. February, 1993.

1996. *Culture in mind: Cognition, culture, and the problem of meaning*. New York: Oxford University Press.

Shweder, Richard A. 1993. The cultural psychology of the emotions. In *Handbook of emotions*, ed. Michael Lewis and Jeannette M. Haviland, 417–431. New York: The Guilford Press.

1994. "You're not sick, you're just in love": emotion as an interpretive system. In *The nature of emotion: Fundamental questions*, ed. Paul Ekman and Richard J. Davidson, 32–47. New York: Oxford University Press.

Shweder, Richard A., and Robert A. LeVine, eds. 1984. *Culture theory: Essays on mind, self, and emotion*. New York: Cambridge University Press.

Smith, C. A., and P. C. Ellsworth. 1985. Patterns of cognitive appraisal in emotion. *Journal of Personality and Social Psychology* 48:813–838.

Solomon, Robert C. 1984. Getting angry: The Jamesian theory of emotion in anthropology. In *Culture theory: Essays on mind, self, and emotion*, ed. Richard A. Shweder and Robert A. LeVine, 238–254. New York: Cambridge University Press.

1993. The philosophy of emotions. In *Handbook of emotions*, ed. Michael Lewis and Jeannette M. Haviland, 3–15. New York: The Guilford Press.

Spinoza, Benedict. 1992 [1677]. *The ethics*, trans. S. Shirley. Indianapolis: Hackett.

Spiro, Melford E. 1984. Some reflections on cultural determinism and relativism with special reference to emotion and reason. In *Culture theory: Essays on mind, self, and emotion*, ed. Richard A. Shweder and Robert A. LeVine, 323–346. New York: Cambridge University Press.

Stearns, Peter N. 1993. History of emotions: The issue of change. In *Handbook of emotions*, ed. Michael Lewis and Jeannette M. Haviland, 17–28, New York: The Guilford Press.

Stein, Nancy L., and Keith Oatley, eds. 1992. *Basic emotions*. Hillsdale, NJ: Lawrence Erlbaum.

Stein, Nancy L., Bennett Leventhal, and Tom Trabasso, eds. 1990. *Psychological and biological approaches to emotion*. Hillsdale, NJ: Lawrence Erlbaum.

Strathern, Andrew J. 1996. *Body thoughts*. Ann Arbor: University of Michigan Press.

Sullivan, Harry Stack. 1953. *The interpersonal theory of psychiatry*. New York: Norton.

Super, Charles M., and Sara Harkness. 1986. The developmental niche: A conceptualization at the interface of child and culture. *International Journal of Behavioral Development* 9:545–569.

Tangney, June Price, and Kurt W. Fischer, eds. 1995. *Self-conscious emotions: The psychology of shame, guilt, embarrassment, and pride*. New York: The Guilford Press.

Thoits, Peggy A. 1989. The sociology of emotions. *Annual Review of Sociology* 15:317–342.

Tompkins, Silvan S. 1962. *Affect, imagery, and consciousness, Volume I, The positive affects*. New York: Springer-Verlag.

1963. *Affect, imagery, and consciousness, Volume II, The negative affects*. New York: Springer-Verlag.

Tooby, John, and Leda Cosmides. 1990. The past explains the present: Emotional adaptations and the structure of ancestral environment. *Ethology and Sociobiology* 11:375–394.

Turner, Terence. 1980. The social skin. In *Not work alone*, ed. J. Cherfas and R. Lewin, 112–140. London: Temple Smith.

Turner, Victor. 1967. *The forest of symbols: Aspects of Ndembu ritual*. Ithaca, NY: Cornell University Press.

Varela, Francisco J. 1991. *The embodied mind: Cognitive science and human experience*. Cambridge, MA: MIT Press.

Varela, Francisco J., Evan Thompson, and Eleaner Rosch. 1991. *The embodied mind: Cognitive science and human experience*. Cambridge: MIT Press.

White, Geoffrey M. 1993. Emotions inside out: The anthropology of affect. In *Handbook of emotion*, ed. Michael Lewis and Jeannette M. Haviland, 29–39. New York: The Guilford Press.

White, Geoffrey M., and John Kirkpatrick, eds. 1985. *Person, self, and experience: Exploring Pacific ethnopsychologies*. Berkeley: University of California Press.

Whybrow, Peter. 1984. Contributions from neuroendocrinology. In *Approaches to emotion*, ed. Klaus R. Scherer and Paul Ekman, pp. 59–72. Hillsdale, NJ: Lawrence Erlbaum.

Wierzbicka, Anna. 1994. Emotion, language, and cultural scripts. In *Emotion and culture: Empirical studies of mutual influence*, ed. Shinobu Kitayama and Hazel Rose Markus, 133–196. Washington, DC: American Psychological Association.

Wikan, Unni. 1990. *Managing turbulent hearts: A Balinese formula for living*. Chicago: University of Chicago Press.

Winnicott, Donald W. 1965. *The maturation process and the facilitating environment*. New York: International Universities Press.

Worthman, Carol M. 1992. Cupid and Psyche: Investigative syncretism in biological and psychosocial anthropology. In *New directions in psychological anthropology*, ed. Theodore Schwartz, Geoffrey M. White, and Catherine A. Lutz, 150–178. New York: Cambridge University Press.

1993. Biocultural interactions in human development. In *Juvenile primates: Life history, development, and behavior*, ed. Michael E. Pereira and Lynn A. Fairbanks, 339–358. New York: Oxford University Press.

Zajonc, Robert B. 1984. On the primacy of affect. *American Psychologist* 39(2):117–123.

Zajonc, Robert B., Sheila T. Murphy, and Daniel N. McIntosh. 1993. Brain temperature and subjective emotional experience. In *Handbook of emotions*, ed. Michael Lewis and Jeannette M. Haviland, 209–220. New York: The Guilford Press.

Part I

Local biology

1 Emotions: You can feel the difference

Carol M. Worthman

That cry – that was Hector's mother I heard!
My heart's pounding, leaping up in my throat,
the knees beneath me paralyzed – Oh I know it . . .
something terrible's coming down on Priam's children.
(Hector's wife Andromache hears wailing at his death: *Iliad* 22:529–532)

And I with the same grief, I died and met my fate.
. . . nor did some hateful illness strike me,. . .
No, it was longing for *you*, my shining Odysseus –
. . .that tore away my life that had been sweet.
(the shade of Odysseus' mother Anticleia: *Odyssey* 11:225–232)

The place of emotion in human experience is presently under careful reconsideration, a long-overdue process which the present analysis aims to advance. As the ancients just quoted clearly expressed and anyone today might recognize through introspection, emotion is both visceral and central to intelligent knowing and acting, contrary to Enlightenment distinctions between feeling and thinking. Furthermore, through the thoroughly embodied aspects of emotion, acutely related above by Andromache, life's vicissitudes wield biological as well as cognitive force that acts on physical as well as mental well-being. Emotion is therefore a matter of life and death, as Anticleia reported, for it mediates not only responses to but also short- and long-term effects of deprivation, neglect, or trauma and loss. Mounting evidence suggests that the kinds and life-long differential distribution of experiences meted out by societies shape the architecture and physiology of cognition, including that of emotional response and state regulation; thus, intra- and inter-cultural variation in emotion has biological concomitants that result in differences in survival and health.

This chapter concerns these aspects of emotion, currently neglected in anthropological discourse. Here, I discuss the ''difference'' that emotions make in the lives of persons, emphasizing their role in cognition and in physical well-being. I also present data that question the isometry between contexts with cultural emotional valence and actual emotional impact on indi-

process	detection, attention learning, memory integration
drive	motivation organization, prioritization recruitment
signal (to self, others)	communication relational representation

Figure 1.1. What emotions are/do

viduals: shared culture does not necessitate shared experience. Competing anthropological accounts of emotion have been concerned with what emotions are (Lutz 1988; Lutz and Abu-Lughod 1990), but asking what they do may take us further by requiring a dynamic explanation (Figure 1.1). Cognitive accounts focus on the signaling dimension of emotions as communicative, relational, representational, involved in situating persons and essential for negotiating and decoding everyday relations (Lazarus 1991; Russell 1991; Zajonc *et al.* 1989; Zajonc 1991). In psychodynamic views, emotions generate drive by being motivational and organizational: they prioritize, and recruit or mobilize action and experience (Levy 1973; Nuckolls 1995; Spiro 1982; Whiting and Whiting 1975a). Social practice-oriented descriptions emphasize contextual determinants of affect and view lived emotion as a product of culture (Goldschmidt 1975; Lutz 1988; Lutz and Abu-Lughod 1990; Markus and Kitayama 1994). But emotions also have information-processing features; they guide knowledge of the world by altering what we notice, influencing rate and content of learning, and evoking recall. Emotions rapidly recruit memories and schemes, and integrate them in cognition and action. These functions are essential to intelligent being-in-the-world.

Much less well studied is the role of emotions in embodiment, namely, as transducers between physical states and experience, as both mediators and dynamic products of the interaction between person and context. The notion of embodiment excites growing attention among anthropologists and social theorists (Csordas 1994), but its weak conceptualization in relation to actual material phenomena (i.e., the body itself) limits its utility for understanding on-the-ground variation in function and well-being. A different view of embodiment will be proposed through notions of *dual embodiment*, which integrates developmental and processual perspectives on emotion; *local biology*, which points to intrinsic nature of biological variation; and *develop-*

mental indeterminacy, the probabilistic relationship of biology and culture to ontogeny, given the biocultural interaction operating throughout development. The present chapter will explore these two dynamic and related roles of emotion, in information processing and embodiment, and apply them to two literatures implicating context-sensitive emotion processes in well-being and health. This exploration of emotion will, not incidentally, touch on the nature of culture and of the relationship of individual to culture, and the biocultural bases of human diversity and commonality.

Ethos and eidos: Feeling and thinking

Bateson's *Naven* (Bateson 1958) made a key contribution to anthropological understanding of the cultural ecology of human experience by seeking to characterize the everyday phenomenological landscapes that produce culturally scripted behavior. *Naven* involved an experience-near, individual-based account of culture that addressed structural-functionalist anthropology's neglect of motivated action and cultural phenomenology, and of the relationship of individuals and culture. Bateson's analysis of Iatmul culture draws a fundamental distinction between *ethos*, or the affective-emotional landscape characterizing members of a culture, and *eidos*, the cognitive-propositional landscape characterizing working cultural logic of members of a culture (pp. 2, 32–33, 220).[1] He links the individual to culture, the existential to the structural, by defining ethos and eidos as involving the "standardized," or shared, affective and cognitive modes of individuals.

Bateson, along with Benedict, Mead, and others, effectively launched psychological anthropology as a comparative phenomenological study of cultural worlds. Nevertheless, anthropology's Batesonian legacy institutionalizes two conceptual impediments to the understanding of emotion in particular, and of culture in general. The first impediment is the distinction between thinking and feeling, reflected in the ethos–eidos dichotomy; the second is the elision of ontogeny in the notion of "standardization," or shared culture. The present chapter seeks to show why these impediments are significant, and how their circumvention or resolution will advance conceptualization of emotion and of culture. The remainder of this section deals with the ethos–eidos issue; subsequent sections will deal with ontogeny and standardization.

Bateson's heuristic distinction between culturally specific domains of ethos (emotional landscape) and eidos (knowledge structures, or "minding") both reflects and reinforces a Western view of emotion (feeling, affect) and rationality (knowledge, thought) as mutually exclusive. The division places emotion and (rational) cognition as separate, mutually exclusive elements in consciousness (Figure 1.2): a conscious state with more "feeling" will have little "thinking," and vice versa. The dichotomy is reflected in the way each

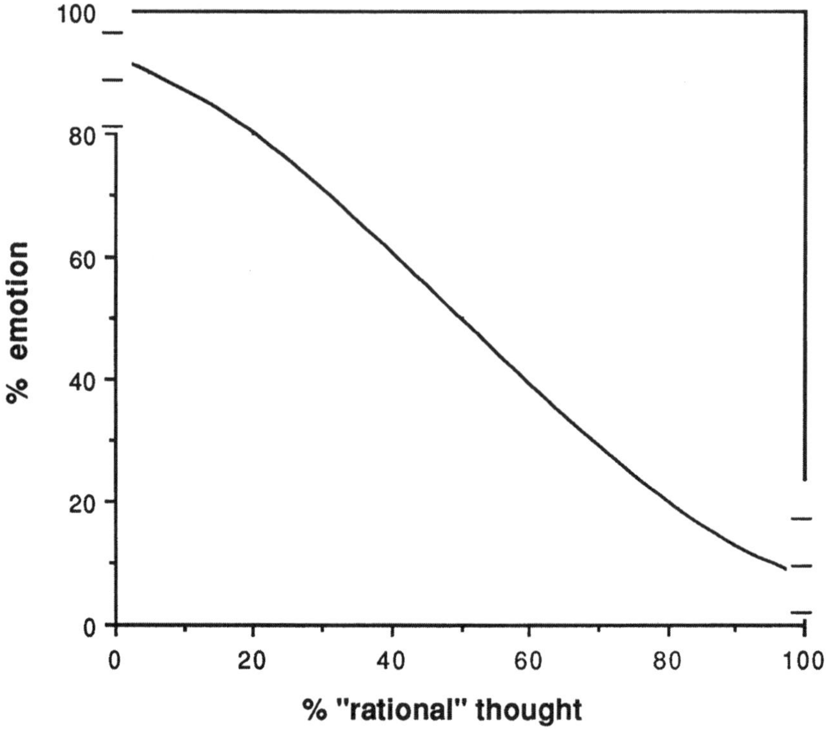

Figure 1.2. Classic Cartesian view of emotion and rational thought, in which the two are mutually exclusive. That is, the degree to which a person is thinking, or rational, varies inversely with the degree to which s/he is in an emotional state. The negative relationship holds true over the mid-range of degrees of emotionality or rationality, but at the extremes of either (very high emotionality or rationality), the opposite state is completely excluded.

has been studied: emotion is examined in terms of states or labels for states, while cognition is approached in terms of information processing. A simplified view of lateralized brain function – with the right hemisphere tuned to non-verbal, emotional, intuitive processes, the left to verbal, rational, and analytic thought – has entered popular culture because it reinforces this division, although the distinction is belied by intrahemispheric specialization and, especially, the functional interdependence of the two hemispheres (Fox 1991; Heller 1990; Silberman and Weingarten 1986). Emotion-thought distinctions are further reinforced by the notion that the two domains are localized in different brain regions: emotions have a ''home,'' characteristically located in the ancient interior basal structures of the brain, the limbic system. Extensive neural linkages between the limbic system and locations throughout the cerebral cortices are often overlooked or subject to interpretations skewed by views of limbic structures as primitive brain and the emotions as inimical to rational thought. Setting aside these important neurological details for the moment to pursue Cartesian logic in terms of the think–feel dichotomy, one can go on to characterize the distribution of experience-states by their feel–think composition on the level of the individual (Figure 1.3). We may then ask (as has frequently been asked; Abu-Lughod 1986; Heider 1991; Menon and Shweder 1994; Rosaldo 1984; Schieffelin 1985) whether and how culture shifts this distribution and exerts characteristic effects on experience and behavior apparent on the population level. Figure 1.3 represents the individual level, but if we take the leap to imagine that these curves represent population distributions in specific contexts, then the landscape, or social distribution of emotion states (analogous to Waddington's ''epigenetic developmental landscape'' [Waddington 1957]) across contexts describes ethos, while the landscape of mindful process in organization and representation of cultural knowledge describes eidos.

Alternatively, what if feeling and thought operate synergistically in much of experience and behavior? (Figure 1.4) Recent advances from cognitive neurobiology and neurology suggest that this is the case (Damasio 1994). Then, a positive relationship would obtain between emotion and conscious processing, with intensity in one enhancing intensity in the other, up to some cutoff. Actual slopes and shapes of the relationship would vary, both by domain and because of temperamental and experience-specific differences. Perhaps this synergy between emotion and thought is essential, that is, structurally integral to information processing (Figure 1.5). The vast majority of sensory information processing takes place preconsciously, which is also where parallel distributed processing occurs: what appears as consciousness from multiple and parallel inputs and throughputs is shaped by relative valences of processing networks. Consciousness rides on the crests of waves in a preconscious ocean: emotions can influence which wave will be ridden. Neurologically, emotions reside in the preconscious, for they center in the limbic system and thalamus, which are secondary and primary routes for incoming sensory information.

Emotions, then, are integral to cognition. First, they are crucial to preconscious processing, for they direct attention, mediate rapid shifts in states of arousal, and thereby shape what is consciously attended to and how closely (Heller 1990; LeDoux 1989; Oatley and Johnson-Laird 1987). Further, emotions participate in memory formation and retrieval, both unconscious and conscious. Emotion-processing areas, such as locations within the amygdala, store memories of emotion events that inform future emotional processing of experience (Aggleton 1992; Damasio 1994). The result is unconscious emo-

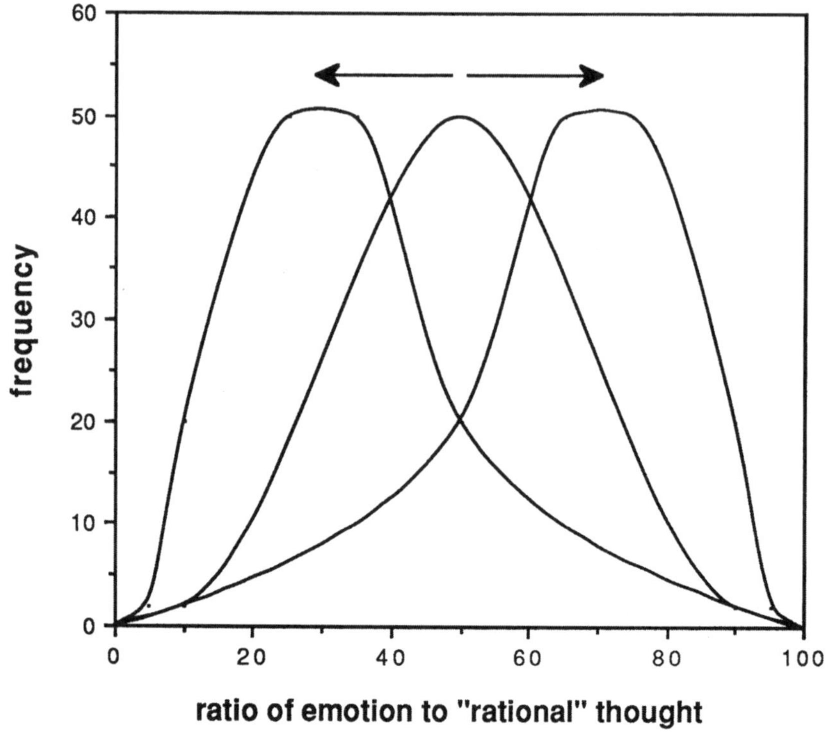

Figure 1.3. Schema extending Cartesian logic to individual temperament or disposition in terms of distribution of emotion/cognition ratios in mental states. The ratio of emotion to cognition or rationality is plotted by the frequency with which an individual is in that state. The arrows at the top indicate that the shapes of the curves, and hence their mode, may be evaluated on an individual basis in relation to cultural ideals, and thus form the basis of culture-specific attributions of temperament. Thus, in a Western view, the curve on the left might represent an ''impulsive'' person, while that on the right might represent a ''controlled'' person. Notions of culture and personality relate to the socialization practices and cultural demands on individual performance as bases for variation in these curves, or rather of population variation in their frequencies.

tional learning. Limbic structures, both amygdala and hippocampus, as well as hormones influenced by affective states, have been linked to modulation of memory and its conversion to long-term storage (de Wied *et al.* 1993; McEwen 1995; McGaugh 1989). Thus, emotion affects propositional learning: it influences what is remembered, inflects how it is remembered, and hence modulates the retrievable information base for future cognition. Addi-

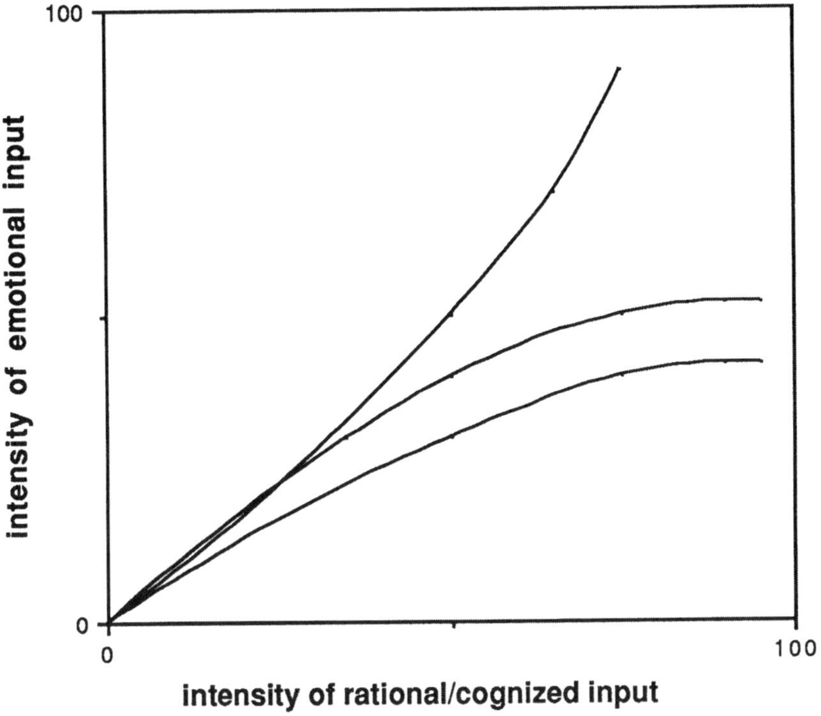

Figure 1.4. A model of emotion as intrinsic to thinking, or information processing, showing a synergistic relationship between intensity of emotional input and intensity of rational input in shaping ongoing information processing (rate and content). Because the numbers of factors under consideration may limit rate of information processing, and because emotion may assist in discounting alternatives (thus reducing computation size and increasing speed), the relationship of emotional and rational inputs to thought is nonlineal. The figure shows that steady emotional state may be required for sustained conscious computation, while very high emotional load may cut off sustained conscious consideration of alternatives or consequences. See also Damasio 1994: 173.

tionally, in their preconscious attention directing and prioritizing functions, emotions may also form a bridge to the unconscious (by definition, that which is and remains outside consciousness, including emotion memories), across which the unconscious "leaks" into thought or purposive action but eludes conscious scrutiny. Emotions may, like other perceptions, become conscious, and emotion experiences are then subject to the same conscious processes of experience, interpretation, schematization, and continuity maintenance as are

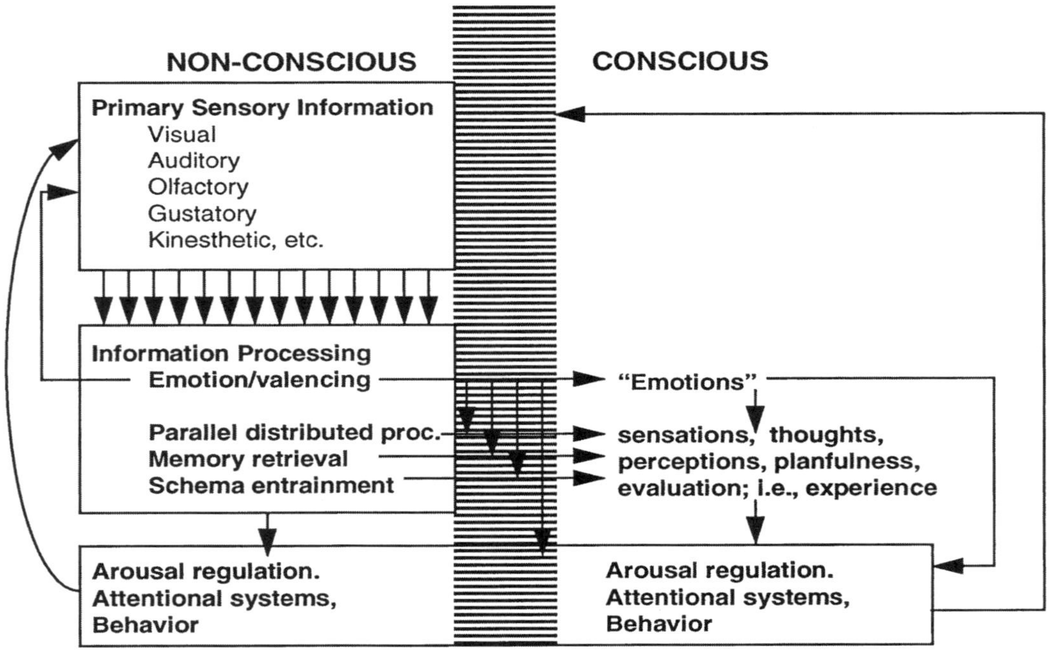

Figure 1.5. A model of relationships among central information processing modes, unconscious or preconscious, and conscious, along with of the role of emotion in trafficking among these modes and prioritizing within them. Notably, considerable peripheral information processing or selection has occurred prior to arrival at the CNS; much of regulatory emotional processing remains backgrounded, outside of consciousness but reflected in efferent outflows.
See also Leder 1990; Porges 1995.

other sensory perceptions or conscious thoughts (Lakoff 1987). Finally, emotions participate, often crucially and definitively, in meaning-making (Shore 1996).

A significant point pertaining to this reconceptualized role of emotion in cognition is the sheer multiplicity and volume of preconscious representations, in relation to what little becomes conscious. For instance, the visual system projects to multiple (likely more than eight) cortical areas that each delineate specific attributes and form representations that then collaborate and compete in composing what is consciously ''seen'' (Changeux 1985). Such parallel distributed processing of various aspects of sensory input in different neural nets greatly enhances the capacity for information extraction. At the same time, what becomes conscious is thus necessarily selective, often highly so: emotion shapes the selection and thereby forms a link in the dialectic between preconscious and conscious, as well as to the unconscious. In short, the input, storage, and processing capacities of the brain are large, consciousness is finite, and a very high functional premium is therefore placed on determining what to pay attention to and what to ignore or background. By attaching valence and weight to inputs and throughputs, emotion plays a key role in directing selective attention and prioritizing cognitive tasks (e.g., LeDoux 1990). It can also influence the apparent speed of cognition by focusing or diffusing attention and altering the intensity of directed cognition.

Moreover, cognitive-emotional lability acts as a medium for both coping and creativity. Selection from multiplicity can be a powerful means to generate flexible, condition-specific cognition to deal with a shifting, complex environment with competing, often conflicting, demands. If we reconsider the multiplicity of preconscious inputs we can, instead of seeing them as competing for conscious representation, view them as generators of diversity that act as grist for moment-to-moment selection in composing consciousness. Without this multiplicity and selection, experience and behavior would be pauperized. Likewise, we may say that the multiplicity of competing or conflicting sources of motivation and meaning are essential to human functioning over a lifetime in a complex, changeable sociable world. At the same time, temperament, or emotional disposition, can enhance experiential continuity in such a world.

In brief, emotions are intimately involved in information processing; they guide knowledge of the world by altering what we notice, enhancing learning, and evoking recall. Emotions also rapidly recruit memories and schemas, and integrate them in cognition and action. Finally, they provide bases for coping and creativity. These functions are essential to intelligent being-in-the-world: via emotions we do, indeed, ''mind.''

Ontogeny and the epidemiology of emotion

The second issue with Bateson's approach, noted above, was that of ''standardization,'' or shared aspects of affect and behavior. This inherently developmental concept implicitly relies on culturally determined commonality of experience to mediate standardization. Bateson's analysis is avowedly synchronic for practical purposes of presentation (Bateson 1958: 3), but development is none the less bracketed at the same time as it is recognized as central. Despite a distinguished history of comparative research on human development by Mead, the Whitings, LeVine, and others, anthropology remains strongly adult-centered. Yet the study of emotion, in particular, would appear to call for a developmental approach, and again, psychological anthropology has a strong history of work in this area (e.g., Whiting and Whiting 1975b; LeVine 1974, 1990; Levy 1984). This analysis builds on and expands that tradition by suggesting that, rather than to search for either the innate universal or the culture-specific features of emotion, we would engage emotion or emotional experience much more comprehensively by examining the interaction of innate and contingent factors in the constitution of emotion. The burden of existing evidence suggests that emotion comprises shared and nonshared elements. Indeed, one human universal appears to be the capacity to generate complex emotional repertoires contingent on experience (Plomin *et al.* 1994). Only a developmental analysis will reveal the dynamics of dispositional and cultural factors which inform adult emotional life, and the pathways by which specific factors exert their effects. In other words, any clarification of the sources of commonalties such as shared affective modes, much less of the sources of cross-individual variation or of cross-cultural diversity in emotions, must ultimately involve development.

An adequate view of emotion would furthermore integrate corporeal and cognitive dimensions, and the relationship of these dimensions as emergent through ontogeny. As discussed in the previous section, most processing of sensory information, including emotional processing, occurs in the unconscious, and thus much emotional experience is literally embodied, outside the realm of consciousness, and indeed often irretrievable for conscious examination (Leder 1990; LeDoux 1994). Such a view implies a distinction between unconsciousness and cognition as one between unconscious and conscious aspects of information processing or thought. Yet both aspects are embodied (that is, they have a material basis), and pursuit of the implications of this point by integrating advances in neuroscience with study of emotional experience, expression, and behavior has yielded exciting insights into the nature of emotion and thought (Churchland 1989; Damasio 1994; Leder 1990; LeDoux 1986).

The remainder of this chapter, then, will proceed to: (1) delineate a scheme that, via development, links the individual to the social-cultural level of analysis, and (2) specify and elaborate this model through the analysis of two well-studied issues, reactivity and well-being, and anger/hostility and life expectancy. These cases are selected not only because they demonstrate biosocial interrelationships in emotional development and function, but also because they remove the discussion from the realm of abstraction. They provide a phenomenological basis for sociocultural analysis through recognition of the truly embodied nature of emotional experiences created by aversive or inequitable conditions in socially constructed human ecologies. Through embodiment, social conditions become translated into physical outcomes that include impairment, suffering, and death. Conversely, such cases also demonstrate the importance of culture, of social conditions, and the experience of those conditions, for construction of meaningful lives and human well-being. That the effect of social conditions on outcomes is probabilistic rather than definitive, also reflects on the relationship of culture to individual.

Dual embodiment and the biocultural bases of local biology

Contemporary culture theory increasingly employs the notion of embodiment, a concept initially advanced by Merleau-Ponty (1962) to indicate the situated-projective relationship of subject to object in perception, and by Bourdieu (1977: 1243) to denote the "socially informed body." Conceptions of embodiment address the persistent conceptual gaps between mind and body, individual and society in both social and cognitive theory. For this reason, and because such gaps have widened with recent ascendance of social determinism in social theory, a more experience-near (Wikan 1991), phenomenological, or embodied approach to relations of individual to society or culture has become increasingly popular (Csordas 1994). As a concept, "embodiment" is applied "not to argue that the human body is an important object of anthropological study, but that a paradigm of embodiment can be elaborated for the study of culture and the self" (Csordas 1990: 53). On the one hand, culture or cultural ecology influences the form and function of the body and is said to be "inscribed" – or embodied – in persons (Figure 1.6) (Braidotti 1994; Broch-Due and Rudie 1993). Examples include simple physical transformations through circumcision or tattooing, and complex modifications such as conditioning (Weinberger 1995) or socially mediated acquisition of culture-specific language skills (Ochs and Schieffelin 1984) that entail permanent modifications in language ability (Changeux 1985). Through this usage of embodiment, culture can be shown to be more than skin deep, to organize corporeal function beyond the level of knowledge or thought. Indeed, some have used the notion of embodiment to extend cultural domination to the body, displace the notion of an innate or separate biological domain, and present the body as an artifact of culture (Butler 1993).

On the other hand, stringent cultural determinism scarcely accounts for human variation, invention and originality, deviance, or dissidence. Culture affects the probability that an individual encounters specific experiences at

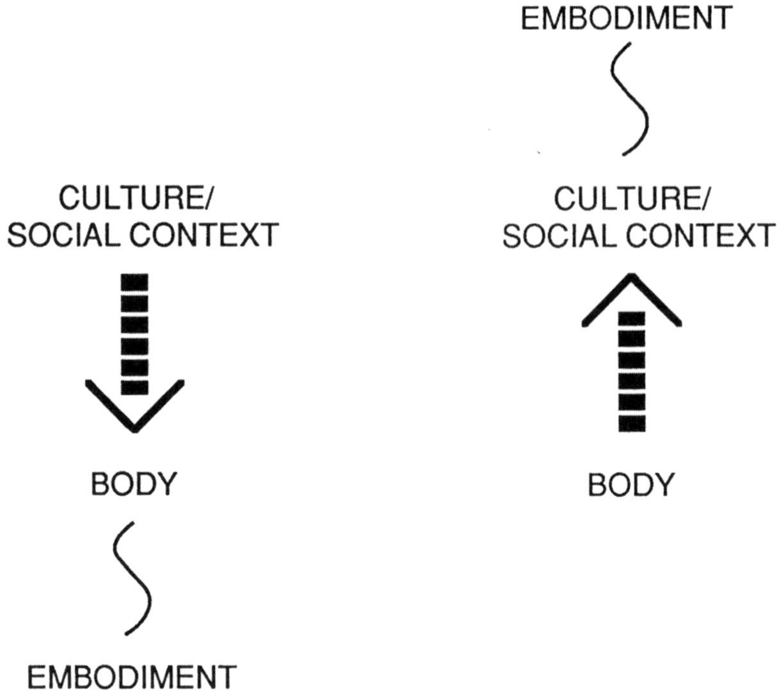

Figure 1.6. Dual embodiment schema

specific times. Within this probabilistic frame, the individual level of experience is determined by historical, idiosyncratic-local constitutional, and stochastic factors that generate very different individual experiences or life histories. For this reason, in Figure 1.6, although the arrow between culture and the body is direct insofar as culture does affect physical ontogeny and function, the arrow between the body and embodiment is wavy, or indeterminate and probabilistic, with respect to specific ways in which individuals are shaped by culture. Embodiment depends on developmental processes, and recent advances in many areas of developmental biology underscore the reliance of ontogenetic processes, by design, on environmental inputs to shape the course of development, from the molecular level upward (reviewed in Worthman 1992, 1993). This feature of organismic design establishes ontogeny as a co-construction of organism and its specific contexts, inputs, and experiences; hence, all biology is ''local'' and ontogeny is to some degree indeterminate, contingent on proximal interactions of individual and environment. Thus, a universal design feature can generate local biology, developmental indeterminacy, and variation (shaped in divergent or convergent ways). Moreover, developmentally emergent individual differences in motivation, perception, behavior, and physical attributes result in differing individual–environment interactions: individuals choose and influence their contexts, are differentially viewed and treated by others, and vary in perception of and responses to their phenomenological worlds. Thus, physical form and function, as well as affect, cognition, and behavior, dynamically co-emerge in the process of development: all these are components of embodiment as they constitute the individual as a set of conditions, dynamics, and actions-in-the-world.

Individuals are themselves social actors who, as members of a culture, participate in its instantiation and continual re-creation, for culture is not an entity disassociable from individual behaviors. Culture depends on practice for reproduction, or re-production. Thus, embodiment exerts phenomenological force and represents a force on, as well as a force in, culture. As culture shapes persons, those persons shape culture. This phenomenon represents the dual, or reciprocal, nature of embodiment (the right side of Figure 1.6): culture is also embodied in the sense that it is represented, re-created and modulated by its individual members, and fundamentally reflects the corporeal domain. Moreover, although the stream of social existence may transcend individuals, it must be actualized through individuals who thereby embody it. In this way, culture may be seen to be accountable, through ontogeny, to individuals through its probabilistic impact on the future affect, cognition, and behavior of those individuals: dual embodiment is the central dynamic in cultural epidemiology.

The notion of dual embodiment may be especially useful for understanding emotion. Emotions are particularly thorny for anthropologists because they require integration of individual and cultural levels of explanation, but they are interesting for just that reason. Emotions involve relational-evaluative stances of individual to situation. Moreover, they effect a crucial link in embodiment of the experiential self by entraining physical states with both individual experience and behavior. Relationships between physical and emotional states have been extensively investigated in psychology, psychiatry, and neurobiology, with a focus on physical concomitants or causes of emotional states (Figure 1.7, top panel). For instance, the study of depression and other mood disorders has focused heavily on identification of the biological factors within persons that cause depressive affect and psychobehavioral dysfunction (Schildkraut 1978; Siever and Davis 1985), with some consideration of reinforcement or feedback from emotional to biological function, largely in terms of how disorder becomes progressive (Gold *et al.* 1988). In other words, risk for becoming depressed is thought to have a genetic-biological

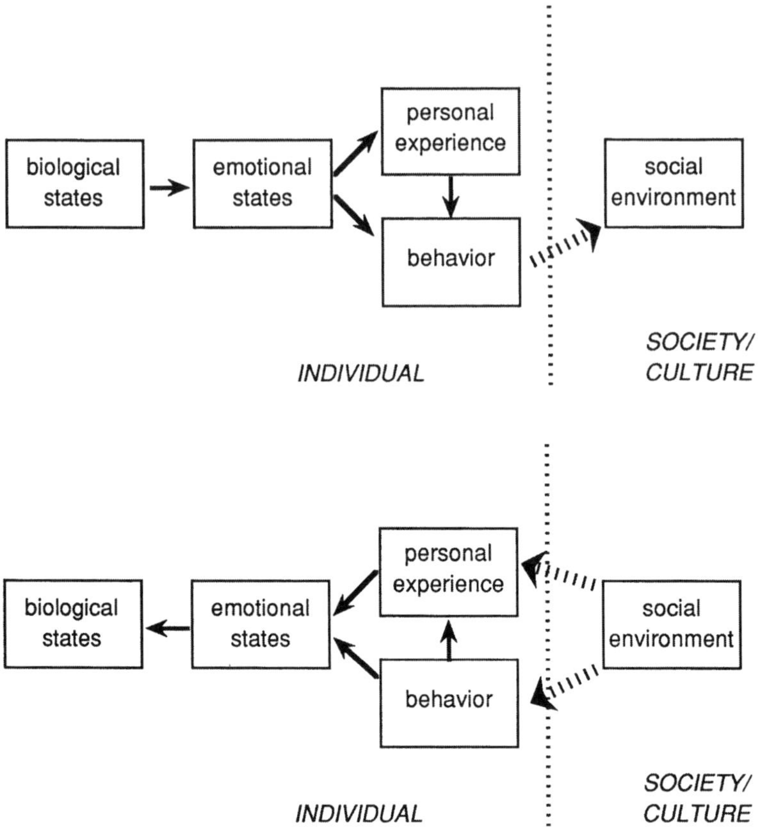

Figure 1.7. Two prevalent, and potentially complementary, models of relationships among biology, experience, and affect in etiology of affective disorders such as depression.

basis, but the biology of being depressed is associated with neuroendocrine and other physiologic states that may be as much the product as the cause of the condition.

The reverse set of linkages, from social experience to physical states via affective experience (Figure 1.7, bottom panel), has been less systematically explored. In the case of depression and other major affective disorders, associations of prevalence and onset with stressful life events have been repeatedly reported (Gold *et al.* 1988). Psychobiological interplay in emotions has been extensively explored under the conceptual umbrella of "stress." Perceived (psychosocial) stress is linked to extensive acute physiological changes (Sapolsky 1992) on even such "fundamental" levels as gastrointestinal activity and immune function, and patterns of stress influence long-term developmental and functional outcomes, including health, survivorship, and physical size. Again, in the case of affective disorder, biological risk factors are viewed not as direct causes of disorder, but as predisposing factors which interact with situational risk factors (Costello and Angold 1995). Informed by this interactive model of affective pathogenesis, clinical treatment has largely aimed to ameliorate individual biology and palliate symptoms, while epidemiologic and public health approaches also aim to uncover social-situational risk factors and to buffer or remove potentially damaging conditions. The approaches are synergistic, but differ profoundly in level of intervention and, thus, political implication: the one targets individual change to alter vulnerability to risk (Kramer 1993), while the other involves social change to alter exposure to risk (Breggin 1994). The goal of the present analysis is to demonstrate how a developmental biocultural approach to emotion yields insights which bear directly on such practical issues of human well-being, but space does not permit pursuit of implications of these insights.

The following two sections apply a biocultural, dual embodiment model through analysis of two substantial literatures concerning individual variation in affect.

Lifespan interactions of temperament and well-being

The complex social world of a long-lived species like humans has its vicissitudes, and everyone must endure their share of loss as well as enjoy a measure of gain. Yet the proverbial cup can be seen as half full or half empty, and events that are disturbing or exciting to one person can be overlooked by or seem uninteresting to another. The individual's interpretation of events, rather than the objective facts themselves, is what constitutes lived experience, the phenomenological world of feeling and knowledge, and the sources of motivation and behavior. If interpretation is key, then understanding the bases of interpretation is crucial. Here, ''interpretation'' has a dually embodied sense as involving not only psychobehavioral but also biological impact of experiences on individuals; moreover, individually characteristic patterns of biobehavioral impact arise developmentally (that is, through time) out of dynamics between the individual and the environment. Neither properties of the environment nor features of the individual are sufficient to explain individual variation in well-being; the interaction between these determines much of that variation. As Jemerin and Boyce put it, in an analytic review of childhood stress and illness: ''individual tendencies in physiologic responses may be seen as the biological analog of behavioral coping, and may thus reflect the operation of meaning at the physiologic level'' (Jemerin and Boyce 1990: 1413). They conclude that ''it may not be possible to understand the individual meaning of an event for a child without careful observation of both behavior and physiology'' (Jemerin and Boyce 1990: 1473). Recent research in behavioral pediatrics and child psychiatry establishes this point most vividly with the observations that stressors themselves account for merely 10 percent of variance in illness outcomes, that a stable subgroup comprising 15–20 percent of children experiences a significantly disproportionate amount of mental and physical morbidity and absorbs over half the medical service use, and that another substantial subgroup of children exposed to environmental risk does not experience poor outcomes (Barr *et al.* 1994; Boyce and Jemerin 1990; Liang *et al.* 1995). Individual and situational factors that exacerbate vulnerability or enhance resilience are currently under intense investigation; findings underscore the centrality of *person-environment* interaction (e.g., Granger *et al.* 1994b, 1996).

Developmental psychologists have investigated the nature and implications of individual differences in emotional valence and interpretive stance toward the world, known as temperament (Lewis 1989; Thomas and Chess 1977). Temperament is viewed as dispositional or innate, that is, seen very early, though etiology is not necessarily genetic. Yet the lived manifestations and consequences of temperament are increasingly understood as the product of person–environment interactions (e.g., Gunnar *et al.* 1992). Accordingly, investigators have sought to distinguish very early patterns in behavioral and concomitant physiological responses to stimuli or stress, and to test their predictiveness of both later reactions to experience and formation of social relationships (Calkins and Fox 1992; Fox 1991; Goldsmith *et al.* 1987; Gunnar *et al.* in press; Kagan and Snidman 1991; see also reviews in Fox 1994).

Temperament likely comprises multiple domains (physiological, affective, and behavioral). Relations across these domains, and of specific vectors within them, can be complex and non-linear. Thus, empirical and conceptual work on temperament is rapidly evolving through synergistic interactions of new data with emerging models, and investigators are clearly aware that current formulations are heuristic simplifications. It is impressive that, despite all these caveats, individual differences in responsiveness to experience, operationalized in terms of ''reactivity,'' have emerged in relation to variation in outcome. Using physiologic (heart rate change, vagal tone, cortisol release) and behavioral (crying, facial expression, movement, social engagability) measures of reactivity, arousal, or responsivity to social or situational novelty (Gunnar *et al.* 1989; Kagan and Snidman 1991; Tennes 1982), maternal separation (Gunnar *et al.* 1992; Kagan and Snidman 1991; Tennes 1982), or physical stress such as inoculation or heelstick (Ramsay and Lewis 1994; Worobey and Lewis 1989), investigators have repeatedly found that some infants and children respond more vigorously to unfamiliarity, uncertainty, frustration, or pain than do others. Further, they report significant, though by no means universal, temporal continuity in individual biobehavioral styles of coping with or responding to experience (Gunnar *et al.* 1989; Gunnar *et al.* in press; Snidman *et al.* 1995).

Kagan and colleagues have intensively studied a minority (15–20 percent) of infants and children who exhibit a biobehavioral pattern of dealing with stress or stimulus termed "reactive-inhibited." Relative to their peers, physiologically "reactive" and behaviorally "inhibited" infants are more easily excited, difficult to soothe, and less readily habituated, while shy or withdrawn children exhibit longer latency to play with unfamiliar objects, slowness to engage with adult strangers, and lassitude or crying during maternal separation (Kagan *et al.* 1987). Physiologic responses to these challenges include high, relatively invariant heart rates, low vagal tone, and exaggerated cortisol response without habituation through repeated experience (Fox 1989; Jemerin and Boyce 1990; Kagan 1992; Kagan *et al.* 1987; Lewis 1992). In reactive-inhibited individuals, familiarity with challenging stimuli may result in behavioral habituation in the absence of physiologic habituation; indeed, physiologic responses may escalate with repeated exposure (Granger *et al.* 1994a; Lewis and Ramsay 1995). Ontogenetic pathways to dissociation of physiologic and behavioral concomitants of experience remain unclear (Gunnar *et al.* 1989; Lewis and Ramsay 1995), but are of high interest from a dual embodiment perspective.

Work by Suomi and colleagues on developmental effects of rearing conditions in rhesus monkeys has provided a rich basis for insight and comparison in this area. In striking parallel to Kagan and colleagues' observations among children, they report that around 20 percent of rhesus exhibit exaggerated responses to situational novelty or brief social separations, characterized by high cortisol and noradrenaline turnover, high and more stable heart rates, and behavioral inhibition (Suomi 1991). Patterns of reactivity show high individual stability over time (Higley *et al.* 1992; Suomi 1991). Their findings suggest that long-term effects exerted by early social experiences vary depending on individual constitution or temperament. Specifically, social, behavioral, and biological outcomes of high-reactive infants are more affected by rearing conditions than those of low-reactive infants: high-reactive rhesus reared by very nurturant foster mothers were behaviorally precocious and showed most rapid adjustment and high social dominance when transferred to large peer groups, whereas those fostered by "average" mothers were socially avoidant and attained low dominance status, and low-reactive monkeys assumed intermediate status irrespective of rearing condition (Suomi 1991).

As a possible substrate for such differences in reactivity, these investigators have identified individual differences in neuroendocrine activity (serotonin

[5-HIAA] and noradrenaline [MHPG] turnover) with significant biparental heritable components (Higley *et al.* 1993). Studies of free-ranging rhesus on Cayo Santiago have shown that a cerebrospinal fluid (CSF) marker of brain serotonin turnover, 5-HIAA, in adolescent macaque males correlated positively with levels of affiliative sociality and time of emigration from the natal troop (Mehlman *et al.* 1995) and negatively with rates of risk-taking, escalated aggression, and wounding (Mehlman *et al.* 1994). Such studies further demonstrated that early physiologic or behavioral responses to social stress or capture predicted antibody titers following immunization (Laudenslager *et al.* 1993). Finally, rearing conditions (peer *vs.* mother) exerted enduring effects on cortisol patterns and neuroendocrine activity (monoamine and noradrenaline turnover) both routinely and during social isolation: peer-reared monkeys exhibited greater physiologic responses to social stress (separation) than did maternal-reared peers (Higley *et al.* 1992).

In sum, studies of rhesus suggest that: (1) individual reactivity can be a product of genetic inheritance or of early experience alike, (2) long-term effects of early experience may be exhibited only under particular conditions, such as specific types of social deprivation or uncertainty; and (3) effects of early experience depend on individual temperament through the interaction of individual reactivity with specific contexts or experiences. Such ''embodied'' styles of relating with the world influence not only behavior patterns and social relations across the lifespan, but also physiologic determinants of health and longevity. The subsequent section will deal with risk for chronic disease, but here one should note that perceived negative stress and life events have been associated with decreased or suppressed immune function, and thus with risk for infectious disease. In a study serendipitously spanning the Loma Prieto earthquake, children with high versus low pre-earthquake immunologic reactivity to kindergarten entry subsequently showed insignificant post-earthquake increases in illness when earthquake impact on parents was low, but illness rates declined sharply in low-reactive and increased markedly in high-reactive children if parent impact was high (Boyce *et al.* 1993). Consequently, variation in child reactivity to mild, normative stress (school entry) emerged as a predictor of illness rates dependent on social conditions (parent distress) following a major stress or stressor. In the many parts of the world where pathogen load and child mortality are high, differential vulnerability to major normative (e.g., weaning) or non-normative (warfare, displacement) stress may attain even greater import for health and survival.

This brief survey of the substantial developmental literature on temperament brings several points to bear on emotion and dual embodiment, and we can begin to discern how divergent biosocial life histories can be constructed through interactions of constitutional and conditional variables. First, individual differences in biobehavioral affective styles of relating to experience (reactivity) create variation in the effects of any given experience. Temperamental variation furthermore comprises degree of reactivity to specific aspects of experience, such as frustration, social loss, or physical discomfort. Reactivity includes threshold to react, duration of reaction or time to restabilization, and ability to habituate to repeated stimulation (Lewis 1989, 1992). Hence, degree of individual variation in impact of an experience, including type, magnitude, threshold, duration, and contingency (habituation) of response, depends in part on specific characteristics of the experience. Second, cultural practices influence the timing, type, and frequency of specific experiences. For instance, maternal workload may allow infants continuous contact over the first two years of life (e.g., Ache; Hurtado *et al.* 1992), or may require early and prolonged maternal separation. Additionally, social variables such as status or role differentiation may create systematic intracultural variation in experience. For example, the timing and abruptness of weaning for Samoan infants may depend on maternal status and number of alternate caregivers (Ochs and Schieffelin 1984). Moreover, the content of alternate caregiving is known to influence infant separation distress (Gunnar *et al.* 1992). Third, culture merely influences the probability of exposure to a given experience or set of experiences; actual individual experience is conditioned by historical, proximate, and stochastic factors. However common their circumstances (e.g., twins) no two individuals will ever have the same set of specific experiences, in type, sequence, or frequency. This leads to developmental indeterminacy with respect to effects of cultural factors such as caregiving and socialization practices. Anthropologists have been slow to appreciate the ontogenetic and cultural opportunities and constraints this situation represents. Fourth, temperament–environment interaction modulates individual phenomenology of even shared experiences. Experiences may be common, culturally marked as normative rather than traumatic (e.g., weaning, brief maternal absences, school entry), but their impact on individuals varies. Predictability of or degree of control over experience may vary not only among cultures but within them along class/status or other social ecologies (Anderson and Armstead 1995). The degree to which maternal versus paternal status affects regulation and predictability of early child experience has scarcely been explored. Fifth, feed-forward ontogenetic processes shaped by person–environment interactions set up future trajectories of actual and lived experience that further interact with the evolving social niche the individual comes to inhabit through both attainment and ascription. Early variation in styles of relating to the world, however attained, sets up different relationships with others, which elicits different treatment by them, which further influences experience and the impact of experience, with implications for future psychosocial and biological outcomes (Gunnar *et al.* 1995, 1997). Variation in situational factors (such as maternal nurturance or household composition) influences the trajectory of this cascade and means that long-term effects of early constitutional affective differences are not a foregone conclusion, but contingent on sociocultural and even stochastic variables.

To conclude this section, the developmental literature on temperament directly supports the central role of emotion in being-in-the-world, for variation in affective responsiveness influences how information is perceived, evaluated, and acted upon, in both the present and the future. It demonstrates the role of biological variation in psychobehavioral variation, and identifies the intersection of person and context as a major determinant of variable outcomes. The next section probes more explicitly how the converse also obtains, that is, how experience conditions the psychophysiology of emotion and behavior regulation, with consequences for psychosocial and physical well-being. In particular, it details evidence concerning the role of emotions as mediators of biological effects of social experience, and traces the dual embodiment of social structural conditions for adversity or inequity.

Hardship, hostility, and health

The example of "hostility" represents a second well-studied exemplar of the influence of social conditions on emotion development, person *vs.* environment interaction in constructions of the life course, and the consequences of these for health (see McCall 1994 for a powerful account). Research in the United States has traced linkages among negative affect, negative experiences, temperament or reactivity, and long-term health outcomes. Specifically, associations of hostility to shortened life expectancy have been persuasively though not definitively documented, and developmental bases for this relationship are emerging (reviewed in Smith 1992; Williams 1994). Hostility has been defined as "a set of negative attitudes, beliefs, and appraisals concerning others [and] . . . connotes a view of others as frequent and likely sources of mistreatment, frustration, and provocation" (Smith 1992: 139). It involves various emotional (anger, irritation, resentment, contempt), cognitive (cynicism, hostile attributions), and behavioral (aggression, antagonism, uncooperativeness) components. Hostility has been related to increased sympathetic activation and cardiovascular reactivity reflected by elevated blood pressure and heart rate under specific social conditions, which conditions are salient interpersonal rather than non-social stressors (Smith 1992). Notably, these associations are more commonly identified for men than for women. Hostility thus appears to increase risk for coronary disease directly, as well as indirectly through its associations with increased risk-taking and health risk behaviors (smoking, caffeine consumption, obesity) (Scherwitz *et al.* 1991).

As with reactivity, hostility can be a product of experience; a variety of contextual factors point to ontogenetic and contextual bases for the emergence of hostility. Although age continuity of individual temperament scores has been consistently supported (Campos *et al.* 1989), not all those who test as reactive in infancy go on to become reactive adults, and initial low-reactives may become high-reactive. Such plasticity argues for contextual effects on temperament. Characteristics of rearing environment have been shown to influence rates of hostility in children and young adults, among whom elevated blood pressure, obesity, hostility, and disruptive behavior have been linked to psychosocial stress and parental harshness or neglect (Anderson *et al.* 1989; Ewart 1991; Lissau and Sorensen 1994; Woodall and Matthews 1989). In addition, hostility is associated with self-reports of diminished positive and heightened aversive interactions in the family (Woodall and Matthews 1989), as well as with elevated resting blood pressure in children. Quality of experience can interact with temperament or reactivity to positive as well as negative effect. In line with the findings on rhesus discussed previously, children with high cardiovascular reactivity experienced high rates of injuries in high-stress settings and low injury rates in low-stress settings (Barr *et al.* 1994); moreover, high-reactive adolescent boys reporting many positive life events also reported far fewer risk behaviors than their peers (Liang *et al.* 1995).

While proximal psychosocial etiologies including disruption of attachment have been advanced to explain these patterns, the larger set of socioeconomic circumstances that influence and at times constrain or disrupt parental behaviors and other determinants of rearing environment should also be considered (see discussions in Chisholm 1996). Rates of hostility are consistently and negatively related to socioeconomic status (SES) (Scherwitz *et al.* 1991), especially in non-whites, among whom poverty associates with particularly high hostility levels (Barefoot *et al.* 1991); once direct and indirect effects of class are removed, African Americans still experience excess mortality. Ironical environments play a role in these effects. From studies with bonnet macaques, Rosenblum and colleagues report effects of predictability of resource availability and maternal foraging requirement on psychosocial development of their infants, and suggest the effects are mediated by erosion of infant attachment through impact on maternal behavioral coping and caregiving (Rosenblum and Andrews 1994). Compared to infants whose mothers had stable and low foraging demand, those whose mothers had variable (high-low) foraging loads showed greater acutc behavioral disturbance, increased behavioral inhibition in novel situations as juveniles (Andrews and Rosenblum 1993), lower social affiliative competence and social subordination as subadults (Andrews and Rosenblum 1994), and evidence that long-term effects are organized by developmental shifts in neuroregulatory noradrenergic and serotonergic systems (Rosenblum *et al.* 1994). Maternal deprivation has previously been associated with acute and long-term alterations in levels and ratios of markers for activity of these two systems in rhesus macaques (Kraemer *et al.* 1989).

Noradrenergic and serotonergic systems are thought to play important roles in environmental monitoring and evaluation, and in behavioral inhibition or restraint for humans (Gray 1982; 1987), so that shifts in the relative activity of these systems could alter styles of perception and behavior, or temperament (Rogeness *et al.* 1992). Diminished monoamine activity has been repeatedly linked to increased cardiovascular reactivity, increased eating, impulsivity, and irritability or aggression (Williams 1994). Serotonergic development shows an unusual, extended developmental window for fiber formation, and a recent exhaustive review suggested that activity- or experience-induced changes in brain neuropeptide levels may influence the final anatomy and physiology of this system (Jacobs and Azmitia 1992). Stress-related hormones (CRH, ACTH, cortisol) (Dunn and Berridge 1990; McEwen *et al.* 1986) have been shown to be important for maintenance (Azmitia *et al.* 1995) and regulation (Chaouloff 1993) of serotonergic neurons, but elevated levels of these hormones shift the balance of 5-HT receptor types implicated in maintaining resilience in affective state (McEwen 1995) and even, in ontogeny, affect serotonergic innervation of the hypothalamus to alter maturation rate and adult behavior (Alves *et al.* 1993).

Neural developmental plasticity, including anatomic and physiologic organization through inputs and throughputs supplied by the environment and the behaving individual, have recently been discovered as central ontogenetic principles of the nervous system. The above line of evidence suggests that ontogeny of neuroendocrine systems regulating arousal, irritability, cardiovascular reactivity, and eating behavior is affected by early stress, and provides a set of possible connections from experience to the biological bases of temperament. Emotion may provide a central mechanism for integration of external conditions (inputs) with internal neurodevelopmental processes and behavior regulation (outputs). Pain or fear and physical stress have been shown to exert permanent effects on sensory processing (Weinberger 1995) and adrenocortical function (Meaney *et al.* 1991), respectively.

Connections of hostility to hardship and then to health risk may contribute to the well-documented relationship of SES to life expectancy in developed countries, a relationship that persists when effects of health care access are removed (Adler *et al.* 1993; Anderson and Armstead 1995) and is strongest where wealth inequities are greatest, as in the United States (Wilkinson 1992). Negative life events occur more frequently and carry greater emotional impact at low SES (Cohen and Wills 1985; McLeod and Kessler 1990); beyond distress, other affective conditions associated with SES include hostility (Barefoot *et al.* 1991; Scherwitz *et al.* 1991) and depression (Murphy *et al.* 1991). In the United States, ethnicity interacts with class to produce exaggeratedly high rates of affective distress, morbidity, and mortality at low levels of SES for African Americans (Anderson and Armstead 1995; Kessler and Neighbors 1986; McCord and Freeman 1990). Due in part perhaps to escalation of wealth inequity in the United States and male vulnerability to developing hostility, SES-related mortality differentials increased strongly in men over recent decades, and only weakly in women (reviewed in Anderson and Armstead 1995).

This section has focused on a case study of situational effects on affective experience and regulation, which effects are mediated by psychobiological processes in development, and also carry implications for health and life expectancy. The case exemplifies, for a particular society at a particular time, the dimension of dual embodiment that concerns cultural effects on the body, but to complete the dual model advanced here requires reciprocal links of individual hostility status to cultural phenomena. Williams (1994) provides striking findings replicated across three independent samples of Americans previously scored for hostility and used in prior investigations of the health-hostility connection: when asked whether they had favored bombing or continuation of economic sanctions during the period prior to the Persian Gulf War of January 1991, three-quarters of individuals with higher hostility scores preferred bombing, while three-quarters of those with lower hostility preferred continued sanctions. Insofar as emotion mediates information processing, monitoring of ongoing conditions, and behavior regulation, an affective foundation of social life is established. The social ecologies encountered by developing individuals inform their future cognition and behavior substantially through emotional pathways, and thus as agents of culture, they come to construct it as it has constructed them.

Emotion and the biocultural interface

An inquiry into the nature and functions of emotion has also led to insights about the nature of culture, the relationship of individual and culture, and the role of biocultural processes in differential human well-being. Emotions are central to reciprocal processes of bringing forward physical states into personal experience and social behavior, as well as of transducing individual social experience into physical states. This dual embodiment instantiates the relationship of individual to culture. That relationship must also be understood ontogenetically, and the above cases suggest the hypothesis that socialization occurs principally through affective, non-conscious routes rather than through rational or conscious means. Through dual embodiment, individuals undergo ''deep socialization,'' in which anatomy, physiology, cognition, and emotion dynamically represent the history of person–environment interactions.

Implications of the above case studies for the present discussion of emotions are direct. First, transparency for actors of cultural construction of everyday life not only relies on internalization of cultural schemas (Shore 1996), but also occurs because things-as-they-are ''feel right'' (Johnson 1987; Leder 1990) Affective normalization occurs even under apparently inimical or aversive conditions, as when poverty and neglect promote hostility, which is then viewed as a property of the person, an aspect of the self, rather than of the situation. Second, because of the centrality of person-environment interaction, the emotional concomitants of any life circumstance must be determined empirically, not inferentially. Impact of sociocultural conditions may be positive or negative, depending on both constitutional characteristics of the individual and specific characteristics of the environment. Third, some roles and other social circumstances are not assigned randomly; rather, individuals self-select or are recruited into them, which, in turn, may influence the relationship between social experience and biology via differential emotional responses. Conversely, experiences shape affective styles, and non-self-selected cultural ecology or microecology also strongly stamps emotional learning, and thereby influences styles of relating to the world. The two latter points imply that individuals do not live in ''culture,'' they live in very specific social microenvironments that are co-constructed through both systematic and idiosyncratic cultural-contextual and individual-physical processes.

We have also traced constitutional (temperament) and situational (hardship) factors in emotion experiences and regulation that, in turn, influence health and survival. In part via affective processes, then, culture influences human capital, both quantitatively (survival), and qualitatively (psychological and physical capacities; mental and physical well-being).

Two important limitations on the present discussion should be noted. For one, the cases and data on humans presented have all been drawn from United States populations. Therefore, the findings and models may be products of specific social and cultural circumstances and require comparative investigation. Little cross-cultural research concerning reactivity is available (but see Lewis *et al.* 1993; Murphy and McGarvey 1994), but what is there suggests that study of population differences in early temperament and later reactivity will be important for developing biocultural models in general and, specifically, unpacking psychosomatic dynamics linking physical and mental health to issues of culture, such as acculturation, class, performance demands, or value systems.

Another substantial limitation is that the data and models presented here are based on differential probability rather than direct causality. That is, the association of hostility with poverty in the United States is not one-to-one: by no means all poor persons become high-reactive or hostile, and not all hostile persons are poor. Rather, those living in poverty have significantly greater rates of hostility than those who do not, and thus may be said to be at greater ''risk'' for becoming hostile. Statistical techniques used to identify such associations cannot draw causal inferences, they merely demonstrate covariance. Moreover, members of a risk group who do not experience the outcome (''positive deviants'') are of possible interest for identifying factors that associate with resistance or resilience in the face of risk.

This probabilistic or epidemiologic perspective could be of considerable use to the study of culture processes, including socialization, as captured in the concept of developmental indeterminacy. Through the dynamic of dual embodiment and using a developmental perspective, the co-constitutive domains of biology and culture have been shown to act in a probabilistic and contingent, and hence non-deterministic manner in effecting individual phenotypes, or outcomes. Such a view helps anthropology to resolve the historical paradox created by expecting shared biology to account for human universals and non-shared culture to drive human variation between populations, while simultaneously expecting shared culture to account for uniformities and non-shared biology to drive variation within them. The concept of local biology (Lock 1995: 370–374), as I use it here, flags how universal features of biology (i.e., environmental expectancy and ontogenetic dependency on external inputs by design) can generate individual biological variation as well as produce uniformity through variation or convergence in experience during ontogeny, and in person-environment interactions. The problem with embodiment as currently conceptualized in anthropology and the humanities lies in an oversimplification of biology: a universal body is predicated on a universal biology, from which it follows that biological variation associated with differences in health, function, or cognition is a product of cultural intervention. Conversely, the probabilistic relationship among culture and individual experience, plus the dynamic interplay between individual biology, cultural constructions of experience, and actual impacts on the individual, leads to considerable individual variation in psychobehavioral outcomes. Nevertheless, shared features in expectable environments of rearing and social life, plus shared features of biological design, create shared environments within and between populations that result in human psychobehavioral universals or universal ranges of variation, while also accounting for greater probability of shared features within populations driven by greater probability of shared experience in certain domains. These insights provide renewed scope for considering the interplay between individual and society, biology and culture. For instance, do individuals with differing temperamental styles experience differential fit with different cultures, so that, for instance, a high reactive individual fares well in one society and very poorly in another? Do behavior, affective, or physical health problems manifest prominently in one society and infrequently in another reflect practices influencing development of emotion and arousal regulation? These are classic concerns of psychological anthropology for which the biocultural model promoted here should provide fresh leverage.

Emotions make the difference in our lives. Not ''just'' feelings, they form an integral part of the biocultural interface, and lie at the heart of human intelligence, sociality, and well-being. Thus, in the present account and other ongoing research, emotions are being rescued from their opposing statuses as universal biological products of ''primitive nature,'' cognitive noise from our animal selves, or as universally variable ''cultural artefacts,'' cognitive icing piped on a culturally constructed cake. Emergence of a developmental biocultural paradigm is central to this promising re-vision that allows us to account for, and work with, the fundamental bases of our similarities and differences, and to apply these new insights to addressing inequities in human health and well-being.

Coda

In closing, the point of this chapter may be brought home by the simple exercise of stepping back to reflect for a moment on knowledge and emotion structures in the context of this essay. Visual and verbal information were combined in contrasting ways. Black and white graphics, value-laden hallmarks of standardized scientific presentation, were used. But the graphic pseudoquantitative models represented not quantitative data or models, but thought experiments about emotion and cognition that cast doubt on the concepts behind them. You were presented with specific studies and findings, framed so as to have a salient and ''this-is-real'' quality, but the argument progressed through assemblage of disparate data bits culled from multiple studies at different analytic levels (molecular to contextual) to form an emergent pattern, like a jigsaw puzzle. A wildly abstracted image of ''mind'' was presented, in which static graphic elements and spatial relations expressed a complex dynamic that, along with the similarly abstract dual embodiment model, comprised the conceptual heart of the chapter which the ''real-world'' data addressed. Throughout, the tension was between the apparent and the real in search of the ''true''; the argument proceeded by bringing up uncertainty, confusion or paradox balanced off by analytic resolution or logical closure, alternating abstract propositions with supporting evidence and capped by summary conclusions. Oscillation between inconsistency and consistency, doubt and resolution, concept and data creates a feeling of progression. Thus, knowledge and emotion structures were completely intertwined in this formal communication, which leaves an ethos–eidos distinction as experientially, if not analytically, uninteresting. The action is in the interplay, as instantiated in the individual. Whatever the social constructions of emotion may be, the individual ''feels'' and therefore ''knows'' the difference that emotions make in the embodied self. Indeed, via embodiment, the person *is* the difference. Like participants in any of the studies mentioned here, you readers, too, comprise a selected group and embody specific ways of knowing-feeling that have, I hope, made communication here possible. Finally, the fact that we can and do communicate in this way defines and redefines (i.e., ''makes'') culture.

Acknowledgments

Ideas presented here were first discussed in papers given at the Society for Psychological Anthropology, 1992, the Emory Mellon Symposium on Emotion, 1993, and the American Anthropological Association annual meetings, 1993. My thanks to the organizers of these symposia (Gilbert Herdt, Bradd Shore, Alex Hinton, respectively) for providing the impetus to develop these ideas, to the W. T. Grant Foundation for Faculty Scholar and grant support, and to student colleagues (Alex Hinton, Donald Smith, Keith McNeal, Jim Rilling) for stimulating conversation on diverse related themes. I also thank John Whiting, Robert LeVine, and Beatrice Whiting for many discussions that likely influence this work. Finally, in many unanticipated but finally important ways, this chapter is both informed by and responds to colleagues in the Consortium on Developmental Psychobiology of Stress, Ron Barr, Tom Boyce, Lonnie Zeltzer, Megan Gunnar, Michael Lewis, Steve Porges, and Chris Coe.

NOTE

1. The metaphor invoked by the notions of cognitive or emotional landscape is similar to that of Waddington's epigenetic landscape (Waddington 1957). Indeed, in the preface to the first edition, Bateson thanks Waddington for having read parts of the manuscript.

References

Abu-Lughod, L. 1986. *Veiled sentiments*. Berkeley: University of California Press.

Adler, M. E., W. T. Boyce, M. A. Chesney, S. Folkman, and S. L. Syme. 1993. Socioeconomic inequalities in health: No easy solution. *Journal of the American-Medical Association* 269:3140–3145.

Aggleton, J. P., ed. 1992. *The amygdala: Neurobiological aspects of emotion, memory and mental dysfunction*. New York: Wiley-Liss.

Alves, S. E., H. M. Akbari, E. C. Axmitia, and F. L. Strand. 1993. Neonatal ACTH and corticosterone alter hypothalamic monoamine innervation and reprodutive parameters in the female rat. *Peptides* 14:379–384.

Anderson, M. B. and C. A. Armstead. 1995. Toward understanding the association of socioeconomic status and health: A new challenge for the biopsychosocial approach. *Psychosomatic Medicine* 57:213–225.

Anderson, M. B., H. F. Myers, T. Pickering, and J. S. Jackson. 1989. Hypertension in blacks: Psychosocial and biological perspectives. *Journal of Hypertension* 7: 161–172.

Andrews, M. W. and L. A. Rosenblum. 1993. Assessment of attachment in differentially reared infants monkeys *Macaca radiata*): Response to separation and a novel environment. *Journal of Comparative Psychology* 107:84–90.

1994. The development of affiliative and agonistic social patterns in differentially reared monkeys. *Child Development* 65: 1398–1404.

Azmitia, E. C., V. J. Rubenstein, J. A. Strafaci, J. C. Rios and P. M. Whitaker-Azmitia. 1995. 5-HT1A agonist and dexamethasone reversal of para-chloroamphetamine induced loss of MAP-2 and synaptophysin immunoreactivity in adult rat brain. *Brain Research* 677:181–192.

Barefoot, J. C., B. L. Peterson, W. G. Dahlstrom, I. C. Siegler, N. B. Anderson, and R. B. Williams. 1991. Hostility patterns and health implications: Correlates of Cook-Medley Hostility Scale scores in a national survey. *Health Psychology* 10: 18–24.

Barr, R. G., W. T. Boyce, and L. K. Zeltzer 1994. The stress-illness association in children: A perspective from the biobehavioral interface. In *Stress, risk, and resilience in children and adolescents*, ed. R. J. Haggerty, L. R. Sherrod, M. Garmezy, and M. Rutter. Cambridge: Cambridge University Press, 182–224.

Bateson, G. 1958. *Naven*. Stanford: Stanford University Press.

Bourdieu, P. 1977. *Outline of a theory of practice*. Cambridge: Cambridge University Press.

Boyce, W. T. and J. M. Jemerin. 1990. Psychobiological differences in childhood stress response. I. Patterns of illness and susceptibility. *Journal of Developmental and Behavioral Pediatrics* 11:86–94.

Boyce, W. T., E. A. Chesterman and N. Martin. 1993. Immunologic changes occurring at kindergarten entry predict respiratory illnesses following the Loma Prieta earthquake. *Journal of Developmental and Behavioral Pediatrics.* 14:296–303.

Braidotti, R. 1994. *Embodiment and sexual difference in contemporary feminist theory*. New York: Columbia University Press.

Breggin, P. R. 1994. *Talking back to Prozac: What doctors won't tell you about today's most controversial drug*. New York: St. Martin's Press.

Broch-Due, V. and I. Rudie. 1993. Carved flesh, cast selves: an introdution. In *Carved flesh/cast selves: Gendered symbols and social practices*, ed., V. Broch-Due, I. Rudie and T. Bleie. Oxford: Berg, 1–39.

Butler, J. 1993. *Bodies that matter*. New York: Routledge.

Calkins, S. D. and N. A. Fox. 1992. The relations among infant temperament, security of attachment, and behavioral inhibition at twenty-four months. *Child Development* 63:1456–1472.

Campos, J. J., R. G. Campos, and K. C. Barrett. 1989. Emergent themes in the study of emotional development and emotion regulation. *Developmental Psychology* 25:394–402.

Changeux, J.-P. 1985. *Neuronal man*. New York: Pantheon.
Chaouloff, F. 1993. Physiopharmacological interactions between stress hormones and central serotonergic systems. *Brain Research Reviews* 18:1–32.
Chisholm, J. S. 1996. The evolutionary organization of attachment organization. *Human Nature* 7:1–37.
Churchland, P. S. 1989. *Neurophilosophy: Toward a unified science of the mind/brain*. Cambridge, MA: Bradford Books/MIT Press.
Cohen, S. and T. A. Wills. 1985. Stress, social support and the buffering hypothesis. *Psychological Bulletin* 98:310–357.
Costello, E. J. and A. Angold. 1995. Developmental epidemiology. In *Developmental psychopathology, Vol. 1: Theory and methods*, ed. D. Cicchetti, D. S. Cohen. New York: John Wiley, 23–56.
Csordas, T. J. 1990. Embodiment as a paradigm for anthropology. *Ethos* 18:5–47.
Csordas, T. J., ed. 1994. *Embodiment and experience: The existentialist ground of culture*. New York: Cambridge.
Damasio, A. R. 1994. *Descartes' error: emotion, reason, and the human brain*. New York: Avon Books.
de Wied, D., M. Diamant, and M. Fodor. 1993. Central nervous system effects of the neurohypophyseal hormones and related peptides. *Frontiers in Neuroendocrinology* 14:251–302.
Dunn, A. J. and C. W. Berridge. 1990. Physiological and behavioral responses to corticotropin-releasing factor administration: Is CRF a mediator of anxiety or stress responses? *Brain Research Reviews* 15:71–100.
Ewart, C. D. 1991. Familial transmission of essential hypertension: Genes, environments, and chronic anger. *Annals of Behavioral Medicine* 13:40–47.
Fox, M. A., ed. 1994. *The development of emotion regulation*. Chicago: University of Chicago Press.
Fox, N. A. 1989. Psychophysiological correlates of emotional reactivity during the first year of life. *Developmental Psychology* 25:364–372.
1991. If it's not left, it's right. *American Psychologist* 46:863–872.
Gold, P. W., F. K. Goodwin, and G. P. Chrousos. 1988. Clinical and biochemical manifestations of depression: Relation to the neurobiology of stress. *New England Journal of Medicine* 319:348–353.
Goldschmidt, W. 1975. Absent eyes and idle hands: Socialization for low affect among the Sebei. *Ethos* 3: 157–163.
Goldsmith, H. H., A. H. Buss, R. Plomin *et al.* 1987. Roundtable: What is temperament? Four approaches. *Child Development* 58:505–529.
Granger, D. A., K. Stansbury, and B. Henker. 1994a. Preschoolers' behavioral and neuroendocrine responses to social challenge. *Merrill-Palmer Quarterly* 40: 190–211.
Granger, D. A., J. R. Weisz, and D. Kauneckis. 1994b. Neuroendocrine reactivity, internalizing behavior problems, and control-related cognitions in clinic-referred children and adolescents. *Journal of Abnormal Psychology* 103:267–276.
Granger, D. A., J. R. Weisz, J. T. McCracken, S. C. Ikeda *et al.* 1996. Reciprocal influences among adrenocortical activation, psychosocial processes, and the behavioral adjustment of clinic-referred children. *Child Development* 67:3250–3262.

Gray, J. A. 1982. *The neuropsychology of anxiety: An inquiry into the functions of the septal-hippocampal system.* Oxford: Oxford University Press.

Gray, J. A. 1987. *The psychology of fear and stress.* Cambridge: Cambridg University Press.

Gunnar, M. R., S. Mangelsdorf and M. Larson. 1989. Attachment, temperament, and adrenocortical activity in infancy: A study of psychoendocrine regulation. *Developmental Psychology* 25:355–363.

Gunnar, M. R., M. C. Larson, L. Hertsgaard, M. L. Harris, and L. Brodersen. 1992. The stressfulness of separation among nine-month-olds: Effects of social context variables and infant temperament. *Child Development* 63:290–303.

Gunnar, M. R., F. L. Porter, C. M. Wolf, J. Rigatuso *et al.* 1995. Neonatal stress reactivity: Predictions to later emotional temperament. *Child Development* 66: 1–13.

Gunnar, M. R., K. Tout, M. de Haan, S. Pierce *et al.* 1997. Temperament, social competence, and adrenocortical activity in preschoolers. *Developmental Psychobiology* 31:65–85.

Heider, K. G. 1991. *Landscapes of emotion: Three cultures of emotion in Indonesia.* Cambridge: Cambridge University Press.

Heller, N. 1990. The neuropsychology of emotion: Developmental patterns and implications for psychopathology. In *Psychological and biological approaches to emotion*, ed. N. L. Stein, B. Leventhal and T. Trabasso. Hillsdale, NJ: Lawrence Erlbaum, 167–211.

Higley, J. D., S. J. Suomi and M. Linnoila. 1992. A longitudinal assessment of CSF monoamine metabolite and plasma cortisol concentrations in young rhesus monkeys. *Biological Psychiatry* 32:127–145.

Higley, J. D., W. W. Thompson, M. Champoux, D. Goldman, M. F. Hasert, G. W. Kraemer, J. M. Scanlan, S. J. Suomi and M. Linnoila, 1993. Paternal and maternal genetic and environmental contributions to cerebrospinal fluid monoamine metabolites in rhesus monkeys (*Macaca mulatta*). *Arch. Gen. Psychiatry* 50: 615–623.

Homer. n.d. *The Iliad.* Transl. R. Fagles. 1990. New York: Viking Penguin.

n.d. *The Odyssey.* Transl. R. Fagles, 1996. New York: Viking Penguin.

Hurtado, A. M., K. Hill, H. Kaplan and I. Hurtado. 1992. Trade-offs between female food acquisition and child care among Hiwi and Ache foragers. *Human Nature* 3:185–216.

Jacobs, B. L. and E. C. Azmitia. 1992. Structure and function of the brain serotonin system. *Physiological Reviews* 72:165–229.

Jemerin, J. M. and W. T. Boyce. 1990. Psychobiological differences in childhood stress response. II. Cardiovascular markers of vulnerability. *Journal of Developmental and Behavioral Pediatrics* 11:140–150.

Johnson, M. 1987. *The Body in the Mind.* Chicago: University of Chicago Press.

Kagan, J. 1992. Behavior, biology, and the meanings of temperamental constructs. *Pediatrics* 90: 510–513.

Kagan, J. and N. Snidman. 1991. Temperamental factors in human development. *American Psychologist* 46:856–862.

Kagan, J., J. S. Reznick and N. Snidman. 1987. The physiology and psychology of behavioral inhibition in young children. *Child Development* 58:1459–1473.

Kessler, R. C. and H. W. Neighbors. 1986. A new perspective on the relationships among race, social class, and psychological distress. *Journal of Health Social Behavior* 27:107–115.

Kraemer, G. W., M. H. Ebert, D. E. Schmidt, and W. T. McKinney. 1989. A longitudinal study of the effect of different social rearing conditions on cerebrospinal fluid norepinephrine and biogenic amine metabolites in rhesus monkeys. *Neuropsychopharmacology* 2:175–189.

Kramer, P. D. 1993. *Listening to Prozac*. New York: Viking.

Lakoff, G. 1987. *Women, fire, and dangerous things*. Chicago: Chicago University Press.

Laudenslager, M. L., K. L. Rasmussen, C. M. Berman, S. J. Suomi, and C. B. Berger. 1993. Specific antibody levels in free-ranging rhesus monkeys: Relationships to plasma hormones, cardiac parameters, and early behavior. *Developmental Psychobiology* 26:407–420.

Lazarus, R. S. 1991. Progress on a cognitive-motivational–relational theory of emotion. *American Psychologist* 46:819–834.

Leder, D. 1990. *The absent body*. Chicago: Chicago University Press.

LeDoux, J. 1989. Cognitive-emotional interactions in the brain. *Cognition and Emotion* 3:267–289.

LeDoux, J. E. 1986. The neurobiology of emotion. In *Mind and brain: Dialogues in cognitive neuroscience*, ed. J. E. LeDoux and W. Hirst. Cambridge: Cambridge University Press, 301–360.

1990. Information flow from sensation to emotion: Plasticity in the neural computation of stimulus value. In *Learning and computational neuroscience: Foundation of adaptive networks*, ed. M. Gabriel and J. Moore. Cambridge, MA: MIT Press, 3–51.

1994. Emotion, memory and the brain. *Scientific American* June: 50–57.

LeVine, R. A., ed. 1974. *Culture and personality: Contemporary readings*. Chicago: Aldine.

LeVine, Robert A. 1990. Enculturation: A biosocial perspective on the development of self. In *The self in transition: Infancy to childhood*, ed. D. Cicchetti and M. Beeghly. Chicago: University of Chicago Press, 99–117.

Levy, R. L. 1973. *Tahitians: Mind and experience in the Society Islands*. Chicago: Chicago University Press.

Levy, R. L. 1984. Culture, emotion, and knowing. In *Culture theory: Essays on mind, self, and emotion*, ed. R. A. Shweder and R. A. LeVine. Cambridge: Cambridge University Press, 214–237.

Lewis, M. 1989. Culture and biology: the role of temperament. In *Challenges to developmental paradigms*, ed. P. Zelazo and R. Barr. Hillsdale, NJ: Lawrence Erlbaum, 203–223.

1992. Individual differences in responses to stress. *Pediatrics* 90:487–490.

Lewis, M. and D. S. Ramsay. 1995. Developmental change in infants' responses to stress. *Child Development* 66:657–670.

Lewis, M., D.S. Ramsay, and K. Kawakami, 1993. Differences between Japanese infants and Caucasian American infants in behavioral and cortisol response to inoculation. *Child Development* 64:1722–1731.

Liang, S.-W., J. M. Jemerin, J. M. Tschann, C. E. Irwin, D. W. Wara, and W. T. Boyce. 1995. Life events, cardiovascular reactivity, and risk behavior in adolescent boys. *Pediatrics* 96:1101–1105.

Lissau, I. and T. Sorensen. 1994. Parental neglect during childhood and increased risk of obesity in young adulthood. *Lancet* 343:324–327.

Lock, M. 1995. *Encounters with aging*. Berkeley: University of California Press.

Lutz, C. A. 1988. *Unnatural emotions*. Chicago: Chicago University Press.

Lutz, C. A. and L. Abu-Lughod. 1990. *Language and the politics of emotion*. Cambridge: Cambridge University Press.

Markus, H. R. and S. Kitayama. 1994. The cultural construction of self and emotion: implications for social behavior. In *Emotion and culture*, ed. S. Kitayama and H. R. Markus. Washington, DC: American Psychological Association, 89–130.

McCall, N. 1994. *Makes me wanna holler: A young black man in America*. New York: Random House.

McCord, C. and H. Freeman. 1990. Excess mortality in Harlem. *New England Journal of Medicine* 322:173–177.

McEwen, B. S. 1995. Stressful experience, brain, and emotions: developmental, genetic, and hormonal influences. In *The cognitive neurosciences*, ed. M. S. Gazzaniga. Cambridge, MA: MIT Press, 1117–1135.

McEwen, B. S., E. R. De Kloet and W. Rostene. 1986. Adrenal steroid receptors and actions in the nervous system. *Physiological Reviews* 66:1121–88.

McGaugh, J. L. 1989. Involvement of hormonal and neuromodulatory systems in the regulation of memory storage. *Annual Reviews of Neuroscience* 12:255–287.

McLeod, J. D. and R. C. Kessler. 1990. Socioeconomic status differences in vulnerability to undesirable life events. *Journal of Health and Social Behavior* 31:162–172.

Meaney, M. J., J. B. Mitchell, D. H. Aitken, S. Bhatnagar, S. R. Bodnoff, J. I. Iny and A. Sarrieau. 1991. The effects of neonatal handling on the development of the adrenocortical response to stress: Implications for neuropathology and cognitive deficits in later life. *Psychoneuroendocrinology* 16:85–103.

Mehlman, P. T., J. D. Higley, I. Faucher, S. S. Lilly, D. M. Taub, J. Vickers, S. J. Suomi and M. Linnoila. 1994. Low CSF 5-HIAA concentrations and severe aggression and impaired impulse control in nonhuman primates. *American Journal of Psychiatry* 15:1485–1491.

1995. Correlation of CSF 5-HIAA concentration with sociality and the timing of emigration in free-ranging primates. *American Journal of Psychiatry* 152:907–913.

Menon, U. and R. A. Shweder. 1994. Kali's tongue: Cultural psychology and the power of shame in Orissa, India. In *Emotion and culture*, ed. S. Kitayama and H. R. Markus. Washington, DC: American Psychological Association, 241–284.

Merleau-Ponty, M. 1962. *Phenomenology of perception*. London: Routledge and Kegan Paul.

Murphy, J. K. and S. T. McGarvey. 1994. Modernization in the Samoas and children's reactivity: A pilot study. *Psychosomatic Medicine* 56:395–400.

Murphy, J. M., D. Oliveri and R. Monson. 1991. Depression and anxiety in relation to social status. *Archives of General Psychiatry* 48:223–229.

Nuckolls, C. W. 1995. The misplaced legacy of Gregory Bateson: Toward a cultural dialectic of knowledge and desire. *Cultural Anthropology* 10:367–394.

Oatley, K. and P. N. Johnson-Laird. 1987. Toward a cognitive theory of emotion. *Cognition and Emotion* 1:29–50.

Ochs, E. and B. B. Schieffelin. 1984. Language acquisition and socialization: Three developmental stories and their implications. In *Culture theory*, ed. R. A. Shweder and R. A. LeVine. Cambridge: Cambridge University Press, 276–320.

Plomin, R., H. M. Chipuer and J. M. Neiderhiser. 1994. Behavioral genetic evidence for the importance of non-shared environment. In *Separate social worlds of siblings*, ed. E. M. Hetherington, D. Reiss, and R. Plomin. Hillsdale, NJ: Lawrence Erlbaum, 1–31.

Porges, S. W. 1995. Emotion: an evolutionary by-product of the neural regulation of the autonomic nervous system. *Psychophysiology* 32:301–318.

Ramsay, D. S. and M. Lewis. 1994. Developmental change in infants' cortisol and behavioral stress response to inoculation. *Child Development* 65:1491–1502.

Rogeness, G. A., M. A. Javors, and S. R. Pliszka. 1992. Neurochemistry and child and adolescent psychiatry. *American Acad. Child. Adolesccent Psychiatry* 31: 765–781.

Rosaldo, M. Z. 1984. Toward an anthropology of self and feeling. In *Culture theory: Essays on mind, self, and emotion*, ed. R. A. Shweder and R. A. LeVine. Cambridge: Cambridge University Press, 137–157.

Rosenblum, L. A. and M. W. Andrews. 1994. Influences of environmental demand on maternal behavior and infant development. *Acta Paediatrica Suppl.* 397:57–63.

Rosenblum, L. A., J. D. Coplan, S. Friedman, T. Bassoff, J. M. Gorman and M. W. Andrews 1994. Adverse early experiences affect noradrenergic and serotonergic functioning in adult primates. *Biological Psychiatry* 35:221–227.

Russell, J. A. 1991. Culture and the categorization of emotions. *Psychological Bulletin* 110:426–450.

Sapolsky, R. 1992. *Stress, the aging brain, and mechanisms of neuronal death*. Cambridge, MA: MIT Press.

Scherwitz, L. W., L. Perkins, M. A. Chesney and G. H. Hughes. 1991. Cook-Medley hostility scale and subsets: Relation to demographic and psychosocial characteristics in young adults in the CARDIA study. *Psychosomatic Medicine* 53:36–49.

Schieffelin, E. L. 1985. Anger, grief, and shame: Toward a Kaluli ethnopsychology. In *Person, self, and experience*, ed. G. H. White and J. Kirkpatrick. Berkeley: University of California Press, 168–182.

Schildkraut, J. J. 1978. Current status of the catecholamine hypothess of affective disorders. In *Psychopathology: A generation of progress*, ed. M. A. Lipton, A. DiMascio and K. F. Killam. New York: Raven Press, 1223–1234.

Shore, B. 1996. *Culture in mind: Cognition, culture, and the problem of meaning*. Oxford: Oxford University Press.

Siever, L. J. and K. L. Davis. 1985. Overview: Toward a dysregulation hypothesis of depression. *American Journal of Psychiatry* 142:1017–1031.

Silberman, E. K. and H. Weingarten. 1986. Hemispheric lateralization of functions related to emotion. *Brain and Cognition* 5:322–353.

Smith, T. W. 1992. Hostility and health: Current status of a psychosomatic hypothesis. *Health Psychology* 11:139–150.

Snidman, N., J. Kagan, L. Riordan and D. C. Shannon. 1995. Cardiac function and behavioral reactivity during infancy. *Psychophysiology* 32:199–207.

Spiro, M. E. 1982. *Oedipus in the Trobriands*. Chicago: Chicago University Press.

Suomi, S. J. 1991. Early stress and adult emotional reactivity in rhesus monkeys. In *The childhood environment and adult disease*, ed. G. R. Bock and J. Whelan. Chichester: Wiley, 171–188.

Tennes, K. 1982. The role of hormones in mother-infant transactions. In *The development of attachment and affiliative systems*, ed. R. N. Emde and R. J. Harmon. New York: Plenum Press, 75–80.

Thomas, A. and S. Chess. 1977. *Temperament and development*. New York: Bruner/Mazel.

Waddington, C. H. 1957. *The strategy of the genes*. London: Allen and Unwin.

Weinberger, N. M. 1995. Retuning the brain by fear conditioning. In *The Cognitive neurosciences*, ed. M. S. Gazzaniga. Cambridge, MA: MIT Press.

Whiting, J. W. M. and B. B. Whiting. 1975a. Aloofness and intimacy of husbands and wives: a cross-cultural study. *Ethos* 3:183–207.

1975b. *Children of six cultures*. Cambridge, MA: Harvard University Press.

Wikan, U. 1991. Toward an experience-near anthropology. *Cultural Anthropology* 6: 285–305.

Wilkinson, R. G. 1992. Income distribution and life expectancy. *British Medical Journal* 304:165–168.

Williams, R. B. 1994. Neurobiology, cellular and molecular biology, and psychosomatic medicine. *Psychosomatic Medicine* 56:308–315.

Woodall, K. L. and K. A. Matthews. 1989. Familial environment associated with Type A behaviors and psychophysiological responses to stress in children. *Health Psychology* 8:403–426.

Worobey, J. and M. Lewis. 1989. Individual differences in the reactivity of young infants. *Developmental Psychology* 25:663–667.

Worthman, C. M. 1992. Cupid and Psyche: Investigative syncretism in biological and psychosocial anthropology. In *The social life of psyche: Debates and directions in psychological anthropology*, ed. T. Schwarz, G. M. White and K. M. Lutz eds. Cambridge: Cambridge University Press, 150–178.

1993. Bio-cultural interactions in human development. In *Juvenile primates: Life history, development and behavior*, ed. M. Pereira and L. Fairbanks. Oxford: Oxford University Press, 339–58.

Zajonc, R. B., S. T. Murphy and M. Inglehart. 1989. Feeling and facial efference: implications of the vascular theory of emotion. *Psychological Review* 96:395–416.

Zajonc, R. S. 1991. *Emotion and adaptation*. Oxford: Oxford University Press.

2 Toward an understanding of the universality of second order emotions

Daniel M. T. Fessler

Introduction

For thirty-two months I studied a community in which much of life revolves around a pair of emotions. Two projects resulted. One, presented elsewhere, is an examination of how and why the given culture shapes and exploits these emotions. The second, presented below, is a consideration of the underlying capacities which make such cultural manipulation possible. Like the other authors in this volume, I hold that the experience of emotion is the combined product of cultural and biological factors. However, rather than explore that synergy, in this essay I attempt to employ the former as a lens with which to view the latter.

I begin with a description of a Malay emotion which appears synonymous with *shame*. However, closer inspection reveals that this emotion can be elicited by two fundamentally different sets of conditions. Moreover, it seems that this duality is a pervasive feature of shame-like emotions around the world. If one adopts the position that the capacity to experience a given type of emotion is the product of evolution, then the duality of shame-like emotions is puzzling, for an evolutionary perspective suggests that each emotion ought to address a discrete facet of life. In order to unravel this puzzle, I search for clues regarding the evolutionary history of shame-like emotions and their opposites, pride-like emotions. I explore the display behaviors and cognitive demands associated with each type of emotion, and conclude that two primitive emotions, which I call Protoshame and Protopride, initially developed in order to motivate the quest for social dominance. I speculate that these emotions served as the foundation for more complex emotions which arose when hominids developed the capacity for a model of mind, that is, the ability to understand that other individuals possess minds like one's own. Such a capacity creates the possibility of a new class of emotions, the second order emotions, which are a reaction to the subjective experiences of other individuals. After examining such first order emotions as *pity* and *envy*, I suggest that Protoshame and Protopride were transformed into two second order emotions, Early Shame and Early Pride, which extended dominance-striving motivations into the new social world created by the advent of the model of mind. However, in addition to enhancing competition, the model of mind also facilitates cooperation. The possibility of significant cooperation resulted in the development of new versions of Shame and Pride which served to motivate conformity rather than rivalry and, in so doing, set the stage for the blossoming of culture as humankind's primary adaptation.

The importance of *malu*

The logic of malu

Dusun Baguk[1] is a semi-traditional fishing village on the southwest coast of Sumatra. Most of the 400 residents describe themselves as *orang Bengkulu asli*, pure exemplars of the Bengkulu, an ethnic group concentrated in and around the city of the same name. The Bengkulu distinguish themselves from both near neighbors such as the Rejang and more distant compatriots such as the Minangkabau on the basis of their distinct dialect of Malay and their emblematic architecture, ritual, cuisine, and performing arts.

Between 1990 and 1993 I conducted fieldwork in Dusun Baguk.[2] A striking feature of life in this community of ninety households is the attention given to one particular emotion: Informants describe a wide variety of behaviors as being the result of a desire to avoid experiencing *malu*. I was repeatedly told that people attended religious services, visited sick neighbors, participated in feasts, purchased consumer goods, and sent their children to school all so that they would not feel *malu* with their neighbors. Likewise, I was informed that people did not eat during prescribed fasting periods, abstained from forbidden pleasures such as alcohol and fornication, avoided ostentatious dress, and even regulated the speed with which they walked because to do otherwise would entail the risk of experiencing *malu.*[3]

My informants told me that people who feel *malu* avert their gaze, stoop, and avoid social interaction. Numerous observations confirmed this portrait. Inspired by Wierzbicka's (1986, 1992) proposals for a metalanguage with which to discuss emotions, and Russell's (1991) and Shaver *et al.*'s (1992) notions of emotion scripts, I collected 305 detailed cases in which informants spontaneously used the word *malu* to describe their own or an Other's emotional state.[4] Focusing on commonalities among some of the more widely discussed cases, I arrived at the following "logic" for *malu*, a set of conditions under which the emotion is experienced:[5]

(1) Ego violates a norm
(2) Ego is aware of his failure
(3) an Other is also aware of Ego's failure
(4) Ego is aware of the Other's knowledge

(5) Other displays hostility and revulsion towards Ego
– OR – Ego assumes that Other experiences hostility and revulsion towards Ego
(6) Ego experiences *malu,* an aversive emotion
The same logic appears to delineate the emotion described by the English term *shame* (cf. Fischer and Tangney 1995), and hence ''shame'' is a reasonable initial gloss for *malu.* However, closer inspection reveals that there are significant differences between the two terms.

Malu *and rank*

The 6-point logic for *malu* presented above can be used to characterize 87.2 per cent of the 305 cases in which informants employed the word *malu.* But what of the other 12.8 percent? A clue as to the nature of the remaining cases lies in informants' statements that the presence of a superior can cause an individual to feel *malu.* Indeed, this experience is so salient that the status of high-ranking individuals is often described not in structural terms, but rather with reference to their capacity to elicit a sense of *malu* in others.

I once watched as an impoverished young fisherman stood with stooped shoulders on the steps of the head of the village's porch, staring at the ground while stammering out his simple request. Witnesses explained his behavior as resulting from intense feelings of *malu.* This case does not conform to the 6-point logic of *malu* described above – failure is the heart of the 6-point logic, yet the fisherman was *malu* despite the fact that he had done nothing wrong. True, being poor might be construed as a failing, but fate is thought to be as important as effort in such matters, and the fisherman's poverty was seen as being no fault of his own. His inferiority was in part due to the fact that he was young, since age is an important factor in the prestige equation in Dusun Baguk, yet being young cannot be seen as a failing of the individual. The 6-point logic simply does not fit cases such as this one. Moreover, all of the 39 anomalous cases are of this type, namely an encounter with a superior.

It appears that there are two facets to *malu*, one premised on failure of some sort, and the other premised on inferiority irrespective of failure or success. But perhaps there is nothing of interest in this finding. Homonymy is common – in English ''bank'' can refer to both a financial institution and the edge of a river. Note, however, that the display behavior associated with the two types of *malu* is identical; looking only at behavior, it is impossible to tell whether an individual feels *malu* because he has failed in a public arena or because he must interact with a superior. Likewise, in both cases informants describe an unpleasant sensation and a wish to flee. No such commonalities link a fiscal bank and a topographic bank. Hence, this is not a case of simple homonymy, but rather one in which two very different situations somehow elicit the same response, a response which is labeled by a single term, *malu*.

Malu resulting from inferiority is only elicited in situations in which a marked disparity between individuals is a salient feature of their interaction. The poor fisherman would not feel *malu* playing volleyball with the head of the village, for in such a situation equality, rather than rank, is a defining feature of the interaction. We can therefore delineate the following supplementary logic for *malu*:[6]

(1) Ego assesses an Other as significantly more important than Ego
(2) Ego must interact with the Other in a situation in which the discrepancy between Ego and the Other is salient for Ego
(3) Ego experiences *malu*, an aversive emotion

This 3-point logic fits all of the cases which are incompatible with the 6-point logic described earlier.

The puzzle of two logics

I will argue that *malu* is a particular instantiation of a panhuman emotion. Holding aside the grounds on which I make this claim, consider what this implies in light of the fact that *malu* has two logics, i.e., a single emotion experience and display can be elicited by two different types of situations. I adopt the position that (a) emotions function as a special way of knowing about how the individual stands in relation to the world (Lazarus 1991; Nesse 1990); and (b) universal features of mind exist because in the past they offered an adaptive advantage to those who possessed them, and this is especially true of emotions (Izard 1977; Plutchik 1980; Tooby and Cosmides 1990). In this perspective, each emotion is thought to "tell" the individual about a particular type of relationship with the world (Nesse *ibid.*), what Lazarus (*ibid.*) has called a "core relational theme." For example, fear is a way of "knowing" that the environment is threatening to the individual. Similarly, the "action tendencies" (Frijda 1986) associated with each emotion serve to somehow improve the individual's position given the particular type of situation which elicited the emotion; running away is a way of mitigating a threat to oneself (Nesse *ibid.*). All of which leads us to ask, if each emotion functions to address a particular type of relationship with the environment, why do two fundamentally different situations both serve to elicit *malu?* The answer lies in the phylogenetic development of Shame, a panhuman emotion. However, before examining this possibility, it is important to consider a second emotion which is significant in Dusun Baguk.

Bangga

The 6-point logic of *malu* revolves around an Other's awareness of Ego's failure. Ego's inadequacies thus distinguish him from other individuals, attracting negative attention. In other words, Ego "stands out." Consider the following discussion concerning the general concept of "standing out":

D.F. – Tell me about that word, *menyolok* (to stand out).

INFORMANT – People who stand out [feel][7] *malu.*

D.F. – But yesterday the speaker at the mosque (an invited guest from the city) wore very fine clothes, didn't that make him stand out?

I – His clothes were nice. They were appropriate.

D.F. – So he [was] not *malu* even though he stood out?

I – No, one can stand out and [feel] *bangga.*

D.F. – So, sometimes standing out causes one to [feel] *malu* and sometimes it causes one to [feel] *bangga*?

I – Right, it depends on the situation. For example . . . if I were to walk from one end of the village to the other wearing shorts, that would stand out and I would [be] *malu* . . .

D.F. – But how can we tell the difference, how can we know what will cause *malu* and what will cause *bangga?*

I – It depends on the situation . . . basically, it depends on what is appropriate, what is customary. If one stands out in a way which is not (appropriate and customary), one [feels] *malu,* but if one stands out in a way which is, then that means one stands out in a good way, and so then one [feels] *bangga.*

Before examining these statements in more detail, it is important to recognize the scope of the phenomenon at issue. Physical attractiveness can produce *bangga,* as can skill at oration and quickness of wit. Hosting a large and impressive feast can make a family feel this way, and having important officials attend the ritual adds to this emotion. Winning an election or a chess game, being known for baking the best cakes, or having many visitors on holidays are all reasons to feel *bangga.* Likewise, the type of house in which one lives can be cause for *bangga,* as can the furniture inside the house, a motorcycle on the porch, and so on. Thus, while the desire to avoid experiencing *malu* is a primary determinant of behavior in Dusun Baguk, the desire to experience *bangga* is also a significant factor.

Informants stress that "standing out in a good way" involves actions which are "appropriate and customary," and which are not "excessive" – one can also "stand out in a bad way." In short, if an individual attracts attention to herself through behavior which cultural standards define as bad, others ridicule or condemn her. Conversely, if she attracts attention to herself through behavior defined as good, others praise her. Hence, just as I described the logic of *malu* in terms of a failing, so too is it possible to delineate the logic of *bangga* in terms of a success (cf. Goddard 1996):[8]

(1) Ego successfully fulfills a norm
(2) Ego is aware of her success
(3) an Other is also aware of Ego's success
(4) Ego is aware of the Other's knowledge

(5) Other displays toward Ego either (i) a positive appraisal and affection, or (ii) a positive appraisal and hostility

– OR – Ego assumes that Other experiences (i) or (ii) toward Ego

(6) Ego experiences *bangga*, a pleasurable emotion

First, note that this logic seems to also characterize the emotion which English speakers label *pride* (cf. Fischer and Tangney 1995). Second, comparing the 6-point logic of *bangga* with the 6-point logic for *malu* reveals that each is the opposite of the other. This suggests an interesting parallel between the two emotions. We can therefore ask whether *bangga* also possesses a 3-point logic which is the opposite of the 3-point logic of *malu.*

Many languages contain character trait terms, labels which describe longstanding features of personality. These terms often address a tendency to experience particular emotions more frequently or with less cause than is common (Lazarus 1991) – a "shy" person feels "shy" more often, and more easily, than others. In Dusun Baguk, the term *bangga* can refer to either an emotion or a character trait.[9] Generally, when the term is used to refer to an emotion, it is the emotion delineated by the 6-point logic described above. However, when informants use the term as a character trait, they are not referring to the excessive experience of this emotion. Informants state quite plainly "He is *bangga* (character trait), he thinks that he is better than others." In other words, the character trait *bangga* describes an individual who excessively experiences an emotion based not on positive evaluation by others, but rather simply on rank.

Although Dusun Baguk is an hierarchically organized community, an ethos of egalitarianism pervades many social situations. Accordingly, there are strong proscriptions against displaying a pleasurable emotion elicited by occupying a position of superiority. Furthermore, the character trait associated with a proclivity to experience this emotion is even more strongly prohibited. In common discourse, this emotion is therefore overshadowed by the proscribed character trait. The character trait *bangga* thus both hides and provides indirect evidence of a rank-related form of the emotion *bangga* – like *malu, bangga* possesses a second logic in addition to the 6-point logic:

(1) Ego assesses an Other as significantly less important than Ego

(2) Ego must interact with the Other in a situation in which the discrepancy between Ego and the Other is salient for Ego

(3) Ego experiences *bangga*, a pleasurable emotion

As was true of the 6-point logic, the 3-point logic of *bangga* is the opposite of that of *malu.* We are thus confronted by a pair of emotions which are opposites, each of which is characterized by two logics. I believe that both the paired nature of these emotions and the existence of their dual logics reflect important features of human phylogeny.

The cross-cultural perspective

The panhuman spectrum of emotion

Levy (1973, 1984) has argued that culture influences the experience of emotion by selectively highlighting or ignoring different aspects of a panhuman spectrum of emotions, processes which he terms *hyper-* and *hypocognizing*.[10] This explains how it is that investigators can come to understand seemingly exotic emotions; we are able to grasp such emotions even though we lack the terms or cultural schemas with which to describe, discuss, and ponder them because we ourselves are capable of experiencing them.[11] This is consistent with a robust finding of cognitive research, namely that cultural/linguistic hypercognizing makes it easier to perceive and think about some things rather than others, but hypocognizing does not preclude perceiving or thinking about anything (D'Andrade 1995; Nisbett and Wilson 1970; Parish 1991).[12]

Levy's approach raises the question as to what the panhuman spectrum of emotion consists of; if we are to truly understand both human beings and culture, we must explain how the inherent capacities of the former interact with the myriad possibilities of the latter. The problem is that nowhere do we have direct access to this spectrum – no matter where we conduct our investigation or who we use as subjects, we can never arrive at a culture-free window into human beings' underlying capacity for emotion.[13]

Exploring universals

Because we can only work with the materials which the world's cultures give us, if we are to delineate the complete set of focal emotions,[14] those principal elements which have universal experiential reality, but which are differentially emphasized across cultures, we must compare the emotions identified in one culture with those identified in another. The goal is to discover core notions which are present in diverse cultures.

In seeking to compare culturally defined emotions across cultures, it is important to distinguish between (i) the "logic" of an emotion (a set of conditions which define when and how the emotion will be experienced); (ii) the subjective experience of an emotion (how the emotion "feels"); and (iii) the display behavior of the emotion (the outward manifestations of emotional experience). The subjective experience of an emotion is extremely difficult to investigate. Hence, in general, investigations of the universality of various emotions fall into one of two categories. Researchers in the social sciences often adopt a *content-based approach* in which emphasis is placed on the context and reasoning which lie behind a given emotion. In contrast, investigators who identify their work with the natural sciences often employ a *display-based approach* in which emotions are defined and compared primarily through their behavioral manifestations.[15] The most rigorous position is that which employs both of these approaches.

Content-based evidence in support of the universality of malu

With some notable exceptions, anthropologists have not employed systematic means for describing emotions. Many ethnographies which touch on questions of emotion do so in an imprecise manner, often using English glosses not as stepping stones, but rather as direct translations, with no admission that translation may itself be a problematic process (Russell 1991). It is therefore difficult to use the ethnographic corpus to test the universality of a particular emotion, as materials are often not directly comparable. Nevertheless, it is sometimes possible to piece together different observations in order to delineate a tentative logic for a particular emotion in a given culture.

After a preliminary survey of the ethnographic literature, I believe that it is possible to identify an emotion equivalent to the 6-point logic of *malu* in the following areas: Ireland (Messenger 1971), Melanesia (Bolyanatz 1994; Epstein 1992; Fajans 1983; Nachman 1982; Strathern 1977), Sri Lanka (Obeyesekere 1981, 1984), Greece (Friedl 1962), Aboriginal Philippines (M. Rosaldo 1983), Aboriginal Central Brazil (Gregor 1977), Japan (Doi 1973; Lebra 1976, 1983; Markus and Kitayama 1991; Miyake and Yamazaki 1995), east Africa (Swartz 1991), Aboriginal Malaysia (Dentan 1978), Nepal (McHugh n.d.; Parish 1991, 1994), Polynesia (Levy 1973), Egypt (Wikan 1980), Aboriginal Australia (Myers 1979, 1986; Tonkinson 1978), Aboriginal Panama (Howe 1986), Mongolia (F. Gil-White, personal communication), and Burma (Spiro 1996).

In contrast to the sketchy material on emotion present in the ethnographic literature, Western clinicians and psychologists have carefully examined a number of emotions. Researchers have constructed a detailed portrait of the emotion *shame* (cf. H. Lewis 1987; Tangney and Fischer 1995). This portrait confirms the presence of an emotion possessing the same 6-point logic as that of *malu.*

With tentative content-based evidence supporting the universality of an emotion characterized by the 6-point logic which I have described for *malu,* I turn now to the question of the universality of the 3-point logic of this emotion. Parish notes that

> The English emotion term ''shame'' seems peculiar in cross-cultural perspective, because it does not seem to be semantically and socially organized in terms of conceptual links with ''timidity,'' ''fear-fright,'' and ''*respect*'' in the way that the emotion

terms often translated by the English word ''shame'' generally do. (1991:332 emphasis added)

Parish could well be describing the 3-point logic of *malu.* Likewise, consider the ancient Greek goddess *Aidos*, ''the personification of modesty, respect, and shame'' (Flexner 1987). The Ilongot word *betang* can be glossed as ''shame, timidity, embarrassment, awe, obedience, and respect,'' (M. Rosaldo 1983), while the Pintupi word *kunta* can be glossed as ''shame, embarrassment, shyness, and respect,'' (Myers 1979). Swartz (1991) has explored the relationship between the feelings of ''shame,'' ''fear,'' and ''respect'' elicited by highly prestigious individuals among the Mombasa Swahili, and Nachman (1982) has made similar observations on Nissan Atoll in Papua New Guinea. F. Gil-White (personal communication) found that the Mongolian word *emeekh* has a prototypical meaning that combines ''respect,'' ''shame/embarrassment,'' and ''fear.'' When I describe the 3-point logic in seminars, North American students and colleagues seem to understand it intuitively. More formally, data collected by Wicker *et al.* (1983) demonstrate the experiential reality of the 3-point logic for English speakers despite the absence of a specific emotion term. In sum, there is evidence that, like the 6-point version of *malu,* the 3-point version is also present in a number of cultures. It would therefore appear that *malu* is a better example of, or window into, one particular panhuman focal emotion than is *shame,* in that the former encompasses more features of the universal pattern than does the latter. To avoid confusion, I will refer to the possibly universal emotion which is characterized by both the 6-point logic and the 3-point logic as Shame (the capital ''S'' indicates that this is not precisely the same concept denoted by the English word *shame*).

Content-based evidence in support of the universality of bangga

Given that content-based investigations indicate that *malu* may reflect a universal emotion, what can be said about *bangga*? At first glance, not much. It appears that the problems which I encountered in exploring the presence of the 3-point logic of *bangga* are not limited to Dusun Baguk. Authors have far more to say about ''proud,'' a term referring to both character and demeanor, than they do about the emotion ''pride.'' The difference between the attention devoted to an emotion resembling *malu* and that devoted to an emotion resembling *bangga* may be due to a number of factors. It is possible that loss looms larger than gain for many peoples (Ketelaar 1993). If this is so, punitive emotions may receive more attention (from both informants and ethnographers) than rewarding ones. However, I content myself with the less tenuous, but still speculative, proposition that, as in Dusun Baguk, a concern with notions such as ''proud'' and ''arrogant'' can be taken as indirect evidence of the presence of an emotion resembling the 3-point version of *bangga.* A number of ethnographers mention these terms (Briggs 1970; Dentan 1978; Gerber 1985; Levy 1973; Romanucci-Ross 1973; Shostak 1983; Wikan 1987). They are also present in some regard in many of the ethnographies cited earlier.

It thus appears that there is indirect content-based evidence of the presence of emotions resembling the 3-point version of *bangga* in many cultures. But what of the 6-point version of *bangga*? Some form of public performance appears to be present in every culture. It seems that performers are often motivated in part by the possibility of applause. Positive evaluation by others, in this case an audience, is precisely the factor which elicits a rewarding emotion in the 6-point logic of *bangga.* Accordingly, while it is admittedly a tenuous form of evidence, the universality of performance may indicate that an emotion resembling the 6-point version of *bangga* is widespread. We can therefore coin a second label, Pride, for the possibly universal emotion described by the 3-point and 6-point logics which characterize *bangga.*

Display-based evidence of universality

I have noted in passing the display behavior associated with *malu.* Below is a more complete description of this display based on observations of many naturally occurring instances (identified as such by informants):

(1) averted gaze
(2) face turned down and away from others
(3) stooped shoulders
(4) shrinking posture
(5) bent-kneed, shuffling gait
(6) reddening of the face and neck
(7) attempts to avoid being seen, culminating in flight[16]

This is the prototypic display behavior which English speakers associate with *shame*, and which psychologists have described in the West (see Fischer and Tangney 1995). In his seminal work on emotion, Darwin (1872) described this configuration and argued that its widespread distribution amounted to evidence of universality. However, Darwin's reliance on anecdotal evidence collected by observers who lacked a uniform method forces us to discount his conclusions, and, unfortunately, no ethological work of equivalent scope has yet touched on this issue. Eibl-Eibesfeldt's comprehensive text (1989) mentions the universality of ''embarrassment'' only in passing. Ekman, the dean of emotion ethology, allows that ''shame-guilt'' and ''embarrassment'' may be universals, but notes that the evidence is still equivocal (quoted in Lazarus 1991).

The dearth of ethological data pertaining to Shame may be due to the fact that most comparative studies focus on facial displays of emotion, yet Shame involves a whole-body display (Lazarus 1991; see Campos *et al.* 1994). As a last resort, we are forced to return to the ethnographic corpus in search of ethological data. Some ethnographers supply us with sufficient ethological data to conclude that the Shame display is present in the region studied (for example, see Dentan 1978; Epstein 1992; Levy 1973; Nachman 1982; Tonkinson 1978). However, the systematic recording of emotion display data is relatively uncommon. Nevertheless, one observation frequently accompanies ethnographic accounts of emic emotions which are characterized by the Shame logic; again and again we are told that individuals who experience this emotion seek to hide their faces and avoid contact with members of their group, to the point that they may even flee. ''When you are ashamed,'' Gregor's Mehinaku informants explain, ''it hurts to be seen'' (1977:221). Less clear-cut is the tantalizing fact that it is common for shameful events to be described in emic terminology as causing a ''loss of *face*.'' In sum, although the display-based evidence relating to Shame is woefully inadequate, the meager data that do exist suggest universality.

Consider the display behavior associated with *bangga*:

(1) eye contact is sought
(2) face is slightly elevated and turned toward others
(3) squared shoulders
(4) erect posture
(5) stiff-legged gait
(6) seeks out opportunities for exhibition

This display is the same as that which English speakers associate with *pride* – compare this description with synonyms which Roget's Thesaurus lists for *pride* and *proud*: ''hold up one's head, hold one's head high, stand up straight, hold oneself erect, never stoop, look one in the face, look one in the eye, erect, stiff-backed, stiff-necked, lofty, swollen, puffed up, nose in the air, look down one's nose'' (Chapman 1977; see Fischer and Tangney 1995; Mascolo and Fischer 1995; Nathanson 1992).

Darwin argued that the *pride* display is universal. However, as I noted, Darwin's methods are less than ideal.[17] Once again we encounter the problem that cross-cultural psychologists have not paid much attention to whole-body emotion displays, while ethnographers have not collected detailed ethological data. Nevertheless, there is some evidence that this display is present in a number of societies, for we find observations such as the following, taken from Lindholm's account of the Swat Pukhtun: ''[Proud men] carry themselves erect, walk with a swagger, and look one another straight in the eye'' (1982:218) (for examples in markedly different cultures, see Chagnon 1983; Weiner 1988). Hence, although the question cries out for serious and

Table 2.1 *Behaviors associated with Shame and Pride*

	Shame	*Pride*
eye contact	avoided	sought
manipulation of apparent body size	smaller than baseline state	larger than baseline state
visibility and social interaction	avoided	sought

extended study by ethologists and cross-cultural psychologists, preliminary behavioral evidence suggests that Pride may be a panhuman emotion.

The phylogenetic origins of Shame and Pride

What the displays tell us

For now, I will content myself with the smattering of data which indicates that it is conceivable and perhaps even reasonable to view *malu* and *bangga* as local instantiations of focal points on the panhuman spectrum of emotion. Natural selection has importantly shaped human emotions. Each emotion thus has, or at one point had, a particular "purpose": each provides a specific adaptive advantage to individuals who are capable of experiencing it. Accordingly, if we assume that Shame and Pride are universal emotions, we can inquire as to the adaptive advantage which these two emotions may have provided at some point in the past. Attempting to answer this question suggests explanations regarding the puzzling features of Shame and Pride, namely why each emotion has two logics, and how this came to be.

The behaviors associated with Shame and Pride are opposites of one another. This holds true on a point-by-point basis, and along the three primary axes which characterize these displays, as illustrated above.[18]

When these behaviors are considered against the backdrop of patterns in primate and mammalian behavior, a central theme appears. In many primates and other species, staring is a component of threat behavior, while gaze avoidance is a component of appeasement behavior (Chevalier-Skolnikoff 1973). Next, in many, perhaps most vertebrates, increasing apparent body size is a component of threat behavior, while decreasing it is a component of appeasement behavior (Eibl-Eibesfeldt 1989). Jolly notes, "Bodily posture is one of the most consistent communicative gestures throughout mammals as a whole. Confident or threatening animals hold themselves straight, look big, and walk with stiff-legged swagger. Submissive ones hunch over, crouch, or lie down'' (1985:208). Lastly, seeking visibility is a central part of many primate threat displays, while avoiding interacting with others or attracting attention to oneself is often a form of submission (Rowell 1966).[19] In sum, if a Martian ethologist were to study human Shame and Pride displays, she would probably conclude that the interactions in which these displays are observed consist of attempts to negotiate or reaffirm issues of dominance and subordinacy.[20]

The congruence of logic and display

We can conceptualize the logic of a given emotion as the set of events which give rise to an assessment of one's standing with regard to a particular facet of the world (Nesse 1990). Social relationships constitute one portion of Ego's interactions with the world. Any given social relationship can have many dimensions, and each of these is addressed by a particular emotion or pair of emotions. For example, one important dimension of a social relationship is the degree to which Ego is positively or negatively inclined toward the Other. This dimension is addressed by the emotions Affection and Hostility. For any given emotion, the logic, feeling, and display are consistent with one another and are mutually reinforcing. The logic of Affection involves ''a desire to help and approach the Other,'' while the logic of Hostility involves ''a desire to hurt and repel the Other.'' The associated displays are consistent with these logics: the Affection display involves an opening up of the face and a masking of threatening characteristics, while the Hostility display involves a closing down of the face and an exaggeration of threatening characteristics (Eibl-Eibesfeldt 1989).

In addition to the degree to which Ego is positively or negatively inclined toward the Other, another important feature of any relationship is the question of rank. We can expect that an emotion or pair of emotions will address this aspect of the relationship, and that this emotion or pair of emotions will be composed of a logic, a feeling, and a display which are consistent with one another. I have argued that the Shame and Pride displays are each well-organized systems of behavior which, drawing on components common across primates, communicate messages of inferiority and superiority, respectively. Consider therefore the 3-point logic of Shame:

(1) Ego assesses an Other as significantly more important than Ego
(2) Ego must interact with the Other in a situation in which the discrepancy between Ego and the Other is salient for Ego
(3) Ego feels something unpleasant

Likewise, recall the 3-point logic of Pride:

(1) Ego assesses an Other as significantly less important than Ego

(2) Ego must interact with the Other in a situation in which the discrepancy between Ego and the Other is salient for Ego
(3) Ego feels something pleasant

In contrast to the 6-point logics with their emphasis on Ego's performance relative to some standard, these logics define a matched pair of emotions centered wholly upon issues of dominance. Hence, unlike the 6-point logics, the 3-point logics are thematically consistent with the displays associated with Shame and Pride, as the displays serve principally to communicate assessments of relative superiority and inferiority. This suggests that *the 3-point logics of Shame and Pride are the original forms of these emotions.*

The above conclusion is further supported by the difference in the complexity of the cognitive demands entailed by the two types of logics. The 6-point logics depend upon Ego's ability to recognize what the Other knows or does not know, a sophisticated capacity found only in humans and perhaps some apes and cetaceans (more on this later). In contrast, the 3-point logics require merely the ability to assess relative superiority, a capacity probably present in most, if not all, vertebrates. Hence, while many ancestral species must have been capable of the information processing required for the experience of emotions based on the 3-point logics, it is only in the evolutionarily recent past that creatures appeared who were capable of experiencing emotions based on the 6-point logics. In sum, based on (a) the congruence between the 3-point logics and the displays, and (b) the relative simplicity of the cognitive demands of the 3-point logics, I propose that the 6-point logics arose at some point after the logic/display configurations of Shame and Pride had already developed. Ultimately, the 6-point logics displaced the 3-point logics and relegated them to a secondary role in both emotions. But before I turn to the events which precipitated this change, we must first consider the origins of the initial 3-point versions of Shame and Pride.

Emotions as goals: the function of Protoshame and Protopride

For clarity, I will refer to the emotions composed of a 3-point logic and a complete display, but lacking the 6-point logic, as Protoshame and Protopride. Although we can view the displays associated with Protoshame and Protopride as derived from earlier threat and appeasement displays, this in no way explains why *feelings* should be associated with the logics that produce these displays. This is not a trivial point, for, at least subjectively, emotions are primarily ''about'' feelings. In both Bengkulu and North America, Shame involves feeling ''small, afraid, dirty, and exposed'' (Holland and Kipnis 1994; Lindsay-Hartz *et al.* 1995; Wicker *et al.* 1983), while Pride involves feeling ''big, happy, shining, and in control'' (Mascolo and Fischer

1995; Nathanson 1992).[21] I will return to these specific feelings later. First, we must consider why feelings exist at all.

Emotions are subjectively distinguished from one another in part on the basis of variation with respect to two criteria, intensity and hedonic aspect (pleasantness/unpleasantness) (Frijda 1986; Plutchik 1980). The salience of these two features in the subjective experience of emotions is what allows emotions to influence action. There are several ways in which emotions can influence action. In the simplest situation, an event occurs which causes Ego to experience an emotion, and, as a consequence of that emotion, Ego acts.[22] We can represent this as

EVENT → EMOTION → ACTION

In this situation, the intensity of an emotion serves to indicate the significance of the stimulus, and hence how dramatic the response should be, while the hedonic aspect indicates whether the reaction should be toward or away from the stimulus. However, even simple creatures learn from experience, and thereafter attempt to avoid events which were unpleasant and to seek out events which were pleasant. In other words, if initially emotions are a reaction to an event, and actions are a consequence of emotions, learning scrambles this sequence, so that individuals act in order to shape events which will cause them to experience particular positive emotions or allow them to avoid experiencing particular negative emotions (Nesse 1990; Parish 1991). We can represent this modified sequence as

ACTION → EVENT → EMOTION

In this situation, *emotional states themselves constitute objectives*, with the characteristics of an emotion influencing action before the emotion is experienced, rather than after. The level of intensity of a particular emotion serves to define its significance as an objective, indicating how hard the individual should strive to achieve it. The hedonic aspect determines whether the objective is a goal (something to be sought) or an anti-goal (something to be avoided).

Each emotion is ''about'' one particular feature of Ego's relationship with her environment. Specifically, the *feelings* of a given emotion act in conjunction with the *logic* of that emotion to create a specific *goal* or *anti-goal* within the range of possibilities which constitutes Ego's relationship with her environment. For example, the logics of Protoshame and Protopride address one aspect of Ego's relationship with an Other, namely the question of who is superior and who is inferior. However, simply knowing that these two possibilities exist does not lead Ego to seek out one and avoid the other. Rather, it is the addition of feelings to these logics which gives them motivational significance: because feeling ''big, happy, shining, and in control'' is very rewarding (it is a high intensity pleasant emotion state), being superior to Others becomes a goal. Conversely, because feeling ''small, afraid, dirty, and exposed'' is very punishing (it is a high intensity unpleasant emotion state), being inferior to Others becomes an anti-goal, something which should be avoided. In short, *because Protopride makes it rewarding to be dominant while Protoshame makes it punishing to be submissive, these emotions shape behavior by leading individuals to strive for higher rank.*

Drives, emotions, and the origins of Protoshame and Protopride

Observations of goal-directed behavior, particularly that which is highly regular across individuals, lead investigators to assume that some factor is responsible for the behavior. ''Drive'' is the name which is often given to such factors. However, if we turn the investigative lens on ourselves and focus on subjective experience rather than external behavior, it seems that we never experience drives *per se.* We act because of emotions, whether it is in anticipation of them or as a consequence of them (Westen 1985). Emotions result in patterned behavior largely because they create goals or anti-goals; the logic of an emotion determines what actions must be taken in order to achieve the desired outcome. When the logics of several emotions complement one another, the patterns in observable behavior become even more noticeable. Viewed in this manner, a ''drive'' has no independent existence – the patterns which lead us to identify such a ''drive'' are produced by sets of emotions.

Because higher rank often corresponds with greater reproductive success, natural selection may have favored a drive for dominance in many species, including humans (Daly and Wilson 1988; Symons 1992; Washburn and Hamburg 1968).[23] We can combine this argument with the earlier observations that (i) drives are composed of emotions, and (ii) Protopride and Protoshame concern issues of dominance. Hence, *the capacity and proclivity to experience Protopride and Protoshame were selected for because these emotions lead individuals to strive for dominance, a behavior which, in the long run, increases reproductive success.*

Early second order emotions and the model of mind

Emotions and the development of a model of mind

In asserting that the 3-point logics preceded the 6-point logics, I noted that the latter require greater cognitive complexity, as they depend upon Ego's ability to recognize what the Other knows or does not know. As discussed above, competition with conspecifics importantly affects reproductive success. The ability to compete in a social arena is significantly enhanced by the capacity to understand that others have minds like one's own, and to think about others' thoughts, that is, to possess and use a *model of mind*, as this furthers the ability to both deceive others and evaluate the sincerity of their threats and friendly overtures (see Byrne and Whiten 1988). In large part this is because an awareness of other minds importantly changes the way in which Ego is affected by Others' emotion displays.

In some cases, emotion displays seem not to be categorically distinguished from other kinds of environmental stimuli, eliciting a direct and apparently automatic response: The ''mock surprise face'' (eyebrows raised, eyes open wide) elicits increased interest from even very young infants, while the ''frown face'' (eyebrows knitted, eyes narrowed) causes infants to avoid interaction (Stern 1977). However, most reactions to emotion displays do not seem to be of this automatic type. I believe that this is primarily due to the importance of a model of mind in human interaction. First, recall that I argued that emotions often function as goals. This assertion is premised on the assumption that creatures remember the experience of emotions, a reasonable supposition given the mounting evidence regarding the critical role played by emotions in the learning process (LeDoux 1994). Second, note that awareness of the physical aspect of oneself (in the reflexive rather than the direct fashion) is presumed to be associated with the presence of a model of mind (Anderson 1984; Gallup 1982). Now, consider the following:

IF (1) Ego can recall emotions which she experienced in the past
AND (2) Ego is sufficiently aware of her own actions to make a connection between her emotion displays and the displays of others
AND (3) Ego is aware that others have minds like her own
THEN (4) Ego is likely to recognize emotion displays not simply as threatening or rewarding stimuli in the environment, but rather as clues to the internal state of the Other.

The clues which displays provide are interpreted on the basis of *empathy*, the formation of an association between the Other's display and Ego's memory of the subjective experience of the corresponding emotion.[24] The ability to make this connection allows Ego to use introspection as a means of predicting how the Other's emotional state may lead to action (Humphrey 1983). Clearly, such predictive abilities are likely to be highly adaptive. Accordingly, this combination of factors probably contributed to selective pressure for the capacity for a model of mind (*ibid.*).[25]

The blending of emotions

Emotions appear to blend like colors from an artist's pallet. This has led researchers to search for ''basic'' emotions, elements equivalent to the primary colors from which all other combinations are created (see Ekman and Davidson 1994). While productive, such an approach holds the danger of leading investigators to discount the fundamental importance and universality of emotions produced by blending (Lazarus 1991). We pause now to consider blended emotions which emerge out of dominance relationships, as understanding these emotions provides insight into the factors which affected the transformation of Protopride and Protoshame.

Up to this point I have contrasted threat behavior with appeasement behavior. This pairing emphasizes the issue of rank as a feature of Ego's relationship with an Other. However, it is also possible to emphasize proximity as a feature of such a relationship. In general, if Ego and an Other interact, it is because they are physically near to one another. From this perspective, the opposite of threat behavior is affiliative behavior: A fundamental feature of Ego's relationship with any Other is the degree to which Ego attempts to drive the Other away or, conversely, the degree to which Ego seeks to cause the Other to be near. With regard to subjective experience, the contrast is thus between Hostility and Affection. Consider the consequences of emphasizing this facet of Ego's relationship with an Other when there is a disparity in rank between the two individuals: Ego can evaluate the Other as either superior or inferior on some specific criteria. In each case, Ego can also experience either Hostility or Affection toward the Other. This produces four possible combinations:

	Hostility toward Other	*Affection toward Other*
Other is superior to Ego	(1)	(2)
Other is inferior to Ego	(3)	(4)

In each of these situations, a unique blend of emotions occurs. I describe these emotions below, and provide content-based and display-based evidence of possible universality in the respective notes: (1) If the Other is superior to Ego on the basis of some criteria, it is because the Other possesses something which Ego does not (strength, size, a beautiful tail, a new car, etc.). Protopride and Protoshame work together to lead Ego to *desire* that which Ego lacks and the Other possesses. Desire or ''wanting'' is probably one of the most fundamental elements on the emotion pallet.[26] In configuration (1), desire for what the Other possesses combines with Hostility toward the Other to produce *envy* (Neu 1980).[27] (2) When the desire to possess that which Ego lacks and the Other possesses combines with Affection toward the Other, Ego experiences *admiration.*[28] (3) Saying that the Other lacks that which is desirable is another way of stating that the Other possesses that which is undesirable (lacking strength means being weak, etc.). Hence, in recognizing that the Other is inferior, Ego can place the Other in the class ''things which are undesirable.'' Unpleasant smells or tastes, or sights which are associated with these, evoke a universal *disgust* reaction involving a pulling back of the lips and a wrinkling of the nose (Ekman 1984; Eibl-Eibesfeldt 1989). Transferring this emotion to the social domain (Darwin 1872) and combining it with Hostility toward the Other produces the emotion *contempt* (Lazarus 1991; cf. Rozin *et al.* 1994).[29] (4) Combining the recognition that "the Other is inferior/lacks that which is desirable" with Affection toward the Other produces *pity.*[30]

The above discussion can be summarized using the 2×2 matrix presented earlier (cf. Krech and Crutchfield 1969) (because I am positing that these four emotions are universal, I use their capitalized forms):

	Hostility toward Other	*Affection toward Other*
Other is superior to Ego	Envy	Admiration
Other is inferior to Ego	Contempt	Pity

The focus of evaluative emotions and the model of mind

There is a subtle difference in focus between the four emotions described above and Protopride and Protoshame. Both Protopride and Protoshame focus on *Ego's position relative to the Other.* In contrast, Envy, Admiration, Contempt and Pity all focus on *the Other's position relative to Ego.* Although both types of emotion are concerned with the class of relationships in which there is a discrepancy in importance between Ego and Other, Protopride and Protoshame center on Ego, while Envy, Admiration, Contempt and Pity center on the Other. This is why, in a given Ego/Other relationship, Ego may simultaneously experience an emotion from the former group and an emotion from the latter group: When Ego is superior to the Other, Ego may feel both Protopride ("I am more important than you") and Contempt ("You are less important than me"). Conversely, when Ego is inferior to the Other, Ego may feel both Protoshame ("I am less important than you") and Envy ("You are more important than me").

Understanding that Envy, Admiration, Contempt and Pity focus primarily on the Other is particularly important if we shift our perspective from that of the individual who experiences these emotions to that of the individual who elicits them. Ego is able to identify when an Other displays Envy, Admiration, Contempt, or Pity toward him.[31] These displays convey messages to Ego about how the Other views their relationship by communicating how the Other views Ego. Envy, Admiration, Contempt and Pity can thus be seen as *messages to Ego about Ego.* And it is here that the capacity for a model of mind becomes significant. If (1) Ego is able to recognize that, just as he assesses Others, so too do Others assess him; and (2) Ego is able to relate the Other's displays to feelings which he himself has experienced toward

Others, then the Other's display of Envy, Admiration, Contempt or Pity offers *a novel perspective from which Ego can view himself* (Harré 1990; Mead 1934). For example, when Ego views the Other's Contempt display, the following two realizations are combined: (1) "The Other is reacting to me," and (2) "The other is feeling Contempt." This combination leads Ego to the conclusion "Aspects of myself may be such as to merit Contempt." As a result of the model of mind, this conclusion may then serve as the stimulus which elicits another emotion.

The process of comparing evaluations of oneself

The model of mind allows Ego to use the Other's emotion display as a means of gaining a different perspective on himself. For example, because Contempt is premised on evaluation, being the target of Contempt gives Ego two perspectives from which he can evaluate himself, his own and the Other's. If Ego believes that he and the Other share the same standards, two possibilities exist. When Ego compares his own evaluation of himself with the evaluation conveyed by the Other's emotion display, the two can either match or fail to match. If viewing himself from the perspective of the Other constitutes an event which can elicit an emotion in Ego, we would expect these two situations (congruent evaluations and incongruent evaluations) to elicit different emotions.[32] Consistent with this expectation, informants in Dusun Baguk repeatedly emphasized that if Ego agrees that an Other's criticism of him is apt, Ego will feel *malu*, but if Ego considers the criticism to be unjust, he will feel *mane* "angry, offended" (cf. Griffin 1995)[33].

Matching evaluations, the 6-point logics, and questions of rank

Informants' statements concerning when Ego will feel *malu* as opposed to *mane* are consistent with the 6-point logic of Shame:

(1) Ego violates a norm
(2) Ego is aware of his failure
(3) an Other is also aware of Ego's failure
(4) Ego is aware of the Other's knowledge
(5) Other displays hostility and revulsion towards Ego
– OR – Ego assumes that the Other experiences hostility and revulsion towards Ego
(6) Ego experiences *malu*, an aversive emotion

The presence of a norm (point (1)) tells us that Ego shares with the Other a standard for behavior. Point (2) tells us that Ego evaluates himself negatively. Points (3), (4), and (5) tell us that Ego is aware that the Other evaluates him negatively. In other words, there is a match between Ego's evaluation of himself and the Other's evaluation of him. But why should this logic hold? That is, what is it about the match between Ego's negative self-evaluation and the Other's negative evaluation of Ego which elicits an unpleasant feeling and a particular display from Ego?

Recall that because high rank improves the individual's reproductive success, selection favors individuals who experience superiority as rewarding and inferiority as punishing. The Other's negative evaluation of Ego is isomorphic with (and may be couched in terms of) the statement "You are inferior to me." If Ego agrees with the Other's negative evaluation of him, he also agrees with the Other's assessment of his position relative to the Other. We are now in precisely the same situation as that which elicited Protoshame, namely there is an obvious and salient discrepancy in rank between the Other and Ego. Accordingly, the same punitive feeling is elicited, "feeling small/being afraid." To this core feeling is added a sense of being befouled or dirty, for Ego has recognized that the Other's Contempt, composed of Disgust and Anger, is justified; in Dusun Baguk, *malu* is linked to a cluster of terms which includes "stained," "dirty," "despised," and so on. Likewise, in describing this sensation, North American English speakers use phrases such as "I felt like dirt," "I had egg on my face," or "I put my foot in my mouth," all expressions related to the feeling of Disgust. Similarly, Strathern's (1977) Melanesian informants explicitly relate Shame to physical revulsion.

The same selective pressures which were responsible for the aversive feelings of Protoshame come into play once more when both Ego and the Other evaluate Ego negatively. Likewise, the same considerations which shaped the Protoshame display force Ego to overtly signal his inferiority to the Other once he has recognized the congruence between the two negative evaluations. The Protoshame display is the ideal vehicle for communicating this message. And this explains how it is that Shame can have two logics: *The 6-point logic of Shame uses both (i) the existence of a shared standard for behavior, and (ii) the ability to see oneself through the Other's eyes in order to create a new means of assessing relative standing. Yet, because the question of relative standing is a very old one, the 6-point logic employs the subjective experience and the behavioral manifestation of an emotion which initially developed with a much simpler logic.*[34] Hence, the two logics share a single form, with one logic governing reactions in certain contexts, and the other governing reactions in other contexts; when Ego is confronted with a vastly superior individual, the old 3-point logic produces the appropriate feelings and display; when Ego concurs with a Contemptuous Other's assessment of him, the more recent 6-point logic kicks in and produces largely the same result. Lastly, given the consistent inverse relationship between Shame and Pride, it should be clear that exactly the same circumstances have resulted in an identical piggybacking in the case of the 6-point logic of Pride and the 3-point logic of Protopride.

Relationships between emotions

First and second order emotions

Envy, Admiration, Contempt and Pity are all *reactions to the characteristics of an Other.* In contrast, Shame is a reaction to the way that an Other feels about Ego. That is, Shame is a *reaction to an Other's reaction to Ego.* Pride, which has the same general structure as Shame, is of the same type. I propose that we thus distinguish between two classes of emotions: *First order emotions* are those which are a reaction to the characteristics of the Other, while *second order emotions* are those which are a reaction to first order emotions – provided that he agrees that it is justified, Ego feels Shame when an Other displays Contempt.[35] We can indicate that a particular first order emotion serves to elicit a particular second order emotion by saying that the former (Contempt, for example) is the *complement* of the latter (Shame, in this case). Two of the four first order emotions are the complements of Shame, and two are the complements of Pride.[36] The following diagram depicts the relationships between the various first and second order emotions:

first order emotions	**Contempt** **Pity**	←(*opposites*)→	**Admiration** **Envy**
	| (*complement*) ↓		| (*complement*) ↓
second order emotions	**Shame**	←(*opposites*)→	**Pride**

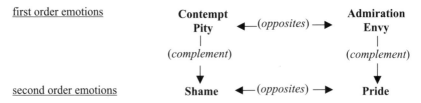

In light of these relationships, we can rewrite the 6-point logics of second order emotions as follows:

Shame

(1) Ego violates a norm
(2) Ego is aware of his failure
(3) an Other is also aware of Ego's failure
(4) Ego is aware of the Other's knowledge
(5) Other displays toward Ego either (i) *Contempt* or (less commonly) (ii) *Pity*
– OR – Ego assumes that Other experiences *Contempt* or *Pity* toward Ego
(6) Ego experiences *Shame*, an aversive emotion

Pride
(1) Ego successfully fulfills a norm
(2) Ego is aware of her success
(3) an Other is also aware of Ego's success
(4) Ego is aware of the Other's knowledge
(5) Other displays toward Ego either (i) *Admiration* or (ii) *Envy*
– OR – Ego assumes that Other experiences *Admiration* or *Envy* toward Ego
(6) Ego experiences *Pride*, a pleasurable emotion

Note that because the model of mind allows Ego to guess at an Other's evaluations of her, it is possible to experience second order emotions as a consequence of an imagined meeting with a real Other, or even as the consequence of an imagined meeting with an imaginary Other. I label these experiences *partially* and *completely psychogenic second order emotions*, respectively.[37] The ability to experience this type of emotion gives the individual an additional competitive edge, as it increases the likelihood that when Ego actually does interact with an Other, Ego's past behavior will have been such as to place Ego in a favorable position. Once again, we see emotions combine with the ability to anticipate the future, and to hold a model of mind, in a manner which increases fitness by furthering the quest for high rank. Hence, we can view completely psychogenic second order emotions as the apex of a process of development that began with the simple rank-related emotions Protopride and Protoshame.[38]

Emotions, cooperation, and culture

Rivalry, audience, and late second order emotions

The story which I have told of the origins and workings of second order emotions is able to account both for facts such as ''Dusun Baguk villagers avoid interacting with high-ranking officials,'' and for facts such as ''Dusun Baguk villagers will go into debt rather than own a bicycle which is inferior to those of their neighbors.'' In short, at this point we have a good understanding of how second order emotions play a part in dyadic relationships, whether they are relationships in which rank discrepancies are firmly established or relationships in which rank discrepancies are being determined. Consider, however, the following case:

It is evening in Dusun Baguk. Families sit on their front porches, relaxing at the end of the day. A young man rides a bicycle down the dirt road in the center of the village. He hits a rock, loses his balance, and falls. Many people, both young and old, laugh and call out to him, making jokes and telling him to look where he's going. He hangs his head, hops back on the bike, and hurriedly peddles away.

The youth has failed to adhere to one or more norms (''Look where you're going,'' ''Young men should be athletic and coordinated,'' etc.). Furthermore, there are Others who, by their comments and their Contempt displays, demonstrate that they are aware of his failure. In other words, the situation is entirely consistent with the 6-point logic of Shame, as is the young man's display behavior. But where is the dyadic relationship? With whom is the young man negotiating rank, that they should show Contempt and he should feel Shame? With the old grandparents who chuckled at him? Unlikely – they are so superior to him that drawing attention to the young man's failings in no way improves their rank. Is he competing with the small children who yelled at him? Equally unlikely – they too are so far removed from him in the hierarchy that even reducing his rank does little to improve their own. True, some of the young man's peers are among those who witnessed his fall, but they are a minority, and, besides, they have no control over the actions of either the very old or the very young. It seems that the relationship is not dyadic at all, in that it is not between Ego and a particular Other. Rather, the relationship is of the type which I noted earlier in discussing the universality of performance, a relationship between Ego and an *audience*. Moreover, it appears that many cases of Shame involve relationships of this type (Baumeister 1982; Buss 1980; Goffman 1959). Furthermore, the same is true of Pride. Clearly, we must reconsider our portrait of second order emotions. But before we can do so, we must return once more to the consequences of the development of the capacity for a model of mind.

Types of cooperation

Webster's defines ''cooperation'' as ''the act of working or operating together to one end; joint operation; concurrent effort or labor.'' In short, to cooperate, individuals must coordinate their efforts. There are two different strategies for achieving this. One way of ensuring coordination of effort is by radically limiting the number of possible reactions to particular stimuli, a strategy employed in social insects. An alternative strategy involves possessing the ability to anticipate the actions of others and shape one's own behavior accordingly. Unlike the ''limited response'' strategy, this approach allows cooperation in an unlimited number of domains. However, it suffers from the problem that, as a species' behavior becomes increasingly flexible and complex, it is more and more difficult for any given individual to anticipate the actions of another individual.

Cooperation and the model of mind

To understand how it is that humans can cooperate despite enormously flexible behavior, we must first consider a number of issues concerning the relationship between present and future action. It seems that even fairly simple animals have *objectives*. However, most creatures are unable to use their knowledge about the existence of objectives to predict the actions of other creatures because they lack a model of mind – knowing about one's own plans for the future does not help one to anticipate others' actions if one does not recognize that they have minds like one's own. Limitations on the ability to predict others' actions limit the possibility of coordinating action. However, the situation changes dramatically when creatures acquire the capacity for a model of mind. Once Ego recognizes that the Other possesses objectives, then Ego can use her knowledge about the Other, about the situation, and about her own objectives to guess at what the Other's objectives might be. In turn, this allows Ego to anticipate the Other's actions in a variety of settings, often far in advance, and, as a result, Ego is able to coordinate her actions with the Other's. Thus, by making it possible for individuals to exploit their knowledge of objectives in order to predict others' actions, the model of mind makes cooperation possible in an unlimited number of domains.

Selective pressure and cooperation

Cooperation can be adaptive in two ways. First, cooperating with Others can further the survival of individuals with whom Ego shares genes. Second, cooperating with Others can benefit the individual directly, either by procuring resources or by reducing the number of competitors. Examples include cooperative hunting and cooperative territorial defense and raiding, all of which have been observed in chimpanzees.[39] Importantly, because participating in cooperative activities increases Ego's inclusive fitness, selection favors the possession of traits which make it possible for Ego to cooperate effectively (Brewer and Caporael 1990).

While Machiavellian factors may have contributed to the initial development of the capacity for a model of mind, once this capacity existed it allowed for heightened cooperation.[40] In turn, the advantages provided by cooperation further increased selective pressure for the capacity for a model of mind.[41] Note, however, that while the model of mind makes extensive cooperation among creatures with highly flexible behavior possible, it does not ensure that individuals will be motivated to behave in a manner which effectively realizes this possibility. Motivation, after all, is primarily the domain of the emotions.

Emotions and the opportunity to participate in cooperative action

Ego's opportunities to benefit from complex cooperative activities depend upon how effective he is as a member of a cooperative group. This is so for two reasons. First, Ego's participation is dependent on the willingness of Others to include him in those activities, and Others' decisions depend upon his past performance. Second, if Ego is allowed to participate, his share of the spoils will likely depend on both his current and his past performance; among Taï chimpanzees, the amount of meat which an individual obtains from a cooperative hunt is primarily determined by the extent of his participation in such hunts, and this is also a factor in meat distribution among some hunter-gatherers (Boesch 1994; Shostak 1983).

Anticipating any joint activity entails forming expectations of the other participants as well as of oneself. A prerequisite for effective participation in activities premised on the coordination of action between individuals is thus the ability to recognize both the Other's objectives and, relatedly, the expectations which the Other holds for Ego. Hence, Ego's past and present success in anticipating Others' expectations of him translates into effective participation in cooperative activities, and effective participation translates into both more frequent inclusion in such activities and a greater share of the spoils.

The ability to anticipate Others' expectations of Ego requires both a model of mind and considerable experience. However, of equal importance, Ego must be motivated to conform to the Other's expectations if he is to perform effectively – simply being able to guess what those expectations consist of has no influence on Ego's efficacy unless he acts on those guesses. Note that only the Other can know how well Ego manages to conform to the Other's expectations. This means that the best way of ensuring that Ego will continually strive to conform to the Other's expectations is for the Other's reactions to have motivational significance for Ego. Motivational significance is accorded a situation when it serves to elicit emotions in Ego, both because those emotions lead to immediate actions and, more importantly, because they serve as goals and anti-goals when Ego is contemplating future action. Hence, it is to Ego's advantage if negative evaluations from the Other elicit painful emotions and positive evaluations elicit pleasant emotions.

Recall that (i) the Other's first order emotions give a message to Ego about Ego, and (ii) these messages are principally concerned with the Other's evaluation of Ego. First order emotions thus constitute an ideal stimulus for the elicitation in Ego of those punishing and rewarding emotions which would give motivational significance to the Other's evaluation of Ego's performance in a cooperative endeavor. Moreover, punishing and rewarding emotions which could be elicited by the Other's first order emotions already exist in the form of second order emotions. In short, the advantages provided by inclusion in cooperative activity may have generated selective pressure which resulted in a novel application of second order emotions. *Whereas initially second order emotions functioned to promote competition, in this new application they functioned to promote conformity to others' expecta-*

tions.[42] In a similar fashion, the social setting in which these emotions were experienced changed as well.

In striving for dominance, Ego competes primarily with individuals who occupy positions near his own in the hierarchy. Accordingly, the prototypic competitive event is dyadic, as Ego struggles to supplant an immediate superior or to hold off a challenge from an immediate subordinate. This means that Ego must be sensitive to the first order emotions of a particular Other, his immediate rival. In contrast, the possibility of cooperative activity creates pressure for Ego to demonstrate his competence to *all* individuals with whom he might someday cooperate – Ego cannot afford to focus only on the reactions of members of the immediate cooperating party, because tomorrow may see opportunities for cooperation with individuals who today are merely observers. Furthermore, provided that minimal communication is possible, Ego must be concerned even with the reactions of individuals with whom he could never engage in cooperative activity, as these individuals might convey a negative evaluation of him to other individuals with whom Ego could cooperate. Hence, *whereas second order emotions were initially elicited by the first order emotions of a single Other who constituted a rival, these same emotions came to be elicited by multiple Others who constituted an audience.*

Late second order emotions and the development of culture

We can distinguish between the initial form of second order emotions and the results of their later modification by terming the former "early second order emotions" and the latter "late second order emotions." Ego's inclusion in cooperative activity is dependent on her ability to meet Others' expectations, and those expectations are, in turn, related to shared standards for behaviors which are relevant to cooperation. As a consequence, the significant adaptive advantage offered by participation in cooperative activities generated selective pressure for an increase in the attention paid to these standards. Late second order emotions were the vehicle through which this increase in attention was achieved. Moreover, because late second order emotions entail a sensitivity to the reactions of all individuals, Ego must be concerned with her performance *vis-à-vis* shared standards when interacting with any other member of her group. It is only a small step from this situation to one in which the shared standards with which Ego is concerned are not limited to the question of cooperative activity – once Ego is concerned with how all Others evaluate her, it is not difficult for shared standards governing other types of behavior to become salient as well. This is because an Other may extrapolate from situations that do not involve cooperation to those that do – an Other may think "If that individual does not follow shared standards in this context, how can I be confident that she will do so if I invite her to engage in cooperative activity?''

I propose that the emotions which, via the reactions of others, rewarded conformity and punished deviance applied equally well to shared ideas which did not involve cooperative action *per se*. Once this step had been taken, the efflorescence of such ideas began. In turn, in an interaction similar to that connecting the model of mind and cooperation, increasing reliance on ideas shared by members of the group as a means of adaptation heightened the selective pressure for the capacity to experience late second order emotions. Hence, *a positive feedback loop arose in which the use of culture and the emotional foundation on which it rested each increased the importance of the other.* Viewed from a behavioral perspective, Shame and Pride became the foundation for a system of social control premised on conformity to cultural understandings, and this allowed for enormous increases in both social and cultural complexity. This led to our modern condition, a state in which we are defined as a species as much by our ability (and proclivity) to experience Shame and Pride as by our reliance on culture as a means of adaptation (cf. Schneider 1977; Scheff 1988).

Both Shame and Pride are the summation of three ''generations'' of emotions. Protoshame and Protopride were primitive emotions which motivated and facilitated the quest for rank. Early second order emotions served the same purpose after the capacity for a model of mind changed the nature of self-evaluation. This capacity also facilitated cooperation, introducing a new target for adaptive patterns of motivation, with late second order emotions being the result. Figure 2.1 summarizes this process.

For both negative and positive versions, all three ''generations'' share a common display pattern and a common subjective experience. As a consequence, the three generations are often emically identified as a single emotion or as a cluster of closely related emotions. However, because each generation has a different focus, Shame and Pride operate in three distinct situations:

(1) Situations of marked superiority or inferiority (the domain of Protoshame and Protopride)
(2) Situations of dyadic rivalry (the domain of early second order emotions)
(3) Situations of conformity to an audience's expectations (the domain of late second order emotions)

Lastly, although these three types of situations are analytically distinct from one another, actual events sometimes involve more than one of the three types, i.e., Shame and Pride can be overdetermined.

Today, the vast majority of the world's societies continue to employ Shame and Pride as the principal mechanisms of social control. In a few societies, particularly those which are large and heterogeneous, these emotions have

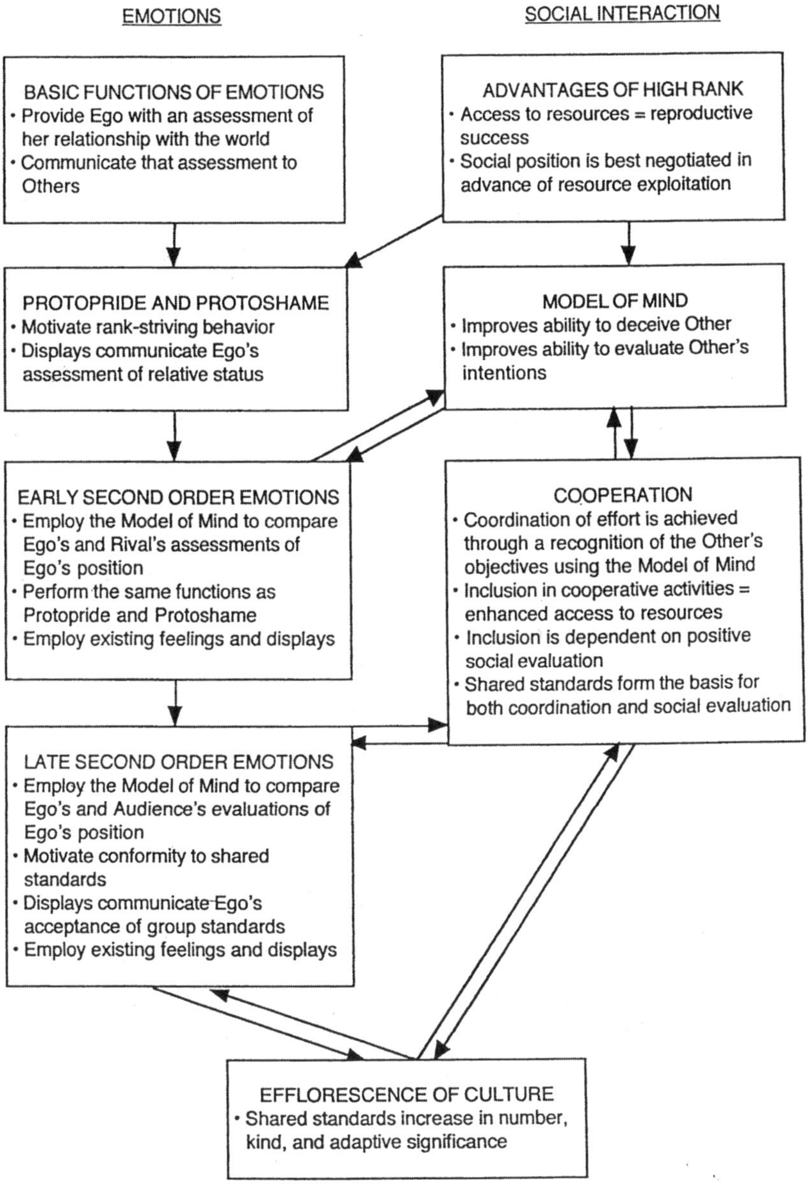

Figure 2.1. The evolutionary interplay of emotions and social interactions.

been partially supplanted by other emotions: Guilt and ''Virtuousness'' serve many of the same functions as Shame and Pride, but differ in that they are not premised on the opinions of an Other. But what these emotions consist of, and how they came to be, is a story for another essay.

Acknowledgments

Versions of this paper were presented in 1995 at the 7th Annual Meeting of the Human Behavior & Evolution Society, June 29–July 2, Santa Barbara, CA, and the Biennial Meeting of the Society for Psychological Anthropology, October 6–8, San Juan, Puerto Rico. I thank the following for their comments on earlier drafts of this paper: Roy D'Andrade, Mel Spiro, Jim Moore, Shirley Strum, Fred Bailey, Alex Bolyanatz, Axel Aubrun, Allen Johnson, Karl Heider, Naomi Quinn, Alex Hinton, Claudia Strauss, Thomas Csordas, Janis Jenkins, and two anonymous reviewers. This article is based on research supported by a NSF Dissertation Improvement Grant, an Hill Fellowship, a Spencer Memorial Fellowship, and grants from the Fulbright-Hays Foundation and the University of California. Jennifer Fessler and Erin Mote importantly assisted in data collection. Research was sponsored by the Social Sciences Division of the Indonesian Institute of Sciences.

NOTES

1. A pseudonym.
2. I entered the field with considerable fluency in Indonesian. Although all but the elderly speak Indonesian, I then devoted the first year to learning the Bengkulu dialect. All discussions cited were held in that dialect.
3. A similarly central role for this emotion has been described in other Malay cultures (cf. Goddard 1996; Heider 1991; Keeler 1983, 1987; Wikan 1987, 1990).
4. Informants were unaware of my interest in emotion, and discussed events either of their own accord, or in response to general requests for explanation (''Why did he do that?'' etc.). For a detailed description of methods, see Fessler 1995.
5. Compare with Goddard's (1996) semantic account of the ''thoughts'' which lead to Malaysian *malu*. The national culture/language of Malaysia, though notably distinct, nevertheless shares many elements with a number of the Malay cultures of Sumatra, including Bengkulu.
6. Elsewhere (1995) I have presented evidence that *segan*, a synonym for *malu* which I gloss as ''respectfully hesitant to act,'' highlights the 3-point logic subsumed within *malu*. Compare with Goddard (1996), Heider (1991).
7. Although the Bengkulu dialect contains a verb, *meraso*, meaning ''to feel,'' this is often dropped. Like other forms of Malay, Bengkulu lacks a ''to be'' verb. Bracketed terms are inserted for clarity.
8. Again I rely on cases involving the spontaneous use of *bangga* in conversation. However, conflict with an egalitarian ethos causes many such statements to refer to a disapproved character trait linked to, but distinct from, an emotion (see text).

Accordingly, as the example indicates, on those occasions when informants were clearly referring to an emotion, I followed a more directive approach than was true with regard to *malu.*

9. This contrasts with the Malaysian case wherein, according to Goddard (1996), terms other than *bangga* are used to refer to "arrogance." In Dusun Baguk these same terms are synonyms for *bangga* (see Fessler 1995). It would be interesting to know whether Malaysian synonym tests revealed the same finding, or whether the two cultures indeed differ in this regard.
10. It is important to distinguish three axes along which emotions can be evaluated:
    (1) Cultural salience – emotions can be *hyper-* or *hypocognized* in a given culture
    (2) Normative value – experiencing (and expressing) particular emotions can be culturally *prescribed* or *proscribed*
    (3) Hedonic value – an emotion can be either *rewarding* or *aversive*

    Many combinations of these variables are possible. For example, in Bengkulu, *malu* is a hypercognized, prescribed, aversive emotion, i.e., it is an unpleasant emotion which is culturally elaborated, and which good people feel in appropriate circumstances (see Gerber 1985; Goddard 1996; Parish 1991).
11. A prominent contemporary position holds that emotions are culturally constructed to such a degree that it is impossible to speak of universals (cf. Lutz 1988). While I concur that culture plays a critical role in emotional experience (see note 12), I believe that the evidence presented herein supports the assertion that shame-like emotions, though differently elaborated and employed by their respective cultures, are premised on a universal experience. Moreover, I question whether our understanding of humanity is advanced by blinding ourselves to such sizable overlap across cultures – there are differences between beagles and bulldogs, but it is impossible to fully understand either if we insist that there is no such thing as a canine *per se.*
12. In addition to questions of hypo- and hypercognizing, culture also interacts with emotion in a number of fundamental ways. Because reality is culturally constituted, culture defines the objects, events, and relationships which elicit emotions. Cultures also include "display rules," understandings which specify when certain emotions should be displayed and how. These issues are important in any cross-cultural study of emotion, but I do not address them here because combining the emphasis on the logic of an emotion with attention to display behavior can sidestep such concerns. See Kitayama and Markus 1994; Mesquita and Frijda 1992; Russell 1991; Scherer 1994; Wierzbicka 1993.
13. Note the word "capacity" here. The human mind and the human reliance on culture coevolved synergistically. Accordingly, fully "emotional" humans are necessarily also fully "enculturated" humans: it is not simply a question of "If only we could strip away the culture, then we would be able to see all of the emotions," as culture is not simply pasted over the human core. Rather, complex emotions probably only emerge through experience in patterned social interactions, and culture is a primary determinant of such patterning (see also Gerber 1985).
14. I intentionally use the word "focal" rather than "basic" here. In the psychological literature, "basic" has come to refer to elementary emotions which can be combined to create more complex or "blended" emotions. I agree that this

distinction between ''basic'' and ''blended'' is a meaningful one. However, I am interested in exploring the universal aspects of emotional capacity rather than simply investigating the most fundamental building blocks of experience. As I will argue later, I believe that a number of ''blended'' emotions are both universal and importantly central to a whole host of complex interrelationships between a number of panhuman emotions.

15. I am polarizing the two approaches in order to emphasize their differences.
16. Cf. Goddard (1996), Heider (1991). The shuffling gait is absent in extreme cases, presumably because it interferes with rapid flight.
17. Darwin's material is further complicated by the fact that he conflates Pride with ''arrogance'' and Shame with ''humility,'' confusing character traits with the emotions upon which they are based. A number of recent authors make the same mistake.
18. The Pride display does not contain an analog of blushing. Space does not permit an explanation of the evolution of blushing, but I will offer one in a future publication.
19. Some forms of submissiveness involve attention-getting, as in posterior presenting in many primates. However, this does not detract from the observation that avoiding attracting attention is often a way of being submissive.
20. See also Gilbert and Trower (1990), Leary *et al.* (1992). Components of these behavioral configurations have also been independently identified as indices of dominance and subordinance in human social relations (Maclay and Knipe 1972; Mehrabian 1969; Weisfeld and Beresford 1982; Zivin 1977). These displays exist because it is always ''cheaper'' to signal superiority or inferiority than to demonstrate it in a contest (see Maynard-Smith 1982; Frank 1989).
21. Note the emphasis on size (feeling ''two inches tall'' or ''ten feet tall,'' in North American colloquialisms), a feature wholly consistent with the *size = importance* equation which serves to unite the displays of Shame and Pride with their respective logics.
22. As many investigators have pointed out, events lead to emotions only because a process of interpretation takes place which gives meaning to those events. Moreover, it is precisely with respect to the process of interpretation that culture exercises a powerful influence (Epstein 1992). While accounting for how such interpretation takes place is an important part of our total understanding of emotions, I hold this question aside.
23. The relationship between dominance and reproductive success is complex, particularly among primates. In contrast to earlier models of a winner-take-all struggle, it is increasingly clear that cooperation is intimately linked to reproductive success, both directly and via the formation of coalitions in the competition for rank (see Ellis 1995 for review; also Pusey *et al.* 1997).
24. It is in regard to the issue of empathy as I have described it here that infants' different reactions to various emotion displays at different ages are of interest. M. Lewis (1995) and Amsterdam and Levitt (1980) have argued that infants only begin to identify themselves in a mirror at the age of 18–24 months. While there is some debate as to the extent to which such mirror tests reveal the presence of a model of mind (see Anderson 1984), it seems clear that if Ego is unable to recognize herself in a mirror, at the very least she lacks the self-reflexive awareness of her own actions (point 2 in the discussion) which is a prerequisite

for making the connection between Others' emotion displays and her own subjective experiences. Hence, if an infant below the age of 18–24 months responds with avoidance to a "frown face," there is good reason to believe that the "frown face" merely constitutes a frightening external stimulus for the child, and is not associated with any claims or plans which the Other may be seen as making.

25. This position is contained within many of the versions of the theory which attributes a Machiavellian origin to the model of mind.
26. It is unclear whether desire is itself an emotion or simply a component of other emotions.
27. This combination is clearly marked in Dusun Baguk, and is found in ethnographies describing widely disparate cultures (e.g., Briggs 1970; Devereux 1939; Epstein 1992; Goddard 1996; Gmelch 1985; Heider 1991; Lindholm 1982; Romanucci-Ross 1973; R. Rosaldo, 1980; Savishinsky 1994; Shostak 1983; Spiro 1996; additional references in Foster 1972). Further evidence of universality is the wide distribution of the notion of the "evil eye," the idea that *envy* causes supernaturally mediated harm to an individual who possesses that which is desired by others (see Dundes 1992; Foster 1972). A number of investigators have argued that *envy* is universal (Foster 1972; Frijda 1994; Lazarus 1991; Schoeck 1969). The *envy* display seems to be similar to that used for *hatred* (intense Hostility) – narrowing of the eyes caused by tensing the muscles below the eyes, thrusting the lower jaw slightly forward, and pulling the corners of the mouth slightly down. *Envy* and *hatred* are probably distinguished largely on the basis of context (Darwin 1872). However, despite extensive ethnographic documentation, little systematic ethological research has been performed on the *envy* display.
28. In Dusun Baguk, there is no term for *admiration* – informants used a more general term meaning "surprised" or "amazed" when asked to describe how they feel in this situation (Darwin argued on ethological grounds that "Admiration apparently consists of surprise associated with some pleasure and a sense of approval" (1872:289) – it would be interesting to see how frequently *admiration* and *surprise* are linked cross-culturally, and to compare such findings with ethological data on the components of the *admiration* display). However, Dusun Baguk contains positive evaluative adjectives, including words like "impressive," and these were often spoken in a tone of voice, and within a larger behavioral scenario, which both I and my informants interpreted as constituting evidence of positive emotion on the part of the speaker. This indicates that Dusun Baguk people can both experience and express *admiration* even if they have difficulty labeling the emotion itself succinctly. Because both ethnographers and ethologists have paid little attention to *admiration*, it is difficult to judge its universality. Nevertheless, I find it significant that *admiration* is clearly experienced even in Dusun Baguk, a place where the domain of ridicule and insults is hypercognized (there are nine words for "stupid"), and people describe their social environment as "a small pond with a lot of crocodiles."
29. Dusun Baguk speakers use a single term for both emotions, distinguishing between the two meanings on the basis of context (cf. Gerber 1975). Many of the ethnographies which describe Pride also mention *contempt.* On the ethological side, Darwin (1872) was convinced of the universality of *contempt*, and this posi-

tion has recently received extensive support (Ekman and Friesen 1986, 1988; Ekman and Heider 1988).

30. As is true of all blended emotions, the ratio of the two elements determines the character of the blend: If the inadequacy of the Other is emphasized and affection plays a minor role, *pity* resembles *disgust.* If the reverse is true, it resembles *love* (pure *affection*) (cf. Lazarus 1991). An emotion resembling *pity* is clearly marked in Dusun Baguk, and, indeed, seems to be hypercognized in many Malayo-Polynesian cultures (Gerber 1985; Heider 1991; Levy 1973), as well as in Japan (Doi 1974). I suspect that a thorough review of the ethnographic corpus will reveal additional evidence of the universality of *pity.* It seems that, as is true of many blended emotions, the display behavior for *pity* is not unique – contextual clues serve to distinguish the *pity* display from that caused by a blend of *sorrow* or *dismay* and Affection. Unfortunately, much of the biological literature which might address relevant issues focuses on the consequences of behavior in this context (the problem of altruism) rather than on the display behavior itself.
31. The importance of context in identifying many of these displays poses no inherent obstacle to their recognition, as Ego is likely to be in a good position to identify the relevant contextual elements.
32. Though otherwise insightful, Goddard (1996) may have overlooked the importance of congruence, as he does not distinguish between (others *knowing* something bad about Ego) and (others [merely] *thinking* something bad about Ego) as elicitors of Malaysian *malu.*
33. Relatedly, if Ego believes that an Other's praise for him is apt, he will feel Pride, but if he disagrees with the Other's assessment of him, he will feel Shame. This is because it is dangerous to be elevated to a position of dominance which one does not deserve, for sooner or later Others will discover one's inadequacies and punish one for the deception. Showing Shame in this situation is thus a way of rejecting the assertion of one's superiority by claiming inferiority. Accordingly, the more lavish and the less deserved the praise, the more Ego will feel and display Shame. This is responsible for everything from the phrase "Oh, you shouldn't have!" when one is given a gift (a common form of tribute) to the red-faced stammering of the honoree at a banquet (cf. Goddard 1996). Lastly, note that the scenarios which informants used in discussing congruence or lack thereof did not involve wide differences in importance between Ego and Other. If the disparity between Ego and Other is great enough, Ego will feel *malu* regardless of his opinion of the other's criticism. This is because in such a situation the 3-point logic of Protoshame overshadows the 6-point logic of Shame.
34. In parallel with this reasoning, it is also possible to identify continuity between the 3-point logic emotions and the 6-point logic emotions at an elementary subjective level. From this perspective, Protoshame and Shame are both emotions in which Ego experiences himself as "bad (in relation to other people)." Because being subordinate and having failed are both ways of being "bad (in relation to other people)" they elicit the same affective sensation. Conversely, both Protopride and Pride are emotions in which Ego experiences himself as "good (in relation to other people)." Because being dominant and having succeeded are both ways of being "good (in relation to other people)" the individual reacts to them with the same positive feeling-about-self (I am indebted to R. D'Andrade and F. Bailey for directing my attention to this; see Parish 1991:331–332).

35. Another way of phrasing this is to say that first order emotions are *emotions about someone*, while second order emotions are *emotions about someone's emotions*. This distinction parallels that which Dennett (1987) draws between first order intentionality (*beliefs about the world*) and second order intentionality (*beliefs about beliefs*). Likewise, Bateson (1972) distinguishes between Learning I (*learning about the world*) and Learning II (*learning about learning*). In each case the process is reflexively turned back upon itself. Moreover, the three processes are probably related in a causal as well as a logical fashion. Consider the following: Before you can know that other people know things (second order intentionality), you must learn that you learn things (Learning II). Why? Well, if a chimp or a child recognizes (learns) that she knows things today which she did not know yesterday, it means that she has stepped outside of her current state and compared it with her previous state. Having seen herself as an actor, it then becomes possible to recognize that other actors must have minds too (Humphrey 1983). In other words, Learning II (the child learns that she has learned things) leads to second order intentionality (the child is aware that she is aware, and hence that others are as well). The model of mind is an organized set of schemas (D'Andrade 1987, 1995). This information structure is constructed via second order intentionality – once one knows that others know things, one can begin to build a representation of how it is that they know things. Part of this model involves emotions: Ego has a representation of other minds which includes not merely the ability to know things the way Ego knows things, but also the ability to feel things the way Ego feels things. Included in this part of the model is the concept that emotions are premised upon evaluation. And it is this feature of the model of mind which allows for second order emotions. So, to experience these special emotions one must have a model of the mind which deals with emotions, and to have a model of mind one must realize that others know things, and to realize that others know things one must realize that one knows things oneself, and to realize that one knows things oneself one must realize that one knows things now that one did not know before, which is another way of saying that one must learn that one learns things. We can summarize this entire sequence by saying that *Learning II makes second order intentionality possible, and second order intentionality makes second order emotions possible.* Phew.
36. Although Pity is premised on a negative evaluation of Ego, and hence can elicit Shame, it does not always do so. It appears that if Ego's situation is dire enough, the desire for assistance overshadows concern with an Other's negative evaluation of Ego.
37. I am indebted to T. Csordas and J. Jenkins for suggesting this term. See also Emde and Oppenheim 1995; Lebra 1983; H. Lewis 1987; Nathanson 1992; Obeyesekere 1984; Parish 1991.
38. Protopride and Protoshame are first order emotions, as they are directly elicited by features of the Other (attractiveness, prestige, skill, etc.) relative to features of Ego, and do not involve an empathic assessment of the Other's subjective state. As noted, first order emotion displays can elicit *other* first order emotions without an empathic process – just as the anger display can elicit fear in a baby, so too can the Protoshame display elicit Protopride in an Other (indeed, this is probably the dynamic present among most nonhuman animals). However, the interaction of emotions is complexified by the presence of a model of mind. Because Proto-

pride and Protoshame displays can provide insight into the subjective state of the Other, Ego can use them as a source of information about himself. For example, Ego may think "I assess myself as having failed, and I assess him as having succeeded. He is holding himself erect and gazing directly at me, therefore he feels Protopride, having assessed me as inferior to him. His assessment thus matches my own, and I therefore feel Shame." Hence, Protopride may act as a complement to Shame, and Protoshame and may act as a complement to Pride.

39. Boesch 1994; Boesch and Boesch 1989; Goodall 1986; Nishida *et al.* 1983.
40. The prevailing view is that opportunities to exploit others were the initial impetus for the development of a model of mind. However, coalitions are extremely important among some non-human primates (see note 23), hence it is possible that *both* opportunities for exploitation and opportunities for cooperation importantly drove the early development of the model of mind.
41. This feedback relationship, like others discussed below, is of the general type described by Cosmides and Tooby (1989).
42. Focusing not on the mechanics of cooperation, but rather on the importance which social living holds for humans as a result of cooperation, Baumeister and Tice (1990), Leary (1990), and Miller and Leary (1992) have proposed that selection has favored a cluster of emotions which serve to motivate individuals to conform to social norms in order to preclude ostracism.

References

Amsterdam, Beulah K. and Morton Levitt. 1980. Consciousness of self and painful self-consciousness. *Psychoanalytic Study of the Child* 35:85–90.

Anderson, James R. 1984. Monkeys with mirrors: Some questions for primate psychology. *International Journal of Primatology* 5(1):81–98.

Bateson, Gregory. 1972. *Steps to an ecology of mind.* New York: Ballantine.

Baumeister, Roy F. 1982. A self-presentational view of social phenomena. *Psychological Bulletin* 91(1):3–26.

Baumeister, Roy F. and Dianne M. Tice. 1990. Anxiety and social exclusion. *Journal of Social and Clinical Psychology* 9 (2):165–195.

Boesch, Christophe. 1994. Cooperative hunting in wild chimpanzees. *Animal Behavior* 48(3):653–667.

Boesch, Christophe and Hedwige Boesch. 1989. Hunting behavior of wild chimpanzees in the Taï National Park. *American Journal of Physical Anthropology* 78(4):547–573.

Bolyanatz, Alexander. 1994. *Matriliny and mortuary feasting among the Sursurunga of New Ireland, Papua New Guinea.* Ph.D. dissertation, University of California San Diego. University Microfilms, No. 94–32-895.

Brewer, Marilynn B. and Linda R. Caporael. 1990. Selfish genes vs. selfish people: Sociobiology as origin myth. *Motivation and Emotion* 14(4):237–243.

Briggs, Jean L. 1970. *Never in anger: Portrait of an Eskimo family.* Cambridge, MA: Harvard University Press.

Buss, Arnold H. 1980. *Self-consciousness and social anxiety.* San Francisco: Freeman.

Byrne, Richard and Andrew Whiten, eds. 1988. *Machiavellian intelligence: Social expertise and the evolution of intellect in monkeys, apes, and humans.* Oxford: Clarendon Press.

Campos, Joseph J., Donna Mumme, Rosanne Kermoian, and Rosemary G. Campos. 1994. A functionalist perspective on the nature of emotion. *The Japanese Journal of Research on Emotions* 2(1):1–20.

Chagnon, Napolean A. 1983. *Yanomamo: The fierce people* (3rd ed.). New York: Holt, Rinehart and Winston.

Chapman, Robert L. ed. 1977. *Roget's international thesaurus* (4th ed.). New York: Harper Collins.

Chevalier-Skolnikoff, Suzanne. 1973. Facial expression of emotion in nonhuman primates. In *Darwin and facial expressions,* ed. P. Ekman, 11–89. San Diego: Academic Press.

Cosmides, Leda and John Tooby. 1989. Evolutionary psychology and the generation of culture, Part II. Case study: A computational theory of social exchange. *Ethology and Sociobiology* 10(1–3):51–97.

Daly, Martin and Margo Wilson. 1988. *Homicide.* New York: A. de Gruyter.

D'Andrade, Roy G. 1987. The folk model of the mind. In *Cultural models in language and thought*, ed. D. Holland and N. Quinn, 112–150. Cambridge: Cambridge University Press.

1995. *The development of cognitive anthropology.* Cambridge: Cambridge University Press

Darwin, Charles. 1965 [1872]. *The expression of emotion in man and animals.* Chicago: University of Chicago Press.

Dennett, Daniel C. 1987. *The intentional stance.* Cambridge, MA: MIT Press.

Dentan, Robert K. 1978. *The Semai: A nonviolent people of Malaya.* New York: Holt, Rinehart, and Winston.

Devereux, George. 1939. Mohave culture and personality. *Character and Personality* 8:91–109.

Doi, Takeo. 1973. *The anatomy of dependence* (trans. John Bester). Tokyo: Kodansha International.

1974. Amae: A key concept for understanding Japanese personality structure. In *Japanese culture and behavior*, ed. T. S. Lebra and W. P. Lebra, 145–154. Honolulu: University of Hawaii Press.

Dundes, Alan, ed. 1992. *The evil eye: A casebook.* Madison, WI: University of Wisconsin Press.

Eibl-Eibesfeldt, Irenaus. 1989. *Human ethology.* Hawthorne, NY: Aldine de Gruyter.

Ekman, Paul. 1984. Expression and the nature of emotion. In *Approaches to emotion*, ed. K. R. Scherer and P. Ekman, 319–343. Hillsdale, NJ: Lawrence Erlbaum.

Ekman, Paul and Richard J. Davidson, eds. 1994. *The nature of emotion: Fundamental questions.* Oxford: Oxford University Press.

Ekman, Paul and Wallace V. Friesen. 1986. A new pan-cultural facial expression of emotion. *Motivation and Emotion* 10:159–168.

1988. Who knows what about contempt: A reply to Izard and Haynes. *Motivation and Emotion* 12(1):17–22.

Ekman, Paul and Karl Heider. 1988. The universality of a contempt expression: A replication. *Motivation and Emotion* 12(3):303–308.

Ellis, Lee. 1995. Dominance and reproductive success among nonhuman animals: A cross-species comparison. *Ethology and Sociobiology* 16(4):257–333.

Emde, Robert N. and David Oppenheim. 1995. Shame, guilt, and the Oedipal drama: Developmental considerations concerning morality and the referencing of critical others. In *Self-conscious emotions: The psychology of shame, guilt, embarrassment, and pride*, ed. J. P. Tangney and K. W. Fischer, 413–436. New York: Guilford.

Epstein, A. L. 1992. *In the midst of life: Ideation and affect among the Tolai.* Berkeley: University of California Press.

Fajans, Jane. 1983. Shame, social action, and the person among the Baining. *Ethos* 11(3):166–180.

Fessler, Daniel M. T. 1995. *A small field with a lot of hornets: An exploration of shame, motivation, and social control.* Ph.D. dissertation, University of California San Diego. University Microfilms, No. 9607–624.

Fischer, Kurt W. and June Price Tangney. 1995. Self-conscious emotions and the affect revolution: Framework and overview. In *Self-conscious emotions: The psychology of shame, guilt, embarrassment, and pride*, ed. J. P. Tangney and K. W. Fischer, 3–22. New York: Guilford.

Flexner, Stuart B., ed. 1987. *The Random House dictionary of the English language* (2nd ed.). New York: Random House.

Foster, George M. 1972. The anatomy of envy: A study in symbolic behavior. *Current Anthropology* 13(2):165–186.

Frank, Robert H. 1989. *Passions within reason: The strategic role of the emotions.* New York: Norton.

Friedl, Ernestine. 1962. *Vasilika: A village in modern Greece.* New York: Holt, Rinehart and Winston.

Frijda, Nico H. 1986. *The emotions.* New York: Cambridge University Press.

Gallup, Gordon G. 1982. Self-awareness and the emergence of mind in primates. *American Journal of Primatology* 2(3):237–248.

Gerber, Eleanor R. 1975. *The cultural patterning of emotions in Samoa.* Ph.D. dissertation, University of California, San Diego. University Microfilms, No. 76–07-808.

1985. Rage and obligation. In *Person, self, and experience: Exploring Pacific ethnopsychologies*, ed. G. M. White and J. Kirkpatrick, 121–167. Berkeley: University of California Press.

Gilbert, Paul and Peter Trower. 1990. The evolution and manifestation of social anxiety. In *Shyness and embarrassment: Perspectives from social psychology*, ed. W. R. Crozier, 144–177. New York: Cambridge University Press.

Gmelch, George. 1985. *The Irish tinkers: The urbanization of an itinerant people.* (2nd ed.) Prospect Heights, IL: Waveland Press.

Goddard, Cliff. 1996. The ''social emotions'' of Malay (Bahasa Melayu). *Ethos* 24(3):426–464.

Goffman, Erving. 1959. *The presentation of self in everyday life.* New York: Doubleday.

Goodall, Jane. 1986. *The chimpanzees of Gombe: Patterns of behavior.* Cambridge, MA: Harvard University Press.

Gregor, Thomas. 1977. *Mehinaku: The drama of daily life in a Brazilian Indian village.* Chicago: University of Chicago Press.

Griffin, Sharon. 1995. Cognitive-developmental analysis of pride, shame, and embarrassment in middle childhood. In *Self-conscious emotions: The psychology of shame, guilt, embarrassment, and pride*, ed. J. P. Tangney and K. W. Fischer, 219–236. New York: Guilford.

Harré, Rom. 1990. Embarrassment: A conceptual analysis. In *Shyness and embarrassment: Perspectives from social psychology*, ed. W. R. Crozier, 181–204. Cambridge: Cambridge University Press.
Heider, Karl. 1991. *Landscapes of emotion: Mapping three cultures of emotion in Indonesia.* New York: Cambridge University Press.
Holland, Dorothy and Andrew Kipnis. 1994. Metaphors for embarrassment and stories of exposure: The not-so-egocentric self in American culture. *Ethos* 22(3):316–342.
Holloway, Ralph L. 1975. *The role of human social behavior in the evolution of the brain.* New York: American Museum of Natural History.
Howe, James. 1986. *The Kuno Gathering: Contemporary village politics in Panama.* Austin: University of Texas Press.
Humphrey, Nicholas K. 1983. *Consciousness regained.* Oxford: Oxford University Press.
Izard, Carroll E. 1977. *Human emotions.* New York: Plenum.
Jolly, Alison. 1985. *The evolution of primate behavior* (2nd ed.). New York: Macmillan.
Keeler, Ward. 1983. Shame and stage fright in Java. *Ethos* 11(3):152–165.
1987. *Javanese shadow plays, Javanese selves.* Princeton: Princeton University Press.
Ketelaar, Timothy V. 1993. *The role of positive and negative affect in cost/benefit perception: An evolutionary-psychological interpretation of Prospect Theory.* Ph.D. dissertation, University of Michigan. University Microfilms, No. 93–32-103.
Kitayama, Shinobu and Hazel Rose Markus, eds. 1994. *Emotion and culture: Empirical studies of mutual influence.* Washington, DC: American Psychological Association.
Krech, David and Richard S. Crutchfield. 1969. *Elements of psychology* (2nd ed.). New York: Knopf.
Lazarus, Richard S. 1991. *Emotion and adaptation.* Oxford: Oxford University Press.
Leary, Mark R. 1990. Responses to social exclusion: Social anxiety, jealousy, loneliness, depression, and low self-esteem. *Journal of Social and Clinical Psychology* 9 (2):221–229.
Leary, Mark R., Thomas W. Britt, William D. Cutlip and Janice L. Templeton. 1992. Social blushing. *Psychological Bulletin* 112(3):446–460.
Lebra, Takie Sugiyama. 1976. *Japanese patterns of behavior.* Honolulu: University of Hawaii Press.
1983. Shame and guilt: A psychocultural view of the Japanese self. *Ethos* 11(3):192–209.
LeDoux, Joseph E. 1994. Emotion, memory and the brain. *Scientific American* June:50–57.
Levy, Robert I. 1973. *Tahitians: Mind and experience in the Society Islands.* Chicago: University of Chicago Press.
1984. Emotion, knowing, and culture. In *Culture theory: Essays on mind, self, and emotion*, ed. R. A. Shweder and R. A. LeVine, 214–237. Cambridge: Cambridge University Press.
Lewis, Helen Block, ed. 1987. *The role of shame in symptom formation.* Hillsdale, NJ: Lawrence Erlbaum.

Lewis, Michael. 1995. Embarrassment: The emotion of self-exposure and evaluation. In *Self-conscious emotions: The psychology of shame, guilt, embarrassment, and pride*, ed. J. P. Tangney and K. W. Fischer, 198–218. New York: Guilford.

Lindholm, Cherry. 1982. Swat Pukhtun family as a political training ground. *South Asia Occasional Papers and Theses*. Ithaca. 8:51–60.

Lindsay-Hartz, Janice, Joseph de Rivera, Michael F. Mascolo. 1995. Differentiating guilt and shame and their effects on motivation. In *Self-conscious emotions: The psychology of shame, guilt, embarrassment, and pride*, ed. J. P. Tangney and K. W. Fischer, 274–300. New York: Guilford.

Lutz, Catherine. 1988. *Unnatural emotions*. Chicago: University of Chicago Press.

Maclay, George and Humphry Knipe. 1972. *The dominant man: The pecking order in human society*. New York: Delacorte Press.

Markus, Hazel Rose and Shinobu Kitayama. 1991. Culture and the self: Implications for cognition, emotion, and motivation. *Psychological Review* 98(2):224–253.

Mascolo, Michael F. and Kurt W. Fischer. 1995. Developmental transformations in appraisals for pride, shame, and guilt. In *Self-conscious emotions: The psychology of shame, guilt, embarrassment, and pride*, ed. J. P. Tangney and K. W. Fischer, 64–113. New York: Guilford.

Maynard Smith, John. 1982. *Evolution and the theory of games*. New York: Cambridge University Press.

McHugh, Ernestine L. n.d. *Situating persons: Honor and identity in the Himalayas*. Paper presented at the 92nd Annual Meeting of the American Anthropological Association, November 17–21, 1993, Washington, DC.

Mead, George H. 1934. *Mind, self and society*. Chicago: University of Chicago Press.

Mehrabian, Albert. 1969. Significance of posture and position in the communication of attitude and status relationships. *Psychological Bulletin* 71:359–372.

Mesquita, Batja and Nico H. Frijda. 1992. Cultural variations in emotions: A review. *Psychological Bulletin* 112(2):179–204.

Messenger, John C. 1971. Sex and repression in an Irish folk community. In *Human sexual behavior*, eds D. S. Marshall and R. C. Suggs, 3–37. New York: Basic Books.

Miller, Rowland S. and Mark R. Leary. 1992. Social sources and interactive functions of emotion: The case of embarrassment. In *Emotion and social behavior*, Vol. 14 *of Review of Personality and Social Psychology*, ed. M. S. Clark, 202–221. Newbury Park, CA: Sage.

Miyake, Kazuo and Kosuke Yamazaki. 1995. Self-conscious emotions, child rearing, and child psychopathology in Japanese culture. In *Self-conscious emotions: The psychology of shame, guilt, embarrassment, and pride*, ed. J. P. Tangney and K. W. Fischer, 488–504. New York: Guilford.

Myers, Fred R. 1979. Emotions and the self: A theory of personhood and political order among Pintupi Aborigines. *Ethos* 7(4):343–370.

1986. *Pintupi country, Pintupi self: Sentiment, place, and politics among Western Desert Aborigines*. Washington, DC: Smithsonian Institution Press.

Nachman, Steven R. 1982. Anti-humor: Why the Grand Sorcerer wags his penis. *Ethos* 10(2):117–135.

Nathanson, Donald L. 1992. *Shame and pride: Affect, sex, and the birth of the self*. New York: W. W. Norton.

Nesse, Randolph M. 1990. Evolutionary explanations of emotions. *Human Nature* 1(3):261–289.

Neu, Jerome. 1980. Jealous thoughts. In *Explaining emotions*, ed. A. O. Rorty, 425–463. Berkeley: University of California Press.

Nisbett, Richard E. and Timothy D. Wilson. 1970. Telling more than we can know: Verbal reports on mental processes. *Psychological Review* 84(3):231–259.

Nishida, Toshisada, Shigeo Uehara, and Ramadhani Nyondo. 1983. Predatory behavior among wild chimpanzees of the Mahale mountains. *Primates* 20(1):1–20.

Obeyesekere, Gananath. 1981. *Medusa's hair.* Chicago: University of Chicago Press.

1984. *The cult of the goddess Pattini.* Chicago: University of Chicago Press.

Parish, Steven M. 1991. The sacred mind: Newar cultural representations of mental life and the production of moral consciousness. *Ethos* 19(3):313–351.

1994. *Moral knowing in a Hindu sacred city: An exploration of mind, emotion, and self.* New York: Columbia University Press.

Plutchik, Robert. 1980. *The emotions: A psychoevolutionary synthesis.* New York: Harper and Row.

Pusey, Anne, Jennifer Williams, and Jane Goodall. 1997. The influence of dominance rank on the reproductive success of female chimpanzees. *Science* 277(8):828–831.

Romanucci-Ross, Lola. 1973. *Conflict, violence, and morality in a Mexican village.* Palo Alto, CA: National Press.

Rosaldo, Michelle Z. 1983. The shame of headhunters and the autonomy of the self. *Ethos* 11(3):135–151.

Rosaldo, Renato. 1980. *Ilongot headhunting 1883–1974.* Stanford, CA: Stanford University Press.

Rowell, Thelma E. 1966. Hierarchy in the organization of a captive baboon group. *Animal Behavior* 14(4):430–443.

Rozin, Paul, Laura Lowery, and Rhonda Ebert. 1994. Varieties of disgust faces and the structure of disgust. *Journal of Personality and Social Psychology* 66(5): 870–881.

Russell, James A. 1991. Culture and the categorization of emotions. *Psychological Bulletin* 110(3):426–450.

Savishinsky, Joel S. 1994. *The trail of the Hare: Environment and stress in a sub-Arctic community* (2nd ed.). Yverdon, Switzerland: Gordon and Breach.

Scheff, Thomas J. 1988. Shame and conformity: The deference-emotion system. *American Sociological Review* 53(3):395–406.

Scherer, Klaus R. 1994. Evidence for both universality and cultural specificity of emotional elicitation. In *The nature of emotion: Fundamental questions*, ed. P. Ekman and R. J. Davidson, 172–175. Oxford: Oxford University Press.

Schneider, Carl D. 1977. *Shame, exposure, and privacy.* Boston: Beacon Press.

Schoeck, Helmut. 1969. *Envy: A theory of social behavior*, trans. M. Glenny and B. Ross. New York: Harcourt, Brace and World.

Shaver, Phillip R., Shelley Wu, and Judith C. Schwartz. 1992. Cross-cultural similarities and differences in emotion and its representation: A prototype approach. In *Emotion*, Vol. 13 *of Review of Personality and Social Psychology*, ed. M. S. Clark, 175–212. London: Sage.

Shostak, Marjorie. 1983. *Nisa: The life and words of a !Kung woman.* New York: Random House.

Spiro, Melford E. 1996. Narcissus in Asia. *Ethos* 24(1):165–191.

Stern, Daniel N. 1977. *The first relationship: Infant and mother.* Cambridge, MA: Harvard University Press.

Strathern, Andrew. 1977. Why is shame on the skin? In *The anthropology of the body*, ed. J. Blacking, 99–110. New York: Academic Press.

Swartz, Marc J. 1991. *The way the world is: Cultural processes and social relations among the Mombasa Swahili.* Berkeley: University of California Press.

Symons, Donald. 1992. On the use and misuse of Darwinism in the study of human behavior. In *The adapted mind: Evolutionary psychology and the generation of culture*, eds. J. H. Barkow, L. Cosmides and J. Tooby, 137–159. Oxford: Oxford University Press.

Tangney, June Price and Kurt W. Fischer, eds. 1995. *Self-conscious emotions: The psychology of shame, guilt, embarrassment, and pride.* New York: Guilford.

Tonkinson, Robert. 1978. *The Mardudjara Aborigines: Living the dream in Australia's desert.* New York: Holt, Rinehart and Winston.

Tooby, John and Leda Cosmides. 1990. The past explains the present: Emotional adaptation and the structure of ancestral environments. *Ethology and Sociobiology* 11(4–5):375–424.

Washburn, Sherwood L. and David A. Hamburg. 1968. Aggressive behavior in Old World monkeys and apes. In *Primates: Studies in adaptation and variability*, ed. P. C. Jay, 458–478. New York: Holt, Rinehart and Winston.

Weiner, Annette B. 1988. *The Trobrianders of Papua New Guinea.* New York: Holt, Rinehart and Winston.

Weisfeld, Glenn E. and Jody M. Beresford. 1982. Erectness of posture as an indicator of dominance or success in humans. *Motivation and Emotion* 6(2):113–131.

Westen, Drew. 1985. *Self and society: Narcissism, collectivism, and the development of morals.* Cambridge: Cambridge University Press.

Wicker, Frank W., Glen C. Payne and Randall D. Morgan. 1983. Participant descriptions of guilt and shame. *Motivation and Emotion* 7(1):25–39.

Wierzbicka, Anna. 1986. Human emotions: Universal or culture-specific? *American Anthropologist* 88(3):584–594.

1992. *Semantics, culture, and cognition: Universal human concepts in culture-specific configurations.* Oxford: Oxford University Press.

1993. A conceptual basis for cultural psychology. *Ethos* 21(2):205–231.

Wikan, Unni. 1980. *Life among the Cairo poor.* London: Tavistock.

1987. Public grace and private fears: Gaiety, offense, and sorcery in northern Bali. *Ethos* 15(4):337–365.

1990. *Managing turbulent hearts.* Chicago: University of Chicago Press.

Zivin, Gail. 1977. Facial gestures predict preschoolers' encounter outcomes. *Social Science Information* 16: 715–730.

3 Steps to an evolutionary ecology of mind

James S. Chisholm

Under the constant influences of the external necessity . . . an internal necessity of thinking evolved, which is nothing else but a copy of the external necessity . . . If one accepts this view as at least partially true, he would admit the fundamental importance of natural science for any logic and theory of knowledge. Natural Science, indeed, would be the Archimedian point for all questions of human knowledge.

Paul Volkmann (cited in Danailov and Tögel 1990:20)

Introduction

This chapter is about the representation of nature in mind, including why we might expect such representations and how they get there.[1] The nature I refer to is as it is conceived by the science of evolutionary ecology; the mind I refer to is the mind of *a priori* categories, cognitive and social-emotional schemas, internal working models, and similar mental constructs. The crux of my argument is that the branch of evolutionary ecology known as life history theory provides a solid foundation for an evolutionary theory of mind – that is, an evolutionary ecological basis for making predictions about the nature and development of cognitive and affective schemas. What follows is an extended thought experiment about sex, evolution, and development in which my goal is to see what life history theory looks like as a theory of mind and motivation.

I begin with some of the key assumptions and concepts of life history theory, focusing on the critical notions of (1) the separate components of fitness; (2) trade-offs, especially the one between current and future reproduction; and (3) the concept of reproductive strategy in general, and Belsky, Steinberg, and Draper's (1991) particular attachment theory model of the development of alternative reproductive strategies in humans. Next, I outline the concept of "time preference" and suggest that it may be part of a psychobiological mechanism for optimizing the trade-off between current and future reproduction. Then I argue that potentially adaptive individual differences in time preference may become represented in cognitive and affective schemas through the attachment process. I conclude with some implications of this life history theory view of mind: (1) that human nature is essentially and biologically local; (2) that the mind is fundamentally an organ of defense; and (3) that one of the mind's major adaptive functions is to put a time value on our schemas for action.

Components of fitness

All organisms have had ancestors. In order for these ancestors to have left descendants (i.e., to have realized a degree of reproductive success or fitness) each one had to have solved the universal requirements of survival, growth and development, and reproduction, which are the major components of fitness. Life history theory is the branch of evolutionary ecology devoted to the study of life cycles and life history traits, which include size at birth, growth rate, age and size at maturity, age- and size-specific reproductive investment and mortality rates, and length of life. It argues that variation in these traits, both between and within species, is largely determined by trade-offs between traits (meaning that an increase in one trait implies a decrease in another). We expect such trade-offs from life history theory's principle of allocation, which holds that organisms have finite resources of energy, information, nutrients, safety, and time to be divided among the often conflicting requirements of the components of fitness: survival and growth and development (sometimes called "somatic effort"), and, once maturity is reached, reproduction (sometimes called "reproductive effort," which includes both "mating effort" [i.e., the production of offspring] and "parenting effort" [i.e., the rearing of offspring]).

The central assumption of life history theory is that selection will favor integrated and correlated[2] anatomical, physiological, behavioral, and developmental traits or mechanisms (i.e., "strategies") for achieving the optimal allocation of resources to survival, growth and development, and reproduction (mating and parenting) from birth to death. Such life history strategies are often referred to as "reproductive" strategies. To non-biologists this may seem a curious narrowing of reference, but it makes sense to evolutionists because while continued survival and adequate growth and development are obvious prerequisites to reproduction, by themselves they contribute nothing to fitness directly. In life history theory a reproductive strategy is thus a suite of functionally integrated anatomical, physiological, behavioral, and developmental traits or mechanisms for optimizing the various trade-offs among the components of, or avenues to fitness, as they arise throughout the life cycle. The main trade-offs that have been analyzed are those between reproduction and survival, reproduction and growth, quantity and quality of offspring, and current reproduction versus future reproduction (Charnov 1993; Roff 1992; Stearns 1992).

Before discussing what seems to be the most important or pervasive of these trade-offs, however – the one between current and future reproduction – it must be emphasized that life history theory's assumption of optimality does not imply any *a priori*, non-contingent definition of optimal design, for what is optimal in one environment is almost sure to be suboptimal in another.[3] Further, the assumption of optimality, while immensely productive, is still only a working hypothesis (e.g., Orzack and Sober 1994; Parker and Maynard Smith 1990). Even more important, however, it is an assumption that compels us always to reconsider our notions of what is "normal" and "pathological" because it requires us to go beyond what is merely statistically average or "normal" for some population and contemplate instead the adaptive significance of the *full range* of variability in some trait; it entails an analytic focus on the potential adaptive function of common individual differences in their local context (see also Caro and Bateson 1986; Williams and Nesse 1991). Because the relationship of the individual to the group is every bit as problematical in evolutionary ecology as it is in the social sciences, I will elaborate on this point with reference to the critical trade-off between current and future reproduction.

Current versus future reproduction

On one hand, while allocating resources to current, or short-term reproduction may reduce the resources available for reproduction in the future, when the probability of death increases substantially with age, younger parents may enjoy greater fitness than individuals who delay reproduction (say, in an attempt to capitalize on longer growth and/or more time for learning). On the other hand, however, when allocating resources to future reproduction (for example, by postponing or slowing reproduction while continuing to grow or learn) does not significantly increase the chance of death before reproduction, older parents may be larger, wealthier, and wiser, and thus better parents, thereby enjoying greater fitness than younger parents.

The critical point is that modern evolutionary ecology does not expect selection always to favor the genetic basis for traits which simply maximize number of offspring in each generation. Instead, under certain circumstances selection is expected to favor traits which minimize the between-generation variance in number of offspring. The end result is not one, but a *variety* of optima – with a major dimension of differences along a continuum with so-called current or short-term reproductive strategies at one end (where the fitness motto might be "minimize chances of lineage extinction by maximizing current reproduction"), and future or long-term reproductive strategies at the other (where the motto might be "maximize future reproduction by minimizing intergenerational variance in number of offspring") (e.g., Gillespie 1977; Lack 1947; Roff 1992; Seger and Brockmann 1987; Stearns 1992; Rubenstein 1982).

There is a growing consensus that mortality[4] rates are among the most important determinants of the optimal trade-off between current and future reproduction. In environments where mortality rates are high or unpredictable, the short-term strategy of maximizing number of offspring in the current generation may be the optimal strategy, because by maximizing the probability of having at least *some* offspring who manage to survive and reproduce it thereby minimizes the probability of ''lineage extinction'' – that is, of one's own genes vanishing entirely from the gene pool. In environments that are safe and predictable, on the other hand, the long-term strategy of consistently producing fewer, high-quality offspring over many generations may be optimal because it can result, ultimately, in more descendants than consistently having large numbers of lesser-quality offspring – who, because of their intrinsic lower ''quality'' and/or lower investment from parents, more often die or fail to reproduce (e.g., Charnov 1993; Charnov and Berrigan 1993; Gadgil and Bossert 1971; Promislow and Harvey 1990, 1991; Roff 1992; Seger and Brockmann 1987; Stearns 1992).

Figure 3.1 provides a graphic illustration of these principles. It is a schematic representation of the reproductive success of each member of two hypothetical lineages, A and B, over four generations. Lineage A occupies a risky, unpredictable, high-mortality environment while Lineage B occupies a safe, predictable, low-mortality environment. For ease of illustration only, I have assumed asexual reproduction. Sexual reproduction would obviously be more realistic, but would also be harder to depict, and would not materially affect the trade-off between current and future reproduction that is illustrated.

The key thing to notice in Figure 3.1 is that while the members of Lineage A enjoy greater short-term or *current* reproduction than those of Lineage B (i.e., a maximum of 3 *vs.* 2 offspring per parent, each generation [to save space only offspring that survive to reproduce are shown]), members of Lineage B nonetheless enjoy greater long-term or *future* reproduction (i.e., a total of 16 *vs.* 9 descendants in the fourth generation). This is because on average 2/3 of the offspring in every other generation of Lineage A fail to reproduce whereas both offspring born each generation in Lineage B survive and reproduce. In other words, while both lineages *average* 2 offspring who survive and reproduce each generation, the between-generation *variance* in the number of offspring doing so is higher in Lineage A than in Lineage B (1 *vs.* 0) – because of Lineage A's more dangerous and unpredictable environment. In effect, Lineage A has traded diminished long-term or future reproduction for greater short-term or current reproduction while Lineage B has done the opposite, sacrificing current reproduction (thereby increasing the

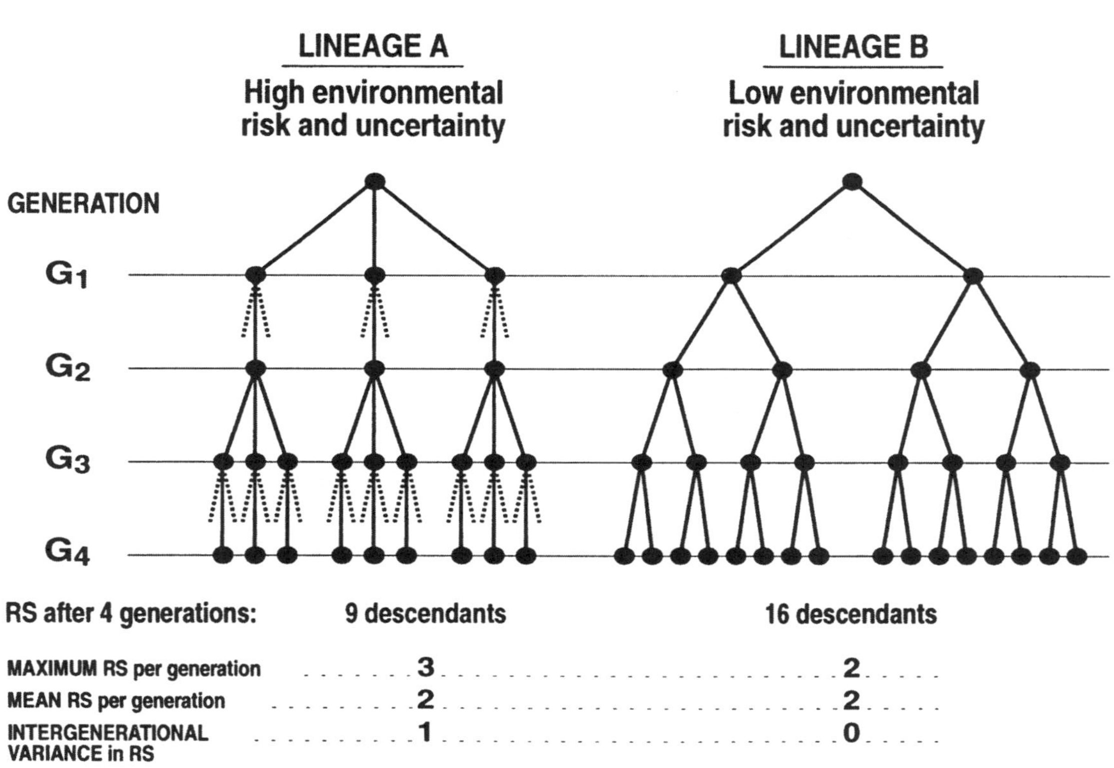

Figure 3.1. Schematic representation of alternative reproductive strategies that illustrates the trade-off between current and future reproduction.

risk of lineage extinction) in return for a greater number of descendants in the future.

When mortality rates are high or unpredictable, in other words, the most important adaptive problem may be the immediate one of avoiding extinction – and Lineage A's short-term, high-fertility reproductive strategy may be the optimal strategy. When mortality rates are low and predictable, on the other hand, there are fewer, or at least less urgent adaptive problems – and Lineage B's long-term, low-fertility, "less is more" reproductive strategy may be optimal. Each strategy, however, works "best" in its own environment. If Lineage A were moved to the low-risk environment its long-term fitness might be as high as that of Lineage B; if Lineage B were moved to the risky environment its long-term pay-off might be as low as that of Lineage A. Therefore, everything else being equal, of these two strategies, "Strategy A" is the optimal strategy in *high mortality* environments while "Strategy B" is the optimal strategy in *low mortality* environments.[5]

The implications of this trade-off between current and future reproduction for evolutionary approaches to the mind and motivation are profound. What it means is that there is no *a priori* best way to measure fitness; fitness is always relative and conditional. Perhaps the biggest problem is *when* to measure it; should we count children, grandchildren, great-grandchildren – or descendants in even more distant generations? How distant? How can we assess today something that theory says cannot properly be measured until some arbitrary point in the future? That is, how can we know today how many descendants an individual will have in the future? In principle, therefore, there can be no *a priori* non-contingent definition of an optimal reproductive strategy; it all depends. And, as we have seen, what it often depends on ismortality rates. If the very possibility of an optimal reproductive strategy depends on environmental conditions (like mortality rates), then optimality itself is inescapably contingent and emergent and is best studied as a dynamic process – whether evolutionary, developmental, or historical (e.g., Gould 1989; Sameroff 1975; Barth 1966). For reasons soon apparent, I will concentrate below on the development of reproductive strategies.

The development of reproductive strategies

It is widely accepted by evolutionary ecologists that under certain conditions selection will favor the genetic basis for phenotypic plasticity, which is the capacity of a single genotype to develop into two or more alternative morphological, physiological, or behavioral phenotypes in response to, or contingent on, environmental influences. Theory, observation, and formal models alike suggest that selection is likely to favor phenotypic plasticity when environmental conditions are "predictably unpredictable" – that is, when socioecological conditions vary so as to present individuals with a *succession* of novel environments – especially when these environments vary more *between* generations than *within* them (e.g., Bateson 1982; Bernardo 1993; Bonner 1980; Boyd and Richerson 1985; Cavalli-Sforza 1974; Fagen 1982; Horn and Rubenstein 1984; Johnston 1982; Rubenstein 1993; Smith-Gill 1983; Stamps 1991; Stearns 1982, 1992; Stephens 1990; West-Eberhard 1989). Such a succession of novel environments seems virtually guaranteed when individuals possess a sophisticated capacity for learning and are surrounded by others who also have this capacity and who continuously generate novel behaviors that are *contingent on one's own* – which is probably a fair image of the ''environment of evolutionary adaptedness'' (EAA) of humans (Bowlby 1969), at least since the Pleistocene. Natural selection for human behavioral plasticity is thus the likely source of human consciousness: the ability to be at least vaguely aware of the workings of one's own mind in order to use that self-awareness as a model for explaining and predicting the behavior of others (Humphrey 1976, 1984: Crook 1988, 1991). The ability to explain and predict the behavior of others has come to be known by its cognitive science name of *theory of mind*, which is ''the capacity to attribute mental states to oneself and to others and to interpret behavior in terms of mental states'' (Baron-Cohen 1995:55). This capacity makes for a peculiarly human ''Machiavellian intelligence'' (Byrne and Whiten 1988; Whiten 1991), which is the capacity to predict social behavior – and by making one's behavior contingent on what others are expected to do, thereby to manipulate it.

However, while hominid evolution is widely conceived as a time of pervasive selection for the cognitive and affective basis for behavioral plasticity, this does not mean that hominid behavioral phenotypes came to wander randomly with respect to their environments. In fact, it seems to me subtly misleading to think of hominid evolution primarily as a time of selection for developmental plasticity because this perpetuates the *tabula rasa* misconception of extreme cultural constructivism that essentially any phenotype is possible for humans. In my view, it is more productive to invoke life history theory's assumption of optimality and to envision hominid evolution instead as a time of particularly intense selection for *optimal* development. An optimal pattern of development is one which maximizes the probability of developing the optimal phenotype in a wide range of environments (e.g., Waddington 1968, 1975). An optimal phenotype, in turn, is one which most often optimizes the various trade-offs among the components of fitness as they arise throughout the life cycle (see also Slobodkin and Rapoport 1974).

It is this notion of trade-offs and the concomitant expectation of a *variety* of optimal reproductive strategies that hold the greatest significance for an evolutionary theory of mind (and that distinguish modern evolutionary ecology most starkly from so-called ''vulgar'' sociobiology). This is because if we accept that optimality is environmentally contingent – that optimality absolutely depends on environmental information – then we have to consider carefully the phenotypic mechanisms for recognizing and responding to environmental contingencies (and replicating the adaptive ones). We must identify, in other words, the mechanisms whereby organisms obtain information about their environments and use that information to make "decisions" about alternative phenotypes (Dennett 1995; Plotkin 1994). These are the mechanisms of development (and history): the countless interactions between genotype and environment that actually produce the phenotype.[6] Because reproduction is the engine that drives evolution, it is the development of the phenotype's capacity for reproduction that commands our special attention – and the reason why the assumption of optimality is most appropriately applied to humans in the realm of reproduction (including, as always, both mating and parenting). We therefore expect selection to have been most assiduous in producing mechanisms for the optimal allocation of reproductive effort (e.g., Gould[7] 1991; Williams 1975). And because we are rapidly coming to understand what an optimal strategy is – and thus what function these mechanisms are supposed to carry out – we are at the brink of being able to identify the actual adaptive mechanisms themselves (see also Barkow 1989; Barkow *et al.* 1992; Tooby and Cosmides 1990).

For example, there is a growing consensus that mortality rates are among the most important determinants of optimality in the critical trade-off between current and future reproduction (Charnov 1993; Hill 1993; Stearns 1992). Selection might be expected therefore to favor phenotypic mechanisms for recognizing and responding to these mortality rates – that is, adaptations whereby the developing reproductive strategies of immature individuals could be adjusted contingently on local mortality rates (see Dennett 1995 for an excellent justification for this expectation). Because adaptations are organizations of cells, tissues, and organs that are patterned with respect to (i.e., adapted to) some feature of an organism's environment, they may be thought of as information about the organism's environment that is literally embodied in its phenotype (e.g., Campbell 1974, 1990; Gottlieb 1991; Lewontin 1982; Lickliter and Berry 1990; Lorenz 1978; Piaget 1971; Plotkin 1982, 1994; Oyama 1985, 1988). Our skeletons, for example, may be thought of as literally embodied, calcified representations of gravity's constant pull; they are "patterned with respect to" gravity. Or, as Plotkin expressed this idea, "[I]nformation or knowledge, in biological terms, describes a *relationship* between the order of the world, whatever that order is, and the answering and reciprocal organization of an organism" (1982:8; original emphasis).

The question then becomes how could juvenile humans obtain the relevant environmental information? How could mortality rates be represented phenotypically – literally embodied? What would children's minds look like if they were designed to recognize and respond adaptively to mortality rates (or any other predictor of the optimal trade-off between current and future reproduction)? It was this assumption (model, image, metaphor) of an "optimal mind" (see also Cosmides and Tooby 1989; Tooby and Cosmides 1990; Barkow, Cosmides and Tooby 1992) that led me to suggest that the attachment theory model of the development of alternative reproductive strategies recently proposed by Belsky *et al.* (1991) might constitute the proximate mechanism (means) for carrying out the ultimate, adaptive function of optimizing the crucial trade-off between current and future reproduction (Chisholm 1991, 1993).

Building on the earlier work of Draper and Harpending (1982), Belsky *et al.* (1991) proposed that the allocation of reproductive effort in adults is at least partly determined by the developmental effects of early psychological stress. Their idea was that when parents or caretakers are themselves under stress – for example, frightened, hungry, and exhausted by war, poverty, and disease – they are less consistently able to provide their children with the kind of sensitive, responsive caregiving so important for the development of secure attachment (loosely defined). As a result of growing up with such a history of insecure attachment relations, with what Bowlby called insecure internal working models (i.e., negative schemas or expectations about self and others in close emotional relations), these children may reach puberty earlier (e.g., Herman-Giddens *et al.* 1988; Jones *et al.* 1972; Moffitt *et al.* 1992; Surbey 1990; Trickett and Putnam 1993) and seem to behave in ways that suggest they are allocating their resources preferentially to mating effort rather than parenting effort – or to their own current reproduction rather than to their own or their offsprings' future reproduction (e.g., Hill *et al.* 1994)

Combining the Belsky, Steinberg, and Draper model with arguments from life history theory about the role of mortality rates in determining the optimal trade-off between current and future reproduction, I proposed that it was because of its sensitivity to local mortality rates (i.e., the direct and indirect effects of loss and fear of loss, both intensely emotional experiences) that the basic anthropoid or hominid attachment process was exposed to novel selection pressures (Chisholm 1991, 1993). I also imagined that hominid children might have come to be developmentally affected by local mortality rates through the ways in which the causes and correlates of local mortality rates affected their parents' behavior and thus the attachment process. While children cannot directly perceive mortality rates, for example, they do seem to construct internal working models of their close emotional relationships on the basis of parental behavior – which, under conditions of stress, is more likely to be "translated" into emotional experience and thereby to foster insecure attachment (e.g., Main 1991; Marris 1991). Parents thus "transduce" the effects on them of the causes and correlates of local mortality rates as they interact with their children. In this way attachment organization might have become a crude index of local mortality rates and thereby also have assumed the "switch" function for entraining the development of alternative reproductive strategies that Belsky and his colleagues proposed[8] (for more details see Chisholm 1996).

In sum, what I envisioned was a model of the development of alternative reproductive strategies in which local mortality rates are indirectly perceived (as "early stress") through children's emotional engagement with their caretakers (as proposed by Belsky *et al.* [1991]), and then represented phenotypically in their internal working models of attachment relations (e.g., Main *et al.* 1985), with systematic later consequences for their allocation of reproductive effort (e.g., Belsky *et al.* 1991; Chisholm 1993, 1995a, 1996). The attachment process (the ontogeny of the balance between fear and love) would then constitute an adaptation (or exaptation [Gould and Vrba 1982]) for optimizing the trade-off between current and future reproduction.

This model captures what I feel is sure to be one of life history theory's chief contributions to cognitive science: a view of the mind as including integrated and correlated cognitive and affective schemas and operations for optimizing trade-offs among the various components of fitness as they arise throughout the life cycle. What I want to do now, however, is to extend this model to include additional threats to fitness besides the mortality rates and experiences of loss on which I focused earlier. To this end I turn now to the concept of "time preference" and outline its relevance to the trade-off between current and future reproduction. Then I suggest how the Belsky *et al.* model of the development of reproductive strategies might provide the mechanism whereby individual differences in time preference came to be represented in cognitive and affective schemas. Last, building on D'Andrade's (1992) arguments about the inseparability of schemas and motivation, I will propose that the adaptive function of these hypothetical schemas is to place a developmentally contingent time value on motivations arising from perceived threats to the various components of fitness.

Time preference

The degree to which a person prefers to receive benefits, rewards, or payoffs now or in the future is referred to as his or her time preference. Known as the "discount rate" in economics, time preference is studied in other disciplines as "impatience," "impulsiveness," "self-control," and "ability to defer gratification." The nature and determinants of individual differences in time preference are critical areas of study, for two reasons. First, they have been shown empirically to have important effects on behavior in many species, including humans. "Impulsiveness," for example, has been implicated in such social and individual concerns as drug addiction, AIDS, teenage pregnancy, high infant mortality rates, crime, and low educational attainment (e.g., Ainslie 1975; Gardner 1993; Lawrence 1991; Leigh 1986; Loewenstein and Elster 1992; Maital and Maital 1977; Rogers 1994; Wilson and Daly 1985). In a classic early study of the source of individual differences in time preference, Mischel (1958, 1961a, 1961b) also found that 7–9-year-old children from father-absent households (frequently associated with "early stress") were more likely to choose a small immediate reward than to wait a week for a promised larger one. Second, time preference seems sure to become an important concept in life history theory because of its potential relevance to the problem of optimizing the trade-off between current and future reproduction. In this context time preference can be thought of as the pay-off in fitness (relative to the population average) at some future date that an organism might require in order to forgo an immediate, current payoff in fitness. This is equivalent to saying, in paraphrased vernacular terms, that "a baby in hand is worth two in the future" (which might be a warning not to forgo any current opportunities to reproduce). When the future seems dangerous or unpredictable it is said to be discounted at a high rate or highly devalued. This makes immediate, short-term payoffs more attractive – which in turn means that it would take impossibly high fertility in the future to compensate for reducing one's fertility in the present.

By this reasoning, the degree to which individuals discount the future might reflect (as state or trait) their own optimal trade-off between current and future reproduction. If the mind is in part adapted to solve the optimization problems that life history theory holds are important, then to study the mind it is surely necessary to study nature (e.g., threats to fitness like local mortality rates). This is because adaptations are "patterned with respect to" nature; literally, they are "fit" (*aptus*) "to" (*ad*) some purpose or use in nature. An adaptation is thus environmental information that has been embodied in (or in the words of both Piaget and Waddington, "assimilated to") the phenotype. Might individual differences in time preference thus constitute facultative adaptations that "bias" or "predispose" individuals to prefer current or future rewards? What is the environmental information that would enable the mind to optimize the trade-off between current and future reproduction, and what are the cognitive and affective operations whereby the mind uses time preference to make optimal "decisions" (not necessarily conscious) about alternative behaviors?

It is widely accepted that individual differences in time preference are heavily influenced by environmental risk and uncertainty (e.g., Clark 1990, 1991; Gardner 1993; Krebs and Kacelnik 1991; Mangel and Clark 1988; Rogers 1994; Seger and Brockmann 1987; Stephens 1990). The specific threats posed by risky and uncertain environments (whether social or physical) apply, however, not just to survival (i.e., to mortality rates, early stress, and the concomitant emotional experience of loss – my original interests), but to all the other components of fitness as well: to growth and development and reproduction (including, as always, both mating and parenting) throughout the life cycle. In other words, although the hypothesis that children are evolved to respond adaptively to threats to their continued survival still seems worthwhile, it is clearly necessary to expand our notion of ''early stress'' to include not just threats to children's survival, but to their growth and development and (future) reproduction[9] as well. The reason is that this focuses our attention on additional sources of individual differences in time preference, which, taken together, might constitute the developmental mechanisms through which information about environmental risk and uncertainty (i.e., threats to fitness) is represented phenotypically and thus available to the psyche (and soma) for optimizing the trade-off between current and future reproduction.

The evolutionary ecology of attachment organization

Viewed from the perspective of life history theory, the attachment process begins to look like an evolved ''developmental system'' (Oyama 1985, 1988) whereby children become predisposed to monitor the most adaptively significant features of their environments (i.e., threats and opportunities affecting their reproductive value) as the basis for optimizing the trade-off between current and future reproduction. Because juveniles cannot reproduce, the most immediate threats and opportunities relevant to their fitness are not those affecting their reproduction, but their survival and growth and development (Chisholm 1996). Because any future reproduction at all is always absolutely contingent on their current survival and growth, selection on hominid juveniles is expected to have favored mechanisms for assessing environmental threats and opportunities affecting their continuing survival and growth and development (that is, their future reproduction) and for allocating their resources accordingly. When threats predominate, it may be optimal to allocate resources to immediate survival (which might actually halt growth, as in non-organic failure to thrive [e.g., Drotar 1991; Monckberg 1992]) or to the ''quantity'' of growth (e.g., to rapid growth or maturation) which may maximize survivorship to reproductive maturity (thereby contributing more to current than to future reproduction [e.g., Pagel and Harvey 1993; Stearns 1992]). When opportunities predominate, however, it may be optimal to allocate resources instead to play, exploration, and learning (i.e., to social-emotional and cognitive development, or the ''quality'' of growth), which are more likely to maximize future reproduction (Bernardo 1993; Fagen 1982, 1993; Johnston 1982; Rubenstein 1993).

The most adaptively significant feature of children's environments must always have been their parents' reproductive strategy – or more precisely, the quality of the parental investment they receive (e.g., Belsky *et al.* 1991; Blurton Jones 1993; Hinde 1982; Lamb *et al.* 1985; Main 1990; Trivers 1974). Building especially on Main's (1990) arguments (but disagreeing with her implication that secure attachment is the ''primary'' developmental strategy, or nature's default), I have argued elsewhere (Chisholm 1996) that the most common individual differences in attachment today arise as facultative adaptations to parental behaviors which during hominid evolution were probably two of the more reliable indicators of threats to juvenile hominid fitness: parents' *inability* to protect or provide for offspring in the face of environmental risk and uncertainty, and parents *unwillingness* (not necessarily conscious) to protect or provide for offspring. In short, I envision individual differences in attachment today as facultative adaptations to parental behaviors which in the past indicated or foreshadowed (1) parental powerlessness and poverty and/or (2) parent–offspring conflict – i.e., neglect, rejection, abuse or infanticide by parents who allocated more of their resources to mating effort, or the production of offspring, than was optimal for the survival or growth and development of individual offspring (Table 3.1 provides a summary of this model).

Along with Dunn (1976), Hinde (e.g., 1982, 1986), Lamb *et al.* (1985) and others, I thus doubt that there is any *a priori*, non-contingent, so-called ''normal'' pattern of attachment. In my view, secure attachment develops today as a facultative adaptation to what we call sensitive, responsive, and accepting parenting because during hominid evolution this style of parenting behavior was a reliable indicator of fitness *opportunities* – i.e., that parents or other caretakers had sufficient resources and motivation to invest in offspring for an extended period. Under the conditions of low environmental risk and uncertainty that would tend to support such parental behavior, life history theory predicts (*ceteris paribus*) that the optimal reproductive strategy will be the high-parenting effort strategy of maximizing future reproduction by investing heavily in a small number of high-quality offspring (e.g., Stearns 1992).

On the other hand, I also venture that the two main types of insecure attachment (so-called Type A, avoidant, and Type C, anxious) may develop today as facultative adaptations to what we call insensitive, unresponsive, and/or rejecting styles of parenting because during hominid evolution such parenting styles were indicators of *threats* to fitness – i.e., high levels of environmental risk and uncertainty that might tend to make parents less able and/or willing to invest in offspring for very long. Thus, in terms of immediate causation, Type C or anxiously attached children are wary of, and preoccupied with their caretakers' moods and intentions because (the evidence

Table 3.1 *Attachment organization as product of interaction between parental reproductive strategies and children's developmental strategies (after Chisholm 1996).*

Attachment classification		Parental reproductive strategy	Child's incipient reproductive (developmental strategy)
A	INSECURE AVOIDANT	Short-term Unwilling to invest High mating effort Dismissing, rejecting of child	Maximize short-term survival Avoid rejecting, potentially infanticidal parent
B	SECURE	Long-term Able and willing to invest High parenting effort Unconditionally accepting, sensitive, responsive to child	Maximize long-term learning (quality of development) Prolong current high level of investment from ''rich'' parent
C	INSECURE ANXIOUS, AMBIVALENT	Short-term unable to invest Parenting effort with inadequate resources Inconsistent, preoccupied, but not rejecting of child	Maximize short-term maturation and learning (''quantity'' [i.e., speed] of development) Increase current low/erratic investment from ''poor'' parent

suggests) their caretakers are often inconsistent. In terms of ultimate causation, however, during hominid evolution such inconsistency may have become reliable information about a caretaker's relative *inability* to invest, because of the caretaker's own inadequate or unpredictable resources, and that anxious, wary preoccupation with parents represents a facultative adaptation for extracting resources from caretakers who are irritable and preoccupied themselves – with fear, hunger, and exhaustion. Likewise, in terms of immediate causation Type A or avoidant children avoid their primary caretakers because (the evidence suggests) their caretakers too often rebuff or reject them. In terms of ultimate causation, however, during hominid evolution such rejection may have become reliable information about a mother's relative *unwillingness* (not necessarily conscious) to invest, because her optimal reproductive strategy was to allocate resources not to parenting, but to the early and/or rapid production of many, relatively low-quality offspring.

The ability and willingness to invest in a child are not dichotomous variables, of course, nor necessarily mutually exclusive. Nonetheless, during hominid evolution they may often enough have been separate dimensions of parental goals or conditions to explain why there seem to be two main kinds of insecure attachment. The reason may be that because essentially all information about both social and physical environmental risk and uncertainty comes to young children through their interactions with their primary caretakers, then from the child's perspective there may be just two kinds of risk and uncertainty – one concerning caretakers' *motives* to maintain investment and the other concerning caretakers' *means* or *opportunities* to maintain investment. The capacity to distinguish between motive and opportunity might have enabled juvenile hominids to differentiate between inadequate parental investment that is due to inadequate parental resources (including inadequate information, time, and safety as well as material resources) and inadequate parental investment due to parent allocating whatever resources they have to mating effort, or the production of additional offspring, rather than to parenting. Anxious (Type C) attachment might thus represent a facultative adaptation to parents who, though willing, lack adequate resources and are hard-pressed to invest. The hallmark of anxious attachment – preoccupation with caretakers' moods and intentions – might thus have functioned to maintain some minimal level of investment from caregivers, and surely hominid parents were from time to time preoccupied with fear, hunger, and exhaustion, as are parents today who have to rear children with limited resources (e.g., Cassidy 1980; Scheper-Hughes 1992). The hallmark of avoidant (Type A) attachment, on the other hand – low expression of affect and literal avoidance of mother – might represent a facultative adaptation to caregivers who, regardless of their ability to invest, are unwilling to invest. And just as modern parents neglect, abandon, and kill their children from time to time (e.g., DeMause 1974; Daly and Wilson 1988; Hausfater and Hrdy 1984; Hrdy 1977, 1987, 1992; Langer 1974; Smuts 1992; van Schaik and Dunbar 1990),[10] so too surely did our ancestors.

Life history theory thus expects information about environmental risk and uncertainty to be embodied phenotypically. The attachment process (the development of love and fear) may be one process whereby this comes about. But now the real work begins. What form does this information take? How is it represented? How does it influence behavior? These questions are what take us now into the mind – the realm of *a priori* categories, cognitive and affective schemas, and internal working models.

Representing risk and uncertainty

John Bowlby (1969) proposed that on the basis of the history of their interactions with their parents children construct internal working models of, first, themselves and their parents, and later, of their social relations in general. These internal working models are generalized expectations about ''self-with-others,'' or trust (the opposite of fear) in the benign availability of others to oneself. Bretherton (1985) notes that Bowlby was led to his concept of internal working model in part by Craik's (1943) theory of mental representations, which states:

> If the organism carries a small-scale model of external reality and of its own possible actions within its head, it is able to try out various alternatives, conclude which is the best of them, react to future situations before they arise, utilize the knowledge of past events in dealing with the present and future, and in every way to react in a much fuller, safer and more competent manner to the emergencies which face it. (1943:61)

But how do we conclude which alternative is *the best*? What is the basis for this evaluation? For Bowlby, as well as virtually all modern theorists of the mind, internal working models or schemas have affective as well as cognitive attributes, so that representations of past events and perceived alternative courses of action have emotional or evaluative components or dimensions. Ultimately, this is because perception itself has an inherent *evaluative* component. In Felicia Pratto's words, ''we are chronically engaged in ascertaining the goodness or badness of stimuli in our environments. . .'' (1994:116); and Henry Plotkin put it this way: ''events in the world are signalled as good or bad, those which we should attempt to attain or avoid, those associated with life and those associated with death'' (1994:208). To perceive *is* to evaluate. Elzanowski (1993) suggests that the neurophysiological source of all human value is what he calls ''value experience,'' which is the positive or negative emotional valence that is universally, innately linked to all perception and sensation (see also Damasio 1994; Mathews and MacLeod 1994). To be understood, Elzanowski argues, ''value experience has first to be accepted as a natural phenomenon, as an objective source of subjectivity'' (1993:272–273).

This is especially true for children. LeDoux (1989, 1995, 1996), for example, notes that a major part of ''value experience'' takes place in the amygdala, at least with regard to evaluating a stimulus as appropriate or not to elicit fear. Because the neural connections between the sensory cortex and the amygdala mature before those between the cerebral cortex and the amygdala, all early memories are essentially *emotional* memories – not explicit, declarative, conscious memories. Moreover, because the earliest emotional memories are laid down prior to the development of connections between the amygdala and the cortex, they are virtually indelible and inaccessible to consciousness. (LeDoux speculates on this basis that ''the role of therapy may be to allow the cortex to establish more effective and efficient synaptic links with the amygdala'' [1995:229].) Finally, because the amygdala sends projections back to the very sensory processing systems from which it receives sensory information, these back-projections may allow the amygdala's habitual evaluations of danger to affect perceptions of the environment.

This may be the neural mechanism whereby a sufficient number of early fearful experiences predispose children to develop negative, fearful, internal working models.

Approaching the evolution of human attachment from the perspective of life history theory, it would seem to be the child's capacity to be reliably affected by his or her early experience that would be the trait under selection.[11] On this view, as mentioned, the attachment process came to function as a developmental "switch" – which Belsky and his colleagues (1991) proposed was "flipped" by the child's experience with early stress (i.e., fear). Whether or not this "switch" metaphor pans out, I think now that we need to include threats to *all* components of children's fitness – not just threats to their survival from the causes of high mortality rates, as I emphasized earlier. I also think it is useful to think of "early stress" in more explicitly ecological terms as "risk and uncertainty," for in theory they are the most important determinants of the optimal trade-off between current and future reproduction.

The next step in my argument is to suggest that it may be useful to think of internal working models as including representations of the past and future that are conceived in terms of life history theory. From this perspective representations of the past might be expected to embody images of the history of local environmental risk and uncertainty – that is, threats to one's fitness that have been experienced phenotypically, emotionally, as pain, fear, loss, rejection, and so forth. On the basis of these amygdala-mediated, emotion-laden images of one's past the mind would create (perhaps in part through back-projections to the sensory cortex) representations (e.g., expectations) of the future – which, because they too are emotion-laden, would have motivational force (conscious or not). On the basis of life history theory I hazard the final suggestion that these emotion-laden representations of the future constitute or include what we call time preference – the degree to which a person prefers or expects rewards, payoffs, or consequences now or in the future. Going further, I speculate that the reason all of this happens is that during hominid (if not mammalian or vertebrate) evolution these mental representations of risk and uncertainty were sufficiently accurate, and their resulting "time preference motivational systems" sufficiently effective in shaping behavior, that the ultimate developmental outcome was usually close enough to the local optimal trade-off between current and future reproduction.

Summarizing briefly, I see internal working models of close emotional relations as phenotypic mechanisms for representing nature (the nature of one's social relations) in the mind and then performing operations on these representations in order to "decide" on one's best course of action. Imagine, for example, a suite of neural mechanisms (for example, LeDoux's emotional memory system) for perceiving environmental risk and uncertainty and then for converting these perceptions into time preferences that are attached to each alternative action schema that is generated. This embodied ''information-with-evaluation'' might provide a means by which the adaptive end of optimizing the trade-off between current and future reproduction could be achieved.

I view the mind from the perspective of evolutionary ecology, which means that I view the mind as evolved to represent certain kinds of environmental information (including one's internal environment) and to carry out certain operations on these representations, especially that of evaluating alternative representations of the future (i.e., the means) in order to arrive at the best solution to a number of universal (and often contradictory) evolutionary problems (i.e., evolution's ends or goals: survival, growth and development, and ultimately reproduction). From a radically different starting place in cognitive anthropology, D'Andrade (1992) has presented a not-dissimilar means–end model for combining cognition (information) and emotion (evaluation, motivation) that may hold promise for a rapprochement between cognitive anthropology and evolutionary psychology (i.e., an evolutionary ecological or life history theory view of mind). D'Andrade envisions a *hierarchy* of schemas:

> This . . . means–ends goal linkage is one principle of schema hierarchy. . . .While there are many possible kinds of linkage through which one schema passes its interpretation to another, it is the topmost level of interpretation which is typically linked to the actions by which an organism operates in its environment. That is, the top-level schemas tend to be goals. . . .At the top of the interpretive system are those which function as a person's most general goals. These might be called master motives – for things like love and work, which instigate action with no more ultimate goal in sight. (1992:30)

While it is obvious that D'Andrade's ''love'' and ''work'' are not the same as the evolutionary ecologist's ''reproductive effort'' and ''somatic effort,'' both love and work are widely conceived to involve a kind of moral *commitment to* the future (e.g., Nussbaum 1994; Solomon 1990; Wilson 1993) – and therefore to constitute action schemas that are *means to* the future. In turn, what D'Andrade terms ''master motives,'' an evolutionary psychologist might think of as the components of fitness. They are not only a person's most general goals, but the most general goals of all living things: achieving the optimal balance between survival, growth and development, and reproduction. The point is that ''love'' and ''work'' and similar concepts and schema theory generally can be, and must be, assimilated into any evolutionary view of mind that aims to be both true and valuable.

Implications and future research

In the space remaining it is possible only to hint at some of the enormous implications that evolutionary ecology and life history theory hold for our understanding of human nature and the mind. By far the most important, in my opinion, is the strong implication that human nature is essentially local. To me, this follows automatically and simply from optimality theory and the concept of trade-offs, especially the critical trade-off between current and future reproduction. Because it is impossible simultaneously to maximize both current and future reproduction (or any other pair of fitness components) there can be no *a priori* optimal reproductive strategy; it depends – on the environment, physical and social. And when environmental conditions are ''predictably unpredictable,'' optimality theory expects that selection will favor mechanisms for developmental plasticity – for adjusting the developing phenotype according to, or contingent on, the environment.[12] This requires mechanisms for recognizing environmental contingencies and using that information to respond to the environment – to develop alternative phenotypes. The more complex these mechanisms become, the more complex becomes one's environment and one's relationship to it – which exerts even more intense selection for obtaining even more and better, fine-grained environmental information. A bird's wing literally embodies ''old'' information about the air its ancestors flew in. This is an adaptive solution because the air the bird flew in while young, and still flies in today, has the same properties as the air of its ancestors. In the same way, our minds literally embody ''old'' information (in the form of *a priori* categories [Plotkin 1994]) about the environments our ancestors lived in. However, because human environments are so complex and change so quickly, our minds seem specially designed to embody also a tremendous amount of ''new'' information about our developmental environments – in order to make predictions about the environments in which we will be reproducing.

Especially for humans, then, the relationship of the genotype to the phenotype is, as Waddington put it, one of ''adaptive *in*determinacy'' (1968:364; emphasis added). The upshot is that humans are quintessentially local animals, adapted to optimize the trade-offs between the components of fitness according to local environmental information. Our genotypes are global but our phenotypes are local – unfinished and thus logically and biologically impossible without local knowledge. Life history theory and its fundamental assumption of optimality thus do not support the extreme reductionist notion of some inner, biological, ''essential'' human nature – except to say that this nature is essentially, biologically, and adaptively local (see also Boehm 1989; Hinton 1993; Worthman 1992). This is an important point, for it points to potential common ground between evolutionary ecology and optimality theory and much of cultural and psychological anthropology (e.g., Geertz 1973, 1983; Shore 1988). It also shows how wrong is the common Marxist complaint that an evolutionary view of humanity ''de-historicizes'' humankind (see Fox 1989:219).[13]

A corollary of the idea that human nature is essentially local – that it emerges *in response to* local conditions – is that the mind is primarily "defensive" in nature, at least early in its ontogeny. This is an old idea, and would not surprise Freud, for example, whose suggestion that personality is composed largely of psychological defense mechanisms is well known. Crook, who also emphasizes the local or "experiential" core of mind, notes that most "theories of identity stress the defensive nature of the processes whereby a human sense of self is achieved" (1988:353). Slobodkin and Rapoport (1974) define adaptation in explicitly dynamic, processual terms as beginning with the organism's recognition of some environmental perturbation, which is defined as the perception of *stress*. If an environmental stressor is an "attack," so to speak, on one's reproductive value, then it will be adaptive and wise to defend oneself against such attacks. The life history view of cognition advanced here suggests that the mind (especially the *young* mind) can be conceived in large part as images or working models of environmental threats – both physical and socioecological (i.e., political and economic) – to the various components of fitness, and schemas (for acting and thinking/feeling) for defending against such threats. Two examples spring to mind: one is Leda Cosmides' (1989; Cosmides and Tooby 1989) suggestion that the mind possesses special "social cognition mechanisms" designed simply to detect "cheaters" in social exchanges. Another is Scheper-Hughes' (1992) moving account of how mothers in impoverished Brazilian shantytowns hedge their emotional bets against the threat of their children's early death (see also Scheper-Hughes 1987).

And from the idea that the mind is primarily or ontogenetically "defensive" in nature, I think it follows that the mind is evolved to place a developmentally contingent time value on the action schemas arising out of the perceived threats to one's fitness. Thus, on the principle that selection tends to favor graded responses to environmental threats or perturbations (e.g., Bonner 1980; Slobodkin and Rapoport 1974), the more threats there are, the more defensive one becomes, and the shorter one's time preference. On the other hand, the fewer the threats to one's fitness, the less defensive one needs to be, and the future assumes greater and greater value. Although he does not discuss threats to fitness, Crook (1988) presents a similar model in which one dimension of human self-awareness is defined as the axis between being focused on a goal in the future ("expectationality"), at one end, and being focused on the on-going present moment ("attentionality"), at the other.[14]

In my view, one of the major goals for future research on the mind that is informed by life history theory should be exploring the actual mechanisms that do all the work. The life history view of mind outlined above might inform us about the mind's work – the problems that nature has posed and the kinds of information that might be needed to solve them – but it does not tell us how the work in fact gets done. We still need to know the actual developmental psychobiological mechanisms that finally produce adaptations, mental as well as physical. My suspicion is that by knowing better the jobs that the mind and body need to do we can narrow the search for these mechanisms.

Fortunately, a number of scholars are already active in this area, where there is growing recognition that soma and psyche have similar problems to solve. For example, Ellison (1990), Peacock (1990, 1991), Worthman (1990, 1993b), and Vitzthum (in press) have each been studying the effects of nutritional and other environmental threats to growth on a variety of subsequent reproductive functions. Each in their own way has come to the overall conclusion that humans seem to have been designed to rely on information from the environment concerning threats to their fitness (in this case growth) as a basis for adjusting the way they allocate resources to survival, growth and development and reproduction in the future. This means that adult reproductive capacity may be adjusted (and perhaps thereby optimized) according to the frequency, duration, and intensity of episodes of malnutrition or disease during development. Ellison (1990) hypothesized that this ''feed forward'' process might come about through the operation of a mechanism for monitoring rates of growth or development. Because rates of growth and development are highly sensitive to environmental threats, he argued, they might thus function as ''bioassays'' on which future conditions for one's soma could be predicted. By analogy with Ellison, I suggested (Chisholm 1993) that one's history of attachment relations might function as a ''socioassay'' on which future socioecological or political-economic conditions for one's psyche could be predicted. By speaking of soma and psyche, of course, I do not mean to perpetuate old-fashioned dichotomous styles of thinking. To the contrary, I hope that by recognizing that they face the same future we may figure out new ways of thinking about how they interact.

Conclusion

Needless to say, the evolutionary model of the mind presented here is a preliminary sketch. Nonetheless, I think it indicates the kind of role that life history theory will play in cognitive science. It provides a fresh evolutionary rationale for the very existence of *a priori* categories, and new conceptual tools for cognitive ethologists, evolutionary epistemologists, and others concerned with the nature of such categories, the origins of knowledge itself, and how nature, and the value that is in nature, become represented in developing minds (e.g., Byrne and Whiten 1988; Greenberg and Tobach 1990; Lorenz 1978; Oyama 1985, 1991; Plotkin 1982, 1994). Such an adaptationist perspective on human nature fosters common ground between evolutionary ecology, psychological and cultural anthropology, and cognitive science.

Finally – and surely paradoxically for some – modern evolutionary theory (especially life history theory) seems to enhance recent arguments that there can be a rational basis for moral sentiments that is independent of received religion, and that the heart of morality itself may be long-term emotional commitment to people's futures (e.g., Dennett 1995; Johnson 1993; Nussbaum 1994; Ruddick 1989; Solomon 1990; Wilson 1993).

Acknowledgments

For helpful advice on earlier versions of this chapter I thank Victoria K. Burbank, Neil Pelkey, Jay Belsky, Sally Stanley, Noel Wescombe and all those who have participated in my yearly seminar "Sex, Evolution, and Development." At the kind invitation of Ben Blount, I first presented this material (almost in its entirety) at the Seventh Annual Cognitive Studies Conference, "Biocultural Approaches to the Mind and Human Development," sponsored by the Institute for Behavioral Research at the University of Georgia, Athens, GA, April 22, 1994. Earlier I had presented portions of this chapter in the symposium "Childhood in Life-History Perspective: Developing Views," organized by Gilda Morelli and Paula Ivey, at the annual meeting of the Society for Cross-Cultural Research in Santa Fe, NM, on February 18, 1994.

NOTES

1. I dedicate this chapter to the memory of Gregory Bateson. In addition to his many contributions to anthropology and cognitive science generally, several years ago, when I was fortunate to take his graduate seminar at the University of Hawaii, he contributed very directly to my own embryonic thoughts about mind and nature. I am obviously indebted to him as well for my title (Bateson 1972), which I have appropriated as a way of honoring his vision of the singular importance of ecology for understanding the mind.
2. Some of an organism's traits are functionally integrated, in the sense that they work together to carry out some developmental, physiological, or psychobiological process which is or was favored by selection; such traits are integrated in a network of adaptive causation – they cause something to happen that may be adaptive. Other traits have no function and do not cause anything adaptive to happen. Instead, they are merely correlated with each other or with other integrated traits (e.g., Stamps 1991; Stearns 1992). The distinction is not always easy to make in practice.
3. Extrinsic, as opposed to intrinsic, mortality rates, are what matter (Stearns 1992). Extrinsic sources of mortality are predation, disease, accidents, and other environmental hazards that are not affected by changes in the allocation of reproductive effort. Intrinsic sources of mortality, on the other hand, are directly affected by allocation decisions, so that, for example, the physiological costs (trade-offs) of early maturation in human females (current reproduction) may include increased

risk for excess weight (Wellens *et al.* 1992) and breast cancer (Apter *et al.* 1989).

4. Nor does the assumption of optimality mean that evolutionary ecologists believe that organisms are perfectly designed, for such is an impossibility. An optimal design is not a perfect design, only the best that can be produced under current conditions, with the available genes, the available resources, and in the available time. Selection cannot produce perfection – the best imaginable – when there is no genetic or developmental basis for achieving it, nor when constrained by a changing environment or inadequate resources (including always-limited time). Moreover, since organisms are comprised of integrated and correlated traits, possessing one or more traits that are the "best available" usually entails trade-offs – physiological costs that make the remaining traits less likely to be optimal. Organisms are thus bundles of compromises among their various traits (e.g., Mangel and Clark 1988; Parker and Maynard Smith 1990; Stearns 1992; Williams 1966). Perfection therefore exists only in the human mind, doomed forever to remain a tantalizing but merely logical possibility.
5. If some individuals in Lineage B's safe, predictable environment were also to gain access to unlimited resources, their optimal reproductive strategy might come to look more like the high-fertility "Strategy A." The reason is that if they had unlimited resources they would be better able to maximize *both* number of offspring (current reproduction) *and* offspring reproductive value (which tends to minimize between-generation variance in number of offspring; i.e., future reproduction). However, since resources usually are limited (and time is always limited), there is usually a trade-off between current and future reproduction, or between mating effort and parenting effort (e.g., Trivers 1974).
6. Early, "vulgar" versions of sociobiology often ignored development – at their peril. Possibly to rationalize their relative inattention to the processes that actually produce the phenotype some have made use of the "phenotypic gambit," which is the simplifying assumption that the relationship between genotype and phenotype is not especially important for understanding adaptation (Grafen 1984; Smith and Winterhalder 1992). But it *is* important, because without an understanding of how phenotypes emerge developmentally from gene–environment interactions we can have no clear picture of the trait that is supposed to be the adaptation (e.g., Bateson 1976, 1982; Gould 1991; Gould and Lewontin 1979; Gottlieb 1991; Hinde 1987; Oyama 1985, 1988, 1991; Scarr and McCartney 1983; Symons 1987; West-Eberhard 1989; Worthman 1992, 1993a). To understand what selection *should* favor it is necessary to test our optimality models against the qualities of real organisms (the "phenotypic gambit"). But to understand what selection *can* favor we must understand how these organisms work – which means understanding the profusion of developmental and historical processes whereby genes and environments mutually construct the phenotype, including the mind and behavior.
7. Stephen Jay Gould, for example, who is occasionally misrepresented as an anti-adaptationist, has argued that the assumption of optimality is most useful for analyzing "explicitly biological traits shared with other related species lacking our cultural richness – e.g. . . .behaviors of sexual and parent-child bonding" (1991:60).
8. To the extent that "emotionality" increased the reliability or efficiency of this switch function, there might have followed selection for even greater emotionality because those who were most sensitive to their early environments might be most

affected by them – and thus be more likely also to adopt the locally optimal reproductive strategy. Greater emotional sensitivity or reactivity might also make children more demanding, or for a longer period. This would tend to exert selection for even greater parental investment, which, as Ruddick (1989) observed, begins with self-control; as she put it, the first part of mothering (for men *and* women, i.e., parenting effort) is "the struggle to be nonviolent."

9. While juveniles cannot yet expend reproductive effort they nonetheless respond to at least some threats to their survival and growth and development in ways that maximize the *future* returns to fertility of resources presently allocated to growth. One of the best non-human examples is that of a kind of East African snail, whose lifespan and/or reproductive rate is usually drastically reduced when it becomes infected with parasites. Minchella (1985) showed that snails that became infected before they were mature responded with an *accelerated rate* of maturation. Similarly, there are reports of earlier maturation in response to psychosocial stress in immature human females (Herman-Giddens *et al.* 1988; Jones *et al.* 1972; Moffitt *et al.* 1992; Surbey 1990; Trickett and Putnam 1993), and some evidence that early-maturing women may have a shorter period of "adolescent subfertility," thereby enjoying higher fecundity, at least early in their reproductive careers (Apter and Vikho 1983).
10. There may be more to so-called avoidant attachment than meets the eye. If the environment of human evolutionary adaptedness often enough included a few potential "allomothers" or substitute caregivers, then seeking out or at least responding positively to such a substitute mother might be (or have been) part of what seems today only a strategy of "avoidance." Because modern industrial, "low density," nuclear families rarely provide children with alternative adult attachment figures, we seldom see them searching for substitute parents – because they're not there. Because they haven't anyone to escape to, all we can see are children avoiding their rejecting caregivers. The strategy of avoiding rejecting caretakers would seem to work best (be optimal) in social environments which provide a number of alternative caregivers for a child to seek out. What we call "avoidant" attachment, in other words, might actually be *failure* to avoid or escape from a rejecting or harmful caregiver.
11. The capacity to be affected in reliable, potentially adaptive ways by one's developmental environment carries with it, of course, the cost or trade-off of increasing the risk of learning or teaching gone wrong, or failing to occur (e.g., Johnston 1982). It is tempting to speculate that our species' various neuroses may be the price we pay for our great learning capacity.
12. Sewall Wright, the leading population geneticist of his day and one of the architects of biology's New Synthesis, put it this way:

    > Individual adaptability [phenotypic plasticity] is, in fact, distinctly a factor of evolutionary poise. It is not only of the greatest significance as a factor of evolution in damping the effects of selection. . . but is itself perhaps the *chief object* of selection. . . The evolution of complex organisms rests on the attainment of gene combinations which determine a varied repertoire of adaptive cell response in relation to external conditions. . . structure is never inherited as such, but merely types of adaptive cell behavior which lead to particular structures in particular conditions. . . (1931:147, emphasis added)

13. There is not space here to develop this idea fully – but briefly, if optimality theory and life history theory suggest that human nature is emergent, naturally selected to be affected by local developmental and historical conditions, then the same is true for male and female versions of human nature: maleness and femaleness would also be importantly emergent and local. On top of a basic primate or mammalian pattern of sex differences in reproductive strategies, natural selection for developmentally contingent phenotypic plasticity would tend to increase the extent of individual differences (especially relative to sex differences) in behavior. Under certain socioecological or political-economic conditions such individual differences would seem to have the consequence of increasing the similarities between male and female reproductive strategies (and decreasing them under others). Using historical data to ground her arguments, Dickemann (1986) has presented an evolutionary ecological model of the development of gender similarities and differences that points out some of these environmental and historical conditions. Whiting and Whiting (1975), in their classic study of the determinants of aloofness and intimacy among husbands and wives, illustrated others. More recently, Smuts (1992) has explored the effects of variation in male control of resources (especially including safety) on male aggression against women and gender relations generally.
14. I also wonder if the evolution of the cognitive capacity to perceive and represent the passage of time and for developmentally contingent individual differences in time preference might be implicated in the evolution of consciousness. To see one's future, one has got to be able to represent oneself in that future (e.g., Humphrey 1976, 1984). Those who were most conscious of themselves and their futures may thus have been more conscious of their own deaths. Having an image of one's own death may require psychological defenses. Intimations of mortality may, of course, be denied (e.g., Becker 1973). But *parents* who denied their own mortality may have had less motivation, and certainly less ability, to allocate resources to their children and their children's children after they had died. Part of the price we pay for our *capacity* to invest in our descendants may thus be the certain knowledge of our own deaths that that capacity entails. Robertson (1991) and Hrdy and Judge (1993) provide many examples of how human activities and institutions can be interpreted as extensions of parenting effort "beyond the family."

References

Ainslie, G. 1975. Specious reward: A behavioral theory of impulsiveness and impulse control. *Psychological Bulletin* 82:463–496.

Apter, D. and R. Vikho. 1983. Early menarche, a risk factor for breast cancer, indicates early onset of ovulatory cycles. *Journal of Clinical Endocrinology and Metabolism* 57:82–86.

Apter, D., M. Reinila, and R. Vihko. 1989. Some endocrine characteristics of early menarche, a risk factor for breast cancer, are preserved into adulthood. *International Journal of Cancer* 44:783–787.

Barkow, J. 1989. *Darwin, sex, and status: Biological approaches to mind and culture.* Toronto: University of Toronto Press.

Barkow, J., L. Cosmides, and J. Tooby. 1992. *The adapted mind: Evolutionary psychology and the generation of culture*. New York: Oxford University Press.

Baron-Cohen, S. 1995. *Mindblindness: An essay on autism and theory of mind.* Cambridge, MA: MIT Press.

Barth, F. 1966. *Models of social organization*. Royal Anthropological Institute of Great Britain, Occasional Paper No. 23.

Bateson, G. 1972. *Steps to an ecology of mind.* New York: Ballantine.

Bateson, P. 1976. Rules and reciprocity in behavioural development.

1982. Behavioral development and evolutionary processes. In King's College Sociobiology Study Group, eds., *Current problems in sociobiology*. Cambridge: Cambridge University Press.

Becker, E. 1973. *The denial of death*. New York: The Free Press.

Belsky, J., L. Steinberg, and P. Draper. 1991. Childhood experience, interpersonal development, and reproductive strategy: An evolutionary theory of socialization. *Child Development* 62:647–670.

Bernardo, J. 1993. Determinants of maturation in animals. *Trends in Ecology and Evolution* 3(5):166–173.

Blurton Jones, N. 1993. The lives of hunter-gatherer children: Effects of parental behavior and parental reproductive strategy. In M. Pereira and L. Fairbanks, eds., *Juvenile primates: Life history, development and behavior*. New York: Oxford University Press.

Boehm, C. 1989. Ambivalence and compromise in human nature. *American Anthropologist* 91:921–939.

Bonner, J. 1980. *The evolution of culture in animals.* Princeton: Princeton University Press.

Bowlby, J. 1969. *Attachment.* Vol. 1. *Attachment and Loss*, New York: Basic Books. (2nd edition published 1982).

Boyd, R. and P. Richerson. 1985. *Culture and the evolutionary process*. Chicago: University of Chicago Press.

Bretherton, I. 1985. Attachment theory: Retrospect and prospect. In I. Bretherton and E. Waters, eds., *Growing points of attachment theory and research*. Monographs of the Society for Research in Child Development No. 209.

Byrne, R. and A. Whiten. eds. 1988. *Machiavellian intelligence: Social expertise and the evolution of intellect in monkeys, apes, and humans.* Oxford: Clarendon Press.

Campbell, D. T. 1974. Evolutionary epistemology. In P. Schilpp, ed., *The philosophy of Karl Popper*. La Salle, IL: Open Court Publishers.

1990. Levels of organization, downward causation, and the selection-theory approach to evolutionary epistemology. In G. Greenberg and E. Tobach, eds., *Theories of the evolution of knowing*. Hillsdale, NJ: Lawrence Erlbaum.

Caro, T. and P. Bateson. 1986. Organization and ontogeny of alternative tactics. *Animal Behaviour* 34:1482–1499.

Cassidy, C. 1980. Benign neglect and toddler malnutrition. In L. Greene and F. Johnston, eds., *Social and biological predictors of nutritional status, physical growth and neurological development*. New York: Academic Press.

Cavalli-Sforza, L. 1974. The role of plasticity in biological and cultural evolution. *Annals of the New York Academy of Science* 231:43–59.

Charnov, E. 1993. *Life history invariants: Some explorations of symmetry in evolutionary ecology*. New York: Oxford University Press.

Charnov, E. and D. Berrigan. 1993. Why do female primates have such long lifespans and so few babies? Or Life in the slow lane. *Evolutionary Anthropology* 2:191–194.

Chisholm, J. S. 1991. Death, hope, and sex: Life history theory and the politics of reproduction. Paper prepared in advance for participants in the Wenner-Gren Foundation International Symposium (No. 113), The Politics of Reproduction. November 1–9. Teresópolis, Brazil.

1992. Putting people in biology: Toward a synthesis of biological and psychological anthropology. In T. Schwartz, G. White and C. Lutz, eds., *New directions in psychological anthropology*. Cambridge: Cambridge University Press.

1993. Death, hope, and sex: Life history theory and the development of reproductive strategies. *Current Anthropology* 34(1):1–24.

1995a. Love's contingencies: The developmental socioecology of romantic passion. In W. Jankowiak, ed., *Romantic passion: A universal experience*. New York: Columbia University Press.

1995b. Life history theory and life style choice: Implications for Darwinian medicine. *Perspectives in Human Biology* 1:19–28.

1996. The evolutionary ecology of attachment organization. *Human Nature* 7(1):1–37.

Clark, C. 1990. Uncertainty in economics. In E. Cashdan, ed., *Risk and uncertainty in tribal and peasant economies*. Boulder, CO: Westview Press.

1991. Modeling behavioral adaptations. *Behavioral and Brain Sciences* 14:85–117.

Cosmides, L. 1989. The logic of social exchange: Has natural selection shaped how humans think? Studies with the Wattson selection task. *Cognition* 31:187–276.

Cosmides, L. and J. Tooby. 1989. From evolution to behavior: Evolutionary psychology as the missing link. In J. Dupré, ed., *The latest on the best: essays on evolution and optimality*. Cambridge, MA: MIT Press.

Craik, K. 1943. *The nature of explanation*. Cambridge: Cambridge University Press.

Crook, J. H. 1988. The experiential context of intellect. In R. Byrne and A. Whiten, eds., *Machiavellian intelligence: Social expertise and the evolution of intellect in monkeys, apes, and humans.* Oxford: Clarendon Press.

1991. Consciousness and the ecology of meaning. In M. Robinson and L. Tiger, eds., *Man and beast revisited.* Washington, DC: Smithsonian Institution Press.

D'Andrade, R. 1992. Schemas and motivation. In R. D'Andrade and C. Strauss, eds., *Human motives and cultural models*. Cambridge: Cambridge University Press.

Daly, M. and Wilson, M. 1988. *Homicide*. New York: Aldine de Gruyter.

Damasio, A. R. 1994. *Descartes' error: Emotion, reason and the human brain*. New York: Grosset/Putnam.

Danailov, A. and C. Tögel. 1990. Evolutionary epistemology: Science philosophy. In G. Greenberg and E. Tobach, eds., *Theories of the evolution of knowing*. The T.C. Schneirla Conference Series, vol. 4. Hillsdale, NJ: Lawrence Erlbaum Assoc.

DeMause, L. 1974. *The history of childhood*. New York: Psychohistory Press.

Dennett, D. C. 1995, *Darwin's dangerous idea: Evolution and the meanings of life.* New York: Simon and Schuster.

Dickemann, M. 1986. Multiple genders and reproductive strategies in humans: Steps toward a radical sociobiology. Paper presented to the Anthropology Colloquium, sponsored by the Department of Anthropology, The Evolution and Human Behavior Program and the Warner-Lambert Lecture Series, Women in Science Program, University of Michigan, Ann Arbor, October 7.

Draper, P. and H. Harpending. 1982. Father absence and reproductive strategy: An evolutionary perspective. *Journal of Anthropological Research* 38:255–273.

Drotar, D. 1991. The family context of nonorganic failure to thrive. *American Journal of Orthopsychiatry* 61:23–34.

Dunn, J. 1976. How far do early differences in mother–child relations affect later development? In P. Bateson and R. Hinde, eds. *Growing points in ethology.* Cambridge: Cambridge University Press.

Ellison, P. 1990. Human ovarian function and reproductive ecology: New hypotheses. *American Anthropologist* 92:933–952.

Elzanowski, A. 1993. The moral career of vertebrate values. In M. Nitecki and D. Nitecki, eds., *Evolutionary ethics.* Albany: State University of New York Press.

Fagen, R. 1982. Evolutionary issues in the development of behavioral flexibility. In P. Bateson and P. Klopfer, eds., *Perspectives in Ethology (Vol. 5).* New York: Plenum.

1993. Primate juveniles and primate play. In M. Pereira and L. Fairbanks, eds., *Juvenile primates: Life history, development and behavior.* New York: Oxford University Press.

Fox, R. 1989. Consciousness out of context: Evolution, history, progress, and the post-post-industrial society. In R. Fox, ed., *The search for society: quest for a biosocial science and morality.* New Brunswick, NJ: Rutgers University Press.

Gadgil, M. and W. Bossert. 1971. Life history consequences of natural selection. *American Naturalist* 104:1–24.

Gardner, W. 1993. A life-span rational-choice theory of risk taking. In N. Bell and R. Bell, eds., *Adolescent risk taking.* Newbury Park, CA: Sage Publications.

Geertz, C. 1973. *The interpretation of cultures.* New York: Basic Books.

1983. *Local knowledge: Further essays in interpretive anthropology.* New York: Basic Books.

Gillespie, J. 1977. Natural selection for variances in offspring numbers: A new evolutionary principle. *American Naturalist* 111:1010–1014.

Gottlieb, G. 1991. Experiential canalization of behavioral development: Theory. *Developmental Psychology* 27:4–13.

Gould, S. 1989. *Wonderful life: The Burgess Shale and the nature of history.* New York: W. W. Norton.

1991. Exaptation: A crucial tool for an evolutionary psychology. *Journal of Social Issues* 47(3):43–65.

Gould, S. and R. Lewontin. 1979. The spandrels of San Marcos and the Panglossian paradigm: A critique of the adaptationist program. *Proceedings of the Royal Society of London* B 205:581–598.

Gould, S. and E. Vrba. 1982. Exaptation – a missing term in the science of form. *Paleobiology* 8:4–15.

Grafen, A. 1984. Natural selection, kin selection, and group selection. In J. Krebs and N. Davies, eds., *Behavioural ecology: An evolutionary approach.* 2nd ed. Sunderland, MA: Sinauer Associates.

Greenberg, G. and E. Tobach, eds. 1990. *Theories of the evolution of knowing: Pro-*

ceedings of the Fourth T.C. Schneirla Conference. Hillsdale, NJ: Lawrence Erlbaum.

Hausfater, G. and S. Hrdy. eds. 1984. *Infanticide: Comparative and evolutionary perspectives*. New York: Aldine de Gruyter.

Herman-Giddens, M., A. Sandler and N. Friedman. 1988. Sexual precocity in girls: An association with sexual abuse? *American Journal of Diseases of Children* 142:431–433.

Hill, E., J. P. Young and J. L. Nord. 1994. Childhood adversity, attachment security, and adult relationships: A preliminary study. *Ethology and Sociobiology* 15(5–6):323–338.

Hill, K. 1993. Life history theory and evolutionary anthropology. *Evolutionary Anthropology* 2(3):78–88.

Hinde, R. 1982. Attachment: Some conceptual and biological issues. In C. Parkes and J. Stevenson-Hinde, eds., *The place of attachment in human behaviour*. New York: Basic Books.

1986. Some implications of evolutionary theory and comparative data for the study of human prosocial and aggressive behaviour. In D. Olweus, J. Block, and M. Radke-Yarrow, eds., *Development of anti-social and prosocial behaviour*. Orlando, FL: Academic Press.

1987. *Individuals, relationships, and culture: Links between ethology and the social sciences*. Cambridge: Cambridge University Press.

Hinton, A. 1993. Prolegomenon to a processual approach to the emotions. *Ethos* 21(4):417–451.

Horn, H. and D. Rubenstein. 1984. Behavioural adaptations and life history. In J. Krebs and N. Davies, eds., *Behavioural ecology: An evolutionary approach* (2nd. ed.). Oxford: Blackwell Scientific Publications.

Hrdy, S. B. 1977. Infanticide as a primate reproductive strategy. *American Scientist* 65:40–49.

1987. Sex-biased parental investment among primates and other mammals: A critical evaluation of the Trivers-Willard hypothesis. In R. Gelles and J. Lancaster, eds., *Child abuse and neglect: Biosocial dimensions*. New York: Aldine de Gruyter.

1992. Fitness tradeoffs in the history and evolution of delegated mothering with special reference to wet-nursing, abandonment, and infanticide. *Ethology and Sociobiology* 13:409–442.

Hrdy, S. B. and D. Judge. 1993. Darwin and the puzzle of primogeniture: An essay on biases in parental investment after death. *Human Nature* 4(1):1–45.

Humphrey, N. 1976. The social function of intellect. In P. Bateson and R. Hinde, eds., *Growing points in ethology*. Cambridge: Cambridge University Press.

1984. *Consciousness regained*. New York: Oxford University Press.

Johnson, M. 1993. *Moral imagination: Implications of cognitive science for ethics*. Chicago: University of Chicago Press.

Johnston, T. 1982. Selective costs and benefits in the evolution of learning. In J. Rosenblatt, R. Hinde, C. Beer and M.-C. Busnel, eds., *Advances in the study of behavior (Vol. 12)*. New York: Academic Press.

Jones, B., J. Leeton, I. McLeod and C. Wood. 1972. Factors influencing the age of menarche in a lower socio-economic group in Melbourne. *Medical Journal of Australia* 21:533–535.

Krebs, J. and A. Kacelnik, 1991. Decision-making. In J. Krebs and N. Davies, eds., *Behavioural ecology: An evolutionary approach (3rd. Ed.)*. Oxford: Blackwell Scientific Publications.

Lack, D. 1947. The significance of clutch size. *Ibis* 89:302–352.

Lamb, M., R. Thompson, W. Gardner, and E. Charnov. 1985. *Infant–Mother Attachment*. Hillsdale, NJ: Lawrence Erlbaum.

Langer, P. A. 1974. Infanticide: A historical survey. *History of Childhood Quarterly* 1:353–366.

Lawrence, E. 1991. Poverty and the rate of time preference: Evidence from panel data. *Journal of Political Economy* 99:54–77.

LeDoux, J. 1989. Cognitive-emotional interactions in the brain. *Cognition and Emotion* 3:267–289.

1995. Emotion: Clues from the brain. *Annual Review of Psychology* 46:209–235.

1996. *The Emotional Brain*. New York: Simon and Schuster.

Leigh, J. 1986. Accounting for tastes: Correlates of risk and time preference. *Journal of Post-Keynesian Economics* 9:17–31.

Lewontin, R. C. 1982. Organism and environment. In H.C. Plotkin, ed., *Learning, Development, and Culture*. London: John Wiley and Sons.

Lickliter, R. and R. Berry. 1990. The phylogeny fallacy: Developmental psychology's misapplication of evolutionary theory. *Developmental Review* 10:348–364.

Loewenstein, G. and J. Elster, eds. 1992. *Choice over time*. New York: Russell Sage Foundation.

Lorenz, K. 1978. *Behind the mirror: A search for a natural history of human knowledge*. New York: Harcourt.

Main, M. 1990. Cross-cultural studies of attachment organization: Recent studies, changing methodologies, and the concept of conditional strategies. *Human Development* 33:48–61.

1991. Metacognitive knowledge, metacognitive monitoring, and singular (coherent) *vs*. multiple (incoherent) models of attachment. In C. Parkes, J. Stevenson-Hinde, and P. Marris, eds., *Attachment across the life cycle*. New York: Tavistock/Routledge.

Main, M., N. Kaplan and J. Cassidy. 1985. Security in infancy, childhood and adulthood: A move to the level of representation. In I. Bretherton and E. Waters, eds., *Growing points of attachment theory and research*. Monographs of the Society for Research in Child Development No. 209.

Maital, S. and S. Maital. 1977. Time preference, delay of gratification and the intergenerational transmission of economic instability: A behavioral theory of income distribution. In O. Ashenfelter and W. Oates, eds., *Essays in labor market analysis*. New York: John Wiley and Sons.

Mangel, M. and C. Clark. 1988. *Dynamic modeling in behavioral ecology*. Princeton: Princeton University Press.

Marris, P. 1991. The social construction of uncertainty. In C. Parkes, J. Stevenson-Hinde, and P. Marris, eds., *Attachment across the life cycle*. London: Routledge.

Mathews, A. and C. MacLeod. 1994. Cognitive approaches to emotion and emotional disorders. *Annual Review of Psychology* 45:25–50.

Minchella, D. 1985. Host life-history variation in response to parasitism. *Parasitology* 90:205–216.

Mischel, W. 1958. Preference for delayed reinforcement: An experimental study of a cultural observation. *Journal of Abnormal and Social Psychology* 56:57–61.

1961a. Delay of gratification, need for achievement, and acquiescence in another culture. *Journal of Abnormal and Social Psychology* 62:543–552.

1961b. Father absence and delay of gratification. *Journal of Abnormal and Social Psychology* 63:116–124.

Moffitt, T., A. Caspi, and J. Belsky. 1992. Childhood experience and the onset of menarche: A test of a sociobiological model. *Child Development* 63:47–58.

Monckberg, F. 1992. Nutrition, emotional factors, and growth. In M. Hernandez and J. Argente, eds., *Human growth: Basic and clinical aspects.* New York: Elsevier.

Nussbaum, M. C. 1994. *The therapy of desire: Theory and practice in Hellenistic ethics.* Princeton, NJ: Princeton University Press.

Orzack, S. and E. Sober. 1994. Optimality models and the test of adaptationism. *American Naturalist* 143:361–380.

Oyama, S. 1985. *The ontogeny of information: Developmental systems and evolution.* Cambridge: Cambridge University Press.

1988. Stasis, development and heredity. In M.-W. Ho and S. W. Fox, eds., *Evolutionary processes and metaphors.* London: John Wiley & Sons.

1991. Bodies and minds: Dualism in evolutionary theory. *Journal of Social Issues* 47(3):27–42.

Pagel, M. and P. Harvey. 1993. Evolution of the juvenile period in mammals. In M. Pereira and L. Fairbanks, eds., *Juvenile primates: Life history, development and behavior.* New York: Oxford University Press.

Parker, G. and J. Maynard Smith. 1990. Optimality theory in evolutionary biology. *Nature* 348:27–33.

Peacock, N. 1990. Comparative and cross-cultural approaches to the study of human female reproductive failure. In T. Zeigler and F. Bercovitch, eds., *Socioendocrinology of primate reproduction.* New York: Wiley-Liss.

1991. An evolutionary perspective on the patterning of maternal investment in pregnancy. *Human Nature* 2:351–385.

Piaget, J. 1971. *Biology and knowledge.* Chicago: University of Chicago Press.

Plotkin, H. C. 1982. Evolutionary epistemology and evolutionary theory. In H. C. Plotkin, ed., *Learning, development, and culture.* London: John Wiley and Sons.

1994. *Darwin machines and the nature of knowledge.* Cambridge, MA: Harvard University Press.

Pratto, F. 1994. Consciousness and automatic evaluation. In P. Niedenthal and S. Kitayana, eds., *The heart's eye: Emotional influences in perception and attention.* San Diego: Academic Press.

Promislow, D. and P. Harvey. 1990. Living fast and dying young: A comparative analysis of life-history variation among mammals. *Journal of the Zoological Society of London* 220:417–437.

1991. Mortality rates and the evolution of mammal life histories. *Acta Oecologica* 12:94–101.

Robertson, A. 1991. *Beyond the family: The social organization of human reproduction.* Berkeley: University of California Press.

Roff, D. 1992. *The evolution of life histories: Theory and evidence.* New York: Chapman and Hall.

Rogers, A. 1994. Evolution of time preference by natural selection. *American Economic Review* 84:460–481.

Rubenstein, D. 1982. Risk, uncertainty, and evolutionary strategies. In *Current problems in sociobiology,* King's College Sociobiology Study Group, eds., Cambridge: Cambridge University Press.

1993. On the evolution of juvenile lifestyles in mammals. In M. Pereira and L. Fairbanks, eds., *Juvenile primates: Life history, development and behavior.* New York: Oxford University Press.

Ruddick, S. 1989. *Maternal thinking: Toward a politics of peace.* New York: Ballantine.

Sameroff, A. 1975. Early influences on development: Fact or fancy? *Merrill-Palmer Quarterly* 21:267–294.

Scarr, S. and K. McCartney. 1983. How people make their own environments: A theory of genotype → environment effects. *Child Development* 54:424–435.

Scheper-Hughes, N. 1987. Introduction: The cultural politics of child survival. In N. Scheper-Hughes (ed.), *Child survival: Anthropological perspectives on the treatment and maltreatment of children.* Boston: D. Reidel Publishing Company.

1992. *Death without weeping: The violence of everyday life in Brazil.* Berkeley: University of California Press.

Seger, J. and H. Brockmann. 1987. What is bet-hedging? In P. Harvey and L. Partridge, eds., *Oxford surveys in evolutionary biology, Vol. 4.* Oxford: Oxford University Press.

Shore, B. 1988. Interpretation under fire. *Anthropological Quarterly* 61:161–176.

Slobodkin, L. and A. Rapoport. 1974. An optimal strategy of evolution. *Quarterly Review of Biology* 49:181–200.

Smith, E. and B. Winterhalder. 1992. Natural selection and decision-making: Some fundamental principles. In E. Smith and B. Winterhalder, eds., *Evolutionary ecology and human behavior.* New York: Aldine de Gruyter.

Smith-Gill, S. 1983. Developmental plasticity: Developmental conversion versus phenotypic modulation. *American Zoologist* 23:47–55.

Smuts, B. 1992. Male aggression against women: An evolutionary perspective. *Human Nature* 3:1–44.

Solomon, R. C. 1990. *A passion for justice: Emotions and the origins of the social contract.* Reading, MA: Addison-Wesley.

Stamps, J. 1991. Why evolutionary issues are reviving interest in proximate behavioral mechanisms. *American Zoologist* 31:339–348.

Stearns, S. 1982. The role of development in the evolution of life histories. In J. Bonner, ed., *Evolution and development.* Dahlem Konferenzen. New York: Springer-Verlag.

1992. *The evolution of life histories.* New York: Oxford University Press.

Stephens, D. 1990. Risk and incomplete information in behavioral ecology. In E. Cashdan, ed., *Risk and uncertainty in tribal and peasant economies.* Boulder, CO: Westview Press.

Surbey, M. 1990. Family composition, stress, and human menarche. In F. Bercovitch and T. Zeigler, eds., *The socioendocrinology of primate reproduction.* New York: Liss.

Symons, D. 1987. If we're all Darwinians, what's the fuss about? In C. Crawford, M.

Smith, and D. Krebs, eds., *Sociobiology and psychology*. Hillsdale, NJ: Lawrence Erlbaum.
Tooby, J. and L. Cosmides. 1990. The past explains the present: Emotional adaptations and the structure of ancestral environments. *Ethology and Sociobiology* 11:375–424.
Trickett, P. and F. Putnam. 1993. Impact of child sexual abuse on females: Toward a developmental, psychobiological integration. *Psychological Science* 4:81–87.
Trivers, R. 1974. Parent–offspring conflict. *American Zoologist* 14:249–265.
van Schaik, C. and Dunbar, R. 1990. The evolution of monogamy in large primates: A new hypothesis and some crucial tests. *Behaviour* 115:31–62.
Vitzthum, V. In press. Resolution of a paradox: The evolution of a flexibly responsive reproductive system. *Human Biology*.
Waddington, C. 1968. The theory of evolution today. In A. Koestler and R. Smythies, eds., *Beyond Reductionism*. New York: Macmillan.
1975. *The Evolution of An Evolutionist*. Edinburgh: Edinburgh University Press.
Wellens, R., Malina, R., Roche, A., Chumlea, W., Guo, S. and Siervogel, R. 1992. Body size and fatness in young adults in relation to age at menarche. *American Journal of Human Biology* 4:783–787.
West-Eberhard, M. J. 1989. Phenotypic plasticity and the origins of diversity. *Annual Review of Ecology and Systematics* 20:249–278.
Whiten, A. (ed.) 1991. *Natural Theories of Mind: Evolution, Development, and Simulation of Everyday Mindreading*. Oxford: Basil Blackwell.
Whiting, J., and B. Whiting. 1975. Aloofness and intimacy of husbands and wives. A cross-cultural study. *Ethos* 3:183–207.
Williams, G. 1966. *Adaptation and Natural Selection*. Princeton: Princeton University Press.
1975. *Sex and Evolution*. Princeton: Princeton University Press.
Williams, G. C. and R. M. Nesse. 1991. The dawn of Darwinian medicine. *The Quarterly Review of Biology* 66 (1):1–22.
Wilson, J. 1993. *The Moral Sense*. New York: Free Press.
Wilson, M., and M. Daly. 1985. Competitiveness, risk taking, and violence: The young male syndrome. *Ethology and Sociobiology* 6:59–73.
Worthman, C. 1990. Socioendocrinology: Key to a fundamental synergy. In T. Zeigler and F. Bercovitch, eds., *Socioendocrinology of Primate Reproduction*. New York: Wiley-Liss.
1992. Cupid and psyche: Investigative syncretism in biological and psychological anthropology. In T. Schwartz, G. White, and C. Lutz, eds., *New directions in psychological anthropology*. Cambridge: Cambridge University Press.
1993a. Bio-cultural interactions in human development. In M. Pereira and L. Fairbanks, eds., *Juvenile primates: Life history, development and behavior*. New York: Oxford University Press.
1993b. The company they keep: Sex differences in maturational timing. Paper presented at the session on Evolutionary Medicine: New Directions and Perspectives, Annual Meeting of the American Association for Advancement of Science. Boston, February 15.
Wright, S. 1931. Evolution in Mendelian populations. *Genetics* 16:97–159.

Part II

Embodiment

4 Music hath charms . . .: Fragments toward constructionist biocultural theory, with attention to the relationship of "music" and "emotion"

Iain D. Edgewater

> I have observed that there are three fundamental types of rhythm to which all meters may be reduced, just as there are four intervals at the base of all the modes; but what kind of life each rhythm is suited to express, I cannot say.
> Well, said I, we shall consult Damon on this question, which metres are expressive of meanness, insolence, frenzy, and other such evils, and which rhythms we must retain to express their opposites. It would take a long time to settle all that.
> It would indeed.
>
> Plato, *The Republic* (trans. F. M. Cornford, Oxford, 1945), 3.400b–c (p. 88)

> Cultures are disciplines that provide codes and social scripts for the domestication of the individual body in conformity to the needs of the social and political order. (Scheper-Hughes and Lock 1987:26)

Introduction

Issues of power have become increasingly important in contemporary social theory, and have inspired much good writing across various disciplines and subtopics in the humanities and social sciences. Speaking very broadly, however, such writing consists mostly of analyses of ways that power relations construct social life, in which the concepts of power and power relations themselves remain implicit and relatively unanalyzed. Analyses that also address what power "is" and how "it" gets things done are less common.[1] While we can all mumble the old Weberian dictum that power has to do with people getting what they want from others, that is about as far as many of us can go.

Below, my first aim is to redress this problem, by modifying Foucault's (1977) conception of how a "microphysics of power" is used to establish disciplinary control over the body. I claim that if the body is manipulated by a "disparate set of tools or methods" (ibid:25–26), i.e., through bodily actions imposed by routines in institutional sites of control, then perhaps understanding more about the biology of this process may not only give a clearer picture of how discipline becomes effective, but also allow us to understand more about the myriad ways in which our bodies are contested zones, and finally to understand more about persuasion, complicity, and empowerment in similar contexts.

A brief clarifying example. It is undeniable that desire for a rich chocolate dessert, which I am experiencing as I type, is sculpted in large measure by the needs of capital for market expansion, and the disciplines of consumption associated with those needs: sellers of rich chocolate desserts must sell their products in order to reproduce and expand the capital spent on making them. Therefore, advertisers create commercials featuring the desserts, usually with sultry saxophone riffs and phrases like ''sinfully delicious'' in the voice-over, all to make them irresistible objects of desire to new customers. However, if it is also true that there is a general predisposition of the human body to prefer sweet, fatty foods remaining from hunter-gatherer days – as is likely the case (Eaton *et al.* 1989) – then it is not *only* a matter of my confectionary desires having been constructed as described above, though this is an integral aspect of the phenomenon. My desire for such desserts (or specifically for Brand X Dessert) can be constructed more easily than, say, desire for cauliflower, because something about my body responds preferentially to sugar and fats. Thus, by acting through bodily avenues which lend themselves to the channeling and cathecting of desire, forms of social control may be comparatively more effective than they might otherwise – in this case, the better for institutions which sell rich chocolate desserts to consolidate their market for such items.

Analysis of less facile examples of how power relationships can have biological aspects (i.e., about one possible modality of power)[2] requires an increased theoretical sophistication that resists predictable cultural or biological reductionisms. Perhaps the political valence of such sophistication accounts for its absence. At any rate, though, biological and cultural theorists can and should find ways to reach across theoretical divides to achieve such sophistication. Unfortunately, while similar holisms are crafted relatively unproblematically in disciplinary interface zones such as public health, or when the culture theory is materialist, special effort is required to bring these camps together otherwise. Below, I make a case for the idea that such effort is worthwhile, not only *vis-à-vis* the issue of power but also because of its potential use in understanding other issues. Making this case persuasively is the second goal of this chapter.

The careful reader will have already surmised, through the references to desire in my dessert example, that *emotion* is a key part of my move toward a constructionist biocultural account of the power/body relationship. The view that emotion is fundamentally involved with social power is not new, though it has made a resurgence recently through a new set of interlocutors (e.g., Lutz and Abu-Lughod 1990; Scheper-Hughes and Lock 1987). I agree generally with their points of view, but also feel they do not go far enough in illustrating ways that emotion, power, and the body are bound up with one another. Making such connections clearer is my third goal.

While it might be interesting to interweave my three goals by continuing to discuss food, I have decided instead to explore murkier territory: music, and its (apparent) emotional effects on its listeners. This is so for two reasons. First, it is easy to see where gaps lie in our knowledge of music's effects – helping build a case for the idea that interdisciplinary work is needed to fill those gaps; and second, because music's effects seem far more general and less automatically positively valenced than food preferences. The argument goes as follows:

(1) Music has a tendency to produce a special effect in listeners – namely, that the contexts with which it is associated are judged more significant, affecting, and important than ordinary contexts. This is a general effect, not dependent upon the particular form of music involved.
(2) This "tendency" is rooted in capacities of the body.
(3) The fact of (1) opens up the possibility that cultural structures, ideologies, and practices may exploit the persuasive nature of music as a resource to effect their own reproduction. Furthermore, this potential may be consciously manipulated by persons or institutions, to aid in achieving desired ends.
(4) We understand the details of (2) very little, so it is to our advantage to study (2), especially as aspects of (2) facilitate the possibility of (3).

In my expansion of this argument below, as the cliché goes, God is in the details. I spend little time making the argument itself, but instead concentrate primarily on arguing for a biological notion of constructionism, for a view of emotion that fits with that notion, and for position (1) above, weaving themes of power and consent throughout. Once these parts are in place, the argument I make follows naturally. Of course there are gaps in evidence and presentation, because there is too much we still do not know about too many things, and in a chapter with so many (apparently) unrelated strands required to build unlikely theoretical bridges, much must necessarily be left incomplete along the way. However, if the chapter succeeds in being even slightly persuasive about the goals set forth above, then I will consider it successful.

Before getting started, I should say a few words about "emotion" and "music," for these are highly problematic concepts on their own, let alone at their intersection. Several other contributors to this volume note, implicitly or explicitly, difficulties involved in giving general definitions of emotion; I refer the reader to their treatments of the issue, for I definitely do not exhaust that issue here. As I go along I do invoke some points I find useful, such as the oft-quoted one about differences between emotional experience, the expression of emotional experience, and the evaluation of such (apparent) expressions. However, I am not concerned here with possible types of emotions, debates about ''basic-level'' versus secondary or derived emotions, and other warhorse issues we students of emotion often fret about. I am primarily interested in emotion's role as a significance marker for its experiencers; in this stance, my biases will become clearer as I proceed.

However, since no other contribution in this volume is explicitly concerned with music, it is worth pinpointing more precisely what I mean by the term. The most obvious problem is deciding what counts as music; in the West alone, the term covers everything from Gregorian chant to ''gangsta rap,'' from Appalachian shape-note singing to the *X-Files* theme, from the cacophonies one finds at websites like www.blackmetal.com to the ''silence'' of John Cage's *4′33″*. Broadening the discussion to the rest of the world only obscures the issues further. I prefer an inclusive view: music consists of sonic phenomena, including silence and pure speech sounds, arranged or highlighted in some way (including random chance framed by performance) by (a) composer(s) and/or performer(s). Thus, music differs from sound in that it is somehow organized; to make use of a crude marxist dualism, music is a product of labor rather than a raw resource of nature. The sound of a waterfall is thus not music, but a recording of its sound, or symbolic enshrinement of its sound, must in some (at least penumbral) sense be so. In general, when I speak of ''music'' below, I have in mind something more like Gregorian chant, ''gangsta rap,'' or the Seattle gamelans with which I sometimes perform than such borderline cases as recorded waterfalls – but I believe the arguments I make incorporate those cases as well. The nature of my arguments, as we shall see, strongly affords this possibility.

Fragments toward . . .

> Why should an archaeology of psychiatry function as an ''anti-psychiatry,'' when an archaeology of biology does not function as an anti-biology? (Foucault 1980:192)

> The loss of transmission from the Galaxy IV satellite last month made some customers realize how much they depended on Muzak. In Lafayette, Indiana, one upset and elderly Burger King customer told the manager: ''Now I just have to sit here and hear myself think.'' (*The Globe and Mail*, June 24, 1998, quoted in *The Risks Digest*, 1984), http://catless.ncl.ac.uk/Risks/19.84.htm#subj15)

Much recent anthropological writing on emotion has reconceptualized its topic so as to concentrate on the many ways in which ''it'' is socially constituted. These reconceptualizations are intended to counter a trend, alleged to exist within Western academic and folk-scientific discourse on emotion, toward viewing emotion as interior and firmly tied to an invariant psychobiology – an essentializing trend considered problematic, among other reasons, because such conceptions of emotion obscure ways in which discourse on/about emotion is deeply involved in the "politics of social life rather than the psychology of the individual."[3] The recent edited volume by Lutz and Abu-Lughod (1990), *Language and the politics of emotion*, is a key reference point in this shift of perspective. In the introduction to their volume, the editors point out that their contributors show how emotion "serves as an operator in a contentious field of social activity, how it affects a social field, and how it can serve as an idiom for communicating, not even necessarily about feelings but about such diverse matters as social conflict . . . gender roles . . . or the nature of the ideal or deviant person" (Abu-Lughod and Lutz 1990:11).

With this direction, the editors have unquestionably taken a positive step. The essays in their volume are quite useful, and the viewpoint they trace out serves as corrective to various aspects of previous emotion theory. However, in their rush to direct attention to social aspects of emotion by delegitimating the idea of an essentialized psychobiological/individual "subject" which "possesses" interiorized "emotions," Abu-Lughod and Lutz have overstated their case – which is to say, they have glossed over the possibility that examination of biological aspects of emotion may contribute to, rather than detract from, their constructionist views. There are typically two main reasons why such glossing-over occurs in constructionist approaches to emotion, both relevant here, and these must be addressed before discussing the positions of Abu-Lughod and Lutz at length, or suggesting how constructionist biocultural accounts of emotion might be articulated.

Criticism of the modernist subject

Criticism of the "subject" as viewed in modernist thought – i.e., the idea of the person as a concrete, unified, coherent reference point with a fixed, continuous identity, which unproblematically expresses "itself," and knows and interprets things-in-the-world as Other (Rosenau 1992:42–61) – is an important part of the postmodern/poststructural theoretical landscape. This is so first and foremost because many contemporary theorists are reluctant to ascribe ontological consistency to *any* construct. These theorists hold that the perception or judgment of such consistencies – "essentialism" – is an artifact of language, an effect produced by discourse which leads us to expect fixity, interiority, and independence-from-context (e.g., Derrida 1976[1967]). "Things" are not fixed outside their discursive construction: "discourses . . . [are not] signs but . . . practices that systematically form the objects of which they speak" (Foucault 1972:49). In this view, since the subject, like everything else, is really constructed by a continual cross-current of discourses, to hold that it is somehow a fixed thing *à la* modernism is simply wrong. Contributing to such error is the fact that the modernist subject is an ideologically charged holdover from Cartesian dualism, made valuable because reification of the individual continues to fit well with capitalist division of labor, and the range of normalizing disciplines in the social milieu associated with it. Criticism of these dynamics is typically linked with criticism of the modernist subject, not only as the product of such disciplines but also as a conduit for the problematic power relations behind them.

Throughout these otherwise useful perspectives, consideration of the biological body is elided, or actively dismissed as unimportant, in large part because the categories of "person," "individual," "self," and "body" are often collapsed into one another as "subject." However, it is possible to separate these categories from one another in useful ways. For example, Neisser (1988) has recently articulated an analysis of the self as multiple, by moving the focus of analysis from the "self" or "selves" as *objects* to different types of *self-knowledge*. Neisser has demonstrated that organismically oriented aspects of knowledge about the body (e.g., proprioceptive knowledge) can be differentiated from the highly culturally variant ways the body is conceived of as an observer and agent (i.e., a "subject"), while acknowledging that these forms of self-knowledge are in constant co-constitutive dialogue with one another. Thus, because the body may coexist with various conceptions of (or ideologies about) "itself," it is not absolutely necessary to conflate the individual existence of the biological body with the subjectivity which that body manifests, nor to extend criticism of the "subject" to studies of the workings of the body.

Of course, if the biological body – once finally teased apart from its associations with the culturally conceived "subject" – is also viewed as fixed and beyond discursive construction, it would still be possible (and necessary) to deploy postmodern/poststructuralist criticisms against that view. However, that move is unnecessary, as it is not true that the body is beyond (at least a type of) discursive construction; but before saying why, I must address the other reason why biology is typically glossed over in contemporary social theory.

Feminist critiques of biological-determinist ideology

Biologically oriented definitions and descriptions of human-being are frequently critiqued in many strands of feminist theory, and, the same category collapses which were shown to be faulty in the previous discussion of postmodernism/poststructuralism play important roles in feminist theory as well. Here, however, these category collapses are important, not so much for the way they might engender problematic feminist theorizing, as for the ways they become the object of study and criticism in themselves. The erroneously collapsed body/identity relationship is often further collapsed together with the category ''female'' as a modality of denigration, configuring problematic constructions of ''woman'' that must be contested. Not only have rhetorics of biology been used to cast women as Other, but they have also been used *à la* the naturalistic fallacy to bolster and justify sexist and heterosexist imagery and practices. Vasseleu (1991:139 n45) notes that:

Nowhere more than in feminist critiques of sexual difference have biologistic arguments been identified and rejected on the grounds of essentialism. As Elizabeth Grosz describes the way in which the term is generally applied in feminist theory: ''Biologism is a particular form of essentialism in which women's essence is defined in terms of their biological capacities . . . Insofar as biology is assumed to constitute an *unalterable bedrock of identity*, the attribution of biologistic characteristics amounts to a permanent form of social containment for women.'' (my emphasis)

Studies of emotion which address biological factors are frequently disparaged by feminists not only because of these issues, but also for the way they frequently invoke the further category collapse bodily = ''female'' = ''emotion(al).'' As Lutz (1990:69) points out, ''qualities that define the emotional also define women'' in much Western thinking. The mutual relationship of the terms in this association consolidates its discursive strength and makes it extremely pernicious. Thus, an understandable movement away from biological approaches to emotion – let alone other issues – has taken place among many feminist scholars.

Fueled primarily by these two strands of objection, biologism is now routinely criticized in arenas beyond them. Thus, by now there is ample precedent for Appadurai (1990:93), when discussing the anthropology of self and emotion, to state as a matter of course that

topographies of the self . . . are variable cultural phenomena. We need to deepen our understanding of *this* variation if we are to retain the force of the insight . . . that emotions are discursive public forms whose special power does indeed draw on embodied experience, *without implying any parsimoniously describable universal biological substrate*. (1990:93; my emphasis)

Such statements are now endemic in many zones of contemporary social theory. But what if biology is not ''unalterable''? Recent approaches which demonstrate the body is not fixed and unchanging in every way, but instead is responsive to – and changes as a result of – experience (e.g., Changeux 1985[1983]; Edelman 1987, 1988; Oyama 1985), indicate that references to the role of biology are not necessarily ''essentialist.'' The fact that biological capacities of the human body are so often depicted by social theorists as static, fixed, and unchanging reveals an unfortunate lack of sophistication that not only ensures social theorists' representations of biology are increasingly disjunct from where biology is actually going, but also surrenders valuable ideological ground in debates about the social importance of biology.

None of the foregoing is intended to imply, of course, that the body is completely plastic. But how plastic is it? Without needlessly reiterating detail better described elsewhere (in this volume, and in the references above), we can note that, although the body continues to be made of certain kinds of "stuff" and is broadly shaped by specific principles of organization, it may be reshaped over time through its experiential trajectory. Some of this reshaping comes through long-term, developmental processes that actually rearrange the anatomical pattern of the body, predominantly early in life. For example, growth and development of the neural system occurs normally through the development of a profusion of connections, which are then selectively pruned as groups of neural connections compete with one another for survival; this process requires the influence of experience to proceed correctly, due to the non-random patterns of strengthening of neural connections induced by experience (Changeux 1985; Edelman 1987, 1988). Thus, the fine neural structure of the body – and especially the brain – is not given by the individual's genetic code, but is instead an *epigenetic* process, governed by the intersection of cellular dynamics (division, development, and death) and the experiences of the body.

However, something like this process, without gross rearrangement and selection of different cellular anatomies, seems to occur with all learning at all times. This second level of neural selection occurs as "during behavior, synaptic connections in the anatomy are selectively strengthened or weakened by specific biochemical processes" (Edelman 1992:84–85). Kandel, after noting how long-term memory formation apparently requires the synthesis of new proteins and the growth of new synaptic connections (1991:1014–1016), goes on to assert that

> [w]ork . . . in simple animals indicates that learning produces structural and functional changes in specific nerve cells. In mammals, and especially in humans, in whom each functional component is represented by hundreds of thousands of nerve cells, *learning is likely to lead to alterations in many nerve cells* and is therefore likely to be reflected in *changes in the pattern of interconnections of the various sensory and motor systems* involved in a particular learning task . . . The cortical maps of an adult are subject to constant modification on the basis of use or activity of the peripheral sensory pathways. Since all of us are brought up in somewhat different environments, are exposed to different combinations of stimuli, and are likely to exercise our motor skills in different ways, *the architecture of our brain will be modified in special ways.* (ibid:1024, 1026; my emphases)

All such changes[4] which result from experience of the world are thus indicative of the continued recreation of the body in dialogue with that experience.

In fact, it is ultimately untenable to separate "body" and "world," or the biological body and the social body, from one another; there is never a time when the biology of the body does not somehow reflect its social context (see also Worthman in this volume).[5] The body is always literally constructed by experience, even though it is from a relatively standardized palette of "stuff," and the degree of construction possible (aside from as-yet unavailable technological interventions) is canalized by constraints of various strengths. As Geertz (1973) made clear long ago, there is no body without experience; its form at any moment is a product of the history of forces shaping it physically and socially, including its effects on itself.

This line of argument is no doubt already too essentialist for some. But the fact that bodily "stuff" is responsive to experience seems vastly more important than the fact that it is postulated as real, or that its constructability occurs within rule-governed constraints. Just as the fact that spoken language is "essentially" composed of sequences of phones transmitted in a temporally linear order does not subvert the creative, fluid, constructed, arbitrary, and pragmatic aspects of such spoken language, so should we see the facts of biology as providing material for enaction of key themes of social constructionism, rather than as contradicting the overly rigidly antiessentialist *a prioris* used to anchor social constructionism up to now (cf. Edgewater, in preparation).

By now, my rather nitpicking discussion should have raised the question: Why *bother* to reinterpret constructionist social theory and human biology in terms commensurable with one another? Aside from whether it is actually *possible* to make all viewpoints mutually translatable – like being able to describe the taste of rich chocolate desserts in terms of quantum mechanics, perhaps feasible though relevant only to rabid totalizers obsessed with theoretical closure for its own sake – what can such translatability actually *do* for us? The only answer is, as always, that addressing some issues of broad interest simply may require perspectives from multiple zones of theory, and lack of theoretical commensurability precludes fruitful work on those issues. While commensurability between biology and constructionist social theory would help avoid such problems – at worst, crudity of conceptualization and outright error, at best, imprecision, vagueness, and subterranean acceptance of concepts ostensibly rejected – with respect to a whole range of issues of mutual interest, I turn to emotion as a particularly clear example of just such an issue.

Let us return to the Abu-Lughod and Lutz (1990) piece mentioned earlier, for it represents a good example of the "at-best" side of the just-mentioned difficulties. First, we can note the authors' statement that

> emotion and discourse should not be treated as separate variables, the one pertaining

to the private world of individual consciousness and the other to the public social world . . . emotion talk must be interpreted as in and about social life rather than as veridically referential to some internal state. . . Emotion can be said to be *created in*, rather than shaped by, speech in the sense that it is postulated as an entity in language where its meaning to social actors is also elaborated. (ibid:11–12)

Thus Abu-Lughod and Lutz articulate a social constructionist position that inveighs against "essentialist" notions of biology and the location of emotions "in" the psyche, consistent with the deemphasis of psychobiology, subjectivity, and individualist approaches they demonstrate elsewhere (cf., e.g., Abu-Lughod 1990; Lutz 1988, 1990). However, Abu-Lughod and Lutz also define "emotional discourses" as those which "seem to have some affective content or effect" (1990:10), and note that "we should view emotional discourse as a form of social action that creates effects in the world . . . that are read in a culturally informed way by the audience for emotion talk" (ibid:12). Thus we can ask: what is the "content"? What is the "effect"? Where is it exerted? Who are the "readers" that are the "audience" for emotion talk, and how do they "read" it? In leaving open the possibility of asking these questions – while de-emphasizing perspectives within which such questions could be addressed – the authors have covertly reintroduced the concept of localized points that register effects and "read" emotion talk.[6] However, such a concept entails, if not subjectivity *à la* the Western individual, at least some notion of the information-processing and significance-assigning (= emotion-experiencing) capabilities of the body, creating the danger of leading precisely back to the psychobiology (if not the subjectivity and individualism) which Abu-Lughod and Lutz intend to decenter.

This conclusion might seem unfair, as the authors declare "the chapters in this book do not deny the force of emotion and subjective experience . . . the reality of emotion is social, cultural, political, and historical, *just as is its current location in the psyche or the natural body*" (ibid:18-19, my emphasis; cf. Appadurai 1990:93, quoted above). But this is the most unambiguous statement the authors make about how to relate discourse and the body to one another; a clear sense of how to reconcile multiple aspects of emotion is not provided. Of course, this gap does not blunt the force of the sociocentric perspective which Abu-Lughod and Lutz are trying to foster; describing body/discourse intercontextualization was not the *raison d'être* of their article, anyway. However, what the gap does do is give away the theoretical high ground by refusing to make clear either (1) how it might be possible to bracket the characteristics of the body, so as to move on to more important (to Abu-Lughod and Lutz) issues of how discourse constructs emotional effects and standardizes culturally defined emotional discourses; or (2) to understand how the characteristics of the body might (be) influence(d by) the characteristics of discourse. Clarifying these issues would be useful because it would forestall the ability of biological (or other) essentialists to argue for reducing emotion to biology/subjectivity/interiority, an ability inadvertently predisposed by subterranean reintroduction of the information-processing, significance-assigning body as a key nexus in the web of emotional discourse effects. The stance of Abu-Lughod and Lutz thus creates a theoretical rift that is more unexplored and incomplete, than real and unbridgeable.

Of course, not everyone will agree such *rapprochement* is necessary. Not all studies in either ''camp'' need be mutually connected. Studies of how emotion discourses fuel power relations in social life – even though such discourses are stereotyped and neither reflect emotional expression nor induce emotional response *per se* (e.g., Appadurai 1990) – typically need not discuss bodily aspects of emotion, just as neuropsychiatric studies of changes in affect after brain injury typically need not address socially constructed aspects of emotion.

Nevertheless, there are times when both approaches are useful for understanding emotion phenomena, and this is where the value in being able to take account of both approaches lies. I address such a case below; but as preparation for that case, no bold new pronouncements are required to show how the necessary synthesis can be achieved, as the answer is nascent in Abu-Lughod's and Lutz' own presentation. If it is true that discourses of emotion have some ''affective content or effect,'' and gain efficacy from this fact, then we can make the connection by asserting that *discourses of emotion exert their (socially constituted) power by virtue of effects they have on the (biological) body.*

The idea that emotional discourses are effective because of their action on individual psyches is hardly novel, but to attempt to recast it in constructionist terms *is* new – and for inspiration about how to proceed we can turn to what I see as the nearest major extant approximation, namely, the work of Michel Foucault. He notes (1977:25–26) how the body can be manipulated by a ''microphysics,'' or a ''disparate set of tools or methods'' – i.e., through bodily actions imposed by routines in institutional sites of control – as a channel for the exertion of power (including, though not limited to, ''political'' power as traditionally conceived). This approach, and the resultant constitution of the body as a node of knowledge formed by such exertions of power, fits well with the reconciliation of biology and constructionism discussed above, and can be appropriated to bolster my amplification of Abu-Lughod's and Lutz' perspective, by treating emotional discourses as ''microphysics of power'' which act on the body.

This is so for two reasons. First, in line with the earlier discussion of how experience affects the body, experience of *any* discourse in which information is learned alters the configuration of the body, however subtly. Such change may be induced from outside the body by others, or by the body acting reflexively under its own agency. Either way, to perceive is to have power exerted upon one's body; to learn is for that power to be effective, as the result of learning is a re-construction of one's body through discursive deployments onto it, and all knowledge is thus (at one level of analysis) the result of biological effect. This does not mean, of course, that the relationship is always one-way or that the body is merely passive (again, see Worthman in this volume); but the dynamic I describe is a key dimension of the embodiment of power, and a useful place to start to understand it. In this way, the mutual convertibility of power/knowledge Foucault describes is always manifest, not only in the social body, but in the total biological/social body over the entire lifecourse (Edgewater in preparation). Emotional discourses would then necessarily be active upon the body as a subset of this dynamic.

This point opens the way for a second and more important point: that the body appears predisposed to be affected by emotional discourses. There is general agreement that emotion's fundamental biological function in animals seems to be the rapid highlighting of input which is highly significant to the health and welfare of the organism (Campos *et al.* 1989; LeDoux 1989), so that action appropriate to survival and/or prosperity may be undertaken quickly. Much recent research (e.g., LeDoux 1989; Zola-Morgan *et al.* 1991) suggests there are separate but parallel stimulus processing systems in the brain, one for processing inputs in a detailed manner, and the other to give a "quick and dirty" view of the selfsame inputs in order to fulfill the rapid-reaction function. It is the latter processing system that appears to be responsible for emotional reactions. As LeDoux (1989:271) notes, this processing system has generalized far beyond its utility for survival situations in animals such as humans: "[T]he brain has a striking capacity to learn and remember the emotional significance of stimuli and events. Affective learning and memory allow us to assign emotional valence to novel stimuli and to change the value . . . previously assigned to a stimulus." Thus, there is complex crosstalk between the two processing systems, and much opportunity for learning, change, and the synthesis of new emotional responses based on other (more "cognitive") knowledge. Lang (1994:87) notes that

> the subcortical circuitry is itself plastic. Simple affective associations are learned and retained in the absence of cortical sensory processing. . . On the other hand . . . connections go back and forth between the amygdaloid complex and higher centers. Thus, associated information at the cortical level can influence (enhance, modulate, reduce) activity in the motivation circuit.

Because these processing systems are continually interacting with each other over very short time spans, "cognition" and "emotion" are virtually always intertwined (cf., e.g., Wikan's [1990] concept of ''feeling-thoughts'' among Balinese). All incoming inputs are thus judged for significance; and emotional discourses, those which address issues of motivational significance ranging from survival situations to intricate cultural meanings, have privileged access to the lifeworld of the experiencer, as an aspect of embodiment.

However, this opens an interesting avenue for exploitation: experiencers may be selectively exploited by social technologies crafted (or evolved) to take advantage of the significance-judging capabilities of their bodies. This is what emotional persuasion is all about. It can trump abstract, more ''purely cognitive'' arguments because ready hooks – i.e., privileged access to motivational aspects of embodiment – exist for persuasive messages to hang onto. When emotionally valenced inputs (also) encode messages pertaining to power-laden social/political/cultural/interpersonal issues, it becomes more likely that judgments of significance will transfer to the associated issues, creating exertions of power not only through increased consideration of those issues, but also through increased valencing of (legitimation of, or reaction against) them (Strauss 1992).

Judgments of significance seem particularly to be facilitated by events including high amounts of somatic/perceptual relevance, presumably as an artifact of their original survival orientation[7] – suggesting that emotional discourses which are very bodily oriented, when linked with (or encoding) politically valenced messages, might be particularly persuasive regarding those messages. However, bodily discourses often color significance strongly positively or negatively, but not both equally well. For example, that the body can experience physical pain *does* predispose techniques exploiting this capability to be effective; such is the fundamental premise of coercive torture. However, pain almost always brands things associated with such contexts (one's torturers, their ideology, etc.) as negative. My introductory chocolate dessert example works in the opposite way: the pleasure experienced in eating the desserts will typically be difficult to link to anything but positive judgments of its associands. Stockholm syndrome and eating disorders aside, such bodily discourses are not labile enough to serve as all-purpose (able to be directed positively and negatively) emotional technologies.

Given this, we can then ask: are there other kinds of strongly bodily based, significance-predisposing (= emotionally affecting) effects which are more subtle, such that strongly positive or negative associations do not derive from them quite so automatically or exclusively, yet nevertheless lend themselves to exploitation – directly by others, or more remotely by large-scale systems of power and domination – through discursive channels? I contend the world of musical and sonic phenomena represents an excellent choice in this regard.

With attention to . . .

Above all, religious specialists master sound; they alone can speak with and hear from animals, ancestors, and otherworld beings. As A. Jackson perceptively observed, ''a deaf ritual specialist is an anomaly whereas a blind one is common enough'' . . . Ritual sound (voice, song, music) serves to *sacralize* space, being, and, above all, time on this world, in order to permit such dialogue. Not only do most rituals begin with sound, but the first evidence of spiritual attendance is usually auditory. (Peek 1994:478–479)

I've got tapes / I've got CDs / I've got my Public Enemy[8] /
My lily white ass / is tickled pink / When / I listen to the music that makes me think . . .

(Red Hot Chili Peppers 1991)

For most of us, it is axiomatic that music has the power to induce emotional response. Though the common view is likely oversimplified, it does seem to be the case that music facilitates articulation of emotional responses to stimuli with which it is paired. While the predispositive rather than automatic nature of this relationship may seem a weakened position regarding associations between music and emotion, it is enough to suggest music may provide an exploitable ''hook'' into our capacity for judging the significance of inputs – in this case, contexts associated with the music.

In order to trace out the nature of music's emotionally predispositive status, it is useful to transit some perspectives which erroneously claim more direct relationships exist. The first which must be dispatched may be called the ''drumming hypothesis.'' Neher (1961, 1962) suggested drum beats might be commonly used as ritual accompaniment because, within certain parameters, they could (as he claimed) directly affect the nervous system to produce an ''auditory driving'' effect, resulting in altered states of consciousness. Since that time, the hypothesis has become rather an article of faith among anthropologists, and has rarely been tested (Ellingson 1986:501f.), although evidence which does exist fails to support it. Ellingson's studies of Tibetan drumming (ibid.) indicate trance occurs in the presence of beats violating Neher's parameters both on grounds of speed (they are far too slow) and symmetry. Erlmann (1982) found similar difficulties for trance behavior among the Hausa. Finally, Rouget (1985) inveighs at length against the drumming hypothesis, noting that

the phenomena in question can occur when drums are struck at a speed varying from . . . twelve beats per second to four beats per second . . . [s]o, unless it is slow, drumming of any kind must therefore be able to trigger 'driving'. . . [but i]f Neher were right, half of Africa would be in a trance from the beginning of the year to the end. (*ibid*:174–175)

While this argument is considered damning by most serious scholars of music, the popularity of the ''drumming hypothesis,'' and the lack of a large body of evidence against it (despite the complete lack of evidence *for* it), have kept it alive unto the present day.

Linking musical form to emotion has also been a major project of Clynes (1977; Clynes and Nettheim 1982). His ''sentics'' theory states that ''(f)or each basic emotion there exists a specific dynamic form (as a brain programme) which can be expressed in a number of modalities – for example, vocalised sound, touch – involving motor action'' (Clynes 1989:328). Emotion can thus be universally expressed and communicated, because the ''dynamic form'' associated with each emotion is a property of the organism, not of cultural convention. Such dynamic forms may also be ferreted out of their various ''modalities,'' including music, and examined for clues about the underlying ''brain programmes'' which support them.

Claims for both music and touch have been tested and found wanting (see, e.g., Nettelbeck *et al.* 1989; Trussoni *et al.* 1988). In the former study, musical snippets Clynes claimed were consistently able to be linked with one of six ''emotions'' (sex, love, joy, grief, anger, and reverence) were retested by the investigators, and his results were either unreplicable (most of the ''emotions'') or artifactual (joy). They suggest Clynes' original work utilized a ''narrowly focused, fixed-choice procedure . . . [in which] half of the stimuli used were sounds widely associated in common experience with the terms attributed to them by Clynes'' (Nettelbeck *et al.* 1989:36). While the ''sentics'' theory is not so popular among anthropologists as the ''drumming hypothesis,'' it has also been propagated somewhat in the popular press as a serious set of research findings (e.g., Ackerman 1990:217).

The issue of conventional associations for music raised above points to the main reason for discounting simple relationships between music and emotion: musical vocabularies are quite culture-bound. Merriam (1964:265–266) notes that

> we in Western culture, being able to abstract music and regard it as an objective entity, credit sound itself with the ability to move the emotions . . . [yet] a piece of music always has a set of social and cultural associations which automatically go with it . . . how can we distinguish the impact of the music sound from the impact of the associations?

Even leaving aside the problem of whether songs take meanings predominantly from their lyrics, Merriam's point presents profound difficulty. For example, the notion that minor keys are intrinsically more ''sad'' than major keys is automatically suspect, because of our entrainment from birth into a musical culture which tells us minor keys are sad. Indeed, musical schemata isomorphic to minor keys are not universally present across the range of traditional musical cultures – and if ''sadness'' was unproblematically stimulated by minor keys, then one might expect more traditional musics to display them, or have similar associations for them where they are found. That such standardizations did not crystallize before the globalization of Western culture suggests conceptually direct music/emotion relationships do not exist.

At first, all this might seem to rule out assertions of music's pan-cultural effects on the human organism. However, it remains very difficult to rule out *some* kind of privileged relationship between sound and emotion. All around the world, musical forms are critically linked with emotionally involving phenomena such as healing systems (e.g., Bahr and Haefer 1978; Laderman 1991; Roseman 1991); worship, ritual, and *rites de passage* (e.g., Jackson 1968; Needham 1967; Peek 1994; Rouget 1985[1980]; Schieffelin 1976); and affect-laden myths and key cultural symbols (e.g., Basso 1985; Feld 1990; Seeger 1987). Given the importance of such phenomena, one might expect their significances to stand alone, without musical accompaniment. We could say the same for more overtly ideological events, such as coronations, military parades, patriotic events of all types – and no protest movement is without its anthems. However, music is virtually always present in all such cases, strongly implying music's effects are ''good to think'' (or, *pace* Wikan, good to feel/think). But how to reconcile this notion with arguments such as Merriam's? How might ways in which music refers to, or causes, something in a relatively non-conscious fashion be separated analytically from associations already existing for those things in conscious, institutionally realized sociocultural contexts?

The only way to ''have it both ways'' is to discard the notion that there is something in *particular* that is referred to by musical stimuli. This idea – most often associated with Langer's (1957[1942]) concept of the ''unconsummated symbol,'' in which the referent of the apparent meaningfulness of the music is supplied by the listener[9] – suggests that while ethnographic observations such as Tuzin's (1984) on the sense of profundity invoked through ritual simulation of thunder by use of bullroarers among the Ilahita Arapesh are undoubtedly correct, there are no pan-human psychophysiological mechanisms facilitating such *specific* associations. More likely, there is some general effect on the organism – let us call it a ''suggestion of significance'' – predisposed by a broad range of sonic (but usually musical) phenomena, which may be harnessed by cultures (or subcultures, or institutions, and so on) to persuade the individual of the significance of things associated with the sounds, by crafting increased likelihood of *general emotional response* whose content is filled in *by* those associations. Such an approach accounts for the variability found across and within cultures regarding what music means, or makes one feel, by preserving Merriam's stress on the importance of cultural context for understanding those meanings and feelings, while also accounting for the fact that all world cultures (subcultures, etc.) seem to use sound (especially music) as a technology for ''spicing up'' whatever messages and events those cultures deem to be of special significance. The ''spicing up,'' in this view, is deployed precisely because it makes cultural messages paired with the sound feel more emotionally relevant – which is to say, it is a culturally enacted exertion of power upon the body, working through bodily mechanisms predisposed to seek significance, to facilitate some type of emotional response to whatever is contiguous to the fount of significance.[10] The political implications of this dynamic, even if it is only *likely* to occur rather than a *fait accompli*, should be obvious: no parades without a band, no worship without a song.

In the contemporary West (at the very least – perhaps now, everywhere) our capacity for perceiving heightened significance for contexts-with-music has become commodified, such that it is now routine, for example, for advertisers to use musical scores, vivid sound effects, and old popular songs (with new product-appropriate lyrics) as part of their attempts to persuade. Of course this is not *always* effective, and of course commercial jingles are not in the realm of the sacred, as is liturgical music, or the melody of the national anthem. Even when experienced out of context, liturgical music stirs a feeling of sacredness, and the national anthem a feeling of patriotism, because the musics are typically paired with things specifically defined as sacred and patriotic, and we learn to channel the action of the music into our response to the things with which it is paired. Commercial jingles do not precipitate quite the same feelings, and we have learned to realize, more or less, what advertisers and other persuaders are up to. But the music still exerts its force – those jingles stay on your mind whether you want them to or not! – and thus its continued usefulness. Advertisers, like religious specialists, political activists, and couples in love choosing a special song, know music is ''sticky,'' and will help keep an association – even a prosaic one – alive long after the associating circumstances are no longer present.[11] And the natural conclusion that most of us draw from the continued presence of an association, however non-consciously encoded, is that it must be an important one.

So far, I have claimed that forming judgments of significance is key to emotional processing, and that a (usually non-conscious) ''suggestion of significance'' may lie at the core of music's emotional effect, making apprehension of such significance the common element between the two. The frequent, pan-cultural use of sound forms, especially music, in contexts judged especially significant by the particular cultures (subcultures, etc.) bearing them is the main reason for asserting such linkage. Furthermore, I have claimed that if music tends to arouse this ''suggestion of significance,'' then it is possible that social institutions – ideologies, key symbols, advertisers in search of marketing edge – may exploit this significance-making capability through music, either intentionally or through bricolage, the better to inculcate their messages into bodies hearing the music associated with them. The natural next question is then: how does it work?

Here is where we must move to artful conjecture, because we still do not have good micro-level information about how the body actually processes musical inputs, much less how they might relate to our hypothetical ''suggestion of significance.'' The ethnographic argument that they must somehow relate is as far as we can go at this time. Virtually no worthwhile research on the musicological/social-scientific plane has gone beyond descriptions of the pragmatics of musical contexts to address how such pragmatics might affect the body through musical action, and only limited research has attempted such questions on the biological-scientific plane. The point is *not* that the music/emotion/significance/power relationships I've suggested do not exist, but that we need more fine-grained research, conducted jointly by biological and cultural researchers, to answer the ''how does it work?'' question.

I will return to that soapbox later. Before doing so, however, it is worth briefly examining some of the evidence, hypotheses, and potentially relevant positions that *do* exist, as they suggest interesting directions for further study of music/emotion relationships, and are in general amenable to my postulations.

Gelernter's ''low focus thought'' and the concept of affect linking

David Gelernter (1994) has recently made a case for reorienting research directions in artificial intelligence toward better understanding of the roles of embodiment, emotion, metaphor and analogy in human thought and consciousness – and, by extension, to attempts to construct machines which would emulate these processes. He claims emotion is key in determining the form and content of our thinking, especially that which occurs at a state he calls ''low-focus.'' Low-focus is the opposite of abstract, analytical thinking; it is a relaxed state wherein the style of thought becomes very concrete, analogical, metaphorical, and stream-of-consciousness – the stuff of creativity, spirituality, and seemingly random leaps of imagination. According to the evidence Gelernter presents, emotion plays a greater role in thinking on this level because analogical relationships are formed not only through detection of common features, metonymy, or other such associational mechanisms (cf. Shore 1996), but also by detecting similar emotional associations for things. This process, which Gelernter calls ''affect linking'' (1994:6–7, 77f.), keys on the idea that

> [t]he *character of the memory as a whole* is subtly captured by the feeling it evokes, by its *emotional content*. But this ''emotional code'' to which a memory is reduced isn't necessarily unique: more than one memory may evoke the same or almost the

same code. This is the basis of affect linking. Two memories that seem completely different might nonetheless evoke the same emotion. At low focus, memories that underlie two adjacent thoughts in a train might be completely different in every detail *except that*, for whatever reason . . . they made you feel the same way when you originally experienced them. (ibid:78–79; emphases in original)

Though Gelernter is primarily concerned with how idiosyncratic ''emotional analogies'' are formed in individual consciousnesses, this mechanism – if it exists – opens a realm of possibilities for institutions large and small to work to forge emotional analogies (or harness previously existing ones) between referents of choice within the minds of individuals, to accomplish their own ends. In other words, if one can be made to feel good about voting for a candidate, purchasing a particular product, worshipping a certain deity, and so forth, the likelihood of that behavior will increase, because the number of possible predispositions (feeling good) for the desired result is increased.

Though Gelernter's claims must be clarified and tested to confirm their explanatory value, we may nevertheless ask: what role might music play with respect to the power potentials inherent in affect linking? Music, Gelernter says, ''induces a series of emotions and each emotion in the series may induce in turn, via affect link, a kaleidoscope of recollections. Low-focus thought accomplishes the same thing directly'' (ibid:99). I have already criticized the idea that music can induce particular emotions, but we can preserve the sense of what Gelernter is talking about by suggesting music induces (or tends to induce) low-focus thought *itself*, in Langerian unconsummated-symbol fashion. If one can be maneuvered into low-focus, or relatively low-focus, thinking when a given message is presented (recall the observation that music is almost always an accompaniment to significant contexts such as ritual), then the ''kaleidoscoping'' concomitant of low-focus thinking – *constantly liable to forge new analogical cues from the environment around it* – will tend to feed off the context of the message, predisposing the possibility that new emotionally analogical links may be spontaneously formed between that context and one's own idiosyncratic thoughts and memories. Music, as a gateway to low-focus processing of information, would thus facilitate such linkages, turning that realm into a stealth zone for discursive contestations at the penumbrae of consciousness.

Raffman's ''cognitive theory of musical ineffability''

Diana Raffman (1988) has sketched an approach to music and emotion which also bears attention, as it focuses on music more directly than Gelernter's approach, and lends itself nicely to hypothesis testing. She claims that

music perception consists in a rule-governed process of computing a series of increasingly abstract mental representations of a musical signal. This scheme enables us to conceive the investigation of musical ineffability as the search for a level of mental representation of whose content we are conscious but cannot make verbal report. Very roughly, it turns out that certain features of the musical signal are likely to be recovered at such shallow processing levels . . . that they fail to be mentally categorized in the manner thought necessary for the learning of verbal labels. Therein lies their ineffability, which I call ''perceptual ineffability.'' (ibid:688)

What is it that is not ''mentally categorized'' as Raffman says? It is all the micro-level features of music that deviate ever so slightly from the culturally systematized scales, harmonies, and other forms that listeners expect on the basis of what they know about music[12] – i.e., the nuances which make up elusive qualities such as ''style,'' and the absence of which makes music sound robotic. It is not that we do not *hear* these variations; but since they stand just outside the rules we learn as members of a given musical culture, they are difficult to describe or even conceptualize clearly. The result of our inability to categorize this ''evanescent corona of unreportable pitches, rhythms, timbres, volumes, and so on, shimmering around the structural frame of the piece'' (ibid:698) is a feeling of ineffability, based on the confusion experienced in dealing with information too dense and irregular for one's culturally entrained listening apparatus.

Presumably, if such effects occur, the resultant feeling of ineffability – a feeling that *something important is going on here, but I don't know what it is* – could be appropriated by the contexts paired with the music, with the unknown ''object'' of the feeling of ineffability being filled in by that context itself. While after some time listeners might become accustomed to the pattern of musical variations, such that the music itself no longer produced fresh feelings of ineffability, by that time those listeners would have been able to form other significant associations with the context in question. (The ineffability effect would also continue to be useful for *new* listeners.)[13] In this way, then, the musical effect could act as a sort of shoehorn for other associations needed to solidify commitment to the context in question, producing an initial ''emotional'' response likely to be read, again because of its Langerian ''unconsummated'' nature, as a response to the associated context itself.

It would be difficult to test Raffman's theory in the field, because of the aforementioned difficulty of separating musical effect from cultural association – though one might get provocative leads by recording various musical performances, analyzing them for ''musical deviance,'' and attempting to correlate such deviance with individual/group-level emotional responses. Similar studies could be done in the laboratory. While positive results would hardly exhaust what remains to be known about music and emotion, they might indicate a basis for the ''suggestion of significance.''

Scraps of tantalizing biological evidence

The idea that music engenders a "suggestion of significance" might lead one to look for ways that music exerts its effects directly through some sort of generalized arousal function, particularly as it might affect the emotional information-processing system described earlier. Unfortunately, we do not yet know enough about music processing circuits even to guess how these might interact with arousal systems in the brain – not fully understood in themselves – or with the affective/attentional priming effects associated with these systems (cf. Tucker *et al.* 1990). Thus, the search for mechanisms of musical significance already requires neurological handwaving at the present state of the art; and so we are once again best grounded in appeals to logic rather than empirical results, because what we do know about music and the body is rather vague.

Music processing seems highly localized in the right hemisphere of the brain (Joseph 1988; Sloboda 1985), but not entirely so, just as language processing is not entirely localized in the left. Furthermore, "various subskills of music have a certain degree of neural independence" (Sloboda 1985:265), and fine-grained aspects of music processing may vary depending upon the training of the listener and the relative importance of various musical components in the sounds being heard (Gates and Bradshaw 1977). Nevertheless, studies of brain-damaged individuals indicate *amusias* (musical processing deficits) occur much more, and with greater severity, with damage to the right hemisphere of the brain (Joseph 1988:636–637).

Studies of "musicogenic epilepsy," an extremely rare reflex epilepsy in which seizures can be induced by musical/sonic stimuli (Critchley 1977; Scott 1977; Vizioli 1989), point toward a privileged role for the temporal lobes of the brain in musical processing, especially the right temporal lobe, because seizures in musicogenic epilepsy patients focus in these regions. As well, studies involving artificial electrical stimulation of the brain by Penfield and Perot (1963) found that musical hallucinations tended to result most frequently from stimulation of superior and lateral surfaces of the temporal lobes, especially the right temporal lobe. Right temporal lobe activity has also been linked not only to musical faculties, but also to religiosity, altered states of consciousness, and other strikingly "emotional" phenomena (e.g., Persinger 1987; Tuzin 1984:582–583). Also of interest is that "unpleasant emotional changes" accompany seizures in musicogenic epilepsy patients (Scott 1977:356).

Such nuggets have been used time and again to suggest natural links between all these qualities, and might similarly seem to buttress my specific postulations about music, emotion, and persuasion. However, the evidence as given does not *firmly* connect these elements and is merely suggestive at this time. We have already gone far afield by alluding to vague concepts such as "religiosity"; we have not discussed brain structures such as the amygdala, a key component of the "emotional" processing system described earlier in the chapter; nor, finally, have we ruled out third-variable possibilities, in which some other aspect of the brain/body further upstream is (also) significant for musical processing (or emotional processing, or both), and merely crosstalks with the temporal lobes (cf. Tuzin 1984:585). While evidence regarding the body's ability to process musical information is accumulating slowly, it is far from clear – and the question of how crosstalk between emotional processing and musical processing might transpire has scarcely been addressed. Much more work needs to be done in this area before *anything* definitive can be said, with regard to my assertions, or in itself.

Conclusion: Music hath charms? On resistance, briefly

> Since music is multiply interpretable, it is effective when there is need for communication between beings who cannot, or will not, bring to a communicative event the same presuppositions about the truth of what is being said. It is this very multiplicity of interpretation and distinction between performer and listener that emphasizes boundaries created by social and cosmological classification, while at the same time paradoxically fusing . . . discourse (Basso 1984:462–463).

"If you have troubles," Valentine declared, "I can give you a piece of advice: Turn on dance music." – (Aleksandr Solzhenitsyn, *The First Circle,* quoted in Perris 1985:v)

To end this chapter, I would like to invoke a story from my own life; but it requires a bit of setup, so the reader will please indulge one last digression. Having been deeply involved in fundamentalist Protestantism in my teens, I participated in various modes of worship and religious expression – but the congregation which most vividly impressed me was one whose practices sprang from Pentecostal traditions long entrenched in the area, despite its nominal association with the Southern Baptist Convention. The juxtaposition yielded worship services pitched somewhere between those poles: charismatic preaching and vigorous congregational response, occasional glossolalia and no snake handling, and – the important element here – free use of instrumental music, including electric guitars and a drum set. The minister and his brothers, along with a changing cast of hangers-on, made up the church "house band," which played old-fashioned hymns and contemporary gospel music alike with a decidedly rock'n'roll beat. Since I was rarely exposed to contemporary music, and practically never to live music, while growing up, this was a particularly striking aspect of the service to me.

A few years later, after completing my painful break with Christianity –

essentially in favor of left-wing politics, probably not such a dramatic leap for me – I found myself in an apartment in Brooklyn for the weekend, full of alcohol and ideology, dancing to the British band New Order with my new comrades, preparing to continue organizing various causes among fellow undergraduates back in Kentucky. Then I realized, dimly: the *thud thud thud* of the drum track strongly reminded me of how the minister's nephew played traps back in that church. There was no (serious) guilt, no particular issues to be resolved: just the knowledge that, somehow, I'd rewired ''feeling the beat'' away from sensation of God's will and the power of the Holy Spirit, into other things – sexual liberation, personal autonomy, a different vision for society.

Later still, after becoming more at ease with my religious history, I realized that not only had I ''rewired'' many things – including music – for new purposes of my own, but that my former congregation had done so as well, in much clearer fashion. While I was there, they constantly spoke of ''using the things of the world for the glory of God,'' but I did not fully appreciate then how much this applied to the music. Although many mainstream styles and genres were used, the ''house band'' had appropriated them all, bent them, molded them to their needs; crafting not signs of alignment with the profane world, but instruments of God's presence, sanctifying the profane and erecting a bulwark against forces of darkness – just as the music had, apparently, helped me reconnect *with* the profane world.

This story does not prove the music/emotion/power relationships I've postulated; there are already far too many associations embedded in its context for it to pass Merriam's test. It remains true that we must ferret out those relationships in more surreptitious, fine-grained ways. Rather, if the effects I've postulated may be (temporarily) assumed, my anecdote suggests that the significance-enhancing function of music may also be appropriated *counter-hegemonically* as a resource to resist domination, i.e., that persons or institutions may appropriate that function as an exertion of power upon *themselves* to reinforce the significance of dissenting points of view. In South Africa, vibrant musical cultures effloresced in conjunction with the anti-apartheid movement; many a Red went to the ramparts with *L'Internationale* filling the air before them; in the 1970s, gay culture bloomed through, among other sites, discos and aural celebrations of the body that rocked them late into the next morning. And in my church, music was used to draw a protective line around things of God, against the onslaught of the profane world. That the music drew from the music *of* that world was a wonderfully ironic twist of religiously animated counterhegemony.

Since music, like all potential channels of communication from the linguistic to the tactile, is part of the semiotic landscape out of which all orientations are formed, its ability to encode power relations must be reckoned with on all sides of any battle of symbolic discourses, at all times. Understanding this ability is thus an important task; aside from the interesting things we might learn about the body, and about how the body and social life meet each other, the potential keys to the nature of power that studies of music and emotion might give us have clear political value for everyone on all sides of all dividing lines.

Here, then, is a clear case where both biological and cultural perspectives are needed to understand fully a very significant human phenomenon, and in the cause of which researchers in such seemingly unrelated perspectives ought to be working together – to examine capacities of the body in detail, not to reduce cultural effects to individual psychophysiology, but rather to show how bodily capacities could facilitate the achievement of certain cultural effects.

The utility of such holism with respect to this problem suggests it might be usefully directed toward an array of similar problems. Thus, the primary goal of this chapter: that the style of theorizing and speculating I've tried to motivate here becomes commonplace, so that scholars of all theoretical persuasions can engage in constructive dialogue, rather than go on uncreatively labeling and dismissing the importance of each other's work.

Acknowledgments

Previous versions of this article benefited from comments by Victor Balaban, Margaret Buck, Samuel Gunto, Ravensara Siobhán Travillian, Alexander Laban Hinton, Carolyn Travillian Jones, Robert Paul, Anne Marie Sereg, Bradd Shore, Dan Smith, E. Jennifer Weil, participants in the Emory University Department of Anthropology spring 1992 Biocultural Seminar on emotion, and four anonymous reviewers for Cambridge University Press. Factual errors, logical problems, or misrepresentations of others' perspectives are my own responsibility. This chapter is dedicated to two men more like brothers to me than any other: first, to Sam Gunto (1952–1994), a scholar and friend who died much too soon, whose advice and guidance are sorely missed; and to Alex Hinton, the editor of this volume, whose faith in me during an ongoing period of intense personal difficulty is a mark of friendship heretofore unexperienced.

NOTES

1. I am indebted to Charles Nuckolls for making this problem clear to me.
2. I do not address every possible modality of "power" in this chapter, nor do I claim every instance of "power" fits Foucault's model. In this chapter I am most concerned with relationships that depend on consolidating the *consent* of those over whom power is exerted. None of my remarks are necessarily illuminative of

other modalities of power, such as those invoked in lockouts of striking workers, blackmail, armed invasion, or political bribery.

3. This quote is from the back cover text of Lutz and Abu-Lughod (1990).
4. To be sure, the process is more complex than described here. Edelman, for example, also stresses how ''selective coordination of the complex patterns of interconnection between neuronal groups by reentry [linkage between representational maps in the brain] is the basis of behavior'' (Edelman 1992:85), and that the long-term processes I called ''rearrangement'' may be interwoven with shorter-term processes of biochemical connection. I have omitted such details here in the interests of brevity.
5. Reproduction itself could be considered a process of construction, eminently social, which merely happens to use a particular palette of biological materials and processes. On a longer scale, processes of evolution could also be seen as constructionist, since their products are continually shaped and reshaped over successive generations, through interactive ''dialogue'' with all other such products in their (also changing) ecological contexts.
6. One factor that exacerbates this problem is the authors' failure to separate clearly the components of *experience*, *evaluation*, and *expression* in emotion-related phenomena. Perhaps Abu-Lughod's and Lutz' arguments could be represented as a shift of focus from the former component to the other two, particularly the latter, with the caveat that ''expression'' need not indicate a ''matching'' interior/experiential state, but may only represent cultural tropes typically identified with themes of emotional expression.
7. As an academic, relatively uninterested in commercial sales practice, I am unlikely to be stimulated by a lecture about that topic; however, a sales representative struggling to make commission in order to support a family will very likely be emotionally stimulated by it. Yet both of us, *ceteris paribus*, will likely be equally stimulated by charging tigers, political torture, or plates of Brand X Chocolate Dessert. Furthermore, stimuli such as the last two, which juxtapose pronounced stimulation of the body with complex cultural meanings, are likely the most affecting of all, as the intercontextualization of multiple modalities of meaning-acquisition yields increased ground for the synthesis – or modification of – meanings (cf. Turner 1967; Shore 1996).
8. An African-American rap group popular in the late 1980s and early 1990s, noted for its politically militant lyrics.
9. Langer claims the ''strength of musical expressiveness'' is that ''music articulates forms that language cannot set forth'' (1957[1942]:233). However, there is no ''vocabulary'' that translates between music and emotion. Rather, music creates emotion-like ''feelings'' in the listener, without requiring these ''feelings'' to have fixed meanings, or actually to ''be'' the emotions they seem to be. The *general similarity* between musical and emotional *forms* induces listeners to bridge the gap, and assume connection: ''music . . . though clearly a symbolic form, is an unconsummated symbol . . . the assignment of one rather than another possible meaning to each form is never explicitly made'' (ibid:240–241). Such references are filled in, if at all, by the hearers of the music – and thus they may experience the express*iveness* of music as emotion, though it is not musical express*ion* of emotion. For Langer, no ''emotional content'' is communicated from performer to hearer.

10. A striking example comes from the aftermath of the Third Reich. Wagner's music was enthusiastically embraced by the Nazis, and was played constantly in the death camps. Years later, when conductor Zubin Mehta programmed an all-Wagner concert in Tel Aviv, public outcry over the program's inappropriateness – spurred by Holocaust survivors for whom the music retained vivid associations – was enormous.
11. Salient examples from even our own rationalized context abound. While rap music has a recitative quality, it is prosodically choreographed, and layered over repetitive rhythms and melodic/harmonic samples; films, even those striving for "gritty realism," use soundtracks; video games typically include musical snippets and sound effects; and so on. If music did not somehow add something to these forms, we would presumably be presented with more spoken word CDs, films without soundtracks, and silent video games – for adding musical elements to them certainly adds expense. The investment must be worthwhile, even for these desacralized products.
12. Cf. Lévi-Strauss (1969[1964]:16) on how Western scales "cook" the "continuous natural realm of sounds into a discontinuous cultural reality" (Roseman 1991:12).
13. Cf. Rumelhart's (1995:152–153) passing remarks – commensurable with Raffman's overall perspective – about how connectionist models of the mind/brain might illuminate the degradation and replenishment of music's emotional effects.

References

Abu-Lughod, Lila. 1990. Shifting politics in Bedouin love poetry. In *Language and the politics of emotion*, ed. Catherine A. Lutz and Lila Abu-Lughod. Cambridge: Cambridge University Press, 24–45.

Ackerman, Diane. 1990. *A natural history of the senses*. New York: Vintage/Random House.

Appadurai, Arjun. 1990. Topographies of the self: Praise and emotion in Hindu India. In *Language and the politics of emotion*, ed. Catherine A. Lutz and Lila Abu-Lughod. Cambridge: Cambridge University Press, 92–112.

Bahr, Donald M. and J. R. Haefer. 1978. Song in Piman curing. *Ethnomusicology* 22(1):89–122.

Basso, Ellen B. 1984. Responses to Feld and Roseman. *Ethnomusicology* 28(3):461–463.

1985. *A musical view of the universe: Kalapalo myth and ritual performances*. Philadelphia: University of Pennsylvania Press.

Campos, Joseph J., Rosemary G. Campos, and Karen Caplovitz Barrett. 1989. Emergent themes in the study of emotional development and emotion regulation. *Developmental Psychology* 25(3):394–402.

Changeux, Jean-Pierre. 1985. *Neuronal man: The biology of mind*. New York: Pantheon.

Clynes, Manfred. 1977. *Sentics: The touch of the emotions*. New York: Anchor.

1989. Evaluation of sentic theory nullified by misunderstood theory and inferior sound: A reply to Nettelbeck, Henderson, and Willson. *Australian Journal of Psychology* 41(3):327–337.

Clynes, Manfred, and Nigel Nettheim. 1982. The living quality of music: Neurobiologic basis of communicating feeling. In *Music, mind, and brain: The neuropsychology of music*, ed. Manfred Clynes. New York: Plenum, 47–82.

Critchley, Macdonald. 1977. Musicogenic epilepsy. (1) The beginnings. In *Music and the brain: Studies in the neurology of music*, ed. Macdonald Critchley and R. A. Henson. London: William Heinemann Medical Books, 344–353.

Derrida, Jacques. 1976 [1967]. *Of Grammatology*. Baltimore: Johns Hopkins University Press.

Eaton, S. Boyd, Marjorie Shostak, and Melvin Konner. 1989. *The paleolithic prescription: A program of diet and exercise and a design for living*. San Francisco: HarperCollins.

Edelman, Gerald M. 1987. *Neural Darwinism: The theory of neuronal group selection*. New York: Basic Books.

1988. *Topobiology: An introduction to molecular embryology*. New York: Basic Books.

1992. *Bright air, brilliant fire: On the matter of the mind*. New York: Basic Books.

Edgewater, Iain D. In preparation. Toward biologically sophisticated social theory: On constructionism, essentialism, and recent developments in biology.

Ellingson, Ter. 1986. Drums. In *Encyclopedia of religion*, vol. 4, ed. Mircea Eliade *et al.* New York: Macmillan, 494–503.

Erlmann, Veit. 1982. Trance and music in the Hausa Bòorii spirit possession cult in Niger. *Ethnomusicology* 26(1):49–58.

Feld, Steven. 1990. *Sound and sentiment: Birds, weeping, poetics, and song in Kaluli expression*. Philadelphia: University of Pennsylvania Press.

Foucault, Michel. 1972. *The archaeology of knowledge and the discourse on language*. New York: Pantheon.

1977. *Discipline and punish: The birth of the prison*. New York: Vintage.

1980. The history of sexuality. In *Power/Knowledge: Selected interviews and other writings*, ed. Colin Gordon. New York: Pantheon, 183–193.

Gates, Anne and John L. Bradshaw. 1977. The role of the cerebral hemispheres in music. *Brain and Language* 4(3):403–431.

Geertz, Clifford. 1973. The growth of culture and the evolution of mind. In *The interpretation of cultures*. New York: Basic Books, 55–83.

Gelernter, David. 1994. *The muse in the machine: Computerizing the poetry of human thought*. New York: The Free Press.

The Globe and Mail, June 24, 1998, quoted in *The Risks Digest*, 1984, http://catless.ncl.ac.uk/Risks/19.84.htm#subj15.

Jackson, Anthony. 1968. Sound and ritual. *Man (n.s.)* 3(2):293–300.

Joseph, R. 1988. The right cerebral hemisphere: Emotion, music, visual-spatial skills, body-image, dreams, and awareness. *Journal of Clinical Psychology* 44(5):630–673.

Kandel, Eric R. 1991. Cellular mechanisms of learning and the biological basis of individuality. In *Principles of neural science,* 3rd ed., ed. Eric R. Kandel, James H. Schwartz, and Thomas M. Jessell. New York: Elsevier, 1009–1031.

Laderman, Carol. 1991. *Taming the wind of desire: Psychology, medicine and aesthetics in Malay shamanism*. Berkeley: University of California Press.

Lang, Peter J. 1994. The motivational organization of emotion: Affect-reflex connections. In *Emotions: Essays on emotion theory*, ed. Stephanie H. M. Van Goozen,

Nanne E. Van de Poll, and Joseph A. Sergeant. Hillsdale, NJ: Lawrence Erlbaum, 61–93.

Langer, Susanne K. 1957 [1942]. *Philosophy in a new key: A study in the symbolism of reason, rite, and art.* Cambridge, MA: Harvard University Press.

LeDoux, Joseph E. 1989. Cognitive-emotional interactions in the brain. *Cognition and Emotion* 3(4):267–289.

Lévi-Strauss, Claude. 1969 [1964]. *The raw and the cooked.* New York: Harper and Row.

Lutz, Catherine. 1988. *Unnatural emotions: Everyday sentiments on a Micronesian atoll and their challenge to western theory.* Chicago: University of Chicago Press.

1990. Engendered emotion: Gender, power, and the rhetoric of emotional control in American discourse. In *Language and the politics of emotion*, ed. Catherine A. Lutz and Lila Abu-Lughod. Cambridge: Cambridge University Press, 69–91.

Lutz, Catherine A. and Lila Abu-Lughod. 1990. *Language and the politics of emotion.* Cambridge: Cambridge University Press.

Merriam, Alan P. 1964. *The anthropology of music.* Evanston: Northwestern University Press.

Needham, Rodney. 1967. Percussion and transition. *Man* (n.s.) 2(4):606–614.

Neher, Andrew. 1961. Auditory driving observed with scalp electrodes in normal subjects. *Electroencephalography and Clinical Neurophysiology* 13(3):449–451.

1962. A physiological explanation of unusual behavior in ceremonies involving drums. *Human Biology* 34(2):151–160.

Neisser, Ulric. 1988. Five kinds of self-knowledge. *Philosophical Psychology* 1(1):35–59.

Nettelbeck, T., C. Henderson, and R. Willson. 1989. Communicating emotion through sound: An evaluation of Clynes' theory of sentics. *Australian Journal of Psychology* 41(1):25–36.

Oyama, Susan. 1985. *The ontogeny of information: Developmental systems and evolution.* Cambridge: Cambridge University Press.

Peek, Philip M. 1994. The sounds of silence: Cross-world communication and the auditory arts in African societies. *American Ethnologist* 21(3):474–494.

Penfield, Wilder and Phanor Perot. 1963. The brain's record of auditory and visual experience – A final summary and discussion. *Brain* 86(4):595–696.

Perris, Arnold. 1985. *Music as propaganda: Art to persuade, art to control.* Westport, CT: Greenwood.

Persinger, Michael A. 1987. *Neuropsychological bases of God beliefs.* New York: Praeger.

Raffman, Diana. 1988. Toward a cognitive theory of musical ineffability. *Review of Metaphysics* 41(4):685–706.

Red Hot Chili Peppers. 1991. ''The power of equality'' on *Blood Sugar Sex Magic.* Warner Brothers W4-26681.

Roseman, Marina. 1991. *Healing sounds from the Malaysian rainforest: Temiar music and medicine.* Berkeley: University of California Press.

Rosenau, Pauline Marie. 1992. *Post-modernism and the social sciences: Insights, inroads, and intrusions.* Princeton, NJ: Princeton University Press.

Rouget, Gilbert. 1985 [1980]. *Music and trance: A theory of the relations between music and possession.* Chicago: University of Chicago Press.

Rumelhart, David E. 1995. Affect and neuro-modulation: A connectionist approach. In *The mind, the brain, and complex adaptive systems (Santa Fe Institute studies in the sciences of complexity, volume XXII)*, ed. Harold J. Morowitz and Jerome L. Singer. Reading, MA: Addison-Wesley, 145–153.

Scheper-Hughes, Nancy and Margaret M. Lock. 1987. The mindful body: A prolegomenon to future work in medical anthropology. *Medical Anthropology Quarterly* 1(1):6–41.

Schieffelin, Edward. 1976. *The sorrow of the lonely and the burning of the dancers.* New York: St. Martin's Press.

Scott, D. F. 1977. Musicogenic epilepsy. (2) The later story: Its relation to auditory hallucinatory phenomena. In *Music and the brain: Studies in the neurology of music*, ed. Macdonald Critchley and R. A. Henson. London: William Heinemann Medical Books Ltd., 354–364.

Seeger, Anthony. 1987. *Why Suya sing: A musical anthropology of an Amazonian people.* Cambridge: Cambridge University Press.

Shore, Bradd. 1996. *Culture in mind: Cognition, culture, and the problem of meaning.* New York: Oxford University Press.

Sloboda, John A. 1985. *The musical mind: The cognitive psychology of music.* Oxford: Clarendon Press.

Strauss, Claudia. 1992. Models and motives. In *Human motives and cultural models*, ed. Roy D'Andrade and Claudia Strauss. Cambridge: Cambridge University Press, 1–20.

Trussoni, Steven J., Anthony O'Malley, and Anthony Barton. 1988. Human emotive communication by touch: A modified replication of an experiment by Manfred Clynes. *Perceptual and Motor Skills* 66(2):419–424.

Tucker, Don M., Kathryn Vannatta, and Johannes Rothlind. 1990. Arousal and activation systems and primitive adaptive controls on cognitive priming. In *Psychological and biological approaches to emotion*, ed. Nancy L. Stein, Bennett Leventhal, and Tom Trabasso. Hillsdale, NJ: Lawrence Erlbaum, 145–166.

Turner, Victor. 1967. Ritual symbolism, morality and social structure among the Ndembu. In *The forest of symbols: Aspects of Ndembu ritual.* Ithaca: Cornell University Press.

Tuzin, Donald. 1984. Miraculous voices: The auditory experience of numinous objects. *Current Anthropology* 25(5):579–589, 593–596.

Vasseleu, Cathryn. 1991. Life itself. In *Cartographies: Poststructuralism and the mapping of bodies and spaces*, ed. Rosalyn Diprose and Robyn Ferrell. London: Allen and Unwin, 55–64.

Vizioli, R. 1989. Musicogenic epilepsy. *International Journal of Neuroscience* 47 (1–2):159–164.

Wikan, Unni. 1990. *Managing turbulent hearts: A Balinese formula for living.* Chicago: University of Chicago Press.

Zola-Morgan, Stuart, Larry R. Squire, Pablo Alvarez-Royo, and Robert P. Clower. 1991. Independence of memory functions and emotional behavior: Separate contributions of the hippocampal formation and the amygdala. *Hippocampus* 1(2):207–220.

5 Emotion and embodiment: the respiratory mediation of somatic and social processes

Margot L. Lyon

> [W]e are everywhere faced with physio-psycho-sociological assemblages of series of actions. These actions are more or less habitual and more or less ancient in the life of the individual and the history of the society.
> (Mauss 1973(1935):85)

> Statements about ''our lived experience of being embodied'' need to be cashed in (as Husserl would say) for evidence that *shows* embodiment to be an experienced fact. Unless and until such experience(s) can be described, the metaphysical (and logical) disjunction between on the one hand an incarnate subjectivity – or lived body – and on the other a Cartesian metaphysics, will remain, and with it the problem of how ''the mental'' and ''the physical'' are in fact united. (Sheets-Johnstone 1990:304)

> Few bodily functions more beautifully illustrate the relationship between thinking and anatomy as does breathing. (Lowry 1967a:3)

Emotion links social and and somatic processes

It must be acknowledged that the term embodiment speaks to physical as well as subjective and social processes. A conceptual framework which takes account of the bodily dimensions of social life is therefore necessary. It is this fundamental question of the embodiment of social life that is addressed in this chapter.

One path for the linking of bodily and social domains is through the study of emotion. Emotion may be understood as a complex construct comprised of a number of ''components.'' It is both embodied and social relational (Kemper 1981; de Rivera 1984; Scheff 1988) and as such, requires the exploration of the question of interrelationships between social and biological being. In a conceptualization of social life as structured relations (in particular historical and cultural contexts) between human bodies, emotion can be seen to inhere in and to be a product of those relations. Emotion thus has a complex mediating role: it is implicate in social and bodily relations and, as a product of structured social relations, it is therefore foundational in the creation of society. Through an understanding of the place of emotion in social life, then, the role of the body as an agent in "world construction" can be clarified and elaborated.[1]

The experience of embodiment is especially present when we *feel*, when we are emotionally engaged in the world, whether or not we are self-consciously aware of that engagement. In this chapter, one bodily capacity linked to feeling will be addressed. This is the respiratory capacity – breathing. The ways in which this bodily function (through both anatomical and physiological mechanisms) is always implicated in the mediation of subjective and somatic being in the context of social and cultural life will be considered. The chapter thus has as its aim the exploration, through the respiratory mechanism, of one dimension of the "somatic" basis of social life.

The relationship between body and society has been a theme in the works of some major theorists including, for example, William James and Emile Durkheim. Marcel Mauss, also, in his "Techniques of the Body," took up the "strong sociological causality" revealed in our bodily actions (1973[1935]:85), addressing the influence of society, culture, and history on bodily being and action. For Mauss, the "habits" (*habitus*) of the body thus formed through this interaction "do not just vary with individuals and their imitations, they vary especially between societies, educations, proprieties and fashions, prestiges. In them we should see the techniques and work of collective and individual practical reason" (1973:73). Mauss calls for a triple viewpoint of biological, psychological and sociological facts and says that even if the action is primarily bodily or biological, it too is subject to the same forces of socialization, imitation, and authority that affect other aspects of social life. Mauss includes in his account the "habits" of breathing (1973:87). The phenomenologist, Buytendijk, following Plessner, similarly acknowledges in his notion of "encounter" the importance of the interrelationship of bodily action and social context: "The forms of (animal) movement are forms of behavior, since they carry visibly in themselves and 'delineate' the relation of the body to the environment and conversely of the environment to the body" (Buytendijk and Plessner quoted in Grene 1968:124). And, the work of the psychologist, William James (1950[1890]), whose writings were known to the French sociological school, was also concerned with the role of habit. James wrote on both the bodily and social bases of habit and argued for its importance in the maintenance of social order.[2]

Mauss's concept of "habitus", later much developed by Bourdieu (e.g., 1977), is important in its indication of the inextricability of bodily and social being, i.e., how the patterning of bodily processes is *part* of our social being. But his treatment of it remains unidimensional in so far as it fails to address the mechanisms through which bodily and social being are intertwined.[3] It is precisely the concept of emotion which can address this issue and thus extend and clarify Mauss's perspective on how the mechanism of "habit" may operate through a process much more complex than the concepts of imitation and socialization can accomodate.

The following material explores how respiratory function can be used to explore the import of emotion in bridging sociocultural and somatic processes. The remainder of this section outlines in brief the perspective on emotion which is taken in the discussion here, and introduces the topic of respiratory function. Section two provides background information on respiratory function and how the nature of respiratory control mechanisms underpin its role in both behavioral and physiological processes. Section three examines how patterns of breathing are linked to emotional agency, including particular examples which illustrate the relationship of respiration to the generation of subjective states in the context of culture and social life. The final section using the conception of "affective order', discusses how respiratory rhythms are one pathway for the continual modulation of emotion in the context of group life, and so are a crucial bodily pathway for the ordering of human social behavior. The chapter as a whole may be seen as a development of Durkheim's point regarding the emotional basis of social life and social action.

Bodily and social relational dimensions of emotion

Emotion is a hypothetical construct which, like the concepts of memory and perception, for example, is based on a number of classes of evidence which may be physiological, behavioral, interpretive, and so forth, and which may include data of many sorts from verbal reports to expressive behavior to peer-group reactions (Plutchik 1984:199). Emotion is thus often described as consisting of a number of components or dimensions both bodily and cognitive (e.g., Scherer 1984:294).[4]

When emotion is dealt with in terms of its social and cultural dimensions, there is a tendency in the relevant literatures to ignore the bodily aspects as irrelevant to analysis. The dominant approach in the social sciences is a social or cultural constructionist one which gives priority to the cultural and social construction of the *meaning* of emotions, the nature of emotional expression, and its control or governance. However, none of the components of emotion – including the bodily – can be understood in isolation from the others, nor can emotion be understood in isolation from the social context – real or imagined – in which it occurs. An adequate approach to emotion, then, should have a place for the various components as well as for how all of these are a function of social relations.

Emotion is integral to our very being. In evolutionary terms, our capacity for the experience, perception, and expression of emotion is associated with the development of increasingly complex forms of social relations. Indeed, the evolution of the affective system is a function of the mediation of social relationships, *not* a primitive relic of our ''animal'' past which has come to be submerged by ''reason'' in human evolution (Reynolds 1981:82, 38). Nor is emotion primarily a primitive urge, as Freud would have it, which when not suppressed or repressed, breaks through to disrupt social functioning. Rather, emotion acts to *organize* human behavior in complex ways, as Leeper (1948) argued early on, and as Scherer's (1984) conception of the components and functions of emotion leads us to see.[5] Further, emotions cannot just be seen as internal states but are a *function* of social relationships. Indeed, they can be viewed as social relationships (de Rivera 1984; de Rivera and Grinkas 1986).[6]

Most of social science cannot be said to be embodied in any real sense. Partly an historical product of divisions between the physical or biological and the social sciences developed in the late nineteenth and early twentieth centuries, such divisions contributed to the shaping of the empirical and theoretical boundaries of the various academic disciplines (Benton 1991). The continued elaboration of and privileged theoretical position given to concepts such as reason and culture in the social sciences both reflects and has ensured the dominance of a cognitivist perspective. The body is excluded from this except as it is socially or culturally constructed, that is, except in so far as it is the subject of thought. Thus, in sociology, an emphasis on rational and structural models has tended to override any impetus to ground them in or link them to bodily processes. In anthropology, the dominant cognitivist or ideational perspectives have meant that the concepts of symbol and of culture have been made to do the work of biological, psychological, and social perspectives (Geertz 1973; Shweder 1984), while leaving them inchoate within the concept of culture itself (Lyon 1995). Such cognitivist approaches have reduced concern with behavior in the larger sense and resulted in a deemphasis of bodily being, the preeminence given to the phenomenological roots of anthropology notwithstanding. When the body is taken up, it tends to be through culturally grounded ideas *about* the body. In anthropology, especially, both body and emotion are frequently subsumed within the culture concept and treated only as productions of culture.[7]

This is not to say that some form of reembodiment of social and anthropological theory has not been a matter of concern in the social sciences. Dennis Wrong, a sociologist, argued as long ago as 1961 for the significance of the human body in the understanding of social processes. The anthropologist, John Blacking, at a conference on the anthropology of the body in 1975, called for an expanded study of the body in the social sciences (Blacking

1977). And, the body has recently reemerged in scholarly writing in structuralist, feminist, and post-modernist accounts (Frank 1990). However, explanation about the body in the social sciences tends to continue to divide along the axis between approaches grounded either in material, biological explanation, or in social and cultural explanation, rather than on the exploration of interrelationships between them in a theoretically productive fashion.[8] This has worked to prevent an adequate consideration of the importance of body *qua* body in social and anthropological theory. The body continues to be treated either as a bounded physical entity, or as a social artifact, rather than as both subject and active agent in the creation of social processes and institutions.

A parallel conceptual division also pervades accounts of emotion. Although there is a growing awareness of the importance of emotion in social life, and emotion is increasingly the object of anthropological and sociological interest (e.g., Lutz and White 1986; Thoits 1989), the emotions literature is frequently organized in terms of a distinction between so-called positivist and constructionist, or universalist and relativist, perspectives. The persistence of the organization of debate along this divide, Kemper's (1981) clarifications notwithstanding, is evidence of a failure in our models of emotion to come to terms with bodily agency.

A bodily example

It is one thing to say that emotion makes possible the conceptualization of how physical being is implicate in social being and vice versa, but a demonstration of this as an ongoing process is more difficult. This task is approached here through a discussion of one particular bodily process, respiration, and how it is implicated in the generation and experience of emotion in social contexts, and how the experience of emotion, in turn, acts back on respiratory functions; for respiratory capacities and emotion are clearly linked.[9] Respiratory patterns are associated not only with internal physiological regulation but with the generation and regulation of feeling states, as well as with the expression of feeling and its communication through various types of movement and vocalization. Through a consideration of examples drawn from the literature on respiration, this chapter seeks to provide a case of how "consciousness" (inclusive of "feeling") may be located simultaneously in the organism and in society and culture, and thus is a basis for understanding the integration of bodily being with social experience and its place in the ordering of social action. Respiration provides a confined domain in which to explore this relationship.

Of all the particular capacities of the body, breathing is unique in that it is the only one which is simultaneously under both autonomic and "conscious" control. For this reason, respiratory function is subject to modulation through either of these channels at all times. This modulation is mostly below the threshold of awareness, and varies complexly in reference to internal physiological factors, environmental factors, type and level of physical activity, and individual and group aspects of subjective social experience. The "dual control" of respiration means that particular patterns or styles of breathing may – in their appropriate social and cultural contexts – come to be differentially associated with particular types of subjective experience. These patterns may be habitual or voluntary, activated directly or indirectly, and be used consciously or unconsciously. Although they are observable primarily in cases of unusual behavior or states, e.g., in trance or ecstasy, the relationship between respiratory patterns and subjective experience is a basic feature of how our bodies function. It is part of the "background" of our bodily being and is implicated in the very basis of social organization.

The purpose of this discussion is not to reduce feeling to respiratory function, nor is it to match particular respiratory patterns and specific experiential states. Indeed, these are not fruitful directions of enquiry, for although there is a physiological dimension to every aspect of being, behaviour can never be reduced to physiological processes (Buytendijk 1950:127).[10] Thus, I am not concerned with the attempt to simply locate explanation about human social behavior in biology, nor to reduce experience and feeling to concepts such as arousal[11] or other states thought to be linked to particular breathing patterns or techniques. Rather, I am concerned with how to simultaneously represent, through emotion, both physiological phenomena and the experiential and active dimensions of those phenomena within the sociocultural context in which they occur.

I thus use the interconnectedness of emotion and respiratory patterns to demonstrate emotion's simultaneous role in linking physiology and society, bodily and social-relational experience. Our bodily being – which takes its forms in terms of its basic capacities for sociality and the establishment of social relations – is crucial in the constitution of society. The interrelationship between respiratory function and emotion is part of that bodily being and thus part of the genesis of "social order."

Respiration, feeling, context

Respiration serves both behavioral and metabolic functions

It is of interest that spirit and breath are represented by a single term in many languages, giving unitary conceptual form to the complex interrelationship of breathing, consciousness, and feeling. In Greek, for example, *psyche* includes both breath and mind, as does the related term *pneuma*.[12] In Sanskrit, *prana* encompasses both breath and soul. In many other languages, terms for breath are closely associated with terms for feeling and emotion (e.g., Onians 1954; Wellenkamp 1988; Roseman 1990). The interrelationships of "mind', emotion, and breath which figure in such linguistic conceptions mirror the complex anatomical and physiological connections that in fact link the human respiratory system and other bodily systems. These interconnections can be understood partly through the fact that the respiratory, cardiovascular, and other organ systems all "share" innervation through the autonomic nervous system, and this system, along with the limbic and hypothalamic areas of the brain, is also of key importance in emotion.[13] Variations in breathing patterns are thus linked to variations in feeling states, both processes being mediated by the autonomic nervous system. Emotional expressivity is also associated with autonomic changes. Ekman *et al.* (1983) have shown that certain changes in facial expression, for example, even quite mechanically generated ones, correlate with different patterns of autonomic activity. Similarly, the work of Lanzetta has demonstrated that there is a correlation between increased autonomic activity and increased facial expressivity (Lanzetta *et al.* 1976 cited in Brown 1991:26).[14]

Respiration provides a framework within which to address the simultaneity of behavioral and autonomic processes, for respiratory mechanisms are harnessed to both autonomous, internal processes and external, socially mediated processes. This happens because respiration is under *both* "voluntary" and autonomic or "involuntary" neural control. The skeletal muscles attached to ribs and between ribs and sternum, which serve to raise and lower and thus expand or contract the rib cage to draw in or expel air, are subject to voluntary control, as can be experienced by intentionally taking a deep breath or holding the breath. These muscles are also innervated by branches of the autonomic nervous system which further provides the major innervation of the smooth (rather than skeletal) muscle of the diaphragm. Breathing is thus also "automatic" as can be experienced by remembering that we do not have to think to breathe. Respiration is the only autonomic function of the body so mediated. Breathing thus serves both metabolic and behavioral systems (Plum 1970:159). Particular respiratory patterns can come to be associated with particular feeling states both by convention and by conditioning, and can be used in the direct manipulation of physiological and subjective states. Further, respiratory patterns and their accompanying manifestations are communicative in both a surface and a deeper sense. They can reveal to an observer clues as to the physiological and subjective state of the person. They are also one of the chief mechanisms mediating the establishment of common interactional rhythms and synchronous behavior in groups.

The point here is that breath is one pathway through which this interrelationship between body, emotion, and social being is constituted and through which it can be explored. It provides an ideal example in that the respiratory function is fundamental to being, i.e., is at all times engaged, and is at all times a reciprocal pathway of communication between bodily and social being. It is implicated in the production of speech, song, all forms of bodily movement, facial expression, and so forth. Respiratory patterns thus cannot be isolated from the wider bodily and psychosocial context of which they are a part. The shared neuroanatomical links with emotion make clear the intimate connections between respiratory patterns and subjective experience without necessitating a concern with arguments about specificity of those relationships. However, this implicate relationship is so much part of our being, both physical and sociocultural, and is so rarely within our conscious awareness, it is difficult to consider at all. The fact that ventilation patterns are continually responding ''automatically'' as well as being acted on, modulated, or manipulated through our actions within various sociocultural contexts, makes it even more difficult to represent.

Respiratory physiology

A brief introduction to the physiology of respiration is provided here as background for subsequent material on the implications of the control and conditioning of respiratory patterns in social context. The physiology of respiration has been well described. Respiration provides for the regulation of gas exchange which provides a supply of oxygen adequate to the metabolic needs of the body and which removes excess carbon dioxide produced in those metabolic processes. The air moved through the lungs comes into proximity to venous blood moved through the lungs by the circulatory system so that gas exchange can take place. Normal breathing (termed eupnoea) is that which meets metabolic demand for the supply of oxygen and the removal of carbon dioxide in reference to the level of activity of the body.[15]

Carbon dioxide, however, *not* oxygen, is the primary stimulus in the functioning of the respiratory system. That is, raised or lowered carbon dioxide levels cause physiological responses. Even small increases in carbon dioxide levels, as for example in underbreathing, cause an increase in ventilatory response (Slonim and Hamilton 1976:133). Thus, if we try to breathe shallowly and infrequently or hold the breath, we eventually experience a powerful urge to take a breath. This urge is due to the build up of carbon dioxide, rather than the lack of oxygen, and the effects this increased carbon dioxide level has on the nervous system. The threshold for hypoxia, oxygen deprivation, is very high and has little effect on ventilation. This can be (dangerously) demonstrated by rebreathing expired air in a closed system in which carbon dioxide is continually removed or absorbed by a chemical filter, e.g., using a gas mask such as used to be commonly available in army surplus stores. In the absence of a build up of carbon dioxide in the rebreathed air, there is little sense of oxygen deprivation until hypoxia is well advanced (Slonim and Hamilton 1976:136–140). However, the resultant hypoxia will eventually cause increasing impairment of function and ultimately unconsciousness. This was dramatically demonstrated on camera by Jonathan Miller in an episode of the British documentary series ''The Body in Question,'' during which Miller used a closed gas mask with carbon dioxide filter to demonstrate his progressive loss of function and eventual near loss of consciousness.

Ventilation in excess of bodily metabolic requirements, that is overbreathing, is termed hyperventilation or hypocapnia (from capnos for smoke referring to carbon dioxide as a byproduct of burning). Contrary to popular understanding, hyperventilation does not result in too much blood oxygen, but rather a lowered level of carbon dioxide. The overbreathing ''washes out'' carbon dioxide and results in a reduction in blood carbon dioxide levels, leading to a decreased partial pressure of carbon dioxide (partial pressure means the amount of one gas relative to that of other gases) in arterial blood. The blood partial pressure of oxygen is only slightly increased in this process. If hyperventilation continues, body tissue stores of carbon dioxide are also reduced.[16]

Effects of overbreathing are rapid and diverse. Most of us have subjectively experienced minor effects of hyperventilation such as dizziness or a sense of lightheadedness when blowing up a balloon or some other inflatable object. The repeated long exhalations used in inflation brings about a reduction in partial pressure of blood carbon dioxide which in turn acts on the nervous system to cause vasoconstriction of both arteries and veins supplying blood to the brain, particularly the neocortex. This leads, in effect, to a mild form of hypoxia, but a brain hypoxia associated with changes in circulation rather than with a deficiency of oxygen in inspired air. This vasoconstriction can be immediate, commencing after only a few seconds of prolonged exhalation, and is mediated by the central nervous system on which the carbon dioxide acts. Thus, carbon dioxide levels are associated with the control of cerebral blood flow, particularly to the forebrain (Lum 1976:203).[17] The subjective experience or expression of emotion often associated with periods of hyperventilation is thought to be facilitated by lowered cortical control associated with reduction of blood flow to this area.

The regulation of gas exchange is under the control of the central nervous system, i.e., the brain and spinal cord, as well as the peripheral nervous system including the autonomic nervous system. The autonomic nervous system originates in the brain in the hypothalamus and branches into two parts as it leaves the spinal cord, the sympathetic and parasympathetic chains. The autonomic system is responsible for the motor innervation of the heart, lungs, diaphragm, digestive tract, other viscera as well as glands and hair follicles. As was noted above, the control of the respiratory system can be seen to be "automatic" in response to internal signals mediated in the lower regions of the brain, including the response to blood carbon dioxide levels. Control of the respiratory system is further subject to behavioral influences which are also mediated by autonomic pathways as well as higher centers of the brain (Plum 1970; 1974).

A discussion of more specific mechanisms of control cannot be attempted here. What is important is that respiratory patterns are determined by complex mechanisms involving both behavioral and neurochemical components.[18] The neural centers implicated in basic functions such as respiration are also important in such processes as emotion, awareness, memory, learning, sensation, and motor control. Plum notes, for example, that in healthy, awake individuals, the cerebral hemispheres do much to control breathing rhythm and depth even when metabolic stimuli vary or are removed (1970:166).[19] This control of breathing is necessary in order to produce and maintain speech, for example, and is also involved in laughing and sobbing (Plum 1974:208).[20] It is the example provided by the behavioral implications of these interconnections which is of concern here.

Subjective associations of variations in respiratory patterns

Attention to the interrelationship between respiration and emotion appears primarily in literature drawn from medicine, psychology, and psychiatry. Its minor import in social science sources will be taken up in Section three. The clinical bias of the former literatures exerts particular constraints, orienting discussion toward problems of the definition and delineation of abnormal states, i.e., the association of abnormal respiratory patterns with what are defined as physical or psychological pathologies. Much of the emphasis is on the parameters of particular ventilatory forms such as hyperventilation and its frequent association with anxiety or panic states, as well as a wide range of physical manifestations. However, the very considerable clinical literature on hyperventilation is useful for the purposes of this chapter in that it addresses the question of the interlocking of respiratory functions and emotion.

As already noted above, the neurophysiological relationship that exists between respiratory stimuli and emotion is partly mediated by the brain and the peripheral nervous system, particularly the autonomic nervous system. Also mentioned was the fact that while the latter is responsible for the routine control of the body's physiological adjustments including heart rate and respiration, it is also associated with what is frequently termed emotional arousal (LeDoux 1986:308). Indeed, the autonomic nervous system and the endocrine system, along with the brain, are the principal physical mechanisms governing emotional response. It is the role of the autonomic nervous system in the mediation of the respiratory drive, via its various connections with other parts of the brain and peripheral nervous system which in turn act on endocrine secretions, which "provides the pathways necessary for the inclusion of altered breathing as part and parcel of emotional experiences" (Johnson 1967:44).

Explicit discussion of relationships between physiological and emotional dimensions of respiration is to be found primarily in the clinical literature on hyperventilation. This tends to divide into work concerned with the definition, description, and differential diagnosis of hyperventilation, and that concerned with delineating what is often termed "hyperventilation syndrome," that is, habitual hyperventilation, considered as indicative of some form of neurosis, primarily anxiety states.[21] Linked to this literature are studies of catharsis and abreaction, also concerned with physiology and the experience of emotion.[22] The concern here is not with debates about the identification and classification of possible syndromes but with the identified effects of hyperventilation.

The particular range of effects associated with overbreathing was first described in the respiratory physiology literature by Haldane and Poulton in 1908 (Bass & Gardner 1985:602; see also Johnson 1967 for a review). The subject also has a long history in medical literature (e.g., Kerr *et al.* 1937; Engel *et al.* 1947). However, according to Lum (1976), despite this considerable early and detailed work, contemporary medical texts rarely include adequate accounts of the wide range of signs – both subjective and observable – associated with hyperventilation. Rather, emphasis tends to be given to the rarely observed acute manifestations, with other signs and symptoms glossed under terms such as "anxiety state" (Lum 1976:196–197) or "panic attacks" (Bass & Gardner 1985:605), thus severing them from their association with patterns of respiration.

Further, because of the simultaneous voluntary and involuntary aspects of respiration, attempts to clinically determine in any precise and refined way an association between overbreathing and particular signs or symptoms cannot be successful. The intentional clinical reproduction of symptoms through forced breathing generally relies on the presence of "the classic triad" of signs associated with hyperventilation ("massive overbreathing, paraesthesiae and tetany" [Lum 1976:375]). Yet the acute signs are, according to Lum, merely the "tip of the iceberg" of a phenomenon that affects at one time or another a significant percentage of the population, as most cases do not present with the signs typical of acute hyperventilation.[23] In an editorial in the *Journal of Psychosomatic Research*, Lum states that the actual signs are frequently unrelated to those thought to be typical of hyperventilation and "may affect any part of the body, and any organ or any system" (1975:375):

''Symptoms may show up anywhere. . .for we are dealing with a profound biochemical disturbance, which is as real as hypoglycemia and more far-reaching in its effects'' (1975:375).[24] It has been suggested recently, for example, that overbreathing may be linked to the symptoms widely associated with chronic fatigue syndrome, with depression, and other common syndromes or disorders.

The various signs or symptoms associated with overbreathing are thus so diverse as to make their summary difficult. A selection of terms associated with its effects are as follows: weakness, malaise, a sense of impending doom, excitement, apprehension, light-headedness, feelings of unreality (floating), dizziness, ringing in the ears, blurred vision, feeling faint, tightness in the chest, inability to breathe deeply, frequent sighing and yawning, palpitation, precordial pain, tightness in the throat, dry mouth, epigastric distress, tingling and numbness in extremities and face, muscle cramps especially in the hands and feet, twitching tremor of extremities, cold moist hands and feet, and so forth (see Johnson 1967:92; Lum 1976:220–224). Symptoms reported, for example, by a study group of military recruits diagnosed as being hyperventilators were: feeling short of breath, difficulty in talking, feeling of breathing ''too much,'' feeling excited for no reason, face numb or tingling, hands tight and hard to open, feeling that everything is unreal, crying for no good reason, laughing for no good reason, tongue numb or tingling (Lowry 1967c:111).[25]

Though the clinical literature tends to give emphasis to negative correlates such as anxiety or panic, Lum argues that in fact anxiety is quite often the product of hyperventilation itself which may be triggered by any number of other factors which go unrecognized by physicians (Lum 1975:380). For example, it has been suggested ''that the loss of voice seen in singers and their conditions of anxiety and stress may be due to hyperventilation'' (Lowry 1967b:16). Or, the association of hyperventilation with crying observed in children who ''thinking tears were warranted but finding them not quite spontaneous, facilitate crying by taking a few deep breaths'' (Lowry 1967b:15–16). Further, triggers for hyperventilation are ''not necessarily associated with fear or anxiety'' (Lum 1976:198): ''Laughter, pleasure, excitement or animated conversation may all do it – even watching the television. Likewise exertion or the malaise of real physical illness. (Lum 1976:198). The point here is that the diversity and range of signs associated with overbreathing provide a clear indication of the variety of physiological and subjective experiences associated with variations in respiratory patterns.

The dominant orientation of the clinical accounts referred to in the above section is, of course, psychological. There are, however, other sources through which to broaden our inquiry. These provide for a better understanding of how basic respiratory functions, through emotion, are implicate in bodily being *and* social being, that is, how ''emotional being'' is constructed within the larger social and cultural context. Such an extension contributes to the further understanding of the embodiment of social processes. The following section takes up some of the ways in which respiratory capacities come to be structured or patterned in social and cultural context.

Respiratory function, bodily agency, and emotion in socio-cultural context

Habits of the body

Viewing respiratory patterns as ''habitus'' in Mauss' terms, we understand that what the clinician seeks to see as symptom of disorder may equally be seen as habit of behavior given form and expression in particular social, cultural, and psychological contexts. At the individual level, even the maintenance of a particular level of blood carbon dioxide is subject to habit. Lum, for example, cites borderline overbreathing in some individuals which acts to keep carbon dioxide levels low such that ''any physical or emotional disturbance may trigger off a chain reaction of increased ventilation, rapidly producing hypocapnic symptoms, alarm engendered by the symptoms, consequent sympathetic arousal resulting in increased ventilation and increased symptoms'' (Lum 1975:380). With repetition, the association between a particular context or stimulus and overbreathing may with repetition take on ''the characteristics of a conditioned reflex'' (Lum 1976:198). Even an individual's very sensitivity to carbon dioxide may be altered by conditioning and thus a factor in hyperventilatory experience, as evidenced by patients who have breathing abnormalities associated with anxiety symptoms, and for whom ''their hypersensitivity appears to be a disorder of conditioning rather than a biochemical alteration'' (Brown 1991:171).

Such habits may be a function of social and cultural forces as well, for patterns of breathing are highly adaptable and readily formed. For the child, breath control is an important part of learning the forms of motor behavior necessary for communication through speech as well as other forms of expression such as song, whistling, etc. This learning is accomplished in ways that are appropriate to the particular psychosocial as well as sociocultural context in which that child exists. As breathing is under voluntary control, ''[w]e may stop, start, vary rate, depth and rhythm, and use either diaphragm or thorax at will. The natural pattern of breathing may therefore be modified by voluntary control and training, and moulded to the dictates of custom, convention or erroneous ideas of 'health' and physical fitness'' (Lum 1976:219). The puffed out chest characteristic of military training, for example, encourages overbreathing through excessive use of the thorax, a "type of breathing more appropriate to exertion, stress or anxiety," but which with continual use "will become as effortless and unconscious as the acquired skills of riding a bicycle, swimming or skating" (Lum 1976:219). The habits of breathing thus entail a reciprocal relationship between body and behavior in sociocultural context; they are a unified feature of being, but one subject to modulation in both "directions." This requires a return to the question of the relational nature of emotion and the importance of the body in that process.

The "capture" of bodily capacities by emotion (and vice versa)

Tomkins states that "[t]he breathing mechanism is continually being captured by the prevailing affective responses" as the "breathing patterns of normal human beings are continually modulated by such affects as fear, joy, depression, grief, startle, distress and anger" (Tomkins 1962:48). This process, as Tomkins emphasizes, is an ongoing one. It is part of the "background" of being. Tomkins could as well have stated it in the reverse, that is, that changes in breathing patterns are associated with the generation of affective responses. The bodily experiences associated with alterations in respiratory patterns are therefore *part* (whether explicitly labeled as such or not) of the embodied awareness of one's subjective state in any relational context, i.e., an aspect of emotion (cf. de Rivera 1984; James 1950 [1890]). Further, the dual control of respiratory capacities already described means that particular techniques of breathing may be used in the facilitation of affective responses and thus of particular types of emotional experience.

The question of the relationship of the bodily components of emotion to emotional experience has theoretical implications which must be acknowledged here. The bodily and perceptual components of emotion cannot in fact be separated from *within* the domain of social action, for together they are partly constitutive of that action. The emphasis on the bodily aspects of emotion requires a reconsideration of ideas which are generally linked to William James. James associated the feeling of emotion with the bodily changes which accompany or follow the perception of some exciting fact (James 1892:375); for example, the sense of heartswelling or tears on listening to poetry or drama or music which moves us, or the sense of one's heart stopping or the breath catching when faced with something frightening. Such bodily changes seem to precede or be simultaneous with the perception of being moved. The experience of bodily awareness which may sometimes precede conscious awareness of a particular emotion and the process of its interpretation can be illustrated by recalling an instance of the experience of strong emotion which was apparently objectless. A common example is the rush of feeling triggered by some stimulus such as a particular odor or sound, which we can only later associate with some past charged event or relational context. Such an approach to emotion sees ''that an emotional state is, fundamentally, the awareness of changes in the state of the body'' (Papanicolaou 1989:xiii). James' approach and its linking with the work of Lange, the so-called James–Lange theory, has frequently been dismissed in favor of more ''cerebrocentric'' theories. Papanicolaou, who reexamined James' model in the light of later evidence, found James' work to be supported (albeit in a somewhat modified form), and found the distinctions made between James' theory and the so-called Cannon–Bard theory (e.g., Cannon 1928) to be grounded in misunderstanding. Papanicolaou recast James' theory as what he termed a ''somatic theory of emotion'' giving place to *both* peripheral bodily and central sources of emotion: '''Somatic', because the object of any emotional experience is the flesh in commotion and not because the brain is any less necessary for instigating that commotion and monitoring it than it is necessary for sensation, movement or external perception'' (Papanicolaou 1989:xiv).[26] The relevance of this here is that such a model can be easily extended to encompass the sociocultural components of the process. The role of the respiratory capacity in the genesis and experience of emotion as explored here supports the importance of such an integrated approach.

The modulation of breathing is thus a bodily capacity closely linked and fundamental to human emotional capacity. It has an important role in almost all areas of human activity including major communicative acts such as talking, crying, singing. Even in sleep, this relationship is said to pertain: ''Asleep as well as awake, man's breathing reflects his emotional state. If something absorbs his interest, his breathing reflects his excitement'' (Slonim and Hamilton 1976:142). ''Indeed, the respiratory system is a major mode of expression for a variety of feelings. The breath-holding of temper tantrums or anger; the singing, humming, or whistling of happiness; the sighing of passion; and the sobbing and crying of sorrow or grief are only a few examples'' (Slonim & Hamilton 1976:142).

Some culturally mediated examples of the relationship between respiratory patterns and subjective states

Particular respiratory patterns are, of course, implicated in any type of organized bodily movement including those used in speech and song, dance, marching, work practices, etc. These patterns, then, are one medium through which to investigate the embodiment of social and cultural life including its affective dimensions. However, as already noted, most sources which explicitly deal with the relationship between breathing patterns and emotion tend to be focused on what are viewed as abnormal physical or psychological states, with the abnormality seen to be located either in incorrect breathing patterns or in psychological states which are thought to be affecting or altering respiratory patterns. Anthropological accounts and other non-clinically oriented accounts which happen to include description of respiratory patterns tend to focus on the implications of specific techniques of breathing for the intentional achievement of particular subjective states in the context of group expression as for example in studies of certain types of religious behaviour, healing, music, dance, or trance. The emphasis is thus on how manipulation of the respiratory capacity may be used to facilitate the experience of particular subjective states.

The relationship between respiratory patterns and emotion is most easily observed in those sociocultural contexts in which the experience of unusual states is facilitated and made manifest. These states may be consciously attributed to the use of a particular technique of breathing or simply to some organized action which acts to establish some respiratory pattern. Examples can be found in contexts involving heightened emotion such as conversion or possession rituals, trance, or practices involving states of calm or quiet as in certain meditation traditions. An obvious example of the latter are the Asian yogic and other meditative techniques in which breath regulation is highly developed.[27] Most studies of meditation techniques have emphasized their psychological effects – the reduction of arousal and the facilitation of calm or restful states. Many yoga practices involve slow, near vital capacity breathing techniques with a pause after both inspiration and expiration. It has been demonstrated that ''voluntary slowing of respiratory rate of subjects under stressful conditions reduced physiological arousal'' (Bass and Gardner 1985:606). Another study supported yogi masters' claims that a form of ''slowed respiration – that is rapid inhalation followed by slow exhalation at a reduced respiratory rate – was an effective technique for reducing physiological arousal when anticipating and confronting a threat'' (Bass & Gardner 1985:606; see also Gellhorn and Kiely 1972:402–404).

Although a general association between levels of arousal and breathing patterns pertains, particular subjective states cannot be matched with particular breathing techniques and their respective autonomic correlates. Subjective states are simultaneously a function of many factors including sociocultural context, psychological factors, etc. Further, no single physiological variable can be said to correlate with any particular level of arousal (Stein 1967:148).[28] Even the equation of underbreathing and overbreathing with the reduction and enhancement of arousal, respectively, is crude as is apparent from detailed studies done on meditation (e.g., Gellhorn & Kiely 1972:402; Cappo & Holmes 1984; Schwartz *et al.* 1978; Wallace 1970).

The obverse of techniques of breath control used in meditation for the lowering of arousal are those which aim to enhance emotional arousal, frequently in pursuit of some expressive state. Many Western, somatic-based, emotive therapies which emphasize the efficacy of emotional expression, such as Reichian[29] or so-called ''neo-Reichian'' or ''neo-gestalt'' therapies, explicitly utilize particular breathing techniques, primarily hyperventilation. A deep, rhythmic combination of diaphragmatic and thoracic breathing is used, for example, in ''rebirthing'' and ''primal therapy'' to facilitate the recall or reexperiencing of emotions and the open expression of these. ''Connected breathing,'' ''holotropic breathing,'' and ''pneumocatharsis'' are popular terms which have been used for such techniques.[30] Such therapies are frequently grounded in ''hydraulic'' models of emotion emphasizing the necessity of emotional release or catharsis. The facilitation of emotional experience and expression seems to operate through the effect of overbreathing on blood carbon dioxide levels which triggers vasoconstriction, leading to a reduction in blood flow to the forebrain and therefore a reduction in neocortical control. The facilitation of emotional expression apparently results from less effective neocortically based monitoring, thus lessening the ability of the conscious mind to ''override'' or integrate emotion within everyday action, enabling a more focused and intense experience and expression of emotion. However, any examination of such techniques and exploration of the bases of their efficacy needs to be undertaken within the study of the larger social and psychological contexts in which they are used.

There are many other relatively mechanical uses of particular breath techniques which could be mentioned in reference to subjective changes. The Lamaze method of breathing used in childbirth to help control pain and facilitate uterine contractions is one of these. Women using the technique commonly report unusual sensations and feelings which may be associated with autonomic changes induced by lowered blood carbon dioxide. It should be noted also that over- or underbreathing is always subject to individual manipulation, including that done intentionally for particular social effects. Charles Darwin and Florence Nightingale, for example, are both said to have exploited the effects of overbreathing to bring on apparent states of syncope or collapse (Lum 1975:220 citing Pickering 1974).

In reference to group phenomena, many forms of ritual illustrate the importance of alterations in respiratory patterns in the generation of group feeling. Accounts which comment directly on bodily aspects of ritual activity are generally concerned with a search for some explanation for what are seen to be unusual states such as ecstasy and trance. William Sargant, a psychiatrist interested in religious behavior, for example, addressed the use of overbreathing and other ''physiological weapons,'' as he termed them, in religious conversion and possession states: ''Fasting, chastening of the flesh by scourging and physical discomfort, regulation of breathing, disclosure of awesome mysteries, drumming, dancing, singing, inducement of panic fear, weird or glorious lighting, incense, intoxicant drugs – these are only some of the many methods used to modify normal brain functions for religious purposes'' (Sargant 1957:79). In *The mind possessed: A physiology of possession, mysticism, and faith healing* (1973), Sargant documents instances of overbreathing in various ritual contexts such as the rhythmic overbreathing used by men of the Samburu and Mole tribes in northern Kenya to bring them to a state of trance during dancing, and the chanting and overbreathing techniques among certain Arabic peoples for trance purposes, the effects of which he compares to those induced by hyperventilation in Western patients (1973:115–118). In a further example, he discusses practices associated with Pocomania, an African-Christian sect in Jamaica and Barbados, who use ''tromping'' or rhythmic overbreathing in order to ''bring down the Holy Ghost'' (1973:166). Sargant's studies stress the importance of emotional excitation and its resolution in forms of abreaction often leading to collapse.[31] He notes: ''Some sects pay more attention than others to a direct stirring up of emotions as a means of affecting the higher nervous system; but few wholly neglect it'' (1957:79).

Studies of healing rituals among the !Kung provide a clear example of the use of overbreathing (Katz 1982). Katz sees the breathing and other techniques of the rituals as generating the transformation of consciousness considered necessary by the !Kung for obtaining healing power (1982:345).[32] The dancers exhibit rapid deep breathing with long exhalations, show trembling and tetany, and are reported to experience sensations of searing pain in the area between the diaphragm and the waist, to feel light, tremble, and feel fear. Katz says that ''!Kia intensifies emotions, be they fear, exhilaration, or seriousness'' (1982:349).

Such states constitute more dramatic examples of the interrelationship of bodily action and affective states in social and cultural context. What is important, however, is that this is a general phenomenon. The role of the establishment and use of common respiratory rhythms in group action is evident in any number of social and cultural contexts. Almost any type of patterned activity that involves organized co-action provides the opportunity for common bodily and affective experience. Roseman, writing on healing rituals among the Temiar, rainforest dwellers in peninsular Malaysia, describes the beating of bamboo tubes which resonate with or mimic bodily and natural rhythms, the effects of which include entrainment or synchronization of bodily rhythms. The sound, she says, ''gains affective power through its rootedness in the rainforest and the body'' (Roseman 1990:241). The synchronization of bodily rhythms including respiratory rhythms could be sought in many other forms of song and chanting. Also, the bodily postures used during song or verbal praise have an effect on respiratory function. For example, in many Christian services, the raising of the arms to reach up and out during singing or praise has an effect on posture and chest capacity and encourages a deeper and more open breathing pattern which, in that context, may have important implications for subjective experience.[33]

The above examples provide clear evidence of the relationship between emotion and variations in respiratory pattern in particular sociocultural contexts. As has been seen, this interrelationship functions generally, not just in special ritual or therapeutic contexts. The relationship between respiration and emotion is foundational and always operative. It is further embedded in other bodily attitudes and thus part of the ''background'' of our being in the social world. The role this association plays in the establishment and maintenance of social relationships must therefore be acknowledged.

The body and ''affective order''

The overall aim of this chapter has been to demonstrate the interlocking relationship between respiratory function, emotion, experience, and action in the context of social life. The first section of this chapter established the study of emotion as a means for conceptualizing the links between bodily and social being. It proposed the examination of how one bodily mechanism, respiration, functions within ongoing social processes in the generation of subjective states, and so is materially implicate in the creation of society as ''social fact.'' The second section (''Respiration, feeling, context'') used a variety of scientific literatures to explain the main features of the functioning of the respiratory mechanism. Section three explored the implications of respiratory patterns in the generation of emotion and subjectivity in sociocultural context. In view of the social-relational ontology of emotion, that is, that it is *generated* in the context of ongoing social life, it is possible to make some further general points about the central place of bodily agency in the generation of subjective experience. Respiration has been explored in terms of how it is shaped (consciously or unconsciously) in structured activity, and how it shapes individual and group response, and in so doing is implicated in our engagement with the world and in the very creation of that world. This final section addresses this latter issue through drawing out some additional points using the notion of synchrony and introducing the concept of an ''affective order.''

References to the structuring or patterning of respiratory function in the context of social relations (and cultural life) can be seen to bear some relationship to discussions of the concepts of rhythm and synchrony in studies of non-verbal communication, in the micro-analysis of interaction, and in physiological sociology more generally (e.g., Byers 1976; Davis 1982; Hall 1983; Barchas 1976; Barchas & Mendoza 1984; Kiritz & Moos 1974). Such studies hold that social life has rhythmic properties. Rhythm in this sense is a form of temporal patterning grounded in both biological and social functions. It is a property of structures, not an entity in itself (Mathiot & Carlock 1982:176), that is, it is a property of groups. ''Rhythm produces the expectation of continuity and changes in rhythm signal new experiences'' (Brown 1991:45). Byers sees the notion of rhythms as a conceptual tool. For him, rhythms ''are process, and they are relationships'' (Byers 1982:139). What is important here is that what is termed rhythm must also be seen in terms of how it is grounded in bodily functions and bodily action, including respiration, heart rate, endocrine system function, etc., as well as the myriad forms of organization of bodily movement, posture, the generation of sound, and so forth.

My argument is thus not merely oriented to how respiratory functions aids in the establishment of interactional rhythms, although in fact respiratory corhythm is an important function of group interaction. Breathing rhythms of group co-members *do* come to be in some synchronous relationship to a dominant rhythm (Johnson 1967:71). And, this synchronous relationship has important communicative functions, both in itself, and because it is implicated in other aspects of behavior such as speech rhythms and intonation patterns as well as movement. But the concern here is to formulate more clearly how emotion is implicated in the mediation of bodily and group processes. Given the intimate interrelationship between respiratory function and emotion, the process of the establishment of the respiratory co-rhythms has obvious affective consequences (and vice versa). The particular respiratory rhythms and their affective consequences are thus a function of the structure of the social relationships to which they pertain, for persons in relation are also bodies in relation (Collins 1981). Significantly, however, such a view does not restrict inquiry to the level of small group or face to face interaction. It can pertain at any level of social relationship, for emotion is part of, is embedded in, the act of being in relationship itself. In emphasizing the place of emotion in social life in this way, one can avoid an implicit reliance on a consensus model of social organization.[34]

As has been demonstrated in preceding sections, the modulation of respiratory function in any context is intimately connected with emotional experience whether or not that experience is consciously perceived. It has been seen that respiratory patterns may be structured within particular emotional contexts, and that alterations in respiratory patterns also act in the generation of the experience of emotion. This experience is only partly explained by the concept of arousal, although the use of particular respiratory patterns in the context of social and cultural action, as in music, dance, vocalization, etc., is one of the chief bodily mechanisms facilitating arousal, just as changes in levels of arousal may result from a person's negative or positive perception of their position in a social setting and so effect changes in respiratory and other bodily functions. Alterations in respiratory patterns thus may be seen to be one of the most important bodily mechanisms through which physical and emotional being are shaped or "tuned" in the context of social relations. This mechanism, implicated as it is in the ongoing forms of action that constitute social and cultural life, is therefore fundamental in the establishment and ordering of social relationships at the material level. That is, it is a fundamental aspect of – and mechanism for – the interlinked and reciprocal ordering of bodily, social, and cultural being.

Emotion organizes human behavior, and it does so in ways that go beyond what may be understood through concepts such as motivation. Durkheim saw that action in groups engendered what he termed a "moral force." Such a force, for Durkheim, is partly grounded in emotion, i.e., emotion which has its origins in particular social forms. These emotions or collective sentiments, for Durkheim, are the basis of the productive power, the efficacy, of society (Durkheim 1915 (1965):406). Durkheim, of course, was concerned primarily with the social ontology of emotions. It is the social ontology of emotion that is of concern here also, but from the perspective of the place of *bodies* in that process. The exploration of respiratory function has been an attempt at understanding how social processes, through emotion, are embodied. Respiration is one bodily capacity that acts to establish an affective order among persons and bodies and therefore is a component in the establishment of social relationships themselves. It provides a bodily mechanism through which both individual and social dimensions of emotion are made manifest.

The implications of the "capture" of respiratory functions by social conditions (and vice versa) are thus far greater than concepts such as emotional engagement or arousal can indicate. Arousal, as already indicated, merely gives emphasis to individual subjective experience or response within a given environment. It is insufficient for it cannot indicate how emotion is implicated in individual and group *agency* in the social life. The continual modulation of respiratory capacities in any given social context provides evidence of how one bodily mechanism is a *part* of the organization of human behaviour simultaneously at both the individual and group levels and how emotion mediates this process. It contributes to the demonstration of how affective organization is grounded in the interaction of physical, psychological, social, and cultural factors.

Acknowledgments

This chapter is based on an article previously published in *Social perspectives on emotion*, vol. II. JAI Press 1994.

NOTES

1. Merleau-Ponty (1962 [1946]) saw the body as an agent in world construction through lived experience. Emphasis in his scheme is on how experience serves as the basis of all knowledge, rather than on the bodily mechanisms through which that experience is given or any role that emotion may have in this process of the apprehension of the world. Merleau-Ponty's account of the foundations of being can thus be extended to encompass how emotion is implicated in bodily agency.

   Emotion has figured more recently in the work of certain phenomenological psychologists. Gendlin, for example, has written on what he terms ''felt meaning'' as opposed to verbal or cognitive meaning. For Gendlin, this ''directly felt, experiential dimension'' is responsible for guiding action and is the basis of meaning, for nothing means except as it ''interacts with felt experiencing'' (Gendlin 1962:1). Gendlin, however, gives emphasis primarily to the conscious experiencing subject although his notion of experience is that it is concrete: ''[R]egardless of the many changes in *what* we feel – that is to say, really, *how* we feel – there always is the concretely present flow of feeling. . ..we *always* have concrete feeling, an inward sensing whose nature is broader [than any] specific idea, wish, emotion, perception, word, or thought'' (author's italics) (1962:11). It is clear from Gendlin's examples, although he deals with the notion of feeling in a restricted sense, that he sees this feeling as bodily through the body's ordered interaction with objects in the environment: ''These objects may or may not be present, yet the body order includes the patterns of interaction that *could* obtain if they *were* present (Gendlin 1962:25). This resonates with Kemper's notion that emotions result ''from real, anticipated, imagined, or recollected outcomes of social relationships'' (Kemper 1978:32). The idea of simultaneity of body sense and emotion is a point that I develop in this chapter.
2. James stated: ''Habit is thus the enormous fly-wheel of society, its most precious conservative agent. It alone is what keeps us all within the bounds of ordinance, and saves the children of fortune from the envious uprisings of the poor. It alone prevents the hardest and most repulsive walks of life from being deserted by those brought up to tread therein'' (James 1950[1890]:121).
3. See Lyon 1997 for a critique of Mauss' concept of habitus, and the further development of the argument regarding the central place of emotion in any analysis of the embodiment of social life.
4. Scherer, a psychologist, lists the following components: ''(a) cognitive appraisal or evaluation of stimuli and situations, (b) the physiological component of activation or arousal, (c) motor expression, (d) the motivational component, including behavior intentions or behavioral readiness, and (e) subjective feeling state'' (Scherer 1984:294). Multiple components, in Scherer's terms, are associated with the multiple functions that the emotional capacity performs, e.g., evaluation of the environment, regulation of the physiological system, preparation for action, communication of intention, and reflection and monitoring (Scherer 1984:297).
5. As Scherer notes, the flexibility of behavioral adaptation in higher animals ''is largely due to the emotion systems'' (1984:295). The existence of the emotion systems has made it possible to ''decouple'' behavioral reaction from events in which they arise such that cognitive-evaluative and other processes intervene.

6. de Rivera, for example, describes what he sees as the three main approaches to the study of emotion: the psychological, the phenomenological and the sociological. The first ''conceives of emotion as a process occurring within an organism located in an environment.'' The second takes the view that ''human emotions are not processes that occur within organisms situated in an objective environment'' but rather ''different ways of being-in-the-world.'' The third perspective, the sociological, for de Rivera, is concerned with how persons exist in relationship with others: ''[E]motion is viewed as a characteristic of the *relationship* between two people'' (1984:116–118).
7. For a critique of anthropological perspectives on emotion, see Lyon 1995. For a treatment of the place of emotion in social theory more generally, see Lyon and Barbalet 1994.
8. Within the biological sciences, there have been a number of attempts to integrate sociological and biological perspectives. In the history of modern biology, for example, there were many who advocated holist approaches as opposed to reductionist or mechanistic approaches, and who sought an understanding of ''the integrative, regulative functioning of physiological systems in ways which required them to think holistically about living organisms'' (Benton 1991:16–17). J. S. Haldane, an early researcher on respiratory function, could be included among those scholars utilizing holistic perspectives.
9. The term respiration includes both the physiological and mechanical processes associated with breathing. Webster's *New Twentieth Century Dictionary* gives the following definition of respiration: ''In physiology, the act, process, or function of breathing; in higher animals, the act by which air is drawn in and expelled from the lungs.''
10. It should also be noted here that I am not arguing for a collapse of the logical distinction between ''mind'' and ''body.'' The two terms represent quite different conceptual categories, not simply two aspects of the same thing (cf. Csordas 1990). As Helmuth Plessner points out, experientially, we both *are bodies* and *have bodies* and experience these two aspects of embodiment quite differently (Plessner 1970 [1941]). This is a point which is also intimately linked to the foundations of the sense of self.
11. The term arousal carries the implication that certain states represent an observable change in reference to ordinary or resting states. Such a manner of use in reference to emotion frequently implies a homeostatic model of emotion wherein emotion is seen as disruptive of ''normal'' homeostatic states. This is not the intention here.
12. See Chapter 3 (''The stuff of consciousness'') in Onians (1954), for a discussion of Greek and Roman concepts of breath and the relationship of breath to thought and emotion.
13. The importance of autonomic interconnections in the functioning of the endocrine and immune systems could also be mentioned here. This would allow the extension of our discussion of embodiment and emotion to the areas of health and illness more generally. On immune networks, see for example Blalock (1984) and Varela *et al.* (1988). See also Lyon 1993 for a review of some of the models of immune system interactions in reference to the place given to social context.
14. The close neurological relationship between respiration and facial expression is apparently grounded in the common phylogenetic origin of the muscles used in

facial expression and those of gill structures in lower animals (Bell 1844; Brown 1991:26 citing Rinn 1984). See also Darwin 1965.

15. Normal resting breath averages 13 to 17 breaths per minute with a tidal volume (''depth'' of breath or amount of air moved) of approximately 500 milliliters per breath. This gives a normal resting volume of 7.56 liters per minute (Slonin and Hamilton 1976:47). Under conditions of muscular exercise, ventilation increases both in frequency and tidal volume.
16. Of the gases which are stored in the various tissues and fluids of the body, carbon dioxide comprises the largest, with major stores in bone and body fluid. A person of 70 kilograms would have approximately 35 liters of stored carbon dioxide, an amount which would equal the bodily metabolic production of carbon dioxide over a period of 140 minutes (Slonin and Hamilton 1976:92–93). If a person hyperventilates so that the total volume of air moved past the alveoli in the lungs is doubled, then the partial pressure of alveolar carbon dioxide ($PaCO_2$) will be halved eventually (after body stores reach a new level) (Slonin and Hamilton 1976:50, 93).
17. Reduction in cerebral blood flow is also related to electroencephalographic changes. Lowry, citing work done by Engel, Ferris, and Logan states:

> They found a direct connection between blood carbon dioxide tension and the frequency of brain waves. An average subject was able to slow his brain to 4 cycles per sec. by rapid breathing of sea level air for 150 sec. Electroencephalogram slowing was most marked when the carbon dioxide level dropped rapidly, when blood sugar was low, when inspired air contained less oxygen than usual, when the patient stood, and following the administration of amyl nitrate and nitroglycerin. With equal amounts of hyperventilation a patient with a high blood sugar level tends to hyperventilate until tetany appears while a subject with a low blood sugar level tends to have marked alterations of consciousness and an earlier spontaneous cessation of hyperventilation. (Lowry 1976b:16–17)

18. These interactions are mediated by the neocortex as well as by lower centers in the brain and nervous system. For example, lower areas of the brain in the brain stem (medulla and pons areas), are in synaptic contact with cranial and spinal nerves, so that the muscles of face, throat, chest, and diaphragm are coordinated for purposes of respiration. But these lower reflex mechanisms include also mechanisms originating in the peripheral nervous system and the cardiovascular system, these latter mechanisms being themselves subject to influences which have their origins in higher centers, i.e., subject to cortical control.
19. The control of behavioral and metabolic functions in respiration, though generally represented as separate, are in fact closely integrated physiological systems operating in parallel. These ''parallel structures'' function at most levels of the brain, with the behavioral portions of control mainly in somatomotor and limbic forebrain structures (Plum 1970:159, 174).
20. Different forms of speech entail different breathing patterns. According to Brown:

> An important function of the rhythm of speech is to allow us to continue to breathe while speaking. We require a complex pattern of breathing movements to modify our respiration so that speech can be produced. This includes movements of the abdomen and chest as well as of the larynx and upper airway. Our breathing must coordinate with the duration and intensity of what we wish to say, and all these factors must be taken into account before we begin to speak. (Brown 1991:39–40)

21. Bass and Gardner (1985) in a review of emotional influences on breathing point out that the category of ''hyperventilation syndrome'' is very problematic as there is no adequate basis for distinguishing it from hyperventilation itself (1985:601). They note that the term was introduced by Kerr *et al.* (1937) to cover an array of symptoms resulting from both anxiety and hyperventilation (Bass and Gardner 1985:602). They state that ''[m]ost of the clinical and physiological features of hyperventilation syndrome can occur in the absence of detectable psychiatric abnormality'' and the authors prefer the term ''idiopathic symptomatic hyperventilation'' (Bass and Gardner 1985:602).
22. Literature on the intentional generation of emotional responses using respiratory stimulus is generally located within work on the use of catharsis or abreaction in therapy. Both Lowry (1967b) and Lum (1976) cite B. I. Lewis on the relationship of hyperventilation to emotion. In patients suffering from anxiety attacks, Lewis found that when he reproduced the symptoms of hyperventilation in patients by pushing on the lower part of the chest to encourage thoracic breathing, after first putting the patient in a similar state of mind to that in which the original attacks occurred, in nearly all ''there was a marked emotional catharsis with weeping and revelation of important historical material'' (Lewis cited in Lowry 1967b:20).
23. Pfeffer notes that hyperventilation is said to affect between 6 and 11 percent of people seen by medical practitioners (1978:47).
24. Because of the wide range of symptoms, Lum notes ''[s]uch patients are often pursued relentlessly with every investigative device known to modern science, and end up with the label of 'anxiety state' '' (Lum 1975:375).
25. The effects of hyperventilation are generally divided according to whether they are central (e.g. alteration of blood gases, cerebrovascular changes, changes in acid–base balance) or peripheral effects (e.g., vasomotor effects such as vasoconstriction of vessels in the skin especially the extremities, reduced blood flow to the gut, etc.). For example, activation of the sympathetic nervous system produced by hyperventilation over a few minutes shows itself in dilated pupils, cold extremities, sweating of palms and axillae, and tachycardia (Lum 1976:207, 210). Whatever the physiological effects, however, it is clear that there is wide scope to the types of subjective experiences associated with these changes.
26. There have been other, earlier arguments for the value of the Jamesian approach. Wenger in 1950 argued for an integration of the findings of Cannon and Bard with those of James and Lange and for their further development: ''Emotion would be continuous, because autonomic activity is continuous, while the state of homeostasis would be regarded as a state of emotion, and we would speak of increased or decreased emotion from this basic pattern'' (Wenger 1950:5).
27. For one introduction to this, see Ewing (1901).
28. Yoga traditions themselves, for example, emphasize the importance of concentration, contemplation, scriptural study, and other practices in pursuit of goals, not just physical techniques which by themselves may lead to ''quite unforeseen and disturbing results such as mental disequilibrium'' (Zaehner 1966:72).
29. Wilhelm Reich, a psychoanalyst concerned with the somatic bases of neurosis, developed the concept of the location of psychological conflict or trauma in the musculoskeletal system as revealed in the carriage and expressions of the body (Kovel 1976:130). Bodily manipulation is said to help make a patient aware of how conflicts are held in the body and aid in their emotional expression, as well

as in the reemergence of early memories. Reich used overbreathing in combination with physical postures or exercises to aid in the expansion of the chest. Lowen, a student of Reich's, states: ''For Reich, then, the first step in the therapeutic procedure was to get the patient to breathe easily and deeply. The second was to mobilize whatever emotional expression was most evident in the patient's face or manner'' (Lowen 1975:19). Describing his own therapy with Reich, he says: ''I would lie on the bed and breathe as freely as I could, trying to allow a deep expiration to occur. I was directed to give in to my body and not control any expression or impulse that emerged'' (1975:19). Many schools of therapy utilize principles described by Reich, often in modified form. Freud and Breuer also, working long before Reich, utilized techniques (mainly hypnosis) designed to achieve abreaction of past trauma in patients.

30. One need only consult catalogs or directories of alternative therapies which are available in any large city for evidence of the many therapeutic techniques utilizing the breath. Grof (1988:170–184) contains a description of the use of ''intense breathing,'' which he terms ''holotropic'' breathing in the context of his own particular therapeutic perspective.
31. There are many studies of abreaction and catharsis in the psychological literature (see Nichols and Zax 1977 and Scheff 1979 for surveys). Scheff (1977, 1979), a sociologist, developed a theory of ritual based on catharsis, i.e., that ritual performs the function of providing a context for ''the appropriate distancing of emotion'' such that individuals can cope with ''universal emotional distresses'' (1977:484). He sees ritual in terms of how it functions in emotional expression: ''Effective ritual is the solution to a seemingly insoluble problem, the management of collectively held, otherwise unmanageable distress. Ritual is unique in that it meets individual and collective needs simultaneously, allowing individuals to discharge accumulated distress and creating social solidarity in the process'' (Scheff 1977:489).
32. A dance is performed which is said to activate *n/um* or energy in those who are healers. The intensification of this energy leads the dancer-healers to experience an enhanced consciousness called *!kia* during which they are able to heal others.
33. This posture also mirrors the bodily disposition of the child who reaches up and outward to embrace or be embraced. Such postures themselves have affective correlates which should be considered as part of the complex of bodily forms which are implicate in both the experience and generation of emotion. See de Rivera (1984) on the bodily disposition of the infant as one basis for a typology of emotions as social relations.
34. As Scheff (1988) has shown in his discussion of the social conformity studies, to be out of ''synch'' with the group of which one is a part can result in shame.

References

Barchas, Patricia. 1976. Physiological sociology: Interface of sociological and biological processes. *Annual Review of Sociology* 2:299–333.

Barchas, Patricia R. and Sally P. Mendoza, eds. 1984. *Social cohesion: Essays toward a socio-physiological perspective*. Westport, CT: Greenwood Press.

Bass, Christopher and William Gardner. 1985. Emotional influences on breathing and breathlessness. *Journal of Psychosomatic Research* 29(6):599–609.

Bell, Sir Charles. 1844. *Anatomy and philosophy of expression.* 3rd edn. (1st edn. 1806).

Benton, Ted. 1991. Biology and social science: Why the return of the repressed should be given a (cautious) welcome. *Sociology* 25(1):1–29.

Blacking, John. 1977. Toward an anthropology of the body. In *The anthropology of the body*, ed. John Blacking. London: Academic Press, 1–27.

Blalock, J. E. 1984. The immune system as a sensory organ. *Journal of Immunology* 132:1067–1070.

Bourdieu, Pierre. 1977. *Outline of a theory of practice.* Cambridge: Cambridge University Press.

Brown, Peter 1991. *The hypnotic brain: Hypnotherapy and social communication.* New Haven and London: Yale University Press.

Buytendijk, F. J. J. 1950. The phenomenological approach to the problem of feelings and emotions. In *Feelings and emotions: The mooseheart symposium*, ed. Martin L. Reymert. New York: McGraw Hill Book Co., Inc., 127–141.

Byers, P. 1976. Biological rhythms as information channels in interpersonal communication behavior. In *Perspectives in ethology II*, ed. P. P. G. Bateson and P. H. Klopfer. New York: Plenum, 141–157.

1982. Discussion. In *Interaction rhythms: Periodicity in communicative behavior*, ed. Martha Davis. New York: Human Sciences Press, Inc., 133–140.

Cannon, W. B. 1928. The mechanism of emotional disturbance of bodily functions. *New England Journal of Medicine* 198(17):877.

Cappo, Bruce M. and David S. Holmes. 1984. The utility of prolonged respiratory exhalation for reducing physiological and psychological arousal in non-threatening and threatening situations. *Journal of Psychosomatic Research* 28(4):265–273.

Collins, Randall. 1981. On the microfoundations of macrosociology. *American Journal of Sociology* 86:984–1014.

Csordas, Thomas J. 1990. Embodiment as a paradigm for anthropology. *Ethos* 18(1):5–47.

Darwin, Charles. 1965[1872]. *The expression of the emotions in man and animals.* Preface by Konrad Lorenz. Chicago: University of Chicago Press.

Davis, Martha, ed. 1982. *Interaction rhythms: Periodicity in communicative behavior.* New York: Human Sciences Press, Inc.

de Rivera, Joseph. 1984. The structure of emotional relationships. In *Review of personality and social psychology: Emotions, relationships, and health.* ed. Phillip Shaver. Beverly Hills: Sage, 116–145.

de Rivera, Joseph and Carmen Grinkis. 1986. Emotions as social relationships. *Motivation and Emotion* 10(4):351–369.

Durkheim, Emile. 1965[1915]. *The elementary forms of the religious life.* New York: The Free Press.

Ekman, P., R. W. Levenson, and W. V. Frieson. 1983. Autonomic nervous system activity distinguishes between emotions. *Science* 221:1208–1210.

Engel, G. L., E. B. Ferris, M. Logan. 1947. Hyperventilation: Analysis of clinical symptomatology. *Annals of International Medicine* 27(5):683.

Ewing, A. H. 1901. *The Hindu conception of the functions of breath: A study in early Hindu psycho-physics.* Dissertation. Johns Hopkins University.

Frank, Arthur W. 1990. Bringing bodies back in: A decade review. *Theory, Culture & Society* 7:131–162.

Geertz, Clifford. 1973. *The interpretation of cultures.* New York: Basic Books.

Gellhorn, Ernst and William F. Kiely. 1972. Mystical states of consciousness: Neurophysiological and clinical aspects. *The Journal of Nervous and Mental Disease* 154(6):399–405.

Gendlin, Eugene T. 1962. *Experiencing and the creation of meaning: A philosophical and psychological approach to the subjective.* Glencoe, IL: The Free Press of Glencoe.

Grene, Marjorie. 1968. *Approaches to a philosophical biology.* New York: Basic Books.

Grof, Stanislav. 1988. *The adventure of self-discovery: Dimensions of consciousness and new perspectives in psychotherapy and inner exploration.* Albany, NY: State University of New York Press.

Hall, Edward T. 1983. *The dance of life: The other dimensions of time.* New York: Anchor Books/Doubleday.

James, William. 1950[1890]. *The principles of psychology.* 2 vols. New York: Dover Publications.

1892. *Psychology.* (An abridgement of *Principles of Psychology.*) London: Macmillan and Co.

Johnson, Cone. 1967. The physiology of hyperventilation. In *Hyperventilation and hysteria: The physiology and psychology of overbreathing and its relationshiip to the mind-body problem*, ed. Thomas P. Lowry. Springfield, IL:. Charles C. Thomas, 34–104.

Katz, Richard. 1982. Accepting ''boiling energy'': The experience of !Kia healing among the !Kung. *Ethos* 10(4):344–368.

Kemper, Theodore D. 1978. Toward a sociology of emotions: Some problems and some solutions. *American Sociologist* 13(1):30–41.

1981. Social constructionist and positivist approaches to the sociology of emotions. *American Journal of Sociology* 87(2):336–362).

Kerr, W. J., J. W. Dalton, P. A. Gliebe. 1937. Some physical phenomena associated with the anxiety states and their relation to hyperventilation. *Annals of International Medicine.* 11:961.

Kiritz, S. and R. H. Moos. 1974. Physiological effects of social environment. *Psychosomatic Medicine* 36:96–114.

Kovel, Joel. 1976. *A complete guide to therapy: From psychoanalysis to behavior modification.* New York: Pantheon.

Lanzetta, J. T., J. Cartwright-Smith and R. L. Kleck. 1976. Effects of nonverbal dissimulation on emotional experience and autonomic arousal. *Journal of Personality and Social Psychology* 33:354–370.

LeDoux, Joseph E. 1986. The neurobiology of emotion. In *Mind and brain: Dialogues in cognitive neuroscience*, ed. J. E. LeDoux and W. Hirst. Cambridge: Cambridge University Press, 301–354.

Leeper, Robert W. 1948. A motivational theory of emotion to replace ''emotion as disorganized response.'' *The Psychological Review* 55(1):5–21.

Lowen, Alexander. 1975. *Bioenergetics.* New York: Penguin Books.

Lowry, T. P. 1967a. Introduction. In *Hyperventilation and hysteria*, ed. Thomas P. Lowry. Springfield, IL: Charles C. Thomas, 3–5.

1967b. The development of the concept of hyperventilation. In *Hyperventilation and hysteria*, ed. Thomas P. Lowry. Springfield, IL: Charles C. Thomas, 5–33.
1967c. A controlled questionnaire study of hyperventilation in military recruits. In *Hyperventilation and hysteria*, ed. Thomas P. Lowry. Springfield, IL: Charles C. Thomas, 105–117.
Lowry, T. P., ed. 1967. *Hyperventilation and hysteria: The physiology and psychology of overbreathing and its relationship to the mind-body problem*. Springfield, ILL: Charles C. Thomas.
Lum, L. C. 1975. Hyperventilation: The tip of the iceberg. *Journal of Psychosomatic Research* 19:375–383.
1976. The syndrome of habitual chronic hyperventilation. In *Modern trends in psychosomatic medicine*. Vol. 3, ed. Oscar Hill. London: Butterworth, 196–230.
Lutz, Catherine and Geoffrey M. White. 1986. The anthropology of emotions. *Annual Review of Anthropology* 15:405–436.
Lyon, M. L. 1993. Psychoneuroimmunology: The problem of the situatedness of illness and the conceptualization of healing. *Culture, Medicine, and Psychiatry* 17(1):77–97.
1994. Emotion as mediator of somatic and social processes: The example of respiration. *Social Perspectives on Emotion* (JAI Press) 2:83–108.
1995. Missing emotion: The limitations of cultural constructionism in the study of emotion. *Cultural Anthropology* 10(2):244–263.
1997. The material body, social processes, and emotion: ''Techniques of the Body'' revisited. *Body and Society* 3(1):83–101.
Lyon, M. L. and J. M. Barbalet. 1994. Society's body: Emotion and the ''somatization'' of social theory. In *Embodiment and experience: The existential ground of culture and self*, ed. T. J. Csordas. Cambridge: Cambridge University Press, 48–66.
Mathiot, Madeleine and Elizabeth Carlock. 1982. On operationalizing the notion of rhythm in social behavior. In *Interaction rhythms: Periodicity in communicative behavior*, ed. Martha Davis. New York: Human Sciences Press. 175–194.
Mauss, Marcel. 1973[1935]. Techniques of the body. Trans. Ben Brewster. *Economy and Society* 2(1):70–88.
Merleau-Ponty, Maurice. 1962[1946]. *The phenomenology of perception*. Trans. Colin Smith. London: Routledge & Kegan Paul.
Nichols, Michael P. and Melvin Zax. 1977. *Catharsis in psychotherapy*. New York: Gardner Press.
Onians, Richard Broxton. 1954. *The origins of European thought about the body, the mind, the soul, the world, time, and fate; new interpretations of Greek, Roman and kindred evidence, also of some basic Jewish and Christian beliefs. . .* 2nd ed. Cambridge: Cambridge University Press.
Papanicolaou, A. C. 1989. *Emotion: A reconsideration of the somatic theory*. New York: Gordon and Breach.
Pfeffer, J. M. 1978. The aetiology of the hyperventilation syndrome: A review of the literature. *Psychotherapy and Psychosomatics* 30:47–55.
Pickering, George. 1974. *Creative malady*. London: Allen and Unwin.
Plessner, Helmuth. 1970[1941]. *Laughing and crying: A study of the limits of human behavior*. Evanston: Northwestern University Press.
Plum, Fred. 1970. Neurological integration of behavioural and metabolic control of

breathing. In *Breathing: Hering-Breuer centenary symposium*, ed. Ruth Porter. London: J. & A. Churchill, 159–175.
1974. Cerebral control of breathing. In *Ventilatory and phonatory control systems*, ed. Barry Wyke. London: Oxford University Press, 208–217.
Plutchik, Robert. 1984. Emotions: A general psychoevolutionary theory. In *Approaches to emotion*, ed. Klaus Scherer and Paul Ekman. Hillsdale, NJ: Lawrence Erlbaum Associates, 197–219.
Reynolds, Peter C. 1981. *On the evolution of human behavior: The argument from animals to man*. Berkeley: University of California.
Rinn, W. E. 1984. The neuropsychology of facial expression: A review of the neurological and psychological mechanisms for producing facial expressions. *Psychological Bulletin* 95:52–77.
Roseman, Marina. 1990. Head, heart, odor, and shadow: The structure of self, the emotional world, and ritual performance among Senoi Temiar. *Ethos* 18(3):227–250.
Sargant, William. 1957. *Battle for the mind*. London: Heinemann.
1973. *The mind possessed: A physiology of possession, mysticism and faith healing*. London: Heinemann.
Scheff, Thomas J. 1977. The distancing of emotion in ritual. *Current Anthropology* 18(3):483–505.
1979. *Catharsis in healing, ritual, and drama*. Berkeley: University of California Press.
1988. Shame and conformity: The deference-emotion system. *American Sociological Review* 53:395–406.
Scherer, Klaus R. 1984. On the nature and function of emotion: A component process approach. In *Approaches to emotion*, ed. K. R. Scherer and P. Ekman. Hillsdale, NJ: Lawrence Erlbaum Associates, 293–317.
Schwartz, G. E., R. J. Davidson, D. J. Goffman. 1978. Patterning of cognitive and somatic processes in the self-regulation of anxiety: Effects of meditation versus exercise. *Psychosomatic Medicine* 40:321–328.
Sheets-Johnstone, Maxine. 1990. *The roots of thinking*. Philadelphia: Temple University Press.
Shweder, Richard A. 1984. Anthropology's romantic rebellion against the enlightenment, or there's more to thinking than reason and evidence. In *Culture theory: Essays on mind, self, and emotion*, ed. R. A. Shweder and R. A. LeVine. Cambridge: Cambridge University Press, 27–66.
Slonim, N. Balfour and Lyle H. Hamilton. 1976. *Respiratory physiology*. St. Louis: C. V. Mosby Co.
Stein, Marvin. 1967. Some psychophysiological considerations of the relationship between the autonomic nervous system and behavior. In *Neurophysiology and Emotion*, ed. David C. Glass. New York: The Rockefeller University Press and Russell Sage Foundation, 145–154.
Thoits, Peggy A. 1989. The sociology of emotions. *Annual Review of Sociology* 15:317–342.
Tomkins, Silvan S. 1962. *Affect, imagery, consciousness. Vol. I. The positive affects*. New York: Springer Publishing Company.
Varela, F. J., A. Coutinho, B. Dupire, N. N. Vaz. 1988. Cognitive networks: Immune,

neural, and otherwise. In *Theoretical Immunology*, ed. A. S. Perelson. New York: Addison-Wesley Publishing Company, 172–185.

Wallace, R. K. 1970. Physiological effects of transcendental meditation. *Science* 167: 1751–54.

Wellenkamp, Jane C. 1988. Order and disorder in Toraja thought and ritual. *Ethnology* 27(3):311–326.

Wenger, M. A. 1950. Emotion as visceral action: An extension of Lange's theory. In *Feelings and emotions: The Mooseheart Symposium*, ed. Martin L. Reymert. New York: McGraw Hill Book Co., Inc., 3–10.

Wentworth, William and James Ryan, eds. 1994. *Social perspectives on emotion, Vol. 2*. Greenwich, CN.: JAI Press.

Wrong, Dennis. 1961. The oversocialized conception of man in modern sociology. *American Sociological Review* 26:183–193.

Zaehner, R. C. 1966. *Hinduism*. London: Oxford University Press.

Part III

Biocultural synergy

6 Affecting experience: Toward a biocultural model of human emotion

Keith E. McNeal

The great natural variation of cultural forms is, of course, not only anthropology's great (and wasting) resource, but the ground of its deepest theoretical dilemma: how is such variation to be squared with the biological unity of the human species? Clifford Geertz (1973:22)

Human emotion: A paradox of sameness and difference

Any perusal of the literature on human emotions is apt to elicit the well-known fight-or-flight response in the interested reader. Research on the emotions is diverse, sometimes conflicting, and very rarely complementary (at least explicitly so). The issue of human emotionality lands one smack in the middle of the familiar Cartesian problem of reconciling bodily (physiological) phenomena with mental (psychological) phenomena. Any discourse on emotion, I hope to show, must deal head-on with interrelated issues concerning cognition, consciousness, and evaluative appraisal. Yet, as Damasio (1994) has recently argued, reason is dependent upon feeling and emotion. This chapter therefore aims to bridge the contributions of biological, psychological, and anthropological research on human emotions, and to initiate a serious dialogue by laying conceptual groundwork for more integrated future discussions. I wish to outline a biocultural model of human emotion that attempts to do justice to emotionality in its full dynamic complexity.

But what does it mean that humans are *biocultural* organisms? Geertz suggests that "man's nervous system does not merely enable him to acquire culture, it positively demands that he do so if it is going to function at all" (1973:68). The rapidly developing postnatal human nervous system is crucially dependent upon sensory input from its environment, and this "developmental microniche" is neurally mediated by experientially derived cognitive schemas.[1] Though Geertz affirms that humans evolved in a synergistic biocultural milieu, he also makes it clear that emotions themselves are "cultural artifacts" (1973:81) which differ significantly cross-culturally. Thus any conceptualization of emotion must account for variation – both its *inter*cultural and *intra*cultural forms. Biological anthropologists tend to see their analytical task as one of explaining axes of variation. Cultural anthropologists often seem more satisfied with simply documenting ''the great natural variation of cultural forms,'' to use Geertz's phrase quoted at the outset. The social scientific literature on emotion tends to oscillate between (a) a psychobiological posture which views emotions as innate, universal psychobiological processes that are invariant across cultural contexts; and (b) a sociocultural constructionist point of view which takes a meaning-centered stance and views emotions as arising from culturally mediated processes which shape emotions in distinctly different ways (Lutz and White 1986; Lazarus 1991). I hope to demonstrate that human emotional dynamics are so complex that they can be analyzed in divergent ways, allowing for *both* universalists and relativists alike to substantiate their claims.

To be sure, cultural anthropologists have good reason for critiquing the psychobiological view which would claim that emotions are everywhere the ''same.'' But biologists and psychologists have equally good reason for critiquing the ''culturally muscular'' perspective of some anthropologists that pushes for a view of emotions as only culturally relative or culturally constructed.[2] I suggest that an explicit synthesis of the varying perspectives might help not only to alleviate some of the debate between these dichotomized points of view, but also to make explanation of variation realistically possible. As Geoffrey Samuel observes: ''Even those who are prepared to accept the reality of mind–body interaction are often much less prepared to accept the conceptual shift that is implied by that interaction'' (1990:96).

A biocultural approach to human emotion has the potential to account for both intercultural commonalities *and* variation by incorporating the bodily basis for emotionality – namely human biophysiology, the structure of the limbic system, and nervous and neuroendocrinological processes. Emotions can be usefully viewed as *fluctuating, biocommunicative states that are elicited contextually through ongoing cognitive processes of evaluation and differentially labeled, emphasized, or ignored through the influence of culture and individual experience.* The human perceptual apparatus continually evaluates the status of the organism in its socioecological niche, so affective feeling-states are implicated in the overall orientational processes of maintaining the organism's well-being in relation to its milieu. By focusing on organismic situational evaluation and intrasubjective labeling, we appreciate the indispensable role of cultural knowledge in the dynamic emotional process, for evaluation and labeling are fundamentally dependent upon experientially learned, culturally mediated cognitive processes. By exploring cross-cultural variation in intersubjective patterns of knowledge and evaluation, one can demonstrate that human emotionality is both contingently variable and yet experientially shared.

A powerful illustration of the role of culturally mediated interpretation in the emotional process can be found in *culture-bound syndromes* (CBSs). Prince and Tcheng-Laroche define a culture-bound syndrome as "a collection of signs and symptoms (excluding notions of cause) which is restricted to a limited number of cultures, primarily by reason of their psychosocial features" (1987:4). The problem of CBSs is a complicated one well beyond the scope of this chapter.[3] I raise the issue, however, to observe that CBSs seem to be a fruitful area of inquiry not only to deal with the issue of interpretive evaluation and labeling in the emotional process, but also because CBSs seem to represent an interesting tension between psychobiological universalism and sociocultural particularism.[4]

Take, for example, the Japanese psychiatric syndrome known as *taijin-kyofu-sho* (TKS) (reviewed by Honda 1983, and Prince and Tcheng-Laroche 1987), which literally means "fear of other people." TKS does not imply that one wants to avoid other persons because one fears them out of threat or intimidation – what a North American might think of as social phobia – but rather because one fears losing the approval of others *by putting burdens upon them or of asking too much of them*. Thus TKS is a social phobia, but it entails a fear of offending or of hurting others (Prince and Tcheng-Laroche 1987:9). Even when this type of social anxiety does not manifest in its extreme form as TKS, we know that "the most frequently experienced negative emotion among the Japanese is a fear of causing trouble or of burdening someone else" (Markus and Kitayama 1994:116). TKS contrasts with Anglo-American psychiatric social phobias or persecutory psychoses; the TKS patient believes that s/he is harming or offending others, and does not believe her/his fear is excessive or unreasonable. The social fears characteristic of TKS make sense in light of Japanese prosocial values of relationality and group interdependence (on Japanese ethnopsychology, see Doi 1981, 1986; Roland 1988; Tobin *et al.* 1989; Markus and Kitayama 1991, 1994; Rosenberger 1992). Thus, TKS fears have to do with not wanting to let others down, putting too much of a burden upon others, being too demanding, and therefore shaming oneself. This is different from modal Anglo-American social fears in which the individual is afraid of not being strong enough or enough of an individual, and therefore is easily intimidated by everyday social interaction. The American cultural value of individualism is reflected in the distinctly high scores of Americans on self-reflexive false uniqueness scales (see Markus and Kitayama 1994).

It would be misguided, I think, to say that TKS and modal Anglo-American social phobias do not have *anything* in common. Precisely because of a pan-human ability to be afraid or fear, and to feel shame and anxiety, it is possible to group together various modalities of "fearing" so that they may be compared and contrasted. To study fear cross-culturally, therefore, one must appreciate both shared existential commonalities *as well as* variation due to the work of sociocultural structuring and elaboration. I have raised the problem of CBSs in order to illustrate that within the complex domain of emotional dynamics one may emphasize either of two divergent perspectives. The universalist points out that fear is a human universal, and even that social phobias are cross-culturally prevalent; a relativist or particularist could emphasize the particular cultural matrix in which a social phobia such as TKS is grounded, emphasizing that social phobias are qualitatively variable and in some sense incommensurable cross-culturally.

From a biocultural standpoint the issue becomes far more interesting: how are particular emotional states embedded, modified, elaborated, or even diminished in particular cultural, intersubjective, personally salient matrices? Instead of asking whether particular emotions are the same or different, it is more interesting and – it would seem – more realistic to explore how the human organism is situated, both individually and intersubjectively, in contexts that significantly influence emotional processing. Consider the findings of Levenson *et al.* (1992) from work with the Minangkabau of West Sumatra, Indonesia: while both American and Minangkabau subjects exhibited similar correlations between mimicked positive and negative facial expressions and corresponding changes in autonomic nervous system activity, *only* Americans tended to report corresponding changes in subjective feeling. The correlation between autonomic activity and related facial expression would seem to suggest some level of neurophysiological organismic wiring shared by both Americans and Minangkabau. Minangkabau subjects most likely had difficulty consciously experiencing or describing such changes in feeling state because they were alone and not in socially appropriate contexts, suggesting complicated interactive affective processes at work. Such data call for a sophisticated processual analysis that bypasses simplistic dichotomies.

This chapter is structured around the paradox of sameness and difference in human emotions. I review fundamental concepts from neurobiology and evolutionary theory, and I attempt to show how *the paradox of sameness and difference is, quite literally, built into the human nervous system.* I address the psychology debate about the primacy of affect, and suggest how this controversy relates to the problem of sameness and difference in human emotions. I readdress the problem of variation in the anthropological literature on emotions, and situate this problem with reference to human learning and culture acquisition. The problematic paradox this chapter addresses is shown to revolve around, as well as find resolution in, the ongoing status of cognitive evaluation and labeling. I end not only with an argument that biologists and psychologists take culture seriously, but also that cultural anthropologists take biology seriously.

In exploring this problematic paradox, for heuristic purposes I develop a computer-processing metaphor by viewing human neurobiology as ''emotional hardware'' and socioculturally learned knowledge as ''emotional software.'' Thus, all humans share a species-level genetic makeup which contributes toward the building of a body equipped for general, pan-human neurobiological processing of affect. But like computer hardware, the human nervous system does not run randomly or on account of its own inherent commands; on the contrary, the nervous system continuously evaluates and processes inputs from the external socioecological niche and from one's internal physiological milieu. Evaluation depends substantially upon the ''software'' of experientially learned knowledge ''stored'' in the nervous system (what cognitive scientists call schemas or neural networks).[5] In other words, organismic interpretive evaluation – whether conscious or not – is always mediated by prior developmental, sociocultural learning. As Worthman puts it, ''the nervous system is *not* preinterpretive'' (1992:153; cf. Neisser 1976). Modulation of nervous system functioning then becomes subject to wide-ranging cultural cognitive variation. Humans have a core set of emotions shaped through hominid evolution that has been selected to respond to recurrent existential situations of human life (Hamburg 1963; Alexander 1990; Tooby and Cosmides 1990). The important key here is that – as neotenous, plastic creatures – humans depend upon intersubjectivity to construe their worlds, and therefore one must always consider the sociocultural side of experience as much as the biological (Hallowell 1955). This becomes acutely apparent when we concede that culture is, at some level, biological and that biology is always culturally situated.

Taking biology seriously

Many non-biologists need to realize that a folk biological view of the body as static and ''written in the genes'' is contrary to the view of modern human biology (see, e.g., Dawkins 1982; Oyama 1985). I discuss neurobiological makeup here because it constitutes the fundamental hardware of emotional processing.

The emotional brain

Around the turn of the century, experimental research found that animals deprived of cerebral cortex exhibited appropriate emotional reactions, seemingly implying that emotional processing was not dependent on neocortical brain structures.[6] In consequence, there was a developing theory from the end of the nineteenth century which postulated – in contrast to the view of William James that there were no special emotional centers of the brain – that different mental faculties such as language or emotion were situated in different parts of the brain (LeDoux 1986; Izard 1990). An extremely important figure for the neuroanatomy of emotions was James Papez who, in 1937, suggested that what was soon to be called the *limbic system* was in charge of the emotional aspects of life. It was known that the reticular formation – which ascends from the brainstem toward the brain and branches out into the cortex – was involved in wakefulness, awareness, integration, and arousal, and that input from various parts of the body converged in the lower parts of the brain and diverged from there out over a range of cerebral regions. The brain was seen as built up, both in the individual and phylogenetically, by successively added layers which cover and integrate lower layers (Vincent 1990:99).

Thus it was in 1937 that Papez proposed a brain mechanism of emotion centered around the hypothalamus.[7] He further postulated that sensory input from the environment reached the thalamus, and from there branched into three separate directions (this idea was accurate – Winson 1985; LeDoux 1986): (a) to the sensory cortex – what Papez called the ''stream of thought''; (b) to the basal ganglia as the ''stream of movement''; and (c) to the hypothalamus, giving rise to the ''stream of feeling.'' Papez proposed that emotions arise via the loop initiated after sensory input is relayed by the thalamus to the hypothalamus. He thought emotional information traveled in a circular fashion from the hypothalamus to the anterior thalamus, cingulate cortex, association cortex, hippocampus, and back to the hypothalamus. The hypothalamus could be activated by direct thalamic relay or indirectly via higher cortical processes, adding emotional coloration to ''raw'' sensory input. Because the association cortex is connected to the hippocampus and hypothalamus, Papez thought cortical processes could elicit downward bodily emotional discharge. Many of these connections have been verified, and – although the whole functional loop is not completely confirmed – Papez's hypothesis has been extremely influential.

In the mid-part of the twentieth century, Paul MacLean, borrowing heavily from Papez's model, put forward the notion of a *limbic system* which serves as the integrating center of internal sensory input and processed inputs from the external environment. This latter segment of the process, in which sensory input from the external environment – both social and non-social – is integrated and entails autonomic nervous functioning, is where one encounters the profound influence of cultural learning. Variation in evaluation of input is influenced by cultural learning and experience, and this has direct relevance for overall affects since evaluation of input is mediated by cognitive knowledge structures variously referred to as cognitive schemas, cultural models, or dispositional representations (see Casson 1983; D'Andrade 1984, 1989, 1990; and Damasio 1994).

MacLean's conception of a hierarchy of three brains – the ''triune brain'' –

was important in that it located the middle, ''visceral'' brain as the seat of emotional functioning.[8] He saw the evolution of the nervous system as having developed according to three basic patterns which he called reptilian, paleomammalian, and neomammalian, each having a ''radically different'' structure and chemistry (MacLean 1980:32; cf. also MacLean 1963). As we shall see in the debate over the primacy of affect, this division of the brain into three domains continues to influence researchers who view affect as stemming from the middle paleomammalian brain structures. Debates about the primacy of affect and the role of cognition often center around the amount of work the paleomammalian brain is considered to do in relation to the neomammalian brain in emotional processing (these issues will be discussed in the following section).

MacLean viewed the reptilian brain as including the reticular formation and striate cortex, and characterized it as the seat of the survival behavior patterns of the individual and the species. The behaviors that it commands are automatic and invariable, mediated by ''innate'' dispositional representations or schemas.[9] One of the major components of the reptilian brain is the striatal complex/corpus striatum, to which most parts of the neocortex and limbic lobe project (MacLean 1980:30). The limbic lobe conforms and molds closely to the corpus striatum; the corpus striatum, in turn, is indirectly connected to the thalamus (which we now know sends information to both limbic structures and the neocortex; LeDoux 1986 and Winson 1985) and other brain structures.

The paleomammalian brain corresponds to what MacLean called the limbic system, which has been referred to as the seat of emotions and motives, and is capable of responding to present information in the light of memories of past information.[10] MacLean characterized the limbic system as a key-ring structure opening upward toward the neocortex and downward toward the brainstem. The best evidence for the limbic system's role in emotional behavior is derived from clinical observations that ''[n]euronal discharges in or near the limbic cortex of the temporal lobe may trigger a broad spectrum of vivid, affective feelings'' (MacLean 1980:20). Case histories of limbic epilepsy indicate that the limbic system is basic for affective feelings of the reality of self and environment, and disruptions of its functions can result in changes of mood, distortions of perceptions, feelings of depersonalization, hallucinations, and paranoid delusions. Limbic seizures tend to spread within but confine themselves to the limbic system, which is why MacLean has frequently referred to the ''schizophysiology'' of the limbic system and neocortex.[11] It is not clear how various sensory and perceptual phenomena are generated by limbic discharges; however, we do know that visual, auditory, somatic, and visceral information reaches respective parts of the limbic lobe by rather direct subcortical pathways (MacLean 1980:23).

It is important to note that sensory information is probably integrated and processed in limbic cortical structures before being passed on to the hypothalamus (*ibid.*:27). The role of the hippocampus is also crucial. Not only is the hippocampus significantly related to memory (Winson 1985), but there is also evidence that hippocampal stimulation – depending on physiological state at the time of stimulation – may have facilitative or inhibitory effects on hormonal release, cardiovascular reflexes, and visceral responsiveness. The hippocampal formation is associated with dreaming and other manifestations of REM sleep, and intero- and exteroceptive information can interact in the hippocampal formation to influence hypothalamic and other brainstem structures involved in the physiological regulation of emotional behavior (MacLean 1980:29–30).

The neomammalian brain is represented by the neocortex, "the brain of anticipation, capable of choosing the response to a stimulus according to what the result will be and also in light of the past" (Vincent 1990:105). This part of the brain is more adaptable and allows higher vertebrates more behavioral freedom. The reptilian brain's striate cortex connects afferent spinal cord neurons with the limbic system and neocortex "which envelop it like a mould" (*ibid.*). The neocortex underwent great expansion relatively late in evolution, and MacLean states that "[t]he evolutionary ascendancy of these systems indicates that *the neocortex is primarily oriented toward the external environment*" (1980:15, italics added). Specific areas of the neocortex are respectively related to the somatic, auditory, and visual systems, and these cortical systems are essential for normal perception. The neocortex makes humans unique, with an extraordinary development of regions specialized for the processing of messages from the outside world and in the ordering of movements. Motor, sensory, associative, and other neocortical areas are regionally specialized but work in conjunction with each other. In MacLean's view, progressive evolutionary encephalization led to a neomammalian brain which is the seat of rationality, functioning relatively independently of the lower brains which it envelops. Vincent, however, warns against a too-rigorous partitioning of different brain areas and their functioning: "It is too much of a simplification to suggest that the reptilian brain marches off to war while the neomammalian brain gives speeches for peace" (1990:105). Damasio (1994), in addition to Plutchik (1980, 1990), has also argued persuasively that the capacity for cognition has evolved in the service of emotions – a psychodynamic view, to be sure.

Current knowledge of the limbic system

The limbic system as currently viewed consists of both cortical and subcortical forebrain structures, and this dovetails with descriptions by Broca, Papez, and MacLean. Cortical areas do not belong to the neocortex but belong to "more primitive zones with less laminar definition than neocortex" (LeDoux 1986:331). Research shows that rich interconnections exist within various subdivisions of a given area and between subdivisions of different areas.

Exteroceptive sensory inputs to the limbic system allow information from the environment to influence limbic activity, and this is mediated by variously derived cognitive schemas. Exteroceptive sensory information reaches limbic areas by two routes. First, this input reaches limbic areas via connections that diverge from ascending sensory projection pathways before reaching neocortical areas (after thalamic relay). *These pathways allow "crude" sensory inputs to reach limbic areas rapidly and without neocortical intervention.* The second path of exteroceptive sensory input is via descending connections from sensory processing areas of neocortex.[12] Each neocortical sensory system sends projections to the hippocampus and amygdala by way of intermediate cortical association zones, and this input is distributed throughout the limbic system. Interoceptive (viscerosensory) inputs, such as from abdominal viscera and the vagus nerve, also reach limbic areas (see Figures 6.1 and 6.2).

There are numerous outputs from limbic areas to autonomic control regions, and many include pathways to the hypothalamus which, in turn, has connections to brainstem areas controlling the autonomic nervous system and to spinal preganglionic motor neurons. Inputs from limbic regions to the hypothalamus allow activity in these areas to influence autonomic nervous activity. The amygdala and insular areas also have *direct* connections to brainstem autonomic regions. "Limbic regions are richly interconnected, thus supporting the notion that limbic areas function as a system" (LeDoux 1986:333). Papez's classic notion that the hypothalamus projects to the anterior thalamus is now well established, as well as cingulate cortex connections with neocortical areas involved in higher-order perceptual and cognitive processing. Outputs of most limbic subsystems are distributed to other limbic areas as well as to hypothalamic exit points (*ibid.*).

We can now see that figures such as Papez and MacLean were not misguided in looking toward mid-brain limbic structures for clues to the neurobiology of emotional information processing. I have reviewed some basic neurobiology in order to demonstrate that the "hardware" of emotional processing is quite complicated and dynamic. I noted that the ongoing modulation of this hardware is importantly mediated by neural schemas derived from individual experience. I will return explicitly to this problem below where I will argue that cognitive schemas built up through experience, and therefore subject to sociocultural mediation, provide a crucial dynamic in the organism's ongoing evaluation of itself in the world. *Variations in culturally mediated evaluation give rise to the variable shaping of bodily feeling states.*

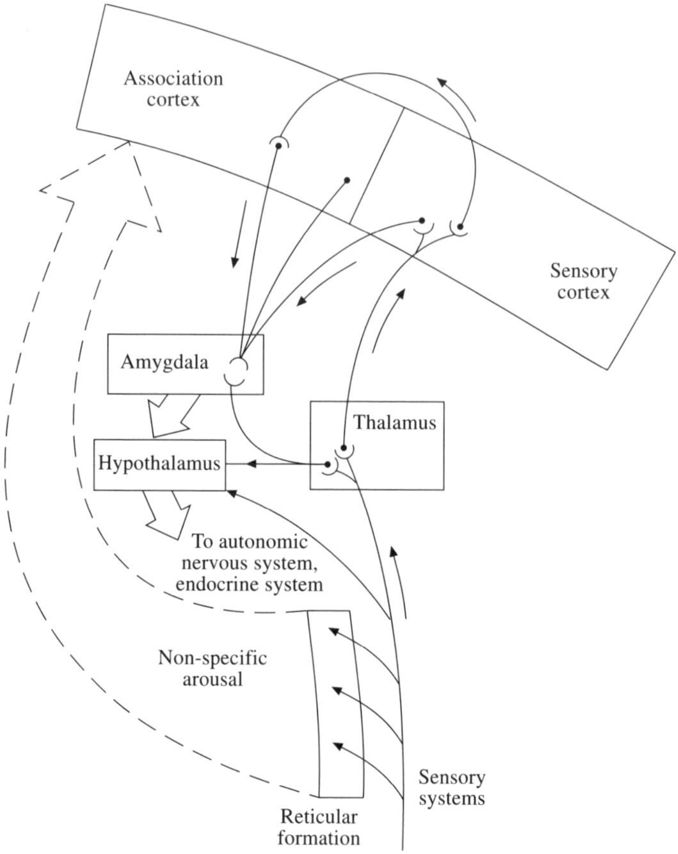

Figure 6.1. A neurobiological model of appraisal.
Source: From Buck 1988, Figure 9.1.

Since the nervous system is not preinterpretive, and indeed is dependent upon cultural cognitive schemas, the neurobiological harddrive of the human body comes under the direct modulation and influence of socioculturally mediated knowledge. Along with Geertz, we come to appreciate the importance of cultural ''software'' as a necessary aspect of human experience. After briefly discussing some ethnographic evidence which suggests why cultural anthropologists might take biology seriously, I will next introduce the psychology debate over the primacy of affect, suggest how it can be resolved, and illustrate the importance of interpretation in the emotional process.

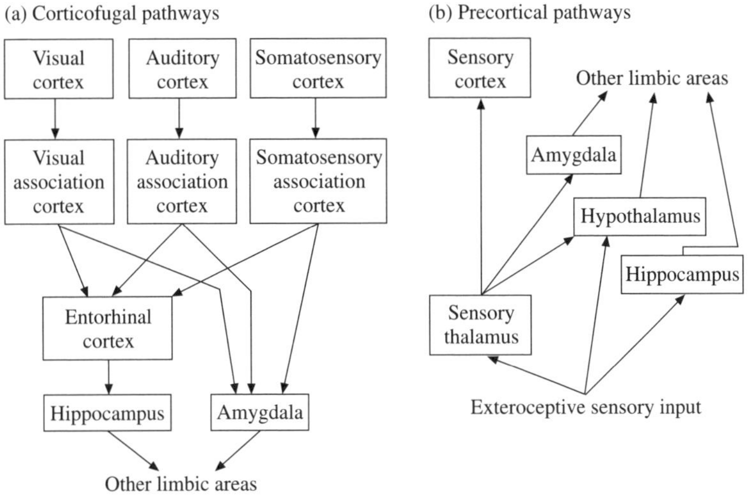

Figure 6.2. Exteroceptive sensory input to the limbic system. Sensory input from the external environment reaches the limbic system by several routes. (a) Sensory nuclei in the thalamus relay incoming signals to sensory receptive areas of the cortex. By way of corticocortical connections, the input is transmitted to modality specific association areas and then by way of transitional cortical areas to the hippocampus and amygdala. Each of these areas has extensive connections with other limbic structures. (b) In addition to relaying incoming signals to cortical receiving areas, some thalamic areas send projections directly to the amygdala and hypothalamus. There is also evidence for direct projections from peripheral receptor organs (retinal ganglion cells) to the hypothalamus and possibly the hippocampus.
Source: From LeDoux 1986, Figure 15.8

Taking biology seriously from an ethnographic point of view

The view articulated in this chapter argues against a radical relativist or purely social constructionist perspective. Indeed, what I believe to be anthropology's most productive contribution to the study of human emotionality is a sophisticated analysis of the paradox of sameness and difference inherent within the domain of the emotions. As Renato Rosaldo has written, ''warnings against facile notions of universal human nature can, however, be carried too far and harden into the equally pernicious doctrine that, my own group aside, everything human is alien to me. One hopes to achieve a balance between recognizing wide-ranging human differences and the modest truism that any two human groups must have certain things in common'' (1989:10).

There is good cross-cultural evidence for shared emotionality across populations, not least of which is the anthropologist's own ability to actually do fieldwork.

We must first of all work *against* the fallacy that serious recognition of cultural variation entails a radically relativist or completely cultural constructionist point of view (cf. Spiro 1984, 1990, 1992; see fn. 2 above). Moreover, ethnographic evidence suggests deeply shared emotional aspects of human phenomenological experience. Consider R. Rosaldo's discussion (1989) of the rage of grief in Ilongot head-hunting. Rosaldo emphasizes it was only after the death of his wife Michelle Rosaldo that he could fully appreciate how Ilongot men would feel such intense rage during bereavement. Rosaldo writes that it was a certain degree of shared experience – losing someone one is deeply attached to – which allowed him to more fully relate to Ilongots and their repertoire of affective experience. Rosaldo, however, nevertheless also points out that his culturally mediated response to his wife's death did not eventually lead him into a head-hunting expedition. Thus here we observe a concrete case of the paradox of sameness and difference in human emotional dynamics, and it is also tribute to an analogous paradox with regard to psychodynamic mechanisms of defense (cf. Nesse and Lloyd 1992).

There are other forms of ethnographic evidence which help triangulate upon the problem of conceptualizing human emotionality in its full complexity. Here I would like to briefly highlight evidence which suggests the importance of appreciating *shared* human emotionality in counterpoint to those aspects of this chapter which argue forcefully for attentiveness to culturally mediated variability. First, studies by Paul Ekman and his colleagues (Ekman 1974, 1980, 1989, 1992; Ekman *et al.* 1983; Levenson *et al.* 1992) have demonstrated seemingly pan-human correlations between facial expression of emotion and autonomic nervous system activity, correlations which I believe should be taken seriously and not swept under the conceptual carpet if one attempts to think hard about emotion and culture. These studies can be related in interesting ways to suggestive relations that have been found between emotion terms and colors. A series of studies since the 1970s of the association between emotion terms and Munsell color chips (discussed in D'Andrade 1990) demonstrates that informants in four different cultures tend to select similar chips out of various arrays as the best examples of translations of the English emotion terms *happy*, *sad*, *angry*, and *frightened*. There is also considerable agreement among all four cultures on which color chips are *good*, *bad*, *strong*, and *weak*. This is the type of provocative cross-cultural evidence that strongly relativistic cultural anthropologists must come to terms with. To be sure, as D'Andrade writes: "This is not to say there are no cultural differences. However, the cultural differences seem to be small compared to the general similarity in emotional response to colors" (1990:74).

Another set of cross-cultural evidence, I think, is important for developing an adequate biocultural model of human emotions: psychiatric syndromes, political economy, and gender. Though this issue deserves a full chapter of its own, it is worth emphasizing cross-cultural epidemiological evidence which documents that women disproportionately suffer from depression relative to men (discussed in Jenkins 1996). Jenkins, Kleinman, and Good (1991) conclude from their review of the available literature on cross-cultural susceptibility to depression that the disproportionate degree of depression among women is likely to be universal. "This disturbing conclusion," Jenkins writes, "must be accounted for in the light of gender inequality conferring less power and status to women relative to men in both Western and non-Western countries" (1996:85). These findings not only point to gender inequalities in the political economy of affect but they also substantiate views (e.g., Nesse 1990b; Nesse and Lloyd 1992) which suggest pan-human emotional responses to social inequality and low status in group hierarchies.

I would like to make one last point with regard to appreciating sameness in the paradox of sameness and difference in human emotional dynamics. Consider the provocative findings of Rosenblatt *et al.* (1976) in their survey of bereavement and emotional expression in seventy-three societies. Using the Human Relations Area Files, the authors found that – in seventy-two of seventy-three societies surveyed – grief was expressed by crying in at least some bereaved persons. The only exception was found among Balinese, whom the authors believe have learned to suppress cathartic and expressive weeping in response to loss and bereavement (see Geertz 1973:360–411 on Balinese notions of personhood and conduct). This survey is particularly interesting in that it revealed almost overwhelming evidence for bereaved crying across seventy-three populations. The problem is what to make of the Balinese exception – does one downplay it, highlight it, or leave it in limbo? If social scientists are to develop an adequate biocultural model of human emotions, I believe that *all* seventy-three societies should be taken seriously. In the Rosenblatt *et al.* survey we encounter powerful reasons to take *both* biology and culture seriously.

Robert Levy's influential work (e.g., 1973, 1978, 1984) in psychological anthropology is helpful in this regard. Levy argued that Tahitians seem to experience that emotion which English speakers label *sadness* as a response to the loss of an important or valued relationship. Levy has referred to this emotional experience as resulting from primary appraisal of an individual's situation. However, for complicated socioecological reasons, Tahitians generally ignore this aspect of pan-human phenomenological experience. In doing so, Tahitians are culturally inclined to label their subjective experience as something other than sadness, usually illness. Thus, in Levy's terms, sadness is "hypocognized" in Tahitian culture, in contrast to anger, which is "hypercognized."

Levy's analysis is very helpful here with reference to the Balinese, and for a fuller biocultural model of human emotion more generally, because his model recognizes ''hard-wired'' human appraisals of situations that lead to pan-human emotional experiences at the *same* time that the model also accentuates the powerful work of culture to shape, elaborate, or ignore certain subjective states. Whereas all humans, in this view, have the capacity to make certain situational appraisals which entail certain phenomenological consequences, culture has an equally powerful and important role in influencing how individuals process, label, and manage such phenomenological consequences. How ''natives'' interpret and label their subjective emotional states has important influences upon all aspects of behavior relating to a given emotional state, and has profound consequences within the intersubjective arenas within which people interact. Thus, the loss of a loved one has both similar *and* dissimilar emotional entailments in different cultural frames, and may set very different behaviors into motion – such as an American getting a psychotherapist, an Ilongot taking part in a head-hunt, or a Trobriand Islander propitiating potentially malevolent spirits of the dead. By acknowledging how universally human situations and the psychobiological dimensions of emotional hardware are differentially ignored or emphasized, we help to facilitate the creation of a ''biologically grounded constructionism'' (cf. Worthman, this volume; Chisholm, this volume).[13]

The primacy of affect problem

The evaluation of sensory input is a crucial component in the elicitation of emotional processes (Levy 1984; Mandler 1984; Westen 1985; Lazarus 1991). As neurobiologist Joseph LeDoux writes: ''[F]or any emotional reaction to an environmental stimulus to take place, the significance of the stimulus must first be assessed. Only on the basis of such an evaluation can the brain regulate the peripheral nervous system in a manner that is appropriate to the meaning of the stimulus. *Stimulus evaluation precedes and constitutes the basis of emotional expression*'' (LeDoux 1986:334–335, italics added). The theory of William James and Carl Lange, by contrast, postulated that an emotional stimulus produces both visceral and skeletal muscle changes, and that these alone are the source of the subjective experience of emotion. They believed there to be no intervening cognition of an emotional stimulus that precedes bodily response; in fact, in their view the bodily response to assessment of sensory input *is* the emotion (*ibid.*:304; see also Buck 1986:285).

Walter Cannon (1931), by contrast, theorized incorrectly that the critical subcortical mechanism involved in assessment and emotional response was the thalamus. He thought that the influence of peripheral bodily changes on emotional experience was quite small. In contrast to James and Lange, Cannon followed the tradition of locating the seat of emotional processing in internal brain structures. Then Papez suggested in 1937 that physical expression of emotion involved the hypothalamus, which, in turn, controlled the autonomic and endocrine systems, while the experience of emotion involved the limbic system. This theory is now widely accepted, as discussed in the previous section, and is consistent with many studies of brain functioning in humans and other animals.

As emotional processing gradually became associated with paleomammalian limbic structures, the thorny issue of the interaction of emotion and cognition emerged. Emotion is often associated with subcortical limbic structures, as is cognition with neocortical functions; it is taken for granted that limbic structures play a crucial role in emotional processing. The contested issue, therefore, has to do with the role of cognition in the emotional process. Different theorists conceive of ''cognition'' in various ways, however, and this variance tends to obfuscate the dialogue concerning the psychology of emotion.

The self-attribution theory of Schacter (Schacter and Singer 1962) postulated that emotions are bodily sensations accompanied by cognitive interpretation. Schacter's theory echoed Papez's view that processing of sensory input diverges, thus giving rise to a stream of feeling and a stream of thought. This perspective is in line with evidence which shows that the significance of a stimulus is often evaluated at subconscious levels, with only the consequences of evaluation reaching consciousness (Zajonc 1980). Strong evidence for unconscious processing also comes from various domains such as non-verbal *emotional contagion* (Hatfield *et al.* 1994).[14] Libet and his colleagues have demonstrated that while incoming sensory information takes just 15–25 milliseconds to reach the brain, we become conscious of it only a half-second *later* (Libet *et al.* 1979). We also know that rapid, even complex, behavioral responses that arise in the interim lag period do so un- or preconsciously (Libet 1978). ''Thus, subjective perception ('consciousness') is in many essential ways a pre-edited, preconscious construct. Recognition that the brain operates through multiple parallel processing, of which subjective consciousness represents only a small segment, has reinforced the notion of a 'plurality of consciousness' '' (Worthman 1992:154). The issue is further complicated by the fact that emotions and behavioral responses are subject to filtering, elaboration, and repression due to culturally constituted *feeling/display rules* (Hochschild 1979; Ekman 1980, 1992).[15]

Some theorists interpret the evidence that a stimulus can be evaluated at subconscious levels and give rise to various feeling-states – that ''feeling does not require thinking'' (Zajonc 1980) – as giving force to the *primacy of affect*. Scholars who assert the primacy of affect believe cognition is secondary to emotion, thus the importance of engaging the psychology debate on the so-called ''primacy of affect'' stems from its relevance to a biocultural theory of emotionality. Unpacking various emphases on affective primacy allows a fully biocultural model to better account for the cultural complexities in emotional variation observed across populations. *If one can demonstrate that emotion is not "primary" but fundamentally modulated by cognitive processes of evaluation and appraisal, then we quickly open up the human emotional repertoire to substantial cross-cultural variation through the role of specifically* cultural *cognition.*

Studies by Robert Zajonc and colleagues suggest that an individual can respond preferentially to stimuli before consciously knowing what those stimuli are (Kunst-Wilson and Zajonc 1980; Zajonc *et al.* 1989; Murphy and Zajonc 1993). Zajonc thus argues that affect occurs prior to, and independently of, cognition. His view is that initial emotional responses – what he calls *preferenda* – are affective information processing mechanisms that are quicker than higher-order symbolic processes and somewhat more innately wired. *Preferenda* are neurally mediated, affective responses which contrast with higher-order *discriminanda* associated with language and symbolic processes (Zajonc 1980:159). Zajonc explicitly argues against what he sees as contemporary psychology's love affair with affect as *post*-cognitive.

Zajonc makes some of his argument on solid ground. Often an organism's first reaction to stimuli is largely "affective," immediate, and not readily available to conscious awareness. These affective reactions tend to be "gross and vague," and they are often immediate and unavailable to conscious, articulate awareness (*ibid.*:154). Zajonc cites Bartlett's groundbreaking work on remembering (1932) in which Bartlett observed that when a subject is asked to remember, it is very often an attitude or mood that is first recalled. More complete recall is then largely reconstructed upon that attitude. Furthermore, social psychological studies also indicate that introspective reports about influences on subjects' evaluations, decisions, and actions can be so unreliable as to not be trusted (Nisbett and Wilson 1977). This seems to support Zajonc's hypothesis that affective responses often take place which do not depend on what he considers "cognition." But the inability to articulate reasons for particular evaluations and decisions does not mean they are made *without* some sort of cognitive appraisal. Expeditious affective responses are possible in part because of *prior* affective-evaluative experience accessible in schematized memory. Zajonc's implicit emphasis on cognition as conscious, "highly symbolically transformed," and able to be articulated is *not* the canonical conceptualization of cognition. At some level Zajonc's subjects must be processing input and making some sort of embodied evaluation of it in order to affect decisions, action, or behavior. And Bartlett himself, as Jerome Bruner observes (1990:57), appreciated the role of culture in mediating memory.

Zajonc develops his argument by making several further observations which are backed by experimental evidence. Affective judgments tend to be irrevocable in that, once formed, an evaluation is not readily revoked. Affective reactions are also dependent on the efficiency of non-verbal channels and difficult to articulate. Based on this reasoning, it seems plausible that affect is fairly independent and often impervious to ''cognition'' as Zajonc defines it. The stimulus features that serve us so well in consciously discriminating, recognizing, and categorizing objects and events may not be useful at all in first evaluating these objects. Zajonc's contrast between *preferenda* and *discriminanda* therefore seems somewhat apposite in describing feeling-laden human responses.

But Zajonc makes a crucial caveat at several places: he explicitly sees himself as dealing primarily with the class of feelings that underlies approach-avoidance distinctions and behavior. ''Thus, for the present purposes, other emotions such as surprise, anger, guilt, or shame, which have been identified in the literature and extensively analyzed by Tomkins, Izard, and others, are ignored'' (Zajonc 1980:152; cf. Murphy and Zajonc 1993). By focusing on *preferenda* Zajonc only deals with conditions of hedonic polarity, that is, pleasant versus unpleasant responses.[16] These are precisely the types of responses which Lazarus (1982, 1984, and 1991) and others have described more as innate reflexes than as emotions. Zajonc's emphasis on hedonically polar affective preferences squares with work on appetitive-avoidance motivational reflex-cortex connections (Lang *et al.* 1992). The latter indeed suggest that pleasant/unpleasant reactions are processed faster than ones elicited by higher-order, symbolic-cognitive appraisal. As stated above, Zajonc's particular conception of ''emotion'' implicitly associates it with being out of awareness or consciousness. His evidence for subconscious, rapid affective processing would then seem to support a dual-processing view of feelings and thought.

I view the debate over the primacy of affect as stemming from differing conceptions of *cognition*. First, we know that much of our neural processing and cognitive process takes place out of conscious awareness. Implicit in Zajonc's conception of cognition is an association with conscious articulation. Although he has stated explicitly that he does *not* limit affect or cognition to conscious awareness, his own studies *do* seem to reflect this implicit assumption in the case of cognition in relation to affect. Consider the Kunst-Wilson and Zajonc (1980) study which showed that subjects, by virtue of repeated suboptimal exposures, developed affective preferences for previously novel Chinese ideographs.[17] Ideographs were first presented under degraded, suboptimal conditions to non-Chinese speakers. Later, the subjects could not distinguish old stimuli from new stimuli during direct recognition memory tests. Yet despite this lack of overt recognition, when asked which of the two ideographs – old or new – they liked better, subjects consistently preferred the previously presented ones. In later studies (Murphy and Zajonc 1993), affective priming was used in which extremely brief suboptimal exposure of images of distinctly pleasant or unpleasant tones preceded optimal presentation of novel ideographs. Priming stimuli had either strong affective content (e.g., faces expressing emotion) or emotionally bland content (e.g., large and small shapes). Stimulus access was manipulated by comparing extremely brief 4 millisecond suboptimal priming exposures with 1 second optimal exposures. By holding all other variables constant, this study demonstrated that suboptimal affective priming consistently explained subjects' later preferential evaluations of the exposed ideographs.

Notice the implicit association of conscious, articulable awareness with cognition in these studies. Because subjects unconsciously processed suboptimal stimulus exposures and this influenced their evaluations of the ideographs, Zajonc reasons that this gives credence to the primacy of affective processing as *prior* to "cognition." Yet this need not be the case. Surely the affective priming stimuli must have been subconsciously evaluated for there to have been affective preference, but this does not mean that the processing was *non*-cognitive. There is nothing about Zajonc's implicit criterion which rules out cognitive processes, especially since we know that sensory input is processed by neocortical, sensory processing centers in conjunction with non-neocortical pathways. Thus, even though Zajonc and colleagues make several statements against associating cognition *necessarily* with consciousness, their reasoning and methodology seem to implicitly contradict these caveats. I do not think that the criterion of "minimal stimulation" (Murphy and Zajonc 1993:735) or the fact that priming is suboptimal makes the priming necessarily non-cognitive. The implicit assumptions in Zajonc *et al.*'s (1989) reasoning make them easy to miss.[18]

Second, the current state of neurobiological knowledge shows that sensory input which reaches the thalamus diverges, and is sent *both* to neocortical sensory processing centers (then down to the limbic system) *and* directly to such limbic structures as the amygdala, hippocampus, and hypothalamus (LeDoux 1986). Such neural circuitry lends evidence neither to the primacy of affect as Zajonc conceives it nor a post-cognitive perspective, but to a complicated, dynamically interactive information processing conceptualization. The direct thalamo-limbic link is shorter than the thalamo-neocortical link, thus it would make sense that some sort of "gross and vague," hedonically polar, preconscious response might emerge faster than a well-processed, evaluated emotional response. The initial response may prime the organism in terms of threshold awareness for further-processed information routed through higher-order cortical processing. Nevertheless, *both* processing loops are probably influenced by developmental experience and culturally mediated evaluation because the development of the nervous system itself is dependent upon learning, and we *cannot* assume the work of culture to be a necessarily conscious process. It is much too simplistic to set up a dichotomy between affective primacy or affect as post-cognitive.

Another important aspect of the issues concerning emotion and the so-called primacy of affect debate concerns how ''evaluation'' is conceived. Richard Lazarus, Zajonc's antagonist in the psychology literature, has developed a ''cognitive-motivational-relational'' theory of emotion which focuses on the process by which certain perceptions of the person–environment relationship are necessary for the elicitation of an emotional response. *Situations must be appraised and evaluated for them to have embodied significance for the organism to respond or react.* In this sense, ''meaning'' is important not necessarily in our usual hypercognized, articulable way, but in the simple sense that the organism is constantly evaluating its status in relation to its context, and these evaluations may or may not take on emotionally significant, personally salient import (see Shore 1996 for a cognitively oriented discussion of human meaning-making).

Zajonc seems to associate evaluation and appraisal with cognition, but, as I have been arguing, we need *not* throw out cognitive processing to focus on the primacy of affect. Zajonc's subjects presumably evaluated suboptimal stimuli at some level in order to have been influenced by them. Equally apparent, sensory inputs must be appraised and evaluated for them to have any meaning for the organism at all. While Zajonc would have to concede that evaluation and appraisal take place, he might argue that evaluative appraisal in primary affective processing is done by subcortical, purportedly ''non-cognitive'' mechanisms. But this would oversimplify the interactive, hierarchical complexity of neural processing outlined above, and there is no reason why *sub*cortical functioning should be considered *non*-cognitive. Because brain neuroanatomy is much more complicated than experimental psychology studies tend to assume, it makes no sense to search for some purely non-cognitive affective processing mechanism. The relatively rapid, hedonically polar preferential responses that Zajonc discusses may indeed be processed initially by thalamo-limbic circuits, and this may result from hippocampal schematic memory input which relates sensory input to past experience.

If Zajonc explicitly states that he is not dealing with more complicated emotional states such as shame, anger, guilt, sadness, etc., then the affects to which he gives primacy may have more to do with innately programmed, polar affective reflexes that stem from existential situations having less to do with socioculturally mediated situations (Lang *et al.* 1992; Lazarus 1991). But to rule out cognitive-evaluative processing from all emotional experience would, in my view, be mistaken and a gross over-simplification.

In the evolution of complex and intelligent species, whose adaptation came to depend greatly on the ability to learn from experience, emotions make possible much greater variability and flexibility than either reflexes or physiological drives. Moreover,

> human emotions are often predicated on complex social structures and meanings that define what is harmful or beneficial and, therefore, require judgment, the ability to learn from experience and the ability to distinguish subtle differences that signify different consequences for well-being. *Appraisal is thus a key factor in the evolution of adaptational processes, including emotion.* (Lazarus 1991:821, italics added)

Lazarus' perspective is in line, then, with our earlier discussion of the evolution of human mental functioning and its dependence on cognitive, often culturally mediated, intersubjectively shared knowledge schemas.

Both Zajonc and Lazarus agree that emotionality has to do with person–environment interactions which implicate the well-being or status of the organismic self. Without a goal or stake in a transaction, the encounter will not generate emotion. This emphasis on the person–environment relationship is a constant among neurobiologists, psychologists, and anthropologists who study emotion (LeDoux 1986; Damasio 1994; Zajonc 1980; Buck 1986; Lazarus 1991; Nesse 1990a; Levy 1984; M. Rosaldo 1984). We may take this aspect of human emotionality as axiomatic. An emotional state, then, is an *index* – in Peirce's semiotic sense – of a particular relation between the person and the external and internal environments.

Our discussion recalls the two contrasting, polar perspectives in emotion theory and research. The universalist position is phylogenetic and centered on imputed innately hardwired, psychobiological universals. The sociocultural constructivist position adopts a relativist stance and is ontogenetic; it assumes the existence of learned variations in the emotional process which emerge in psychosocial development. By including the processes of evaluation, appraisal, and labeling into our emotion theory, we can begin to resolve the tension in this false dichotomy. This is why the primacy of affect problem is relevant to a biocultural model of human emotionality – how one conceptualizes the relations between emotion, cognition, biology, and culture has crucial theoretical implications for the weight given to each domain and thus for our explanatory understandings of human experience.

It is plausible that there is a fundamental subset of experiences that are pan-human, and for which there are relatively ''hard-wired'' emotional responses. Such emotions constitute psychobiological universals. As Lazarus points out, if two persons make the same appraisal, then they will experience the same emotion (1991:825). This type of response is in accordance with studies conducted by Ekman and his colleagues on seemingly species-universal correlations between facial expression and autonomic nervous system activity discussed above (Ekman 1974, 1980, 1989, 1992; Ekman *et al.* 1983; Levenson *et al.* 1992). Certain existential experiences are universal in that they are part of the human condition and – at the greatest abstract level – do not vary cross-culturally. Evolutionary psychologists would say that they have been shaped within the human *environment of evolutionary adaptedness*. Thus, it is in the context of such pan-human, core existential situations that natural selection has acted in the selection of particular emotion complexes (Hallowell 1955; Hamburg 1963; Alexander 1990; Tooby and Cosmides 1990).

Kagan (1978) has also asserted that such pan-human existential situations exist, calling them *human universal incentive events*. ''It is likely that there is a small set of incentive conditions, as interpreted by cognitive processes, that guarantees that certain states are likely to occur (perhaps must occur) in all settings in which children are raised by and live with human beings'' (Kagan 1978:32). Such incentive events include encounters with discrepant events, detection of inconsistency or deviation between acquired standards or between the standard and behavior, loss of a target object to which the person has established a response routine, anticipation of danger, harm, or an event with which the subject cannot cope, etc. ''Since some cultures present unique incentives not present in all locales, some affective states are unique to a community'' (*ibid.*:33).

Lazarus approaches the tension between universals and particulars similarly. During their life-course, all people, regardless of culture, are likely to have had all the basic relational experiences, that is, all the *core relational themes* for the emotions characteristic of human life. Being human presents typical experiences which everyone must evaluate and manage, such as: (a) being slighted or demeaned (for anger); (b) facing existential threats (for anxiety); (c) experiencing irrevocable loss (for sadness); (d) transgressing a moral imperative or causing harm (for guilt); (e) failing to live up to a collective ego ideal (for shame), etc. (Lazarus 1991:826). Cross-cultural variation emerges as a result of the ways these core relational themes are evaluated and labeled in their particular contexts, since their evaluations are based upon learned, intersubjectively shared meaning systems (culture). Variation also emerges in important ways due to culturally mediated variation with respect to how subjective affective states are labeled, elaborated, or ignored. Thus, variation in emotion becomes manifest first in divergent beliefs and motives in relation to particular situations, and second, in group and individual differences in labeling and coping. *If we have established that the appraisal/evaluative process is a crucial component in the elicitation of emotional states, then culturally constituted interpretive schemas or labels would give rise to variations on relational themes. Conceptual room is provided for both the psychobiological universals in emotion and the variations based on sociocultural influences that shape the personalities of the members of a population whose experiences are both common and variable.*

Lazarus proposes, therefore, that humans are biologically constructed in such a way that encountering any of the basic relational experiences, and personally appraising them as such, will elicit the experience of the emotion linked to the appraised meaning – regardless of how they are labeled or explained, and whether or not they become conscious. Randolph Nesse argues for a similar view of particular emotions having been selected via natural selection for their adaptive fit in relation to particular person–environment situations (1990a; cf. also Weinrich 1980). In this way, neurologically intact persons should be able to experience the full spectrum of human emotionality. I agree with the general thrust of Lazarus' argument, however I am inclined to give more force to the ethnopsychological shaping, elaboration, or ignoring of emotion states – that is, the work of culture. This issue is, nevertheless, one of emphasis.

We know that diverse cultural settings make different sense of life's events, and cultures do this frequently by emphasizing or amplifying different aspects of general human problems. This is why Briggs (1970) and M. Rosaldo (1984) argued that Utku Eskimo and Ilongot respectively do not feel anger in the way that Westerners do, and why Geertz stated for Balinese that the "passions are as cultural as the [social institutional] devices; and the turn of mind . . . that informs the one informs the other" (1980:124).[19] We must be careful that these types of ethnographic interpretations do not lead to misguided theoretical assertions. It does not make sense to claim that Eskimos never feel anger as some of Briggs's readers have claimed, or that "Ilongot 'anger' differs [totally] from our own" (M. Rosaldo 1984:150). Yet it also seems implausible to claim that Eskimos and Ilongots get angry the same way, for example, as an Anglo-American would (cf. Solomon 1984 and Lakoff and Kovecses 1987 on Anglo-American models of anger). My argument is that we need *not* try to decide the issue in one extreme way or the other. Precisely what is most needed in the cross-cultural analysis of emotionality is a perspective which seeks to illuminate how core relational themes are variously elaborated, shaped, and/or diminished (e.g., Levy 1978; Harkness and Super 1983, 1985; Hochschild 1983; Gerber 1985; Lindholm 1988; LeVine 1990; Parish 1991). This is the crucial point made by Levy (1984) who emphasizes a dynamic, interactive process involving primary and secondary stages of appraisal and culturally mediated cognitive evaluation – a process which deserves more sophisticated analyses of covert and overt knowing, hierarchies of evaluation, appraisal, and cultural labeling, and therefore issues of hyper- and hypocognition. Indeed, from the biocultural perspective I am developing here, the entire domain of *knowing* itself is a processual, intersystemic, and quite complicated process.

By appreciating the roles of cognitive appraisal and labeling in the emotional process without the necessity of tying consciousness with cognition, we can avoid getting caught up in the primacy of affect controversy and we make a persuasive case for the role of cultural cognition in mediating cross-cultural variation of the emotional process (see Buck 1990 for another related discussion of the Zajonc–Lazarus debate). This is especially the case when we keep in mind the complex neuroanatomical connections which include *both* thalamo-limbic and thalamo-neocortical pathways. These pathways seem to represent a neurobiological correlate to the oscillating pendulum between psychobiological universals and sociocultural particulars. Neural information is concurrently and interactively processed through both major pathways, and this has great import for the way intraorganismic communication is embodied and behavior is motivated. Unfortunately, we know very little about these complicated information transduction processes, and therefore there is still a great deal of research to be done. The point is that various events, circumstances, or behaviors – depending upon sociocultural context – may or may not be construed as threatening or joyful. When the mental apparatus makes such an evaluation, this ''cognitive'' information becomes transduced into neurophysiological and endocrine effects, a process which often happens before the evaluation is presented into conscious subjective perception. Thus we may observe relativism at the cultural cognitive ''software'' level of knowing yet concurrent universalism at the neurobiological ''hardware'' level.

The picture drawn here demonstrates that the neurobiological hardware involved in the processing of affect is dynamic and highly complex. The ongoing neural evaluatory apparatus continually interprets and assesses hierarchies of incoming stimuli from both the external and internal environments, and thus we find a complicated processual dynamic of fluctuating biocommunicative feeling states under constant modulation and assessment, labeling and management. The perspective on emotion developed here asserts that this constant modulation and assessment of bodily hardware is significantly mediated by experiential and cultural cognitive schemas. I contend that such schemas constitute the software side of emotional processing, so now we shall turn briefly to look at the primary importance of cultural cognition in the variable processing of affect.

Taking culture seriously

If a pan-human set of psychobiologically programmed affective responses are built into the organism, and these affective responses are elicited via evaluative appraisal in relation to the organism's contextual situation, it is understandable that the anthropologist focuses on variation in the culturally influenced evaluative processes which contribute to variable modulation of emotional feeling states. The ''data'' which the anthropologist observes are the wide-ranging, culturally construed worlds in which various peoples live and perceive. Because various populations can define and interpret situations differently – or perhaps emphasize various aspects of situations differently –

our human suite of emotional responsivity can be elicited, shaped, or diminished in diverse ways. This does not exclude the wide range of *common* existential situations, or core relational themes, that humans experience and share cross-culturally. This view is supported both by contemporary views of the evolution of neocortical structures which influence responses that are more hard-wired in lower brain structures, and also by the complex neuroanatomical picture of sensory processing outlined above. Continuing with the computer metaphor, different sets of data are processed in various ways by the same set of hardware contained in the central processing unit of the nervous system. Depending upon the ''program'' being used by the processing unit, peripheral input is read, interpreted, and ''run'' differently.

Any consideration of the psychosocial dynamics of emotionality must take account of the important fact that humans are characterized by a prolonged infantile helplessness and dependency, a fact which relates to the presence of *neoteny* – juvenilization resulting from dissociation and retardation of ancestral rates of shape change (Shea 1989:69) – in human ontogeny and phylogeny. Stephen Jay Gould has asserted that ''[t]he early stages of ontogeny are a reservoir of potential adaptation'' (1977:397), and he believes we should *not* focus on morphology in assessing the adaptive significance of neoteny. He states that the developmental temporal delays themselves are the most significant feature of human heterochrony, and that primitive hominids had already evolved an extended childhood. ''We [humans] belong to an order of mammals distinguished by their propensity for repeated single births, intense parental care, long life spans, late maturation, and a high degree of socialization . . .'' (*ibid.*:399–400). Delayed postpartum development is a key feature in our common hominid heritage in comparative phylogenetic perspective, and is particularly expressed in extended childhood and late maturation. The newborn human child is a particularly dependent creature among placental mammalian infants, and the child requires intense parental care for many years; this childhood flexibility persists during more than a decade of necessarily close contact with adults. Thus there is a certain adaptive premium placed on *learning* in humans as opposed to innate response (*ibid.*:400–1; Jacobson 1969; Geertz 1973; Shatz 1993; Damasio 1994).[20]

Childhood is a highly significant time for the organization of ontogenetic trajectories which emerge out across life history. Infancy and childhood are important periods when salient emotional attachments develop, when particular experiences take on influential import, when significant interpersonal relations become habituated, and when orientational tendencies begin to sediment. Such processes interact with other axes of development such as physiology, nutrition, timing of maturation, and, importantly, acquisition of language and culture. Such a developmental view is indispensable once one appreciates that the infant is primarily an affective being, and that various emotions emerge as they become adaptive in the life of the infant (Izard 1978, 1979; Rosenblum 1978). Izard points out that the emotion system is the primary motivational system for humans, and that emotions constitute principal organizing factors in consciousness. It is crucially important to appreciate that various affects – with their consequent biobehavioral shifts – emerge across human maturation, with each one becoming important for particular types of learning. Put succinctly, socialization itself is motivated. It is thus important to view emotions as evolved proximate mechanisms for learning, socialization, and the ongoing calibration of social relations, and in this sense they are proximate products in the evolution of social relationality (cf. Trivers 1971, 1974).

Because the human infant is born into the world with much developing to do, it is significant that learning and acquisition take place in a world of communicative inputs (Rogoff 1990; Shore 1996), a point which deserves deep appreciation.[21] Gould (1977:401) notes that Jacobson identified a neurological basis for the importance of delayed development called neural shaping or sculpting, and this process has been emphasized by many others (e.g., Changeux 1985; Kandel and Hawkins 1993; G. Hinton 1993). The complexity of neuronal development must also be appreciated in light of the fact that nerve cells do not reproduce by cell division, but simply die (Konner 1982:397). Thus in counterpoint to appreciating human plasticity, one must also stress that the nervous system has been designed to develop a certain maturational inflexibility which in turn calibrates cognitive-perceptual organization and socialization.[22] What we have then is an affectively driven organizational process of learning that slowly begins to decelerate sometime in late childhood or adolescence. This has import for the current topic because it presents an ontogenetic perspective on the developmental, sociocultural "programming" of organismic neurobiological hardware. The acquisition and internalization of cognitive schemas leads to more or less variation in the way one's world is construed, and therefore of the evaluation of perceptual stimuli and the labeling of subjective affect states.

Given the developmental "biopsychocultural" view of mental function that has been sketched here, it should be clear that the universalist cannot deny cross-cultural variation nor can the relativist deny commonalities in the emotional process. But since I have reviewed some of the neurobiological evidence for universal hardware, and demonstrated the primacy of evaluative appraisal in the modulation of feeling states, I would now like to explore the various ways culturally mediated knowledge constitutes a mutually important dimension of the emotional process. I recall an anecdote concerning an Orthodox Jewish restaurant patron who experienced wrenching convulsions of disgust upon learning that s/he had just ingested a meal containing pork. While there is nothing inherent in the meat which would elicit a disgust reaction from a non-Jewish observer's perspective, it is precisely the interpreted moral world of the patron that makes disgust in this situation a salient and overwhelmingly "natural" reaction. If the "introduction of a single fact" (Kagan 1978:37) can be responsible for changing the emotional valence of a situation, we cannot then underestimate the crucial role of interpretation in the emotional process. This is particularly important, and thus even more complex, when we consider that the "introduction of a single fact" may often take place unconsciously.[23]

If our interpretive evaluations of ourselves in the world did not play a crucial role in the emotional process, our *imagined* worlds would also not prove particularly salient. Schutz (1962) describes "finite provinces of meaning" as temporary, contained experiences in which the person has suspended his/her participation in an intersubjective world of "paramount reality" to participate in alternative, circumscribed worlds of meaning. Schutz's best-known examples of finite provinces of meaning include the religious experience of the mystic, the transcendent abstractions of pure mathematics, and the experience of the audience member as s/he is drawn into the world of a play as the curtain is raised. It is precisely our ability to imagine, identify, empathize, and project that makes such finite provinces of meaning possible. Would we consider the emotional experience of a captivating drama an insincere one? Because humans can construct and emotionally participate in imagined sociocultural worlds, we should not fail to appreciate the role of interpretive evaluation in the emotional process. We might think of culture, then, as an intersubjective process of imagination.

This is illustrated beautifully in children's playtime. Like the vicarious participation of the audience in a captivating drama, play is often a process in which roles and identities defined by a society's worldview are instantiated and explored in a safe, alternative "play" world. Children act out situations and roles they observe those around them taking part in – situations and roles which seem taken-for-granted by others. And we know that children can experience the full range of emotions in their playtime activities. This is why play can often not only represent a safe arena for psychosocial exploration, but also act as a salient pathway for self-initiated socialization (Kelly-Byrne 1989). The child is not just acting out the rules or injunctions which s/he is taught by parents, peers, or significant others; in playtime children represent and manipulate situations and identify with the characters and roles imagined in the play. In this way, the child's experience of a normative moral world becomes "experience near," to use Geertz's (1984) version of Heinz Kohut's phrase.

This is analogous to the moral worlds of religious cosmologies. Through imagined identification and participation, the religious believer inhabits a world that becomes personally salient and real. Otherwise, we would not be able to explain the faithful supplicant of the Blessed Virgin Mary. Only by imagining this superhuman figure – and knowing her existence to be real – could a devotee of Mary find actual *embodied* solace through belief, supplication, and ritual. I use the religious world of culturally postulated superhuman agents as an illustration of interpretation because religious belief and action are based on knowledge and evaluation. The "sensory input" in this system is the belief and perception that there is a trusted, sacred, motherly figure who will look after and take care of the faithful supplicant, perhaps as the mother of one's childhood may have filled the same role (see Spiro 1978 on the subjective developmental foundation for belief in superhuman religious agencies).

Consider further the importance of interpretation for the processes of ritual healing and contemporary psychotherapy (Kleinman 1988; Frank 1991 [1961]; Csordas 1994). Kleinman has highlighted the process of evaluative transformation, indicating that successful healing therapies – of whatever sort – are often predicated upon effecting deep changes in the ways one knows, and therefore perceives, the world. To a certain extent, this process is one of interpretive reformulation; the problem (anxiety, neurosis, etc.) leading to the healing process can largely emerge as a result of the ways the subject interprets his/her status in the world and then acts upon it. Effective therapy requires a thorough reworking of the patient's problematic, habituated ways of knowing, including reinterpretations of past experience (Lock 1987). Yet "cognitive" reformulation in Zajonc's sense is usually not enough; the most successful therapy is always embodied in the sense that as the process of reinterpretation proceeds, powerful catharses, feelings, etc. accompany the reinterpretive process. These embodied correlates of reinterpretation make the healing process personally salient and hopefully long-lasting.

Thus far I have discussed the importance of culturally mediated evaluation for the ongoing dynamics of emotional processes. I noted that new information can drastically change one's emotional valence, and furthermore that the ontogenetic trajectory of human development and the configuration of neurological maturation lends force to the argument that culture must be taken seriously. Humans live their lives in ongoing processes of learning from experience, inferring causalities, and acquiring cultural schemas which shape the interpretive process. I prefer to emphasize modal patterns of intersubjectively shared knowledge because such a view allows room for individual variation along intercultural and intracultural axes (Schwartz 1978, 1992; Shore 1996). This is important for our consideration because *it is precisely these personal stocks of intersubjectively shared knowledge schemas that inform and influence the evaluatory processes of appraisal and intersubjective processes of labeling. Variation in cultural learning and personal experience, then, translates into variation in emotional experience.* Cross-cultural variation emerges as a result of the various ways human beings appraise core relational themes in particular socioecological contexts, appraisals which are significantly dependent upon learned, intersubjectively shared meaning schemas – in a word, culture.

The variability of cultural learning – and therefore appraisal and labeling – means that indeed, from a certain point of view, complexes of affective states *can be* somewhat different from each other. Yet a focus on the analysis of context and interpretive meaning, i.e., the "software," emphasizes certain aspects of the emotional process over others (what A. Hinton [1993] refers to as "intellectual metonymy"). Biological researchers have trained their analytical focus on a seemingly less variable level, namely the "hardware" levels of arousal and neurobiological function. If we are to go beyond simple reductionistic dichotomies, we must take biocultural insights to heart and focus our attention on more complicated processes of elaboration, shaping, and diminishing. We would therefore do well to use Levy's notions (1984) of culturally constituted hyper- and hypocognition. His view of the evaluating and labeling individual agent is echoed in the dynamic view sketched in this chapter. Researchers seem to be unable to adequately model complex, interactive relationships between learning (cultural, idiosyncratic, and biogenetic), experience, cognition, memory, and emotion. I suggest that research and work in these directions will enhance the sophistication of our understanding concerning the complexity of emotional functioning. Such complexity demands systematic, integrated biocultural attention.

Conclusion: Emotion as a biocultural phenomenon

I have emphasized neoteny and temporal retardation in human development because of the adaptive significance of learning in human life. Connected in importance is the crucial shaping and socializing process the human organism undergoes. Plasticity would not have any adaptive significance – and would indeed entail severe disadvantages – were it not for the ontogenetic, orientational calibration of the organism's central nervous system. To use the crude computer metaphor elaborated here, our central nervous system (hard drive) has evolved the ability to internalize and access a tremendous amount of information, but this central processing unit must be given instructions (software) in order to evaluate, label, and generate appropriate responses for a particular socioecological environment (i.e., selecting appropriate physical and/or mental behavior). Enculturation and individual idiosyncratic experience are important processes whereby the organism's central processing unit is actively oriented toward its behavioral environment.

This computer metaphor bears a kindred relation to Randolph Nesse's

(1990a) evolutionary explanation of emotions which suggests that emotions might heuristically be seen as "software of the mind." Nesse appreciates that human emotions each have situational-functional specificity, and that they have therefore been shaped by natural selection because they provide the motivational undergirding for increased fitness in particular contexts. This emphasis on situationally specific selection is important since it concurs with guiding principles of contemporary evolutionary theory. In Nesse's view, emotions are "specialized modes of operation shaped by natural selection to adjust the physiological, psychological, and behavioral parameters of the organism in ways that increase its capacity and tendency to respond adaptively to the threats and opportunities characteristic of specific kinds of situations" (1990a:268). This emphasis on the correspondence between a specific emotion and specific situations dovetails well with Lazarus' (1991) emphasis on core relational themes and Kagan's (1978) emphasis on human universal incentive events discussed above.

It is within this theoretical context that Nesse suggests a view of emotions as *software* of the mind, a perspective which contrasts with the model of emotion proposed in this chapter. In Nesse's view, "emotions provide for the mind what software programs provide for the computer. A computer is ineffective until software programs are loaded to adjust its various parameters to the needs of a particular task" (Nesse 1990a:269). I differ with Nesse in some important respects by preferring to view human affective neurobiology as the "various parameters" (i.e., hardware) which need programming and adjusting. Such emotional-motivational complexes become situationally oriented both toward the external environment and intrapsychically. It is more plausible, then, to consider emotions as "hardware executions" that have been contextually selected within the human environment of evolutionary adaptedness, and that it is rather socioculturally mediated, experiential learning that is the software of the mind.[24] This seems more appropriate given the particular evolution of human ontogeny. In fact, Nesse's emphasis on situational context supports the view that emotions are "hardware" that gets shaped by the "software" of learning, experience, and evaluation. The emotional hardware must be "programmed" in order to function effectively in the service of the organism's well-being *in a particular socioecological milieu.* Thus, emotions are *not* software but hardware managed by cognitive evaluatory processes.[25]

Take, for example, the development of phobias discussed by Nesse (*ibid.*:271). He states that agoraphobia develops because of repeatedly experienced panic in situations with specific cues. Learning what situations to be agoraphobic in can be ontogenetically adaptive. That people can develop idiosyncratic agoraphobias to situations/cues that seem non-adaptive to others sheds light on the fact that emotions are contextually shaped via experience and learning. At a further level of remove, that emotional hardware – hardware in the sense that it is ''made''/selected to ''run''/ function in reference to experiential, schema-mediated ''instructions'' – needs shaping, development, and modification supports the argument that it has been adaptive for humans to be flexible and shaped socioculturally and experientially. In the case of agoraphobia, the emotion of fear is the psychobiological response elicited by a particular cue or context; it is precisely because agoraphobias can develop in association with a wide range of situational cues that I contend that emotion (in this case, fear) is an aspect of organismic hardware. In the ontogenesis of a phobia, fear is modulated in specific, contextual ways, just as software programs on the computer instruct the central processing unit how to run and what algorithms to execute. Problems arise when social situations or environments change so quickly that the way individuals are enculturated during a particular generation is less applicable or even non-adaptive in later socioecological contexts during the individual's own lifetime. Problems also arise within specific sociocultural matrices when individuals, as the result of particular individual experiences, develop non-modal habits of evaluation (as in the Japanese syndrome of *taijin-kyofu-sho* discussed in the introduction, for instance). But this does not change the fact that the emotion fear has relatively constant psychobiological and experiential ramifications which are elicited along variable axes of individually idiosyncratic and cross-culturally variable learned experiences. This is important to appreciate because ''developmentally, experientially and circumstantially contingent variation is precisely what evolutionary biological theories of social phenomena are about'' (Daly and Wilson 1994:261).

I have used the computer metaphor in reference to emotionality because the image of software is heuristically useful in directing research toward examining the complicated ways sociocultural forces influence learning, evaluation, memory, and experience. Such a focus enables us to examine the profound work of culture. The ethnographer, in a sense, observes and analyzes cultural software in dynamic interaction with the central processing of emotions. Many focus on the feeling-state aspect of emotions, but since feeling-states occur continuously in experience they cannot necessarily be taken as the defining characteristic of the emotional process. This is why focusing *only* on changes in feeling-states is of relatively minimal analytic value. *To analyze emotions we therefore need to place changes in feeling-states within their dynamic environmental, developmental contexts, taking into consideration the culturally mediated cognitive processes of evaluation, labeling, and interpretation involved.*

Variation in human emotionality can be seen as stemming (a) from the ontogenetic history which has shaped the individual (or group of individuals) to relate, interpret, and react to socioecological interactions in various ways, and (b) from the culturally mediated knowledge schemas which influence perception and cognition in particular ways. This interpretive and experiential variation, however, is always deeply embedded in – and indeed made possible by – the neurobiological apparatus of the common human organism. It is only with these sorts of complicated considerations in mind that we may begin to reconceptualize ourselves out of the conundrum of emotions in social science. I have endeavored to take biology more seriously as a fledgling effort to answer the call for cultural anthropologists to take biology more seriously (e.g., Paul 1987), not only so that our thinking on human matters might become more sophisticated but also to counter some biologists' and sociobiologists' disregard for the work of culture.

Acknowledgments

This chapter evolved from work supported under a National Science Foundation Predoctoral Fellowship and has greatly benefited from my intellectual interaction with Carol Worthman, who introduced me to biology not so very long ago. I wish to thank Carol, Mark Ridley, Charles Nuckolls, Bradd Shore, and the anonymous reviewers for their helpful comments and pointed questions regarding my thinking on the problem of human emotionality. Thanks also to Alex Hinton who not only asked me to contribute this working paper to the current volume but also provided crucial feedback. Not least, many thanks to Mark Padilla and Donna Murdock, both of whom provided feedback upon my last-minute coercion. I am, of course, solely responsible for the views articulated here.

NOTES

1. The notion of cognitive schema or model has been variously defined, but for our purposes here Casson's description serves as well as any other: ''Schemata are conceptual abstractions that mediate between stimuli received by the sense organs and behavioral responses . . . not all stimuli are stored in memory; rather, schemata are employed to provide 'a general impression of the whole' and to construct (or reconstruct) 'probable details' '' (1983:430). On the notions of developmental niche/microniche, see Super & Harkness (1986) and Worthman (1995) respectively.
2. I have adopted the apt phrase ''culturally muscular'' from Robert Hefner (personal communication). Bradd Shore (1996) makes the important point that it is a common anthropological fallacy to view cultural practices and beliefs as random or arbitrary if they are not universal. ''If cultural practices and beliefs are not fully determined or universally shared, the fallacy goes, then they must be arbitrary and thus infinitely variable.'' Thus, the ''assertion of unmotivated arbitrariness in human affairs where what is meant is actually the indeterminacy

of conventional arrangements invites all sorts of misguided attacks on the nihilism implicit in 'cultural relativism' '' (Shore 1996:37–38).

3. See Hahn (1995:40–56) for a fuller discussion of the conceptual problem of CBSs.
4. I should state at the outset that the contrast between psychobiological universalism and sociocultural particularism is a guiding heuristic for discussing the wide-ranging literature on emotions. The poles represent a continuum, really, and this opposition is admittedly somewhat of a false dichotomy in itself, for universalists such as Izard and Ekman acknowledge cultural variation as well as biological universals, and sociologists such as Kemper (e.g., 1981) acknowledge biological universals as well as cultural particulars. Lutz is another ''culturally strong'' researcher who has mentioned that she does not completely outlaw the role of biology (1988). I would agree with Lazarus (1991) that the differences are largely matters of emphasis and the central focus of their research. On the conceptual difficulties of navigating between the poles of universalism and particularism, see the dialogue between Murray, Button, and Wierzbicka (Murray and Button 1988; Wierzbicka 1988).
5. After this chapter was substantially written, I discovered a kindred conceptual metaphor using computer terminology. Robert LeVine *et al.* (1994) develop a comparative perspective on child development, socialization, culture acquisition, and parental behavior using the notions of ''organic hardware,'' ''ecological firmware,'' and ''cultural software.'' Our mutual perspectives are similar in spirit, though I was not aware of LeVine and colleagues' model when I developed the biocultural perspective on emotion presented in the current chapter.
6. The famous injury of Phineas Gage and experiments with monkeys showed that there are regions of the brain which govern our sentiments and emotional relations with the world, just as there are others which deal with perceptions and movements (Vincent 1990; Damasio 1994). Current knowledge of the limbic system presented in this chapter comes from Kupfermann (1991), Winson (1985), LeDoux (1986), and Buck (1990).
7. The hypothalamus functions as a neuroendocrine informational integration, coordination, and transduction center.
8. I would like to emphasize my dissatisfaction with the tradition of identifying the limbic system as the emotional *center* of the brain for, as I hope my discussion will show, I conceptualize emotions as processual phenomena constituted by multiple domains. It is certainly true that limbic structures play a crucial role in information integration, contributing to the analysis of afferent inputs (both interoceptive and exteroceptive, that is, respectively interior to and exterior to the body), and their transduction into various types of outputs. My contention, however, is that emotions are processes which involve appraisal of the organism's status in relation to its microniche, and that embodied translations of this appraisal (feeling-states) orient the organism to its situation by recruiting appropriate behaviors to meet particular demands and providing the substrate for subjective experience.
9. I put ''innate'' in scare quotes because it is important to recall Gregory Bateson's observation (1972) that genetic selection in evolution is *itself* a process of learning.
10. It is important to note that fluctuating bodily affect states can also draw one's

attention *back* to particular self-environment situational concerns that have *passed* from consciousness; i.e., because there is an array of shorter and longer transductive bodily processing loops (such as direct sympathetic nervous innervation or longer hypothalamo-pituitary-adrenal neuroendocrine pathways), various fluctuating bodily states can actually prompt the organism's attention back to a prior concern or evaluation made concerning the organism's status in relation to the socioecological environment. Damasio (1994) calls this somatic marking. D'Andrade (1981) has briefly made a similar point but without the biology.

11. Carol Worthman (personal communication) has pointed out that this neuroanatomical state of affairs constitutes a biological basis for human ambivalence
12. Este Armstrong (1994) has recently observed that there is overwhelming evidence indicating that most sensory information comes to the limbic system from the most highly processed, multimodal, "feed-forward" cerebral parts of the brain ("areas related to symbols and language"). The input which originally reaches neocortical sensory processing areas is relayed there by the thalamus (see Armstrong's contribution to this volume). This is an important fact to keep in mind below with the question of the primacy of affect.
13. I heartily thank one anonymous reviewer for helping me clarify the importance of keeping appraisal and labeling conceptually distinct, and I further thank this reviewer for suggesting the felicitous phrase "biologically grounded constructionism." The phrase is particularly apt for what I am trying to convey here, and I can only wish that I had thought of it myself.
14. Shibutani (1961:164) has called attention to the finding reported in studies of aphasia (loss of ability to use words) and Parkinson's disease (where there is loss of ability to express emotion) that it is easier to understand a person suffering from aphasia than one with Parkinson's disease. This accentuates the importance of non-verbal emotional gesture and expression in the communication of meaning, even without language. When no emotion is expressed, one cannot tell how the speaker feels about what s/he is saying, creating difficulty in understanding or even misunderstanding – a point also made by Bateson (1972).
15. For these reasons – combined with the crucial observation that multiple, ongoing, even conflictual emotional processing rather than single, serial processing seems to be the most realistic view of human mental functioning – a psychodynamic view of the human mental apparatus seems to me incontrovertible (see Paul 1987, 1990; Nesse 1990b; and Nesse and Lloyd 1992 on the mutual relevance of evolutionary theory and psychoanalysis).
16. An important note should be made concerning *hedonic polarity*. As MacLean states, "affects differ from other psychological information by being imbued with a *physical* quality, of *either agreeable or disagreeable nature*" (1980:12, italics added); this is the quality of hedonic polarity. It is plausible to view emotional affects from the standpoint of organismic self-preservation given that all our emotions have either positive or negative polar valence. This suggests that the hedonic polarity of emotional states has evolved through natural selection because the polarity contributes toward evaluating the contextual environment in regard to its fitness implications (cf. Whiten n.d.; Nesse 1990a; and Nesse and Lloyd 1992 for similar views). Silvan Tomkins has distinguished what he sees as nine basic affects, one of which – surprise/startle – is considered neutral with regard to

hedonic polarity. Whether this is the case or not does not affect the nature of the argument concerning the evolutionary significance of affective polarity.

17. *Suboptimal* means stimulus exposure which is so brief that the subject has no conscious awareness of the prime.
18. Consider this concluding statement: ''Within this supposition, the processing of affective information seems, at least within the constraints of the present experiments, *to have an earlier access than the processing of information that is not affective in nature*'' (Murphy and Zajonc 1993:736, italics added). The italicized portion illustrates how easily Zajonc and colleagues elide non-cognitive affect with any type of processing that is *out* of awareness.
19. ''[A]ffects, whatever their similarities, are no more similar than the societies in which we live . . .'' (M. Rosaldo 1984:145). Rosaldo's statement illustrates her ''culturally muscular'' view of the emotions. To be fair to Rosaldo, however, she does admit that there is overlap between various social shapings of emotion, and she generally seems to struggle with the problem of the dichotomy between universals and particulars. But despite her struggle she emphasizes discourse and how people talk about situations as the determinant of ''the life of feeling,'' and tends to side with a culturally deterministic perspective (see Spiro's critique, 1984).
20. Though it has been an important adaptation, human plasticity has to be relatively fixed or set in its own turn, and this is what socialization/enculturation is all about. On the potential problems resulting from plasticity, see D'Andrade (1981, 1990) and Konner (1982:397).
21. For this reason Shore characterizes the human brain as an *eco-logical brain* (1996).
22. See also Konner (1991) on the maturation of brain myelination in relation to behavioral development. It is highly suggestive to note that the limbic system myelinates around 8 years of age (Konner, n.d.).
23. Consider an experience of Catherine Lutz during her fieldwork on the Ifaluk atoll in Micronesia (1988). Upon being awakened one night by the entrance of an ''intruder'' into her hut, she screamed for help. In the cultural reality of Ifalukers this was a socially sanctioned conduit for initiating sexual relations, thus Lutz's screams brought laughter from the islanders. Or consider that Sambia men of Papua New Guinea hold their noses during sexual intercourse with women because of the perceived disgusting odor of women's genitalia (Herdt 1990); this is the same scent that men in other cultural contexts may find arousing.
24. Because of the current chapter's emphasis on the situationally specific shaping of emotions in natural selection, and its contention that affective-emotional states are somewhat psychobiologically hardwired but contingent upon variable evaluations and culturally influenced perceptions that are made concerning the status of self-in-microniche, the present view is akin to that of evolutionary psychologists John Tooby and Leda Cosmides. They argue that the mind is not a social product nor ''an externally programmed general-purpose computer, lacking a richly defined evolved structure'' (Tooby and Cosmides 1992:24). But of course the human mind *is* in some sense a *social* product for the very reasons discussed in this chapter. However, being a social product does *not* necessarily imply a tabula rasa view of the human mind. Lest there be any confusion – as I hope my discussion has illustrated – my view of the human mind is far from that of a

purely externally programmed general-purpose computer; the intricate complexity derives from a ''richly defined evolved structure'' that is yet dependent upon shaping, modification, and socioculturally mediated variation in cognitive evaluation.

25. Let me emphasize here, for the sake of clarity, that the current view is similar to Nesse's in the sense that we both use computer metaphors to model an understanding of human emotionality, *however* I am proposing that emotions are *not* software of the mind. By contrast, human affective neurobiology is the ''hardware'' that is run using the ''software'' of personal knowledge schemas developed through cultural and idiosyncratic experience.

References

Alexander, Richard. 1990. Epigenetic rules and Darwinian algorithms: The adaptive study of learning and development. *Ethology and Sociobiology* 11:241–303.

Armstrong, Este. 1994. How symbols become meaningful. Paper read at Annual American Anthropological Association Meetings, Atlanta, Georgia.

Bartlett, F. C. 1932. *Remembering*. Cambridge: Cambridge University Press.

Bateson, Gregory. 1972. *Steps to an ecology of mind*. New York: Ballantine.

Briggs, Jean L. 1970. *Never in anger: Portrait of an Eskimo family*. Cambridge, MA: Harvard University Press.

Bruner, Jerome. 1990. *Acts of meaning*. Cambridge, MA: Harvard University Press.

Buck, Ross. 1986. The psychology of emotion. In *Mind and brain: Dialogues in cognitive neuroscience*, ed. J. E. LeDoux and W. Hirst, 275–300. Cambridge: Cambridge University Press.

1988. *Human motivation and emotion*, 2nd ed. New York: Wiley.

1990. William James, the nature of knowledge, and current issues in emotion, cognition, and communication. *Personality and Social Psychology Bulletin* 16:612–625.

Cannon, Walter B. 1931 Against the James–Lange and Thalamic theories of emotion. *Psychological Review* 31:281–295.

Casson, Ronald. 1983. Schemata in cognitive anthropology. *Annual Review of Anthropology* 12:429–462.

Changeux, Jean-Pierre. 1985. *Neuronal man: The biology of mind*. New York: Pantheon Books.

Csordas, Thomas J. 1994. *The sacred self: A cultural phenomenology of charismatic healing*. Berkeley: University of California Press.

Daly, Martin and Margo Wilson. 1994. Evolutionary psychology of male violence. In *Male violence*, ed. John Archer, 253–88. New York: Routledge.

Damasio, Antonio R. 1994. *Descartes' error: Emotion, reason, and the human brain*. New York: Putnam.

D'Andrade Roy G. 1981. The cultural part of cognition. *Cognitive Science* 5:179–196.

1984. Cultural meaning systems. In *Culture theory: Essays on mind, self, and emotion*, ed. R. Shweder and R. LeVine, 88–119. Cambridge: Cambridge University Press.

1989. Cultural cognition. In *Foundations of cognitive science*, ed. M. Posner, 795–830. Cambridge, MA: MIT Press.

1990. Some propositions about the relations between culture and human cognition. In *Cultural psychology: Essays on comparative human development*, ed. James Stigler, Richard Shweder, and Gilbert Herdt, 65–129. New York: Cambridge University Press.

Dawkins, Richard. 1982. *The extended phenotype: The gene as the unit of selection*. San Francisco and Oxford: W. H. Freeman.

Doi, Takeo. 1981. *The anatomy of dependence*. Tokyo: Kodansha International.

1986. *The anatomy of self*. Tokyo: Kodansha International.

Ekman, Paul. 1974. Universal facial expression of emotion. In *Culture and personality: Contemporary readings*, ed. Robert LeVine, 8–15. New York: Aldine de Gruyter.

1980. Biological and cultural contributions to body and facial movement in the expression of emotion. In *Explaining emotions*, ed. A. Rorty, 73–102. Berkeley: University of California Press.

1989. The argument and evidence about universals in facial expressions of emotion. In *Handbook of psychophysiology: Emotion and social behavior*, ed. H. Wagner and A. Manstead, 143–163. New York: Wiley.

1992. Facial expressions of emotion: New findings, new questions. *Psychological Science* 3:34–38.

Ekman, P., R. Levenson, and W. Friesen. 1983. Autonomic nervous system activity distinguishes between emotions. *Science* 221:1208–1210.

Frank, Jerome. 1991 [1961]. *Persuasion and healing: A comparative study of psychotherapy*. Baltimore and London: Johns Hopkins University Press.

Geertz, Clifford. 1973. *The interpretation of cultures*. New York: Basic Books.

1980. *Negara: The theatre state in nineteenth-century Bali*. Princeton, NJ: Princeton University Press.

1984. "From the native's point of view": On the nature of anthropological understanding. In *Culture theory: Essays on mind, self, and emotion*, ed. R. Shweder and R. LeVine, 123–136. Cambridge: Cambridge University Press.

Gerber, Eleanor. 1985. Rage and obligation: Samoan emotions in conflict. In *Person, self, and experience: Exploring Pacific ethnopsychologies*, ed. G. White and J. Kirkpatrick, 121–167. Berkeley, CA: University of California Press.

Gould, Stephen Jay. 1977. *Ontogeny and phylogeny*. Cambridge, MA: Harvard University Press.

Hahn, Robert A. 1995. Culture-bound syndromes unbound. In *Sickness and healing: An anthropological perspective*, 40–56. New Haven, LT: Yale University Press.

Hallowell, A. I. 1955. The self and its behavioral environment. In *Culture and experience*, 75–110. Philadelphia: University of Pennsylvania Press.

Hamburg, David A. 1963. Emotions in the perspective of human evolution. In *Expression of the emotions in man*, ed. Peter H. Knapp, 300–317. New York: International Universities Press.

Harkness, Sara and Charles M. Super. 1983. The cultural construction of child development: A framework for the socialization of affect. *Ethos* 11:221–231.

1985. Child–environment interactions in the socialization of affect. In *The socialization of emotions*, eds. M. Lewis and C. Saarni, 21–36. New York: Plenum Press.

Hatfield, Elaine, John Cacioppo, and Richard Rapson. 1994. *Emotional contagion*. Cambridge: Cambridge University Press.

Herdt, Gilbert. 1990. Sambia nosebleeding rites and male proximity to women. In *Cultural psychology: Essays on comparative human development*, eds. J. Stigler, R. Shweder, and G. Herdt, 366–400. Cambridge: Cambridge University Press.

Hinton, Alexander L. 1993. Prolegomenon to a processual approach to the emotions. *Ethos* 21:417–451.

Hinton, Geoffrey E. 1993. How neural networks learn from experience. In *Mind and brain: Readings from* Scientific American, 113–124. New York: W. H. Freeman and Company.

Hochschild, Arlie Russell. 1979. Emotion work, feeling rules, and social structure. *American Journal of Sociology* 85:551–575.

1983. *The managed heart: Commercialization of human feeling*. Berkeley: University of California Press.

Honda, Y. 1983. DSM-III in Japan. In *International perspectives on DSM-III*, ed. R. L. Spitzer, J. B. W. Williams, and A. E. Skodol, 55–76. Washington: American Psychiatric Press.

Izard, Carroll. 1978. On the ontogenesis of emotions and emotion-cognition relationships in infancy. In *The development of affect*, ed. M. Lewis and L. Rosenblum, 389–413. New York: Plenum Press.

1979. Emotions as motivations: An evolutionary-developmental perspective. In *Nebraska symposium on motivation*, 1978, 163–199. Lincoln, NE: University of Nebraska Press.

1990. The substrates and functions of emotion feelings: William James and current emotion theory. *Personality and Social Psychology Bulletin* 16:626–635.

Jacobson, Marcus. 1969. Development of specific neural connections. *Science* 163: 543–547.

James, William. 1890. *The principles of psychology*. New York: Holt.

Jenkins, Janis H. 1996. Culture, emotion, and psychiatric disorder. In *Medical anthropology: Contemporary theory and method*, revised ed., ed. C. Sargent and T. Johnson, 71–87. Westport, CT: Praeger.

Jenkins, Janis H., Arthur Kleinman, and Byron Good. 1991. Cross-cultural aspects of depression. In *Advances in affective disorders: Psychosocial aspects*. Vol. I, ed. L. Beckert and A. Kleinman, 136–160. Hillsdale, NJ: Erlbaum.

Kagan, Jerome. 1978. On emotion and its development: A working paper. In *The development of affect*, ed. M. Lewis and L. Rosenblum, 11–41. New York and London: Plenum Press.

Kandel, Eric and Robert Hawkins. 1993. The biological basis of learning and individuality. In *Mind and brain: Readings from* Scientific American, 40–53. New York: W. H. Freeman and company.

Kelly-Byrne, Diana. 1989. *A child's play life: An ethnographic study*. New York and London: Teachers' College Press.

Kemper, T. D. 1981. Social constructionist and positivistic approaches to the sociology of emotions. *American Journal of Sociology* 87:337–362.

Kleinman, Arthur. 1988. *Rethinking psychiatry: From cultural category to personal experience*. New York: Free Press.

Konner, Melvin. 1982. *The tangled wing: Biological constraints on the human spirit*. New York: Henry Holt and Company.

1991. Universals of behavioral development in relation to brain myelination. In *Brain maturation and cognitive development: Comparative and cross-cultural perspectives*, ed. K. Gibson and A. Petersen, 181–223. New York: Aldine de Gruyter.

n.d. Presentation given at the Emory Anthropology Department Mellon Symposium on Culture and the Evolution of Human Latency, Spring 1995.

Kunst-Wilson, W. R. and R. B. Zajonc. 1980. Affective discrimination of stimuli that cannot be recognized. *Science* 207:557–558.

Kupfermann, Irving. 1991. Hypothalamus and limbic system. In *Principles of neural science*, 3rd ed., ed. E. Kandel, J. Schwartz, and T. Jessell, 735–760. New York: Elsevier.

Lakoff, George and Zoltan Kovecses. 1987. The cognitive model of anger inherent in American English. In *Cultural models in language and thought*, ed. D. Holland and N. Quinn, 195–221. Cambridge: Cambridge University Press.

Lang, Peter, Margaret Bradley, and Bruce Cuthbert. 1992. A motivational analysis of emotion: Reflex-cortex connections. *Psychological Science* 3:44–49.

Lazarus, Richard. 1982. Thoughts on the relations between emotion and cognition. *American Psychologist* 37:1019–1024.

1984. On the primacy of cognition. *American Psychologist* 39:124–129.

1991. Progress on a cognitive-motivational-relational theory of emotion. *American Psychologist* 46:819–834.

LeDoux, Joseph. 1986. The neurobiology of emotion. In *Mind and brain: Dialogues in cognitive neuroscience*, ed. J. LeDoux and W. Hirst, 301–354. Cambridge: Cambridge University Press.

Levenson, R, P. Ekman, K. Heider, and W. Friesen. 1992. Emotion and autonomic nervous system activity in the Minangkabau of West Sumatra. *Journal of Personality and Social Psychology* 62:972–988.

LeVine, Robert. 1990. Infant environments in psychoanalysis: A cross-cultural perspective. In *Cultural psychology: Essays on comparative human development*, ed. J. Stigler, R. Shweder, and G. Herdt, 454–474. New York: Cambridge University Press.

LeVine, Robert, Suzanne Dixon, Sarah LeVine, *et al.* 1994. *Childcare and culture: Lessons from Africa*. Cambridge: Cambridge University Press.

Levy, Robert I. 1973. *Tahitians: Mind and experience in the Society Islands.* Chicago: University of Chicago Press.

1978. Tahitian gentleness and redundant controls. In *Learning non-aggression*, ed. A. Montagu, 222–235. New York: Oxford University Press.

1984. Emotion, knowing, and culture. In *Culture theory: Essays in mind, self, and emotion*, ed. R. Shweder and R. LeVine, 214–237. Cambridge: Cambridge University Press.

Libet, B. 1978. Neuronal vs. subjective timing for a conscious sensory experience. In *Cerebral correlates of conscious experience*, ed. P. A. Buser and A. Rougeul-Buser, 69–82. Amsterdam: North-Holland.

Libet, B., E. W. Wright, B. Feinstein, and D. K. Pearl. 1979. Subjective referral of the timing for a conscious sensory experience. *Brain* 102:193–224.

Lindholm, Charles. 1988. The social structure of emotional constraint. *Ethos* 16:227–246.

Lock, Margaret. 1987. DSM-III as a culture-bound construct: Commentary on "culture-bound syndromes and international disease classification." *Culture, Medicine, and Psychiatry* 11:35–42.

Lutz, Catherine. 1988. *Unnatural emotions: Everyday sentiments on a Micronesian atoll and their challenge to Western theory*. Chicago: University of Chicago Press.

Lutz, Catherine and Geoffrey White. 1986. The anthropology of emotions. *Annual Review of Anthropology* 15:405–436.

MacLean, Paul. 1963. Phylogenesis. In *Expression of the emotions in man*, ed. Peter H. Knapp, 16–35. New York: International Universities Press.

1980. Sensory and perceptive factors in emotional functions of the triune brain. In *Explaining emotions*, ed. A. Rorty, 9–36. Berkeley, CA: University of California Press.

Mandler, George. 1984. *Mind and body*. New York: W. W. Norton & Co.

Markus, Hazel and Shinobu Kitayama. 1991. Culture and the self: Implications for cognition, motivation, and emotion. *Psychological Review* 98:224–253.

1994. The cultural construction of self and emotion: Implications for social behavior. In *Emotion and culture: Empirical studies of mutual influence*, ed. S. Kitayama and H. Markus, 89–130. Washington, DC: APA.

Murphy, Sheila and R. B. Zajonc. 1993. Affect, cognition, and awareness: Affective priming with optimal and suboptimal stimulus exposures. *Journal of Personality and Social Psychology* 64:723–739.

Murray, D. W. and Gregory Button. 1988. Human emotions: Some problems of Wierzbicka's ''Simples.'' *American Anthropologist* 90:684–686.

Neisser, Ulrich. 1976. *Cognition and reality*. San Francisco, CA: W. H. Freeman.

Nesse, Randolph. 1990a. Evolutionary explanations of emotions. *Human Nature* 1:261–289.

1990b. The evolutionary functions of repression and the ego defenses. *Journal of the American Academy of Psychoanalysis* 18:260–285.

Nesse, Randolph and Alan Lloyd. 1992. The evolution of psychodynamic mechanisms. In *The adapted mind: Evolutionary psychology and the generation of culture*, ed. J. Barkow, L. Cosmides, and J. Tooby, 601–624. New York: Oxford University Press.

Nisbett, R. E. and T. D. Wilson. 1977. Telling more than we can know: Verbal reports on mental processes. *Psychological Review* 84:231–259.

Oyama, Susan. 1985. *The ontogeny of information: Developmental systems and evolution*. Cambridge: Cambridge University Press.

Papez, James W. 1937. A proposed mechanism of emotion. *Archives of Neurology and Psychiatry* 38:725–743.

Parish, Steven M. 1991. The sacred mind: Newar cultural representations of mental life and the production of moral consciousness. *Ethos* 19:313–351.

Paul, Robert A. 1987. The individual and society in biological and cultural anthropology. *Cultural Anthropology* 2:80–93.

1990. What does anybody want?: Desire, purpose, and the acting subject in the study of culture. *Cultural Anthropology* 5:431–451.

Plutchik, Robert. 1980. A general psychoevolutionary theory of emotion. In *Emotion: Theory, research, and experience*, vol. I, ed. R. Plutchik and H. Kellerman, 3–33. San Diego, CA: Academic Press.

1990. Emotions and psychotherapy: A psychoevolutionary perspective. In *Emotion: Theory, research, and experience*, vol. 5, ed. R. Plutchik and H. Kellerman, 3–41. San Diego, CA: Academic Press.

Prince, Raymond and Françoise Tcheng-Laroche. 1987. Culture-bound syndromes and international disease classifications. *Culture, Medicine, and Psychiatry* 11(1):3–19.

Rogoff, Barbara. 1990. *Apprenticeship in thinking: Cognitive development in social context.* New York: Oxford University Press.

Roland, Alan. 1988. *In search of self in India and Japan: Toward a cross-cultural psychology.* Princeton, NJ: Princeton University Press.

Rosaldo, Michelle Z. 1984. Toward an anthropology of self and feeling. In *Culture theory: Essays in mind, self, and emotion*, ed. R. Shweder and R. LeVine, 137–157. Cambridge: Cambridge University Press.

Rosaldo, Renato. 1989. Grief and a headhunter's rage. In *Culture and truth: The remaking of social analysis*, 1–21. Boston: Beacon.

Rosenberger, Nancy, ed. 1992. *Japanese sense of self.* Cambridge: Cambridge University Press.

Rosenblatt, Paul C., R. P. Walsh, and D. A. Jackson. 1976. *Grief and mourning in cross-cultural perspective.* New Haven: HRAF Press.

Rosenblum, Leonard. 1978. Affective maturation and the mother–infant relationship. In *The development of affect*, ed. M. Lewis and L. Rosenblum, 275–292. New York: Plenum Press.

Samuel, Geoffrey. 1990. *Mind, body and culture: Anthropology and the biological interface.* Cambridge: Cambridge University Press.

Schacter, S. and J. Singer. 1962. Cognitive, social, and physiological determinants of emotional state. *Psychological Review* 69:379–399.

Schutz, Alfred. 1962. *The problem of social reality*, Collected Papers, vol. I. The Hague: Martinus Nijhoff.

Schwartz, Theodore. 1978. Where is the culture?: Personality as the distributive locus of culture. In *The making of psychological anthropology*, ed. G. Spindler and L. Spindler. Berkeley: University of California Press.

1992. Anthropology and psychology: An unrequited relationship. In *New directions in psychological anthropology*, ed., T. Schwartz, G. White, and C. Lutz, 324–349. Cambridge: Cambridge University Press.

Shatz, Carla. 1993. The developing brain. In *Mind and brain: Readings from* Scientific American, 15–26. New York: W.H. Freeman and company.

Shea, Brian. 1989. Heterochrony in human evolution: The case for neoteny reconsidered. *Yearbook of Physical Anthropology* 32:69–101.

Shibutani, Tamotsu. 1961. *Society and personality.* Englewood Cliffs, NJ: Prentice-Hall.

Shore, Bradd. 1996. *Culture in mind: Cognition, culture, and the problem of meaning.* New York: Oxford University Press.

Solomon, Robert C. 1984. Getting angry: The Jamesian theory of emotion in anthropology. In *Culture theory: Essays on mind, self, and emotion*, ed. R. Shweder and R. LeVine, 238–254. Cambridge: Cambridge University Press.

Spiro, Melford E. 1978 [1967]. *Burmese supernaturalism.* Philadelphia: ISHI.

1984. Some reflections on cultural determinism and relativism with special reference to emotion and reason. In *Culture theory: Essays on mind, self, and emotion*, ed. R. Shweder and R. LeVine, 323–346. Cambridge: Cambridge University Press.

1990. On the strange and the familiar in recent anthropological thought. In *Cultural psychology: Essays on comparative human development*, ed. J. Stigler, R. Shweder, and G. Herdt, 47–61. Cambridge: Cambridge University Press.

1992. A critique of cultural relativism, with special reference to epistemological relativism. In *Anthropological other or Burmese brother?: Studies in cultural analysis*, 3–52. New Brunswick, NJ: Transaction.

Super, Charles M. and Sara Harkness. 1986. The developmental niche: A conceptualization at the interface of child and culture. *International Journal of Behavioral Development* 9:545–569.

Tobin, Joseph, David Wu, and Dana Davidson. 1989. *Preschool in three cultures: Japan, China and the United States*. New Haven: Yale University Press.

Tooby, John and Leda Cosmides. 1990. The past explains the present: Emotional adaptations and the structure of ancestral environments. *Ethology and Sociobiology* 11:375–424.

1992. The psychological foundations of culture. In *The adapted mind: Evolutionary psychology and the generation of culture*, ed. J. Barkow, L. Cosmides, and J. Tooby, 19–136. New York: Oxford University Press.

Trivers, Robert. 1971. The evolution of reciprocal altruism. *Quarterly Review of Biology* 46:35–57.

1974. Parent–offspring conflict. *American Zoologist* 14:249–264.

Vincent, Jean-Didier. 1990. *The biology of emotions*, translated by J. Hughes. Cambridge: Basil Blackwell, Inc.

Weinrich, James. 1980. Toward a sociobiological theory of the emotions. In *Emotion: Theory, research, and experience*. Vol. I, ed. R. Plutchik and H. Kellerman, 113–138. San Diego, CA: Academic Press.

Westen, Drew. 1985. *Self and society: Narcissism, collectivism, and the development of morals*. New York: Cambridge University Press.

Whiten, Andrew. n.d. The evolution and development of emotional states, emotional expressions and emotion-reading in human and non-human primates. In *Emotions: A biocultural perspective*, ed. B. Shore and C. Worthman (forthcoming).

Wierzbicka, Anna. 1988. Semantic primitives: A rejoinder to Murray and Button. *American Anthropologist* 90:686–689.

Winson, Jonathan. 1985. *Brain and psyche: The biology of the unconscious*. New York: Vintage Books.

Worthman, Carol. 1992. Cupid and psyche: Investigative syncretism in biological and psychosocial anthropology. In *New directions in psychological anthropology*, ed. T. Schwartz, G. White, and C. Lutz, 150–178. Cambridge: Cambridge University Press.

1995. Biocultural bases of human variation. *International Society for the Study of Behavioral Development (ISSBD) Newsletter* 27:10–13.

Zajonc, R. B. 1980. Feeling and thinking: Preferences need no inferences. *American Psychologist* 35(2):151–175.

Zajonc, R. B., S. Murphy, and M. Inglehart. 1989. Feeling and facial efference: Implications of a vascular theory of emotions. *Psychological Review* 96:395–416.

7 Making symbols meaningful: Human emotions and the limbic system

Este Armstrong

Symbolic capabilities are critical for our human cultural way of life. The latter adaptations encompass behaviors that create and channel our interactions with the physical, interpersonal, and mental environments surrounding us. Although scientists have yet to determine exactly how the brain constructs and manipulates symbols, we do know that structures in the forebrain, particularly the cortex and thalamus, are crucial for these capabilities. As a consequence, more research has been aimed at elucidating the evolutionary history of these regions than other spheres, such as the limbic system, that portion of the brain responsible for the elaboration, integration, and coordination of our emotions.

Analyses of the limbic system have long been recognized as being important for understanding human emotions *per se*, the limits they place on human behavior and social organization (Armstrong *et al.* 1987; Heath 1963; Heath *et al.* 1955; Isaacson 1974; Kling and Steklis 1976). It is my contention that the limbic system is critical for the human capacity of making symbols as real and important (if not more so) as structures and systems in the physical and interpersonal realms. New and powerful perspectives on both the human use and elaboration of symbols and the cultural constructions of emotions will emerge as the interactions between the emotional centers of the brain and the cognitive, neocortical ones are analyzed. The analysis in this chapter provides such a perspective. In doing so, comparative neuroanatomic data about the size and connections of different components of the limbic system are analyzed for their support of or conflict with hypotheses about the role of emotions in human symbolism.

In this essay, emotions are neither considered as isolated neurophysiological states nor as wholly culturally determined, but it is recognized that two forces, societal and biological, are *perforce* integrated (Armstrong 1991; Armstrong *et al.* 1987: Laughlin 1987; Hinton 1993). It is the premise of this chapter that without interaction between limbic and cortical structures, we would neither be symbol bearing animals nor have symbolic objects, behaviors, and relationships influence our emotions. This chapter investigates how human emotions can be both neurophysiologically based yet concerned with symbols. Irrespective of whether the latter concern language, ideas, social relationships, or objects, symbols trigger emotions and, in turn, become actualized by them. The thesis draws upon comparative evidence showing that emotional centers enlarged during human evolution within the context of stable cortical-limbic connections, thereby providing humans with a brain in which symbols interest, motivate, and satisfy many of our desires.

The limbic system

Human emotions and their neurological base, the limbic system, are frequently typified as being phylogenetically old. It has been asserted that the enlargement and increased complexity of human cortical association areas contrast with the conservation of emotions and the limbic system (MacLean 1982). In this paradigm, the functions of the limbic system, emotions, are thought of as being less important for human behavior than they are for other primates. A further extension of these ideas is that human cognition evolved by either extricating cortical circuits from limbic ones, and thereby freeing them, or by inhibiting the latter (Geschwind 1965; Jurgens 1982; Yakovlev 1971).

Other scientists question that paradigm and instead suggest that the emotional centers of the brain have not become less important, but play new roles in human behavior (Laughlin and d'Aquili 1974; Reynolds 1981; Steklis and Raleigh 1979). One paradigm suggests that during human evolution, the emotional centers of the brain evolved into a circuitry that reifies symbols (Armstrong 1991), a role that depends on the interactions of limbic and cognitive structures. A corollary of this model is that a major function for the human limbic system is to elaborate, modulate, and inhibit culturally defined objects and relationships. To do this, the physiological states called emotions must interact with symbolic thought processes.

The limbic system is a heterogeneous collection of cortical and subcortical forebrain structures that are grouped together by functional considerations (Figure 7.1). Major cortical structures include the cingulate gyrus and hippocampus and their respective fiber bundles: the cingulum and fornix. Noncortical structures include two telencephalic (arising from the embryonic cortical mantle) complexes, the amygdala and the septum, and several diencephalic structures, like the anterior and mediodorsal thalamic nuclei and the mammillary bodies of the hypothalamus. The diencephalic nuclei have major connections with the telencephalic limbic structures. Major subcortical fiber tracts include the stria terminalis, the mamillothalamic tract and the medial forebrain bundle (Papez 1937; MacLean 1952, 1982; Isaacson 1974; Armstrong 1991).

As an integrated circuit, the mammalian limbic system broadly functions

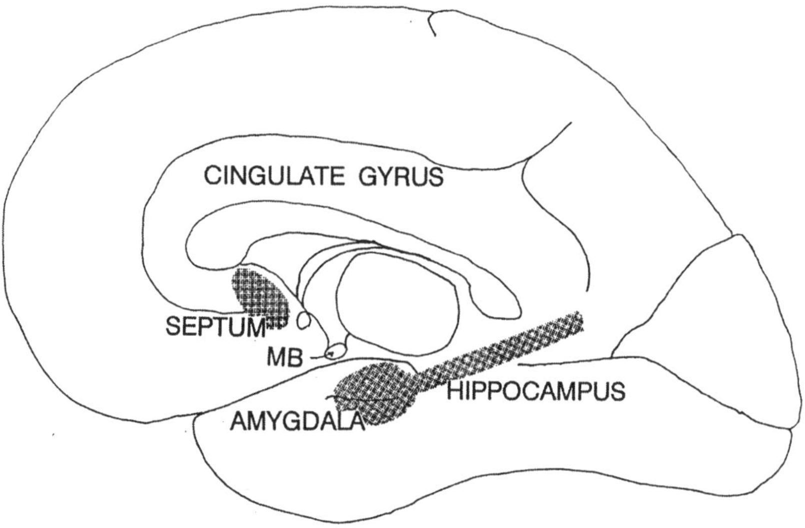

Figure 7.1. Line drawing of a hemisected human brain. The limbic structures are labeled. MB = mamillary body. The septum, amygdala, and hippocampus are covered by cortex and are not actually seen in a hemisected preparation.

to determine the significance of stimuli. In extreme events, the limbic system coordinates the "flight or fight" syndromes. In non-human animals, limbic activity is associated with observable and measurable behaviors of feeding, olfaction, fighting, sex, and memory (MacLean 1990; Squire and Zola-Morgan 1991; Isaacson 1974). As befits a region of the brain integrating information about the environment so that the appropriate visceral reactions can be implemented, limbic structures not only monitor highly processed synchronic information, but are responsible for retrieving past situations and ensuring that present experiences are saved. Memory access and formation involve limbic circuits. Although learned motor skills do not use limbic regions, linguistically mediated and other symbolic systems do (Squire and Zola-Morgan 1991).

In addition, limbic activities directly and indirectly affect visceral effector mechanisms via the autonomic nervous system, levels of hormones, and general states of arousal as well as body posture and facial expression. The behaviors can be observed and studied in animals as well as in humans, but obviously only in people can subjective feelings be stated. Stimulation in and around the amygdala, for example, produces displays of aggression and defensive reactions in animals and feelings of apprehension, anxiety, fear, and anger in humans (Heath and Mickle 1955; MacLean 1990). By contrast, stimulation in the septal region elicits increased sociability and neural self-stimulation in animals and feelings of well-being and sexual arousal in humans (Heath 1963; Heath and Mickle 1955; Isaacson 1974).

Although these subjective feelings and their underlying neurophysiological states can be artificially elicited out of context, normally these human behaviors are regulated and influenced by cultural traditions. No emotion is free from cultural proscription and prescription and every symbol can be attached to emotions. If a symbol is of interest to us, it carries an emotional valence. A cultural way of life could not have evolved unless human emotional and symbolic capabilities interacted.

The degree of cultural determinacy for subjective states and feelings continues to be debated (reviewed by Lutz and White 1986; Myers 1990; Hinton 1993). It is my position that human feelings are not restricted to coloring cerebral events, a statement that implies that colorless activity and thoughts exist as well, but are critically important in providing people with the capacity to focus on and reify symbols. Conversely, cultural symbols, relationships, and configurations can modulate, by activating or inhibiting, different levels of activity in emotional centers. These capabilities are necessary for a cultural life. Because symbols can grab our attention and influence our behavior, an analysis of the limbic system and its interactions with the neocortex is necessary to clarify how emotions can both be neurophysiological states yet vary by culture and social context. In turn, these understandings can help elucidate the limits and complexities of biological and cultural interactions.

Evolution of the limbic system

Several conceptual and biological aspects of the limbic system, the neurological basis of emotions, are reviewed here. A consideration of the paradigm that our emotions are primitive behaviors elaborated from parts of the brain which have not evolved will be examined by analyzing quantitative neuroanatomic data. Next, the altered proportions of olfactory structures will be analyzed. They manifest alterations that have pushed the sizes and proportions away from those of other primates, illustrating that under appropriate selection pressures vast changes in limbic structures could, and did, occur. I will conclude with a brief assessment of how conserved patterns of corticolimbic interconnections allow the emotional centers of the human brain to monitor and process symbolic information. These interactions are probably also the major neurological substrate by which increased complexity of social organization and cognition are linked (Byrne and Whiten 1988; Humphrey 1988; Jolly 1966). Because this linkage lies outside the purview of this essay, the association of increasing social and cognitive complexities will be discussed only briefly. The major thrust of this essay is that the use of symbols to interact with the physical, social, and mental worlds means that emotions are stimulated and constrained by culturally defined worlds.

Is the human limbic system conservative or derived?

Statements that the limbic system is phylogenetically old (MacLean 1952, 1982), imply a fixity of structure and function; namely, that our emotions remain similar to those of other mammals. If this paradigm is accurate, one prediction would be that human neurophysiological states of emotions would be universal and primitive, activated by similar stimuli and elaborated and expressed the same way. One proponent of the idea that the human limbic system did not evolve after our ancestors separated from those of the great apes, Paul MacLean, has promulgated a paradigm in which the human brain is a triune one. In this conceptualization, the human brain is viewed as being constructed from a hierarchy of three brains: a protoreptilean, a paleomammalian (limbic system), and a neomammalian one. According to the triune brain model, the limbic system or paleomammalian brain has a distinct mentality, which is a common denominator in all mammalian brains, and unlike the neomammalian brain (neocortex), the paleomammalian emotional centers did not enlarge or change during human evolution (MacLean 1952, 1982).

The *scala naturae* approach of the triune brain paradigm assumes that the organization of the paleomammalian brain is equivalent in all mammals and that they can be ranked as to how advanced or retarded they are along a single scale. Rabbits, cats, monkeys, and humans are contrasted as though each formed a stage or grade that all mammals passed through to reach a higher level. In this conceptualization, no divergence by organization exists. Differences are along a single scale, and the emotional centers of primates, including humans, are considered to have an immutable paleomammalian configuration. Only the mushrooming of the neocortex, an event that occurred after the limbic system stabilized, is said to distinguish the evolution of the human brain (MacLean 1952, 1982).

Morphometric analyses of limbic and other neural structures allow this hypothesis and its corollaries to be tested. If the sizes of limbic structures in human and ape brains were the same, support for the triune brain hypothesis would be strengthened. Such support would lend credence to the idea that human emotions are primitive behaviors, shared with apes and other primates, and are unlikely candidates for the elaboration and modulation of culturally dependent feelings. Enlargement of the emotional centers, on the other hand, would suggest that other evolutionary hypotheses are more likely.

When neural structures among apes and humans are compared, a mosaic of quantitative relationships is observed. Since no new neural structures distinguish human from ape brains (Armstrong 1990), quantitative analyses are necessary to detect evolutionary shifts. Traits in the human brain are considered derived if morphometric differences in size or shape distinguish them from their counterparts in ape brains. The interpretation of what represents a significant amount of difference depends in large part on whether the size or shape of the human structure is that expected according to rules of scaling. That is, if the size of a given structure is associated with the overall size of the brain or body among non-human primates, and if that relationship predicts the observed human one, then the major evolutionary selection was one of maintaining a quantitative link.

Morphometric data show that a few regions in the human brain are regressed (absolutely smaller than the homologous regions in apes' brains), some are conserved (have the same size), most scale according to brain weight, and a few are relatively enlarged (Armstrong 1982, 1990). In this regard, limbic regions resemble those of other neural systems. Structures in the limbic system also vary in how far they deviate from absolute and relative sizes found in non-human primates, suggesting differential selection pressures on components within the limbic system.

Comparative studies of the visual system, the best analyzed neural system, can provide an evolutionary perspective on how the human brain differs from those of other primates, and can be used as a foil for examining changes in the emotional centers of the brain. We know, for example, that the functional units of the visual cortex are numerous columns extending across the cortical depth. Each column stretches from the outer (pial) surface of the cortex to the inner white matter. Primate visual cortex is specialized in having about four times more neurons within a given column than found in any other mammalian taxon or in other parts of the primate cortex (Rockel *et al.* 1980). This trait is conserved in the human brain; that is, it is found in human, ape, and monkey brains. In fact, as shown by the similarities of structures, functions, and quantities of neurons dedicated to the basic abstracting of visual stimuli, the visual system from the retina to the primary visual cortex is conserved in the human brain (Stephan 1969; Armstrong 1979, 1990). Although a vast expansion of the brain occurred during human evolution (the human brain is about three and a half times bigger than that of apes), the primary visual cortex is the same size in human and ape brains. On account of the similarity in size and neuronal architecture among humans and apes, the visual structures of the retina, thalamus, and primary visual cortex are considered evolutionarily conserved. The parts of the visual cortex concerned with higher order analysis of visual perception, on the other hand, have undergone an unknown amount of evolutionary change and are considered derived (Armstrong 1990; Passingham 1973).

Thus a given neural system can manifest both conserved (shared) and derived (unique) morphometric traits. The presence of one does not preclude the other. Furthermore, the conservation of a neural feature among non-human primates does not prevent evolutionary changes of it in the human (or in any other taxon) brain, nor does the presence of a primate-derived feature mean that this trait necessarily evolved further during human evolution. What is true for the visual system can be observed in other neural systems, like the limbic and cognitive systems.

Regions in the human brain involved with emotions, that is, structures of the limbic system, show a mosaic of alterations. A few limbic components have regressed in size and are absolutely smaller than those found in other, smaller brained primates (see below, pp. 263). Most limbic complexes have enlarged to the size predicted on the basis of the increase in brain size, but in the human brain a few have increased to sizes bigger than that predicted by brain size.

To date, only one limbic region, Area 13 of the orbital frontal cortex, has been found to be conserved in size among humans and apes (Semendeferi *et al.* 1998). Thus, a pattern of conservation similar to stabilization seen in regions of the visual and auditory systems (Armstrong 1979, 1980, 1982) and as predicted by the triune brain hypothesis (MacLean 1952, 1982) is possible, but rarely observed in the limbic system. During human evolution, selection pressures have not stabilized the sizes of the emotional centers of the brain, but have either diminished or, more frequently, enlarged them.

Structures in the human limbic system that are bigger than those in apes have generally maintained a conserved histological architecture, suggesting a preservation of patterns of connections and forms of interaction (Andy and Stephan 1976; Armstrong 1986; Zilles *et al.* 1986, 1987; Stephan *et al.* 1981, 1987). Analyses of the posterior cingulate gyrus, a region highly interconnected with other limbic structures and with multimodal cortex (Mesulam *et al.* 1977; Armstrong 1990) provide an example. The measurements show that the absolute amount of space for interneuronal connections (neuropil) distinguishes the human region from those of apes and Old World monkeys. Other aspects of the cellular architecture remain unchanged. The constancy in cellular architecture supports the idea that the number of connections increased without a massive repatterning of connections (Zilles *et al.* 1986; Armstrong *et al.* 1986).

Furthermore, the observed conservation of cortical organization among human, ape, and Old World monkeys is not a limitation of the methodology used. The same techniques showed significant differences in cortical architecture between prosimians and anthropoids and between New World monkeys and Old World monkeys. In these instances, morphometric shifts are accompanied by detectable architectural differences (Armstrong 1986; Armstrong *et al.* 1986; Zilles *et al.* 1986). Similarities in architecture among human, ape, and Old World monkey brains found in many centers of the limbic system suggest that these three taxa share a common organization of those neural functions.

Despite the architectural conservation that is found in most of its components, the human limbic system does not fit the criteria necessary for a conserved neural system. Its unique aspects include absolute regression in particular populations of neurons, especially those concerned with olfaction. At the same time, other limbic populations enlarged (see below, Figure 7.2). Like the neocortex, the sizes of most emotional centers scale according to brain weight and have numbers of neurons that are expected on the basis of brain weight. A few human limbic complexes have evolved an excess number of neurons for the size of the brain (Armstrong 1980, 1982, 1986, 1990, 1991). The morphometric data illustrate the evolutionarily derived nature of the human limbic system. The enlargement of the emotional centers means an increased number of neurons and space is available for elaborating and refining their associated functions, particularly memory and emotions.

Olfaction has a relatively small input into the human limbic system

In the mammalian brain, olfactory stimuli are relayed into the perirhinal areas of cortex where they have both direct and indirect access to limbic regions, particularly the amygdala, entorhinal cortex and parts of the orbitofrontal cortex. As a group, primates have relatively small olfactory structures (Stephan *et al.* 1981), a trait that probably characterized primates since the Eocene (Gurche 1982) or may have arisen later in phylogeny through regression (Clark 1959; Martin 1973).

Among extant primates, the sizes of olfactory bulbs are significantly associated with brain size, but the relative size of the olfactory apparatus separates anthropoids from prosimians. Given a similarly sized brain, anthropoids have absolutely smaller olfactory bulbs than prosimians (Stephan *et al.* 1981). In this instance, humans do not continue the trend established among non-human anthropoids. The size of the human olfactory bulbs matches those from monkeys with brain weights close to 100 grams (*Homo sapiens* olfactory bulb = 114 mm^3; *Cercopithecus mitis* with a brain weight of 75 grams has an olfactory bulb of 117 mm^3. By contrast, the common chimpanzee and gorilla have olfactory bulbs that are 257 and 316 mm^3 respectively (data from Stephan *et al.* [1981]). The small absolute size of the human olfactory bulbs is a case of regression.

Despite the fact that the olfactory system has a direct input into the emotional centers of the brain, it does not follow that limbic nuclei are regressed in either absolute or relative size. Most of them are not. These and data from other sensory and motor systems argue against the idea that the sizes of

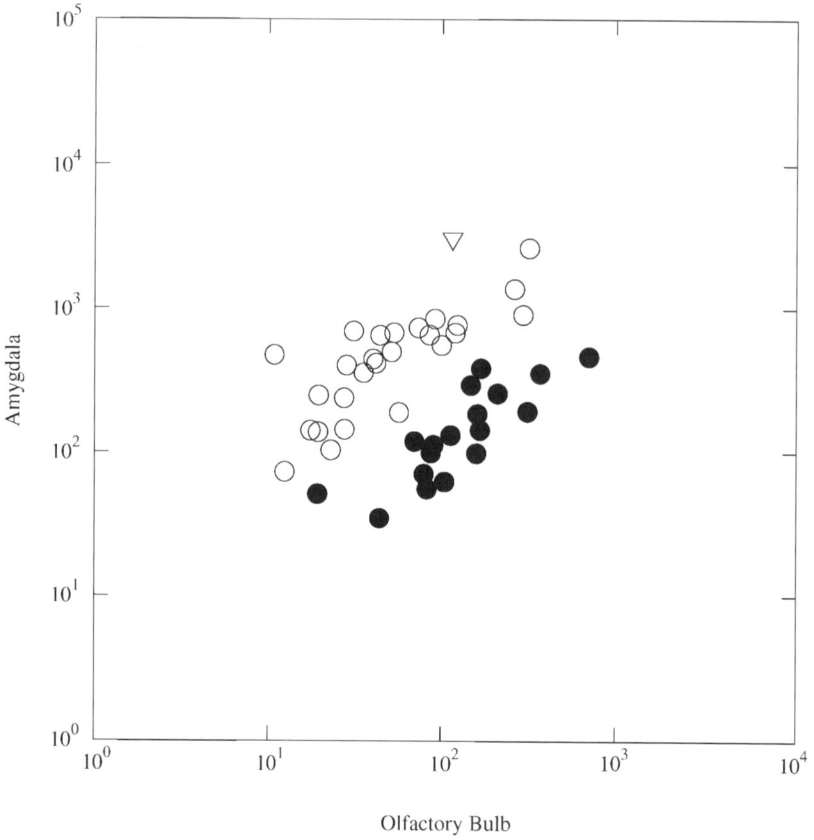

Figure 7.2. Graph of amygdala size as a function of olfactory bulb size. Prosimians are filled circles, monkeys and apes are open circles and the human value is the triangle. The closest primate to the human is the gorilla. *Source*: Data from Stephan *et al.* 1981.

peripheral structures, such as skin and muscles, control the sizes of brain structures or that of the total brain (Jerison 1973). Rather, peripheral inputs are one of many influences (Armstrong 1991).

To give an example, the sizes of limbic structures can be studied as a function of the olfactory bulb size. In both anthropoids and prosimians, bigger olfactory bulbs are associated with larger amygdalae, one of the limbic structures that is also a target for incoming olfactory fibers. At the same time, however, anthropoids have smaller olfactory bulbs for the same sized amygdalae than prosimians (Figure 7.2). Studying the size of the amygdala as a function of those of olfactory bulbs reveals that the human amygdala is greatly enlarged for an anthropoid. Although primary and secondary olfactory afferents synapse within the amygdala, other connections and selective pressures have produced an enlarged human amygdala. The proportions of afferents have changed.

No quantitative analyses of the amygdala's neuronal architecture have yet been undertaken. Descriptive work clearly identifies homologous regions in human and non-human primate brains (de Olmos 1990), but whether the altered proportions of non-olfactory-to-olfactory inputs has a measurable impact on the organization of perikarya remains to be determined. The above morphometric data predict a significant architectural shift (more than a simple increase in neuropil) will be observed in a comparative study of human and non-human anthropoid amygdala.

Given the direct olfactory input into the emotional centers of the brain, an unchanged or expanded size of limbic structures coupled with a decreased olfactory input means that more limbic neurons are free to process other forms of stimuli. Another way to state this is that an amygdala of the same size will have more space allocated for processing non-olfactory information in an anthropoid brain than in a prosimian one. Except for a few small nuclei, like the septal nucleus *pars triangularis* (Andy and Stephan 1976; Armstrong 1991), the reduced size of the olfactory input has not produced smaller limbic structures.

The decrease in absolute size of the human *pars triangularis* shows that limbic nuclei can be reduced (Armstrong 1990). Neural structures do not passively enlarge just because the brain in which they are embedded becomes bigger. Whether the decrease in the size of the human *pars triangularis* reflects a decrease in sensory information or is the result of interference with newer functions is not clear. In any case, the fact that human limbic regions enlarged signifies that these neurons are involved in critical processes. Indeed, the sizes of regions involved with emotions are highly correlated with the size of the brain (Armstrong 1991), a rough statement that their interactions are important for functions in widespread regions.

Both the decrease of olfactory input into the limbic system and the expansion of numbers of neurons and neuropil within it suggest that the human limbic system is a derived structure. The human limbic system is capable of abstracting, processing and synthesizing more non-olfactory information than can the homologous centers in the brains of other primates. In these features, changes in the limbic system resemble those of the neocortex. Conservation of the major forms of non-olfactory neural architecture in limbic structures suggests that, although more information is being processed in the human brain, the basic patterns of abstraction, integration, and elaboration are shared with apes.

Neurobiology supports a cultural definition of emotions

One characteristic of the anthropoid limbic system is that the multimodal cortex serves as its predominant source of information. As sensory systems abstract and relay stimuli, the resultant information flows into the cortex, where it is further analyzed and processed in both parallel channels and serial nodes. The vast majority of signals are processed hierarchically, first in the primary cortex and then fed forward to various unimodal association regions, regions which process information from only one sensory modality albeit in diverse functions and circuits. Information reaches multimodal cortex (cortex that receives information from more than one sensory modality) after it is processed in various unimodal regions (Pandya and Selzer 1982; Pandya *et al.* 1988). In these processes, feedforward connections promote the activation of downstream neurons and cellular columns, and contrast with feedback connections, which help monitor and correct activities but do not promote the spread of activity into new regions. The various feedforward connections of different circuits eventually bring information to multimodal cortex. Thus the most highly processed information occurs in multimodal association regions.

Not all information is processed using the same chain, however, and cognition requires the simultaneous activation of several sets of neurons, the precise identity of the sets changing as the tasks alter (Roland and Friberg 1985; Goldman-Rakic 1988). In the human brain, complex and symbolic thinking routinely activate regions within several multimodal lobules. While the reproducibility of activating the same small and discrete regions in different individuals has been overwhelmed by the individual variation present in both the brain and the tasks, larger cortical regions, like the inferior parietal lobule or lateral prefrontal cortex, are consistently activated. Anatomical studies of anthropoid brains show that these regions are highly interconnected with each other and with the limbic system.

In the primate cortex, the superior temporal, inferior parietal, and lateral prefrontal cortex have been identified as areas where sensory modalities are brought together. Further, functional studies in the human brain show that these regions are activated during complex symbolic tasks, such as language, suggesting that a synthesis of information occurs within and/or among the regions (Bachman and Albert 1990). Anatomical studies of these cortical areas indicate that inputs coming from separate modalities end in different lamina within the same column or in alternating columns within the same area (Goldman-Rakic 1988). In both cases the information is juxtaposed, but because of the architecture of cortical columns, the former is thought to elicit a more powerful response than the latter (Edelman 1987).

A perspective on how culture can define neurophysiologically based emotions can be gained by analyzing the integration of symbolic and limbic circuitry. Because language is the best studied symbolic system of the human brain, I shall briefly summarize the association of language with different nodes of multimodal cortex. Issues of lateralization are more complex than previously thought, particularly when the linguistic tasks become complex (Bachman and Albert 1990), and are not considered here. The interaction of language with the brain's emotional centers models how other symbolic systems, like kinship roles or specific definitions of justice, for example, can trigger, assuage, or otherwise influence our subjectively felt emotions.

The superior temporal multimodal cortex forms part of Wernicke's area and has long been implicated in the comprehension of language. Although some scientists interpret this cortex as responding to sounds whether or not they are symbolic (Roland and Friberg 1985), others think that the evidence is strong that this cortex makes lexical and not just phonemic or syntactic distinctions. The interaction between this multimodal cortical region and the limbic system may be particularly important for learning and retrieving vocabulary (Van Hoesen and Damasio 1987; Damasio and Damasio 1989; Wise *et al.* 1991). One arm of information feeds forward from this region through nodes in the superior temporal multimodal cortex to synapse in limbic regions of the medial temporal lobes (Pandya and Selzer 1982; Pandya *et al.* 1988; Squire and Zola-Morgan 1991). The limbic structures of the hippocampus and amygdala are powerfully influenced this way.

The inferior parietal region, which in the human brain includes parts of the angular and marginal gyri, is another multimodal region that has been implicated in understanding language. Like the superior temporal cortex, the inferior parietal cortex is activated during complex symbolic tasks as part of a distributed system that includes both temporal and lateral prefrontal regions (Roland and Friberg 1985). Its major feedforward connections are to the prefrontal cortex and the posterior cingulate gyrus, a major center of the limbic system (Mesulam *et al.* 1977).

The lateral prefrontal cortex has been called the executive center of the brain. It receives information from the posterior multimodal association cortices, such as the superior temporal and inferior parietal gyri, and, among other tasks, it organizes long-term planning, adjustment to and meeting social goals by monitoring the social appropriateness of actions and their attainment. A variety of regions within the prefrontal cortex are activated during cognition; the more complex the task, the more likely it is that some portion of the prefrontal cortex will be activated (Roland and Friberg 1985). Although connected to other cortical regions by feedback mechanisms, its feedforward output is primarily to the supplementary motor cortex and to the limbic anterior cingulate cortex (Goldman-Rakic 1988). The anterior cingulate gyrus is a limbic structure, which not only processes cortical information, but through its interactions with the hypothalamus and other centers regulating hormone levels and the autonomic nervous system, has a direct role coordinating the outward expressions of emotions.

Thus the three best-studied multimodal regions of the cortex are interconnected with each other and send efferents into the limbic system. The similarity of cellular architecture among human and non-human anthropoid limbic cortex (Armstrong 1986; Armstrong *et al.* 1986; Zilles *et al.* 1986) suggests that this cortex maintains the anthropoid monkey pattern of accessing most of its information from multimodal regions. Likewise architectural studies of Tpt, a multimodal cortex, show many similarities among human and non-human anthropoids. The similarities are especially strong in layer III, the source and target of many corticocortical connections (Buxhoeveden *et al.* 1996). The conservation of the anthropoid pattern of neural connection means that language, our preeminent symbolic system, not only organizes human social and physical worlds, but also structures stimuli for the emotional centers of the brain. The input, being direct, is powerful.

Likewise, the conservation of neural feedback mechanisms predicts that the modulation and expression of human emotions is influenced by cultural systems. Because these connections have a less powerful influence on multimodal cortex than the latter has on the limbic system, the expressive features of emotion are less open to cultural influences.

The above neurobiology may also underlie the phenomenon of increased complexities in cognition being linked with the increased complexity of social organization in the primate order (Byrne and Whiten 1988; Cheney and Seyforth 1990; Humphrey 1988; Jolly 1966). As mentioned above, features of social organization are strongly associated with limbic structures (Armstrong 1980, 1990; Armstrong *et al.* 1987; Kling and Steklis 1976), and cognition with association cortex (Damasio and Damasio 1989; Bachman and Albert 1990; Geschwind 1965). The feedforward and feedback circuitry between multimodal and limbic cortices also enhances the likelihood that a linkage between social organization and cognitive capabilities should occur in primates. Indeed, the pattern of major connectivity between multimodal and limbic cortices appears to be the base for the behavioral adaptive radiation among primates. Like other adaptive radiations, the linkage between social organization and cognitive capabilities is not scalar (or linear) among primates, but has variant forms in diverse clusters of primates. Significant architectural differences in structures where limbic and multimodal influences are commingled are found between prosimians and anthropoids, between New World and Old World monkeys and between humans and other hominoids (Armstrong 1986; Armstrong *et al.* 1987; Buxhoeveden *et al.* 1996; Zilles *et al.* 1986). Thus, one expectation would be that these primate clusters comprise different variants of the primate multimodal-to-limbic architectural paradigm. In this regard, further studies in the cingulate cortices, particularly ones that take into account lateralization and handedness, would be most welcome.

The social and biological construction of emotions

The existence of the neurophysiological states of emotions does not preclude a cultural definition of emotions: the neuroanatomic data reviewed above predict that both biological and social forces are important. That is, studies of neural connections show that those portions of the brain responsible for the construction and comprehension of symbolic systems preprocess the major stimuli coming into emotional centers. Symbols, of all forms, can stimulate the limbic system. Given that symbols are culturally variant, it follows that the elicitation, maintenance, modulation, and inhibition of feelings also vary between cultures and by contexts within a culture.

Anger, for example, is associated with activity in and around the amygdala (Heath and Mickle 1955; Kling and Steklis 1976; MacLean 1990), and is elicited and elaborated differently in different social contexts (Myers 1990). The stimuli, being symbolic, vary between societies and according to relational contexts within a society (Lutz and White 1986; Myers 1990). The existence of cultural rules and constraints does not deny the existence of emotional centers of the brain; rather they show that the stimuli with which the limbic system works is predominantly symbolic. The basic anthropoid pattern of neurobiologic connections, wherein the most highly processed cortical information is fed forward into the limbic system, accounts for this feature. Additionally, the enlargement of human limbic structures supports more graded responses and enhanced processing of that information than found in other anthropoids.

A more detailed picture of structure–function relationships within the human brain will strengthen our understanding of how emotions resemble and differ from other forms of cognition. Studying the interaction between emotions and symbols will help clarify how humans reify symbols, giving meaning to arbitrary relationships, objects, and sounds (Armstrong 1991). Integration between limbic and multimodal cortex is crucial in determining the fixity or fluidity of socially derived meanings.

The neural circuitry supporting the interaction among varied cognitive and emotional centers, as well as within both sets, can be influenced through patterns of use, particularly when the infant is young (Edelman 1987; Hinton 1993; Diamond 1991). Whether more constraints (less flexibility for modulating impulses) exist in the emotional centers than in the multimodal cortex remains to be determined, but the observed differential in size and in neuronal architecture would suggest so. Multimodal cortex, containing many more neurons and connections than the limbic structures, has the potential to modify information and elaborate responses in more diverse ways. It is logical to think, therefore, that neocortical and cognitive structures have more flexibility than do the smaller emotional centers. How the major differences in architecture between multimodal cortex and limbic regions (multimodal cortex is six-layered neocortex, while limbic structures vary from six layers in the posterior cingulate gyrus areas 23 and 31 to three-layered hippocampal allocortex to the non-layered but telencephalic structures like the amygdala) affect functioning is as yet unresolved.

The basic patterning of connections and sizes of neural structures cannot, of course, explain particular forms of behavior whether the behaviors in question are symbolic or emotional. Histories of the cultural traditions, ontogenetic modeling (Hinton 1993), and synchronic contextual configurations must be analyzed if specific patternings of behaviors are to be explained.

The neurobiologic data show, however, that not all stimuli have an equal influence on our emotional centers. The vast preponderance of information received by the limbic system is culturally defined. Emotions are not added to cognitive processing of symbols nor are the latter added to primitive states of feeling. Rather the interactions construct meanings, and, for human beings, meanings are always composed within a cultural milieu. Our brains make it impossible for it to be otherwise.

References

Andy, O. J., and Heinz Stephan. 1976. Septum development in primates. In *The septal nuclei*, J. F. DeFrance, ed. New York: Plenum Press, 3–36.

Armstrong, Este. 1979. A quantitative comparison of the hominoid thalamus. I. Specific sensory relay nuclei. *American Journal of Physical Anthropology* 51:365–381.

1980. A quantitative comparison of the hominoid thalamus. II. Limbic nuclei, *anterior principalis* and *lateralis dorsalis*. *American Journal of Physical Anthropology* 52:43–54.

1982. Mosaic evolution in the primate brain: Differences and similarities in the hominoid thalamus. In *Primate brain evolution: methods and concepts*, ed. E. Armstrong and D. Falk. New York: Plenum Press, 131–161.

Armstrong, Este. 1986. Enlarged limbic structures in the human brain: The anterior thalamus and medial mamillary body. *Brain Research* 362:394–397.

1990. Evolution of the brain. In *The human nervous system*, ed. G. Paxinos. San Diego: Academic Press, 116.

Armstrong, Este. 1991. The limbic system and culture: An allometric analysis of the neocortex and limbic structures. *Human Nature* 2:117–136.

Armstrong, Este, K. Zilles, G. Schlaug, and A. Schleicher. 1986. Comparative aspects of the primate posterior cingulate cortex. *Journal of Comparative Neurology* 253:539–548.

Armstrong Este, M. R. Clarke, and E. M. Hill. 1987. Relative size of the anterior thalamic nuclei differentiates anthropoids by social organization. *Brain, Behavior and Evolution.* 30:263–271.

Bachman, D. L. and M. L. Albert. 1990. The cerebral organization of language. In *Cerebral cortex* ed. A. Peters and E. G. Jones. Vol. 9. New York: Plenum Press. 213–255.

Buxhoeveden, Daniel, William Lefkowitz, Peter Loats, Este Armstrong. 1996. The linear organization of cell columns in human and nonhuman anthropoid Tpt cortex. *Anatomy and Embryology* 194:23–36.

Byrne, R. and A. Whiten, eds. 1988. *Machiavellian intelligence.* New York: Oxford University Press.

Cheney, D. L. and R. M. Seyforth. 1990. *How monkeys see the world.* Chicago: University of Chicago Press.

Clark, W. E. LeGros. 1959. *The antecedents of man.* Edinburgh: Edinburgh University Press.

Damasio, H. and A. R. Damasio. 1989. *Lesion analysis in neuropsychology.* New York: Oxford Press.

De Osmos, Jose S. 1990. *Amygdala in the human nervous system*, ed. G. Paxinos. San Diego: Academic Press. 583–710.

Diamond, M. C. 1991. Environmental influences in the young brain. In *Brain maturation and cognitive development: Comparative and cross-cultural perspectives*, ed. K. R. Gibson and A. C. Petersen. NY: Aldine de Gruyter, 107–124.

Edelman, G. M. 1987. *Neural Darwinism: The theory of neuronal group selection.* New York: Basic Books.

Geschwind, N. 1965. The disconnexion syndromes in animals and man. *Brain* 88: 237–294, 585–644.

Goldman-Rakic, P. 1988. Changing concepts of cortical connectivity: Parallel distributed cortical networks. In *Neurobiology of neocortex*, ed. P. Rakic and W. Singer. New York: John Wiley, 177–202.

Gurche, John. 1982. Early primate brain evolution. In *Primate brain evolution: Methods and concepts*, ed. E. Armstrong and D. Falk. New York: Plenum Press, 227–246.

Heath, R. G. 1963. Electrical self-stimulation of the brain in man. *American Journal of Psychiatry* 120:571–577.

Heath, R. G., R. R. Monroe and W. A. Mickle. 1955. Stimulation of the amygdaloid nucleus in a schizophrenic patient. *American Journal of Psychiatry* 111:862–863.

Hinton, Alexander L. 1993. Prolegomenon to a processual approach to the emotions. *Ethos* 21:417–450.

Humphrey, N. K. 1988. The social function of intellect. In *Machiavellian intelligence*, ed. R Byrne and A. Whiten. New York: Oxford University Press.

Isaacson, R. L. 1974. *The limbic system.* New York: Plenum Press.

Jerison, H. J. 1973. *Evolution of the brain and intelligence.* New York: Academic Press.

Jolly, A. 1966. Lemur social behavior and primate intelligence. *Science* 153:501–506.

Jurgens, U. 1982. Amygdala vocalization pathways in the squirrel monkey. *Brain Research* 241:189–196.

Kling, A. and H. D. Steklis, 1976. A neural substrate for affiliative behaviour in non-human primates. *Brain Behavior and Evolution* 13: 216–238.

Laughlin, C. D. 1987. Neurognosis: A biogenetic structural theory of culture and cognition. *Biology Forum* 81: 137–139.

Laughlin, C. D. and E. G. d'Aquili. 1974. *Biogenetic structuralism*. New York: Columbia University.

Lutz, C. and G. White. 1986. The anthropology of emotions. *Annual Review of Anthropology* 15:405–436.

MacLean, P. D. 1952. Some psychiatric implications of physiological studies on frontotemporal portion of the limbic system. *Electroencephalogram and Neurophysiology* 4:407–418.

1982. On the origin and progressive evolution of the triune brain. In *Primate brain evolution: Methods and concepts*, ed. E. Armstrong and D. Falk. New York: Plenum Press, 291–316.

1990. *The triune brain in evolution: Role in paleocerebral functions*. New York: Plenum Press.

Martin, R. D. 1973. Comparative anatomy and primate systematics. *Symposia of the Zoological Society of London* 33:301–337.

Mesulam M.-M., G. W. Van Hoesen, and D. N. Pandya. 1977. Limbic and sensory connections of the inferior parietal lobule (area PG) in the rhesus monkey: A study with a new method for horseradish peroxidase histochemistry. *Brain Research* 136:393–414.

Myers, F. R. 1990. The logic and meaning of anger among Pintupi aborigines. *Man* 23:589–610.

Pandya, D. N. and B. Selzer. 1982. Intrinsic connections and architectonics of posterior parietal cortex in the rhesus monkey. *Journal of Comparative Neurology* 204:196–210.

Pandya, D. N., B. Selzer, and H. Barbas. 1988. Input–output organization of the primate cerebral cortex. In *Comparative Primate Biology 4: Neurosciences*, ed. H. D. Steklis and J. Erwin. New York: A. R. Liss. 39–80.

Papez, J. W. 1937. A proposed mechanism of emotion. *Archives of Neurology and Psychiatry* 38:725–744.

Passingham, R. E. 1973. Changes in the size and organization of the brain in man and his ancestors. *Brain, Behavior and Evolution* 11:73–90.

Reynolds, P. C. 1981. *On the evolution of human behavior*. Berkeley: University of California Press.

Rockel, A. J., R. W. Hiorns, and T. P. S. Powell. 1980. The basic uniformity in structure of the neocortex. *Brain* 103:221–244.

Roland, P. E. and L. Friberg. 1985. Localization of cortical areas activated by thinking. *Journal of Neurophysiology* 53:1219–1243.

Semendeferi, K., E. Armstrong, A. Schleicher, K. Zilles and G. van Hoesen. 1998. Limbic frontal cortex in hominoids: A comparative study of area 13. *American Journal of Physical Anthropology* 106:129–155.

Squire, L. R. and S. Zola-Morgan. 1991. The medial temporal lobe memory system. *Science* 253:1380–1386.

Steklis, H. D. and M. Raleigh. 1979. Behavioral and neurobiological aspects of primate vocalization and facial expression. In *Neurobiology of Social Communication in Primates*. New York: Academic Press. 257–314.

Stephan, Heinz. 1969. *Quantitative investigations on visual structures in primate brains*. Proceedings of the 2nd International Congress of Primatology 3:3442.

Stephan, H., H. D. Frahm, and G. Baron. 1981. New and revised data on volumes of brain structures in insectivores and primates. *Folia Primatologia* 35:1–29.

1987. Comparisons of brain structure volumes in insectivora and primates, VII: Amygdaloid components, *Journal für Hirnforschung* 28:571–584.

Van Hoesen, G. W. and A. R. Damasio. 1987. Neural correlates of the cognitive impairment in Alzheimer's disease. In *Higher functions of the nervous system, the handbook of physiology*, ed. F. Plum. Bethesda: American Physiological Society, 871–898.

Wise, R., F. Challot, V. Hadar, K. Fristen, and E. Hoffnet. 1991. Distribution of cortical neural networks involved in word comprehension and word retrieval, *Brain* 114:1803–1817.

Yakovlev, P. I. 1971. A proposed definition of the limbic system. In *Limbic system and autonomic regulation*, ed. C. H. Hockman. Springfield, IL: C. C. Thomas, 241–283.

Zilles, K., E. Armstrong, G. Schlaug and A. Schleicher. 1986. Quantitative cytoarchitectonics of the posterior cingulate cortex in primates. *Journal of Comparative Neurology* 253:514–526.

8 Brain and emotion relations in culturally diverse populations

Lee Xenakis Blonder

Introduction

In the introduction to their edited book *The adapted mind. Evolutionary psychology and the generation of culture*, Barkow, Cosmides, and Tooby (1992) point out that, unlike the natural sciences, the social and behavioral sciences lack vertical integration. That is, they are not mutually consistent nor are the theoretical principles of the social and behavioral sciences compatible with those of the natural sciences. Within cultural anthropology in general, and ethnopsychology in particular, overt philosophical barriers to vertical integration exist. These barriers are variously termed cultural constructionism or extreme cultural relativism, both of which represent variants of cultural determinism (see Spiro 1986; Blonder 1991). In a review article entitled ''The anthropology of emotions,'' Lutz and White (1986:417) confirm the presence of the nature–culture dichotomy in ethnopsychology: ''[p]erhaps the most fundamental difference among recent studies of emotional understanding is in the degree to which emotions are granted an a priori pancultural status as opposed to being seen as culturally created.'' In describing the biological approach to emotions, Lutz and White (1986:407) state that ''emotions are treated as material things; they are constituted biologically as facial muscle movements, raised blood pressure, hormonal and neurochemical processes, and as 'hard-wired' instincts making up a generic human psyche.'' In contrast, ethnopsychology emphasizes ''the *primary* importance of cultural meaning systems in emotional experience'' (p. 417; italics in the original). While biological approaches to emotion do not necessarily exclude the influence of cultural processes, cultural constructionism is usually incompatible with biological explanation.

In a widely cited article ''The Mindful Body: A Prolegomenon to Future Work in Medical Anthropology,'' Scheper-Hughes and Lock (1987:30) state that ''biomedicine is still caught in the clutches of the Cartesian dichotomy and its related oppositions of nature and culture . . .'' In an attempt to describe an integrated approach to mind and body, Scheper-Hughes and Lock settle on emotions as the ''missing link . . . capable of bridging mind and body, individual and society.'' They further state: ''It is sometimes during the experience of sickness, as in moments of deep trance or sexual transport, that mind and body, self and other become one'' (p. 29). While for the biocultural-ist such a view might represent a welcome concession toward an integrative stance, from the perspective of cognitive neuroscience this view springs from dualist assumptions insofar as it proposes that mind and body are unified only during select experiences. In the non-dualist perspective, mind and body are unified in the brain, and this unity is a *prerequisite* to all classes of thought and behavior, not merely emotions (see Blonder 1991 for further discussion).

This brief discussion brings me to my premise, which is that emotions, like all human thought and behavior, are brain mediated. While the brain is programmed by genes to develop in a way that is characteristic of the species, the form and function of the mature nervous system are dependent upon the amount and timing of gene expression, developmental neurobiological mechanisms, and the type and amount of environmental stimulation to which the individual is exposed. Learning, of which enculturation is a part, is constrained by the properties of the central nervous system and occurs via the alteration or modulation of neural circuits. Given these conditions, several important questions emerge in adopting a biocultural perspective on emotion. First, ''how much neuroplasticity is built into human emotional systems?'' In other words, ''to what extent are emotional systems allowed to vary?'' Second, ''to what extent are brain and emotion relations stable across a variety of cultural, linguistic, and ethnic groups?'' Third, ''what aspects of intra- and intercultural variation are meaningful in influencing the neural organization of emotions?'' At present, considerably more research must be carried out in order to fully answer these questions. However, some answers to these questions will be given in the review and discussion that follows.

My first question, ''to what extent are emotional systems allowed to vary?'' can be addressed through comparison of descriptions of emotional behavior undertaken in a wide variety of cultures. This approach to anthropological research was delineated by Ward Goodenough in his formulation of the concepts emic and etic and in his book *Description and comparison in cultural anthropology* (1970). Unfortunately, little descriptive and comparative research has been carried out on emotion. This lack of research is in part attributable to the postmodern influence in anthropology which dismisses scientific empiricism as ideology. Such a view effectively precludes the potential contribution of anthropology to a neurobehavioral theory of emotions.

My second and third questions, ''what aspects of intra- and intercultural variation are meaningful in influencing the neural organization of emotions,'' and ''to what extent are brain and emotion relations stable across a variety of cultural, linguistic, and ethnic groups?'' require more direct methods of assessing brain and emotion relations. This assessment is a difficult task, given the techniques currently available in neurobehavioral research. It is noteworthy that the tendency toward decontextualization in such research is, to some extent, a function of the methodological constraints present in all studies of human brain and behavior relations. That is, only a limited number of experimental methods are currently available by which to study the neural substrates of human behavior and emotion. Those that are available are fraught with technological constraints.

The primary method by which brain and behavior relations have been studied is through the ablation paradigm. In this paradigm, behavioral, cognitive, and emotional processing is studied in individuals who have suffered circumscribed injury to the cerebral cortex or subcortical structures – usually through a stroke, head injury, or brain tumor. The assumption is that if damage to a particular region or neural network is consistently associated with a particular behavioral deficit or cluster of deficits, then that region is involved in the mediation of the disrupted behaviors. While neuroanatomic demarcation of the damaged area can be approximated through clinical neurologic examination, localization is more reliably performed using a computed tomography (CT) or a magnetic resonance (MR) scan.

One can also use techniques to activate structures in the left or right cerebral hemisphere, then examine the extent of activation using a neuroimaging modality such as brain electrical activity mapping (BEAM) (Duffy *et al.* 1979), positron emission tomography, single photon emission tomography, regional cerebral blood flow, or functional magnetic resonance imaging. Some of these modalities do not have high anatomic resolution, hence one may be limited to examining left versus right hemisphere differences in activation or differences within hemispheres by lobe. One can also examine brain and behavior relations using dichotic listening or tachistoscopic techniques. In both these techniques properties of the visual or auditory systems allow one to direct stimuli to the left or right hemisphere. Response accuracy as a function of side of administration of stimuli is used to infer hemispheric specialization.

The protocols that are successful in cerebral activation studies are those that can be administered while the subject is reclining in a scanning device. Likewise, stimuli used in tachistoscopic or dichotic listening tasks must be capable of administration via visual or auditory modalities while the subject looks through a viewfinder or listens through headphones. These conditions limit the types of stimuli that can be presented and the aspects of emotion that can be studied. Neuropsychological studies involving brain damaged patients are less restrictive, since they do not require a person to be immobilized in a device. However, to insure accurate anatomical localization of lesion and attribution of behavior, the research participants should have had a CT scan or an MR scan. As is readily apparent, direct methods of examining brain and behavior relations in humans are expensive, technologically intensive, and do not lend themselves easily to field research, particularly if the field is not within relatively close proximity to a university or a tertiary medical center.

While these constraints limit the opportunity to undertake neurobehavioral research among remote populations, there are hospitals and universities in many industrialized nations that have the technology required to support such work. In the discussion that follows, I will review investigations of the neuropsychology of human emotion with special emphasis on cross-cultural findings. In some cases the research is designed to examine the effect of an aspect of emotion that varies between cultures on brain organization. In other studies, there is no intent on the part of the investigators to consider the effect of cultural context on the aspect of emotion under study.

Research on the neuropsychology of emotion has focused on several dimensions, including non-verbal communication or affect displays (facial expression, intonation or prosody in speech), lexicosemantic representations, emotional imagery, physiologic arousal, and mood. While these dimensions of emotion are interrelated in the experience of the individual, neuropsychological research has shown that they are mediated by a variety of cortical and subcortical brain regions, and can be fractionated (Bowers *et al.* 1993). Although neuropsychological studies of emotion have been conducted in a variety of countries, very few investigators examine or even consider in discussion the possible influence of cultural factors on the neuropsychological organization of emotion. Thus, I have attempted to describe findings by indicating in which populations consistencies, or lack thereof, have been observed. I have also reviewed the handful of studies that actually sought to examine the effect of a cultural (usually linguistic) variant on the neural organization of emotions. For purposes of examining neurocultural interactions as they pertain to emotions, the latter approach is more effective.

Non-verbal communication of emotion

Prosody

For over a century, it has been known that structures in the left cerebral hemisphere control phonology, morphology, syntax, and semantics in most individuals (see Dingwall and Whitaker 1974, for a review). Left hemisphere predominance in linguistic processing has been documented in a wide variety of languages, although there is some evidence that it is enhanced by the acquisition of a phonologically based orthography (see Blonder 1991 for a review). Within the last two decades, research in American, Chinese, Danish, French, German, and Italian populations indicates that the *right hemisphere* plays a dominant role in the production and comprehension of emotional prosody. Dichotic listening studies in normal individuals show a right hemisphere advantage in the perception of emotional intonation (Carmon and Nachshon 1973; Ley and Bryden 1982). Clinical research has shown that patients with damage to the right hemisphere are unable to discriminate emotions communicated through intonation and lack emotional prosodic variation in speech (Heilman *et al.* 1975; Tucker *et al.* 1977; Ross 1981; Benowitz *et al.* 1983; Hughes *et al.* 1983; Heilman *et al.* 1984; Ehlers and Dalby 1987; Craca *et al.* 1990; Blonder *et al.* 1991).

Within the last twenty years, considerable cross-linguistic data has emerged suggesting that the hemispheric organization of pitch, rhythm, timing, volume, and duration of utterance is dependent upon the extent to which these features are used in segmental phonology. When these features of the speech wave function phonemically, as in tone languages, they engage left hemisphere processors. When these features extend over greater lengths of utterances to convey emotional meaning, they are processed by the right hemisphere. Thus, for example, dichotic listening studies, in which differing auditory stimuli are simultaneously presented to the two ears, show a right hemisphere advantage in the perception of emotional intonation in neurologically normal speakers of English (Carmon and Nachshon 1973; Ley and Bryden 1982). Clinical research on both American English and Chinese speakers has demonstrated that patients with lesions in the right hemisphere lack prosodic variation in speech and are unable to comprehend the meaning of emotional intonation (Heilman *et al.* 1975; Tucker *et al.* 1977; Ross and Mesulam 1979; Ross 1981; Weintraub *et al.* 1981; Benowitz *et al.* 1983; Hughes *et al.* 1983; Heilman *et al.* 1984; Shapiro and Danly 1985). By contrast, investigations of hemispheric processing of vocal pitch in speakers of tone languages have shown that when pitch contrasts make phonemic distinctions they are processed by the left hemisphere (Van Lancker and Fromkin 1973; Naeser and Chan 1980; Gandour and Dardarananda 1983; Packard 1986). These studies suggest that the neural pathways involved in the processing of fundamental frequency differ according to the extent to which fundamental frequency is phonologically distinctive.

In discussions of the evolution of language, most theorists consider only the segmental system. This focus may account for the prevalent belief that human language is qualitatively different from non-human primate communication. Yet if one integrates findings from neuropsychology, linguistics, and primatology, it becomes apparent that the prosodic system may represent an intermediary link in the emergence of propositional language. For example, empirical research in linguistics suggests that certain aspects of prosody show universal regularities and intrinsic sound-meaning correspondences. In particular, Bolinger (1980) reports that end-shifting of emphatic stress is a regular feature of languages as diverse as Chontal (Mexico), Kunimaipa (New Guinea), Tagalog (Philippines), and Western Desert (Australia). In three surveys of some 250 languages, terminal pitch rises have been found to characterize questions in 70 percent of languages examined (ibid.). While some theorists consider question intonation an example of grammatical prosody, Bolinger (1972:233) notes that questions are an expression of a speaker's uncertainty or curiosity, "which is suspiciously close to emotion." Psycholinguistic experiments have found that listeners are able to identify emotions communicated in unfamiliar languages through intonation contours alone (Uldall 1960; Kramer 1964; Scherer 1974). From an ontogenetic perspective, intonation is the first subsystem of language that an infant is capable of mastering (Lenneberg 1967; Lecours 1975). Taken together, these studies suggest that emotional intonation may be under tighter genetic control than propositional language.

This hypothesis is further supported by similarities in non-human primate vocalizations and human intonation. From a behavioral perspective, non-human primate calls rely heavily on variations in pitch, amplitude, and rhythm and these sounds tend to grade into one another in a continuous fashion, much like human intonation. In addition, it is thought that relative to propositional language, non-human primate calls and human intonation are more iconic than arbitrary. From a neuroanatomic perspective, subcortical structures of the limbic system, basal ganglia, and thalamus predominate in the control of both monkey vocalizations and emotional response (Jurgens 1979). Likewise, humans with Parkinson's disease, a neurologic condition that primarily affects dopaminergic transmission in the limbic system, basal ganglia, and thalamus, have disturbances in the production and perception of intonation (Scott *et al.* 1984; Blonder *et al.* 1989). These homologies in neurobehavioral relations suggest that emotional prosody is a more primitive subsystem of human language.

One can speculate that the neural substrates of prosodic features shifted during hominid evolution as the left cortical language zones evolved. Meaningful contrasts in vocal pitch, rhythm, amplitude, and duration were selectively incorporated into the rapidly evolving segmental system. The right hemisphere, together with the phylogenetically older substrates of vocal communication, the limbic system, basal ganglia, and thalamus, assumed preferential control over suprasegmental phonology. Having originated as the principal channel of communication, and the subsystem of language most closely related to vegetative functions, prosody and other aspects of paralanguage assumed a secondary role in communication. This speculation is reasonable given the selective advantage conferred by the segmental system and its expanded capacity to encode and transmit information.

Facial Expression

There have been numerous studies of the neural mediation of facial expression. These studies have been undertaken in American, Canadian, Danish, French, German, Italian, and Swiss populations and generally support the view that the right hemisphere predominates in the perception of facial expressions of emotion (Sackheim *et al.* 1978; Ley and Bryden 1979; Borod and Caron 1980; DeKosky *et al.* 1980; Benowitz *et al.* 1983; Natale *et al.* 1983; Bowers *et al.* 1985; McLaren and Bryson 1987; Ehlers and Dalby 1987; Laurian *et al.* 1991; Roschmann and Wittling 1992). A much smaller number of investigations into hemispheric asymmetries in the control and perception of facial affect support a divalent model, such that the left hemisphere mediates positive emotion and the right negative (e.g. Dimond *et al.* 1976; Reuter-Lorenz and Davidson 1981). However, there have been several failures to replicate these findings (see Gainotti *et al.* 1993 for a review). For example, Etcoff (1984) found a similar error pattern by right hemisphere damaged (RHD) patients in similarity judgments of positive and negative emotions. Left hemisphere damaged (LHD) subjects did not differ from controls on this task, nor did they show deficits in the recognition of positive emotional states. In a Swiss study, Laurian *et al.* (1991) found a right hemisphere superiority as measured by EEG in the identification of both positive and negative emotional faces. Likewise, Canadian researchers McLaren and Bryson (1987) showed a left visual field (LVF), right hemisphere superiority by a group of male and female university students in the perception of positive and negative emotional faces. Natale, Gur, and Gur (1983) presented happy, sad, and mixed chimeric faces to normal American subjects via tachistoscope. They found an overall LVF (right hemisphere) superiority in the identification of emotional valence and a right visual field (RVF) bias toward judging ambiguous emotions as positive. No such bias was found in the LVF.

As a result of limitations in the methods available for inferring localization of cerebral function, little is known concerning the precise intrahemispheric regions involved in the processing of facial emotion. Fried *et al.* (1982) undertook electrical stimulation mapping in humans and found that naming the emotional expression on faces was disrupted with stimulation of the right middle temporal gyrus while facial recognition was altered during stimulation of the right parieto-occipital junction. Rapcsak *et al.* (1989, 1993) reported two individuals who sustained selective deficits in naming facial emotion following lesions in the middle temporal gyrus of the right hemisphere. Cancelliere and Kertesz (1990) mapped cerebral infarcts on CT scans and found that most individuals with deficits in the comprehension of facial affect had sustained damage to the basal ganglia and the anterior temporal lobe. However, Blonder *et al.* (1989) failed to find deficits in the identification of facial emotion in a group of subjects with hemiparkinsonism, suggesting that basal ganglia dysfunction may be insufficient to cause impairment in facial emotion processing. Recently, Adolphs *et al.* (1994) reported evidence that the human amygdala is involved in the interpretation of fear as displayed on the face. They described a woman who had bilateral damage to the amygdala and had a concomitant disturbance in the processing of affective faces, particularly those faces expressing fear. Young *et al.* (1995) also found that identification of facial emotion was disturbed following partial bilateral amygdalotomy. These results are consistent with animal research showing that the amygdala is involved in emotional behavior (LeDoux 1992, 1993). In particular, LeDoux (1986) has shown that the amygdala has extensive connections with the thalamus and the cortex and is involved in pre- and post-processing of emotionally charged stimuli.

There is some evidence that hemispheric lateralization in the perception of facial emotion may be influenced by the directionality of the script one learns. Vaid and Singh (1989) compared native speakers of Hindi (left to right readers), native speakers of Arabic (right to left readers), a group of bidirectional readers (Hindi/Urdu) and a group of non-literate speakers of Hindi/Urdu in the ability to perceive facial emotion. The stimuli consisted of pairs of composite faces in which two half-faces expressing differing emotions (happy, neutral) were presented free-field. Past studies had shown that normal right-handed individuals tend to select the emotion expressed on the right half of the face (the viewer's left) as more intense than the same emotion placed on the left side of the face (the viewer's right), supporting right hemisphere predominance in the perception of facial emotion. Vaid and Singh (1989) found a significant left visual field preference in the Hindi subjects only (left to right readers), suggesting that the acquisition and directionality of an orthography influences the hemispheric substrates of facial emotion perception. In particular, the acquisition of a right-to-left script may attenuate an intrinsic right hemisphere specialization. Alternatively, the acquisition of a left-to-right orthography may shift to the right what would have been a bihemispheric function. Given that Hamilton and Vermeire (1988) found right hemisphere specialization among split-brain monkeys and Morris and Hopkins (1993) showed evidence of right hemisphere advantage in chimpanzees in the perception of facial expressions, the former hypothesis seems more tenable. In another study using a population of unilateral stroke patients recruited from the Department of Surgery at the Banaras Hindu University, Mandal *et al.* (1992) found no differences in the perception of facial affect as a function of hemispheric side of lesion. Stroke patients in general performed less well than controls, and among stroke patients those with anterior damage were significantly more impaired than those with posterior damage. The authors did not discuss the possibility that cultural or linguistic differences contributed to these findings, however.

Numerous studies have shown that the right hemisphere is specialized in the *production* of facial affect (see Borod 1993 for a detailed review). Some investigators have shown that emotions, particularly negative emotions, are expressed more intensely on the left side of the face in normal individuals during both posed and spontaneous conditions, indicating right hemisphere control (Sackheim *et al.* 1978; Borod and Caron 1980; Dopson *et al.* 1984; Moskovitch and Olds 1982). Several studies of spontaneous facial expression in brain-injured patients also support a right hemisphere predominance. In a study involving patients with unilateral right or left hemisphere damage, Buck and Duffy (1980) videotaped normal controls plus patients with RHD, LHD, or Parkinson's disease while each individual watched a set of emotionally laden slides. Raters then viewed the videotapes, categorized the subjects' expressions, and rated their expressivity on a seven-point scale. Findings revealed that RHD and Parkinsonian patients were rated as significantly less expressive than LHD aphasics and normal controls. These results were confirmed in several studies by Borod and colleagues (see Borod 1993 for a review) who also found reduced emotional facial expressivity following unilateral damage to the right hemisphere. Blonder *et al.* (1993) studied the production of facial expressions during videotaped interviews and found that right hemisphere damaged patients were less expressive than left hemisphere damaged patients or normal controls. In particular, RHD patients smiled less than the other two groups. Reduced facial expressivity and smiling were not a manifestation of dysphoria, since these patients did not report depression.

The participants in the studies of facial expressivity described above were American. Two studies involving Italian subjects that used the Facial Affect Coding System (FACS) (Ekman and Friesen 1975) failed, in part, to replicate these findings. Caltagirone *et al.* (1989) examined the ability of LHD and RHD patients and a group of normal controls to produce posed facial expressions of emotion. They found no differences between the three groups in this capability. Mammucari *et al.* (1988) found no differences between LHD and RHD patients in spontaneous facial responsivity to emotional movies, although, in comparison to LHD patients and normal subjects, RHD patients did show reduced gaze aversion to an unpleasant movie, suggesting that they failed to process the negative emotions depicted. Recently, however, Hauser (1993) reported that the right hemisphere predominates in the control of emotional facial expression in rhesus monkeys, suggesting that human population differences in the hemispheric processing of emotional facial expression do not result from genetic variation between ethnic groups. In the case of the human studies, methodologic differences rather than cultural influences on the hemispheric processing of facial emotion, probably account for the divergent findings (see Buck 1990; Borod 1993).

Neural control of verbal emotional communication

Based on studies of facial affect processing in Western and non-Western cultures, Ekman and colleagues (see Ekman 1972 for a review) posit that the emotions of happiness, sadness, fear, anger, surprise, and disgust are universal. Ekman (1972) further proposes the existence of a facial affect program located in the nervous system of all human beings, which links particular emotions with particular facial muscular movements. While the six emotions named above are considered by Ekman (1972) to be innate, the elicitors of this affect program and the rules of display are thought to be socially learned and culturally variable. This view has been criticized by cultural anthropologists studying emotion. For example, M. Rosaldo (1983:136) cautions anthropologists interested in emotion against "starting (*à la* Ekman [1974]) with presumed psychological universals and 'adding culture on.'' Others note that not all languages have words corresponding to these English emotion terms. For example, Polish does not have a word that exactly corresponds to our word disgust and the Aboriginal Australian language Gidjingali does not make a lexical distinction between fear and shame (Wierzbicka 1986). Wierzbicka (1986) questions whether researchers who were native speakers of Gidjingali or Polish would claim fear, shame, and disgust as fundamental emotions as do Izard and Buechler (1980). In her study of emotion words on Ifaluk, Lutz (1986) noted that of thirty-one emotion terms isolated for analysis, only eight were adequately glossed by an English emotion word. Just one, the lexical equivalent of disgust, represents one of Ekman or Izard's universal emotions. The remaining twenty-five words required two or more English emotion descriptors to convey meaning. In sum, anthropologists consider English emotion terms, like those of any other language, a folk taxonomy, rather than representative of universal concepts or basic psychological realities. Based on the dissimilarities in lexical domains of emotion cross-linguistically, Wierzbicka (1986) states: "If we want to posit universal emotions we need to do it in terms of a language independent semantic metalanguage, not in terms of English folk words for emotions . . . A considerable amount of lexical data collection, and of serious semantic analysis, is needed before any tenable universals in the area of emotion concepts can be plausibly proposed." However, as psychophysiologists point out, the assumption that common language representations of emotion are isomorphic to emotional experience is problematic (Öhman and Birbaumer 1993). Thus, the emotions of happiness, sadness, fear, anger, surprise, and disgust may be universally experienced and expressed non-verbally but not universally lexicalized. In this sense, the domain of emotion may be analogous to that of color, for which cross-cultural variation in lexical descriptors is not indicative of population differences in the capacity to perceive colors.

While Ekman and colleagues (see Ekman 1972) and Izard and Buechler (1980) use a typological approach to emotions, others consider the domain from a dimensional perspective. In semantic analyses of the domain of emotions in non-brain-damaged subjects, the most consistent finding is that of a two-dimensional model encompassing pleasant–unpleasant and level of arousal (Engen *et al.* 1957, 1958; Stringer 1967; Russell 1980; Russell and Bullock 1985). Osgood, May, and Miron (1975) provided cross-cultural evidence for three dimensions labeled evaluation (positive, negative), potency (powerful, weak), and activity (active, passive). Although Lutz (1986) observed that Ifaluk emotion words were defined and sorted according to the social situation within which the emotion occurred, informants' clustering of emotion words approximated the dimensions of evaluation and potency identified by Osgood, May, and Miron. Typological versus dimensional representations of emotion reflect in part differences in methodological approach to the subject matter (see Fillenbaum and Rapoport 1971). However, lexical and facial depictions of ''discrete'' emotions appear to map onto a circumplex model such that these two conceptualizations are mutually compatible (Russell 1980; Russell and Bullock 1985).

Semantic experiments comparing left and right-brain-damaged subjects and normal controls have found abnormalities limited to the left hemisphere damaged aphasic groups for most domains investigated (Grossman and Wilson 1987; Koemeda-Lutz *et al.* 1987). Most studies, however, have not examined classification patterns of categories for which the right hemisphere is thought to be specialized.

In a tachistoscopic study involving the capacity of the normal right and left hemispheres to identify emotional words, Graves, Landis, and Goodglass (1981) found a LVF advantage in males but not females. In a companion experiment using alexics, Landis *et al.* (1982) showed preferential reading of emotion words compared to non-emotional, suggesting right hemisphere participation in the lexical representation of emotion words. Using a triadic comparison methodology, Semenza *et al.* (1986) found that right hemisphere damaged patients recruited at the University of Padua, Italy, differed from normal controls in the clustering of emotion words. Borod and colleagues (1992) found that American RHD patients were impaired in the ability to discriminate and identify emotional words and sentences. Blonder and Boster (1996) found that American RHD subjects showed significantly less consensus than normal controls on similarity judgment tasks involving emotional face photographs, emotional words, emotional non-verbal expression terms, and tool photographs. In similarity judgments of tool words, color words, and color swatches, RHD and control performance was comparable. These results suggest that the right hemisphere contributes to the processing of both facial and semantic representations of emotion. However, in a multidimensional scaling analysis involving similarity ratings of pairs of emotional faces and emotion terms, Etcoff (1984) found that American RHD patients differed from LHD and hospital controls in judgments of emotional faces but not emotion words.

Blonder, Bowers, and Heilman (1991) sought to investigate whether the impairment in the *comprehension* of emotional prosody and facial expression that had been previously documented in right hemisphere damaged patients involved lexicosemantic representations of emotion as well. We asked American right hemisphere damaged patients, left hemisphere damaged patients, and normal controls to judge the emotional meaning of sentences describing non-verbal expressions (e.g., ''He smiled'') and sentences describing emotional situations (e.g., ''Children tracked dirt over your new white carpet''). We found that right hemisphere damaged subjects performed normally in their ability to infer the emotion conveyed by sentences describing emotional situations. However, these patients were impaired in relation to both left hemisphere damaged patients and normal controls in the ability to judge the emotional meaning of *sentences* depicting facial, prosodic, and gestural expressions. We interpreted these results to mean that the right hemisphere may house lexical-semantic representations of *non-verbal expressions* and that right hemisphere lesions either destroy these representations or prevent them from being activated. In another study, we showed that right hemisphere damage selectively disrupts the ability to imagine emotional facial expressions, lending some support to the proposition that the ability to comprehend the meaning of verbal descriptions of non-verbal expressions may require the formation of a mental image of these expressions (see Bowers *et al.* 1991).

Additional studies have examined the capacity of the right hemisphere to produce verbal expressions of emotion. Bloom *et al.* (1990) studied the production of emotional discourse in a small number of RHD, LHD, and non-hemisphere damaged (NHD) American subjects and found that RHD patients produced words of lower emotional intensity than the other two groups. Cimino *et al.* (1991) found that the emotional content of stories produced by American RHD patients in response to single word cues was reduced in comparison to normal controls.

In sum, available data from American and Italian studies suggest that the right hemisphere is involved in the processing of lexicosemantic representations of emotions, although the findings are less consistent than those regarding comprehension and production of facial and prosodic emotion.

Neural mediation of mood

While structures in the right hemisphere play an important role in non-verbal communication of emotion, portions of the frontal lobes in both hemispheres participate in emotional state and personality. These observations date to the case of Phineas Gage, a nineteenth-century New England railroad worker who sustained severe injury to the frontal lobes when an iron tamping bar penetrated his skull (Harlow 1868). Gage's physician described his patient's behavior after the injury in the following light: ''He is fitful, irreverent, indulging at times in the grossest profanity (which was not his custom), manifesting but little deference for his fellows, impatient of restraint or advice when it conflicts with his desires . . .'' (Harlow 1868:339–340).

Since the time of Gage, researchers have repeatedly documented the role of the frontal lobes, in particular the limbic system, in emotional behavior. The limbic system comprises the phylogenetically more ancient cortices that form the medial surface of the cerebral hemispheres. Numerous studies in non-human primates have demonstrated aberrant emotional behavior (rage, hypersexuality, placidity) following lesions to various structures in the limbic system (see Heilman *et al.* 1993, for a review). Lishman (1968) described the behavioral symptoms associated with frontal lobe damage as ''including one or more of the following symptoms in severe degrees: lack of judgment, reliability or foresight; facetiousness, childish behavior, disinhibition, and euphoria.''

Mood disturbances have also been noted to accompany unilateral damage to the cerebral hemispheres in studies of Americans, French, and Italian subjects. Babinski (1914), Hecaen *et al.* (1951), and Denny-Brown *et al.* (1952) observed that right hemisphere damaged patients were often indifferent or emotionally flat. Terzian and Cecotto (1959) and Alemà and Donini (1960) found that barbituration of the left hemisphere often resulted in a depressive-catastrophic reaction, while anesthetization of the right hemisphere often results in a manic-euphoric reaction (see Gainotti *et al.* 1993 for a review). Gainotti (1972) noted that depressive-catastrophic reactions tend to follow damage to the left hemisphere while indifference or euphoria characterizes right hemisphere disease. Similarly, Robinson and colleagues (1981, 1982) evaluated over 100 randomly selected stroke patients and found an increased incidence of post-stroke depression in patients with left-sided brain injury. Within that group, severity of depression was positively correlated with the proximity of the lesion to the anterior frontal lobe. In a more recent study, Robinson and colleagues

(1984) again found highest mean depression scores among anterior left hemisphere damaged patients, but they also showed that within the right hemisphere damaged group, anterior lesions were associated with inappropriate cheerfulness while posterior infarcts were associated with depression. These investigators have postulated that the high incidence of depression accompanying anterior frontal lobe infarcts is related to disruption of asymmetric catecholamine innervation in these regions. In contrast to these findings on Western subjects, a Japanese study found that barbituration of the left hemisphere produced euphoric reactions in all subjects (Tsunoda and Oka 1976). Tsunodo and Oka (1976) interpret this to mean that emotion is lateralized differently in Japanese and Western brains. If true (and I know of no replications), it is unclear whether genetic or cultural-linguistic factors underlie the differences.

Numerous cases of pathological emotional expression following brain injury have also been reported. In most instances, however, the relationship between emotional expression and mood is unclear. Sackheim and colleagues (1982) reviewed 119 published case reports of pathological laughing and crying accompanying neurologic disease and found that crying was associated with destructive lesions of the left hemisphere and laughing with those of the right hemisphere. The opposite pattern was found in cases of epilepsy: pathological laughing was associated with a left hemisphere seizure focus and pathological crying with a right hemisphere focus. The authors interpret this to mean that: (a) destructive lesions result in disinhibition of contralateral brain regions while irritative lesions excite ipsilateral centers; and (b) the left hemisphere subserves positive emotion while the right mediates negative emotion.

Gainotti, Caltigarone, and Zoccolotti (1993) have suggested that the depressive reactions often observed in patients with left hemisphere damage are psychologically appropriate reactions to the disabilities incurred. On the other hand, the indifference reaction often shown by right hemisphere damaged patients constitutes an emotionally inappropriate response to disability. Consistent with this interpretation are reports dating to Babinski's observations published in 1914, concerning three patients with right hemisphere damage who denied the existence of their hemiplegia. Babinsky coined the term ''anosognosia'' to describe this syndrome. Critchley (1966) later identified a related disorder which he labeled ''anosodiaphoria.'' In this syndrome, also associated with right hemisphere damage, patients are aware of their hemiplegia but emotionally indifferent to it. Recently, Blonder and Ranseen (1994) found that a group of American subjects with right hemisphere damage were aware of their difficulties in cognitive and emotional processing, but this awareness did not cause them to suffer from depression.

Hemispheric mechanisms of arousal

Numerous studies have identified arousal as a component of emotion (see above). Levels of physiologic activation and arousal may influence an individual's capacity to experience emotions (see Heilman *et al.* 1993 for a review). Ekman *et al.* (1983) and Levenson *et al.* (1991) found an emotion specific pattern of autonomic nervous system response in young and old American subjects. These findings were replicated in a group of Minangkabau, a matrilineal Muslim culture in West Sumatra (Levenson *et al.* 1992; see Heider, this volume). Studies of neural mechanisms of activation and arousal indicate that the right hemisphere may mediate readiness to respond bilaterally (Heilman and Van Den Abell 1979). Moreover, impairments in reaction time are greater after right than after left hemisphere stroke (Howes and Boller 1975; Coslett *et al.* 1987). Heilman and colleagues (1978) measured galvanic skin response to electrical stimulation in the hand ipsilateral to the lesion and found that RHD patients had significantly greater reductions than LHD patients. Morrow *et al.* (1981) found that RHD patients had reduced galvanic skin response to neutral and emotional stimuli. Coslett and Heilman (1986) showed that men with RHD were significantly more likely to suffer from reduced libido and sexual potency than patients with left hemisphere damage. In a study of normal German university students, Wittling (1990) found greater increases in systolic and diastolic blood pressure in females during right as opposed to left hemisphere viewing of an emotionally positive film.

Summary and conclusions

In summary, available data regarding the neural control of human emotions suggest that: (1) The right hemisphere mediates the expression and comprehension of emotional prosody and facial expression; (2) The right hemisphere houses lexicosemantic representations of non-verbal communicative signals and may play a role in the comprehension and production of verbal emotion more generally; (3) The right hemisphere predominates in the control of physiologic arousal; (4) The frontal lobes including the limbic system are particularly involved in the control of emotional behaviors that we consider to form personality characteristics; and (5) the two hemispheres may differentially contribute to emotional state or mood. With the exception of lexicosemantic representations of emotions, most of these functions have a long evolutionary history and their neural substrates show homologies with those of non-human primates. In particular, there is evidence that the limbic system and basal ganglia in both non-human primates and humans control aspects of emotional behavior. Furthermore, right hemisphere predominance in the production and perception of emotional facial expression may predate the emergence of hominids.

Based on the data reviewed in this chapter, one can formulate provisional answers to the questions posed in the introduction. First, in answer to the question "to what extent are brain and emotion relations stable across a variety of cultural, linguistic, and ethnic groups?" one can conclude that, to the limited extent that these relationships have been studied in varying cultural and ethnic groups, they seem relatively stable. The stability of these relationships is further evidenced by non-human primate studies in which the same pattern of neural organization of an emotional function (i.e. facial emotion processing) has been shown. This does not mean that features of emotional communication cannot be harnessed by a culture group to mark social boundaries or power relations (e.g., see Irvine's [1990] discussion of linguistic emotional markers of social class among the rural Wolof community in Senegal), but that one would not expect, on the basis of available evidence, to find variability in the neural organization of emotion based on variability in the sociocultural rules that govern or restrict emotional communication. However, one might expect to find a difference in neuronal or synaptic density associated with the elaboration of a particular emotional function by a cultural group or subgroup. This expectation is based on evidence from studies of learning and memory showing that experience can influence neural circuitry (see Introduction, p. 274).

In answer to the question "what aspects of intra- and intercultural variation are meaningful in influencing the neural organization of emotions?" these studies show that language structure is as yet the only aspect of intra- and intercultural variation that has been identified as meaningful in influencing the neural organization of emotions. The patterns of variation in brain and emotion relationships, to the limited extent that they have been documented, seem to be most influenced by gross differences in language structure, rather than variation in cultural practices. To date, no cross-cultural differences in the neural organization of emotions has been found to exist within or between Euro-American culture groups. This finding, that linguistic structure influences neural mechanisms of emotional processing, is interesting in itself and suggests that features of emotional communication develop in concert with language acquisition at the level of the neural substrate.

I also posed the question, "how might culture be better incorporated into these studies?" With the exception of gross differences in language, it is apparent that researchers have not paid particular attention to the effects of inter- and intracultural variation on brain and emotion relations. Furthermore, most brain and emotion studies, like the majority of research in neuropsychology, are laboratory based, and use as the source of data, psychological tests and unidimensional, decontextualized stimuli, rather than observations of natural behavior. This is both an outgrowth of the technomethodological constraints in assessing brain and behavior relations and a methodological tradition based largely in experimental psychology. In conclusion, there are several obstacles to overcome in undertaking neurocultural studies of emotion. These include: (1) the methodological difficulties involved in undertaking brain and emotion studies using real-life situations as the data source; (2) the ethnocentric tendency on the part of cognitive neuroscientists to make general statements about human brain and emotion relations based on a limited number of cultural samples; (3) the lack of sensitivity to issues of cross-cultural variation among researchers participating in the brain and emotion enterprise; and (4) philosophical barriers to biocultural integration coupled with a lack of neurobiological sophistication among ethnopsychologists.

Acknowledgments

Portions of this chapter are taken from Blonder 1991. Human Neuropsychology and the concept of culture. *Human Nature* 2:83–116. The author gratefully acknowledges the editorial assistance of Sherry C. Williams, ELS, Stroke Program, Sanders-Brown Center on Aging, University of Kentucky.

References

Adolphs, R., D. Tranel, H. Damasio, and A. Damasio. 1994. Impaired recognition of emotion in facial expressions following bilateral damage to the human amygdala. *Nature* 372:669–672.

Alemà, G. and G. Donini. 1960. Sulle modificazioni cliniche ed elettroencefalografiche da introduzione intracarotidea di iso-amil-etil-barbiturato di sodio nell 'uomo. *Bolletino della società italiana di biologia sperimentale* 36:900–904.

Babinski, J. 1914. Contribution á l'étude des troubles mentaux dans l'hémiplégie organique cèrèbrale (anosognosie). *Revue Neurologique* 27:845–848.

Barkow, J. H., L. Cosmides, and J. Tooby, eds. 1992. *The adapted mind: Evolutionary psychology and the generation of culture*. New York: Oxford.

Benowitz, L. I., D. M. Bear, R. Rosenthal, M. M. Mesulam, E. Zaidel, R. W. Sperry. 1983. Hemispheric specialization in nonverbal communication. *Cortex* 19:5–11.

Blonder, L. X. 1991. Human neuropsychology and the concept of culture. *Human Nature* 2:83–116.

Blonder, L. X. and J. D. Ranseen. 1994. Awareness of deficit following right hemisphere stroke. *Neuropsychiatry, Neuropsychology, and Behavioral Neurology* 7: 260–266.

Blonder, L. X., R. E. Gur, and R. C. Gur. 1989. The effects of right and left hemiparkinsonism on prosody. *Brain and Language* 36:193–207.

Blonder, L. X., D. Bowers, and K. M. Heilman. 1991. The role of the right hemisphere in emotional communication. *Brain* 114:1115–1127.

Blonder, L. X., A. Burns, D. Bowers, R. W. Moore, K. M. Heilman. 1993. Right hemisphere facial expressivity following natural conversation. *Brain and Cognition* 21:44–56.

Blonder, L. X. and J. S. Boster. 1996. Judged similarity of emotions following right hemisphere stroke. *Twenty-ninth annual winter conference on brain research.* Snowmass, CO, January.

Bloom, R. L., J. C. Borod, L. K. Obler, and E. Koff. 1990. A preliminary characterization of lexical emotional expression in right and left brain-damaged patients. *International Journal of Neuroscience* 55:71–80.

Bolinger, D. 1972. *Intonation*. Harmondsworth: Penguin.

1980. Intonation and nature. In *Symbol as sense*, ed. M. Foster and S. Brandes. New York: Academic Press, 9–23.

Borod, J. 1993. Cerebral mechanisms underlying facial, prosodic, and lexical emotional expression: A review of neuropsychological studies and methodological issues. *Neuropsychology* 7:445–463.

Borod, J. and H. Caron. 1980. Facedness and emotion related to lateral dominance, sex, and expression type. *Neuropsychologia* 18:237–241.

Borod, J. C., F. Andelman, L. K. Obler, J. R. Tweedy, and J. Welkowitz. 1992. Right hemisphere specialization for the identification of emotional words and sentences: Evidence from stroke patients. *Neuropsychologia* 30:827–844.

Bowers, D., R. Bauer, H. Coslett, and K. Heilman. 1985. Dissociation between the processing of affective and nonaffective faces in patients with unilateral brain lesions. *Brain and Cognition* 4:258–272.

Bowers, D., L. X. Blonder, T. Feinberg, K. M. Heilman. 1991. Differential impact of right and left hemisphere lesions on facial emotion and object imagery. *Brain* 114:2593–2609.

Bowers, D., R. M. Bauer, and K. M. Heilman. 1993. The nonverbal affect lexicon: Theoretical perspectives from neuropsychological studies of affect perception. *Neuropsychology* 7:433–444.

Buck, R. 1990. Using FACS vs. communication scores to measure spontaneous facial expression of emotion in brain-damaged patients: A reply to Mammucari *et al.* (1988). *Cortex* 26:275–280.

Buck, R. and R. J. Duffy. 1980. Nonverbal communication of affect in brain-damaged patients. *Cortex* 16:351–362.

Caltagirone, C., P. Ekman, W. Friesen, G. Gainotti, A. Mammucari, L. Pizzamiglio, and P. Zoccolotti. 1989. Posed emotional expression in unilateral brain damaged patients. *Cortex* 25:653–663.

Cancelliere, A. E. B. and A. Kertesz. 1990. Lesion localization in acquired deficits of emotional expression and comprehension. *Brain and Cognition* 13:133–147.

Carmon, A. and I. Nachshon. 1973. Ear asymmetry in the perception of emotional non-verbal stimuli. *Acta Psychologia* 37:351–357.

Cimino, C. R., M. Verfaellie, D. Bowers, and K. M. Heilman. 1991. Autobiographical memory: Influence of right hemisphere damage on emotionality and specificity. *Brain and Cognition* 15:106–118.

Coslett, H. B. and K. M. Heilman. 1986. Male sexual function: Impairment after right hemisphere stroke. *Archives of Neurology* 43:1036–1039.

Coslett, H. B., D. Bowers, and K. M. Heilman. 1987. Reduction in cerebral activation after right hemisphere stroke. *Neurology* 37:957–962.

Craca, A., M. Del Prete, P. Fiore, G. Balestroni, and G. Megna. 1990. Psychopathological aspects and emotional behavior in right brain-damaged patients. *Italian Journal of Neurological Sciences* 11:465–469.

Critchley, M. 1966. *The parietal lobes*. New York: Hafner.

DeKosky, S., K. M. Heilman, D. Bowers, and E. Valenstein. 1980. Recognition and discrimination of emotional faces and pictures. *Brain and Language* 9:206–214.

Denny-Brown, D., J. S. Meyer, and D. Horenstein. 1952. The significance of perceptual rivalry resulting from parietal lesions. *Brain* 75:434–471.

Dimond, S. J., L. Farrington, and P. Johnson. 1976. Differing emotional responses from right and left hemispheres. *Nature* 261:691–692.

Dingwall, W. O. and H. A. Whitaker. 1974. Neurolinguistics. *Annual Review of Anthropology* 3:323–356.

Dopson, W. G., B. E. Beckwith, D. M. Tucker, and P. C. Bullard-Bates. 1984. Asymmetry of facial expression in spontaneous emotion. *Cortex* 20:243–252.

Duffy, F. H., J. L. Burchfiel, and C. T. Lambroso. 1979. Brain electrical activity mapping (BEAM): A method for extending the clinical utility of EEG and evoked potential data. *Annals of Neurology* 5:309–321.

Ehlers, L. and M. Dalby. 1987. Appreciation of emotional expressions in the visual and auditory modality in normal and brain-damaged patients. *Acta Neurologica Scandinavica* 76:251–256.

Ekman, P. 1972. Universals and cultural differences in facial expressions of emotion. In *Nebraska symposium on motivation*, ed. J. Cole. Lincoln: University of Nebraska Press.

1974. Universal facial expressions of emotion. *Culture and personality: Contemporary Readings*. ed., R, Levine, Chicago: Akline, 8–15.

Ekman, P. and W. V. Friesen. 1975. *Unmasking the face*. Englewood Cliffs, NJ: Prentice-Hall.

Ekman, P., R. W. Levenson, and W. V. Friesen. 1983. Autonomic nervous system activity distinguishes between emotions. *Science* 221:1208–1210.

Engen, T., N. Levy, and H. Schlosberg. 1957. A new series of facial expressions. *American Psychologist* 12:264–266.

1958. The dimensional analysis of a new series of facial expressions. *Journal of Experimental Psychology* 55:454–458.

Etcoff, N. L. 1984. Perceptual and conceptual organization of facial emotions: Hemispheric differences. *Brain and Cognition* 3:385–412.

Fillenbaum, S. and A. Rapoport. 1971. *Structures in the subjective lexicon*. New York: Academic Press.

Fried, I., C. Mateer, G. Ojemann, R. Wohns, and P. Fedio. 1982. Organization of visuospatial functions in human cortex: Evidence from electrical stimulation. *Brain* 105:349–371.

Gainotti, G. 1972. Emotional behavior and hemispheric side of lesion. *Cortex* 8:41–55.

Gainotti, G., C. Caltagirone, and P. Zoccolotti. 1993. Left/right and cortical/subcortical dichotomies in the neuropsychological study of human emotions. *Cognition and Emotion* 7:71–93.

Gandour, J. and R. Dardarananda. 1983. Identification of tonal contrasts in Thai aphasic patients. *Brain and Language* 18:98–114.

Goodenough, W. H. 1970. *Description and comparison in cultural anthropology*. Chicago: Aldine.

Graves, R., T. Landis, and H. Goodglass. 1981. Laterality differences for visual recognition of emotional and non-emotional words. *Neuropsychologia* 19:95–102.

Grossman, M. and M. Wilson. 1987. Stimulus categorization by brain-damaged patients. *Brain and Cognition* 6:55–71.

Hamilton, C. R. and B. Vermeire. 1988. Complementary hemispheric specialization in monkeys. *Science* 24:1691–1694.

Harlow, J. M. 1868. Recovery after severe injury to the head. *Publication of the Massachusetts Medical Society (Boston)* 2:327–346.

Hauser, M. D. 1993. Right hemisphere dominance for the production of facial expression in monkeys. *Science* 261:475–477.

Hecaen, H., J. de Ajuriaguerra, J. Massonet. 1951. Les troubles visuoconstructifs par lésion pariéto-occipital droit. *Encephale* 40:122–179.

Heilman, K. M. and T. Van Den Abell. 1979. Right hemisphere dominance for mediating cerebral activation. *Neuropsychologia* 17:315–321.

Heilman, K., R. Scholes, and R. Watson. 1975. Auditory affective agnosia. *Journal of Neurology, Neurosurgery, and Psychiatry* 38:69–72.

Heilman, K. M., H. D. Schwartz, R. T. Watson. 1978. Hypoarousal in patients with the neglect syndrome and emotional indifference. *Neurology* 28:229–232.

Heilman, K. M., D. Bowers, L. Speedie, and H. B. Coslett. 1984. Comprehension of affective and nonaffective prosody. *Neurology* 34:917–921.

Heilman, K. M., D. Bowers, and E. Valenstein. 1993. Emotional disorders associated with neurological disease. In *Clinical Neuropsychology*, ed. K. M. Heilman and E. Valenstein. New York: Oxford, pp. 461–497.

Howes, D. and F. Boller. 1975. Simple reaction times: evidence for focal impairment from lesions of the right hemisphere. *Brain* 98:317–332.

Hughes, C. P., J. L. Chan, and M. S. Su. 1983. Aprosodia in Chinese patients with right cerebral hemisphere lesions. *Archives of Neurology* 40:732–736.

Irvine, J. T. 1990. Registering affect: Heteroglossia in the linguistic expression of emotion. In *Language and the politics of emotion*, ed. C. A. Lutz and L. Abu-Lughod. New York: Cambridge, 126–161.

Izard, C. and S. Buechler. 1980. Aspects of consciousness and personality in terms of differential emotions theory. In *Emotion: theory, research and experience. Vol. 1: Theories of emotion*, ed. R. Plutchik and H. Kellerman. New York: Academic Press, 165–187.

Jurgens, U. 1979. Neural control of vocalization in nonhuman primates. In *The neurobiology of social communication in primates*, ed. H. D. Steklis and M. J. Raleigh. New York: Academic Press, 11–44.

Koemeda-Lutz, M., R. Cohen, and E. Meier. 1987. Organization of and semantic access to memory in aphasia. *Brain and Language* 30:321–337.

Kramer, E. 1964. Elimination of verbal cues in judgments of emotion from voice. *Journal of Abnormal and Social Psychology* 68:390–396.

Landis, T., R. Graves, and H. Goodglass. 1982. Aphasic reading and writing: possible evidence for right hemisphere participation. *Cortex* 18:105–112.

Laurian, S., M. Bader, J. Lanares, L. Oros. 1991. Topography of event-related potentials elicited by visual emotional stimuli. *International Journal of Psychophysiology* 10:231–238.

Lecours, A. 1975. Mylogenetic correlates of the development of speech and language.

In *Foundations of language development*, ed. E. H. Lenneberg and E. Lenneberg. Vol. 1. New York: Academic Press, 121–135.

LeDoux, J. E. 1986. Sensory systems and emotion. *Integrative Psychiatry* 4:237–248.

1992. Emotion as memory: anatomical systems underlying indelible neural traces. In *The handbook of emotion and memory: research and theory,* ed. S. A. Christianson. Hillsdale, NJ: Erlbaum Associates, 269–288.

LeDoux, J. E. 1993. Emotional memory systems in the brain. *Behavioral Brain Research* 58:69–70.

Lenneberg, E. 1967 *Biological foundations of language*. New York: Wiley.

Levenson, R. W., L. L. Carstensen, W. V. Friesen, and P. Ekman. 1991. Emotion, physiology, and expression in old age. *Psychology and Aging* 6:28–35.

Levenson, R. W., P. Ekman, K. Heider, and W. V. Friesen. 1992. Emotion and autonomic nervous system activity in the Minangkabau of West Sumatra. *Journal of Personality and Social Psychology* 62:972–988.

Ley, R. and M. Bryden. 1979. Hemispheric differences in recognizing faces and emotions. *Brain and Language* 7:127–138.

1982. A dissociation of right and left hemisphere effects for recognizing emotional tone and verbal content. *Brain and Cognition* 1:3–9.

Lishman, W. 1968. Brain damage in relation to psychiatric disability after head injury. *British Journal of Psychiatry* 114:373–410.

Lutz, C. 1986. The domain of emotion words on Ifaluk. In *The social construction of emotions*, ed. R. Harré. Oxford: Basil Blackwell, 267–288.

Lutz, C. and G. M. White. 1986. The anthropology of emotions. *Annual Review of Anthropology* 15:405–436.

Mammucari, A., C. Caltagirone, P. Ekman, W. Friesen, G. Gainotti, L. Pizzamiglio, and P. Zoccolotti. 1988. Spontaneous facial expression of emotions in brain-damaged patients. *Cortex* 24:521–533.

Mandal, M. K., H. S. Asthana, S. C. Tandon, S. Asthana. 1992. Role of cerebral hemispheres and regions in processing hemifacial expression of emotion: evidence from brain-damage. *International Journal of Neuroscience* 63:187–195.

McLaren, J. and S. E. Bryson. 1987. Hemispheric asymmetries in the perception of emotional and neutral faces. *Cortex* 23:645–654.

Morris, R. D. and W. D. Hopkins. 1993. Perception of human chimeric faces by chimpanzees: evidence for a right hemisphere advantage. *Brain and Cognition* 21:111–122

Morrow, L., P. Vrtunsky, K. Youngjai, F. Boller. 1981. Arousal responses to emotional stimuli and laterality of lesion. *Neuropsychologia* 19:65–71.

Moskovitch, M. and J. Olds. 1982. Asymmetries in spontaneous facial expressions and their possible relation to hemispheric specialization. *Neuropsychologia* 20:71–81.

Naeser, M. A. and S. W. Chan. 1980. Case study of a Chinese aphasic with the Boston Diagnostic Aphasia Exam. *Neuropsychologia* 18:389–410.

Natale, M., R. E. Gur, and R. C. Gur. 1983. Hemispheric asymmetries in processing emotional expressions. *Neuropsychologia* 21:555–565.

Öhman, A. and N. Birbaumer. 1993. Psychophysiological and cognitive-clinical perspectives on emotion: Introduction and overview. In *The structure of emotion*, ed. N. Birbaumer and A. Öhman. Seattle: Hogrefe and Huber, 3–17.

Osgood, C. E., W. H. May, and M. S. Miron. 1975. *Cross-cultural universals of affective meaning*, Urbana, IL: University of Illinois Press.

Packard, J. L. 1986. Tone production deficits in nonfluent aphasic Chinese speech. *Brain and Language* 29:212–223.

Rapcsak, S. Z., A. W. Kaszniak, and A. B. Rubens. 1989. Anomia for facial expressions: Evidence for a category specific visual-verbal disconnection syndrome. *Neuropsychologia* 27:1031–1041.

Rapcsak, S. Z., J. F. Comer, and A. B. Rubens. 1993. Anomia for facial expressions: neuropsychological mechanisms and anatomical correlates. *Brain and Language* 45:233–252.

Reuter-Lorenz, P. and R. J. Davidson. 1981. Differential contributions of the two cerebral hemispheres to the perception of happy and sad faces. *Neuropsychologia* 19:609–613.

Robinson, R. and T. Price. 1982. Post-stroke depressive disorders: A follow-up study of 103 patients. *Stroke* 13:635–641.

Robinson, R. and B. Szetela. 1981. Mood change following left hemisphere brain injury. *Annals of Neurology* 9:447–453.

Robinson, R., K. L. Kubos, L. B. Starr, K. Rao, and T. R. Price. 1984. Mood disorders in stroke patients. Importance of lesion location. *Brain* 107:81–93.

Rosaldo, M. Z. 1983. The shame of headhunters and the autonomy of self. *Ethos* 11:135–151.

Roschmann, R. and W. Wittling. 1992. Topographic brain mapping of emotion-related hemispheric asymmetries. *International Journal of Neuroscience* 63:5–16.

Ross, E. 1981. The aprosodias. *Archives of Neurology* 38:561–569.

Ross, E. and M. M. Mesulam. 1979. Dominant language functions of the right hemisphere? Prosody and emotional gesturing. *Archives of Neurology* 35:144–148.

Russell, J. A. 1980. A circumplex model of affect. *Journal of Personality and Social Psychology* 39:1161–1178.

Russell, J. A. and M. Bullock. 1985. Multidimensional scaling of emotional facial expressions: similarity from preschoolers to adults. *Journal of Personality and Social Psychology,* 48:1290–1298.

Sackeim, H., R. C. Gur, M. Saucy. 1978. Emotions are expressed more intensely on the left side of the face. *Science* 202:434–436.

Sackeim, H., A. Weinman, R. C. Gur *et al.* 1982. Pathological laughing and crying: functional brain asymmetry in the expression of positive and negative emotions. *Archives of Neurology* 39:210–218.

Semenza, C., M. Pasini, M. Zettin, P. Tonin, P. Portolan. 1986. Right hemisphere patients' judgments of emotions. *Acta Neurologica Scandanavica* 74:43–50.

Scheper-Hughes, N. and M. M. Lock. 1987. The mindful body: A prolegomenon to future work in medical anthropology. *Medical Anthropology Quarterly* 1:6–41.

Scherer, K. 1974. Acoustic concomitants of emotional dimensions: Judging affect from synthesized tone sequences. In *Nonverbal communication*, ed. S. Weitz. New York: Oxford University Press.

Scott, S., F. Caird, and B. Williams. 1984. Evidence for an apparent sensory speech disorder in Parkinson's Disease. *Journal of Neurology, Neurosurgery, and Psychiatry* 47:840–843.

Shapiro, B. and M. Danly. 1985. The role of the right hemisphere in the control of speech prosody in propositional and affective contexts. *Brain and Language* 25:19–36.

Spiro, M. E. 1986. Cultural relativism and the future of anthropology. *Cultural Anthropology* 1:259–286.

Stringer, P. 1967. Cluster analysis of nonverbal judgements of facial expressions. *British Journal of Mathematical and Statistical Psychology* 20:71–79.

Terzian, H. and C. Cecotto. 1959. Determinazione e studio della dominanza emisferica mediante iniezione intracarotide di Amytal sodico nell'uomo. I. Modificazioni cliniche. *Bollettino della Società Italiana di Biologia Sperimentale* 35: 1623–1626.

Tsunoda, T. and M. Oka. 1976. Lateralization for emotion in the human brain and auditory cerebral dominance. *Proceedings of the Japanese Academy* 52:528–531.

Tucker, D., R. Watson, and K. M. Heilman. 1977. Discrimination and evocation of affectively intoned speech in patients with right parietal disease. *Neurology* 27:947–950.

Uldall, E. 1960. Attitudinal meanings conveyed by intonation contours. *Language and Speech* 3:223–234.

Vaid, J. and M. Singh. 1989. Asymmetries in the perception of facial affect: Is there an influence of reading habits? *Neuropsychologia* 27:1277–1287.

Van Lancker, D. and V. Fromkin. 1973. Hemispheric specialization for pitch and ''tone'': Evidence from Thai. *Journal of Phonetics* 6:19–23.

Weintraub, S., M. M. Mesulam, L. Kramer. 1981. Disturbances in prosody: A right hemisphere contribution to language. *Archives of Neurology* 38:742–744.

Wierzbicka, A. 1986. Human emotions: Universal or culture-specific? *American Anthropologist* 88:584–594.

Wittling, W. 1990. Psychophysiological correlates of human brain asymmetry: Blood pressure changes during lateralized presentation of an emotionally laden film. *Neuropsychologia* 28:457–470.

Young, A. W., J. P. Aggleton, D. J. Hellawell, M. Johnson, P. Broks, and J. R. Hanley. 1995. Face processing impairments after amygdalotomy. *Brain* 118: 15–24.

Part IV

Systems theory

9 Outline of a bioculturally based, ''processual'' approach to the emotions

Alexander Laban Hinton

> But what is difficult to understand, as long as Ilongot ''anger'' is construed within our analytic frame, is how and why the Ilongots concerned could be content with what to me appeared the sort of outcome that could only lead to renewed conflict . . . [T]he failure of my vision – of how ''anger'' grows and is resolved – to comprehend their very real success in keeping ''anger'' from disrupting bonds of kin suggests that in important ways their feelings and the ways their feelings work must differ from our own . . . [A]ffects, whatever their similarities, are no more similar than the societies in which we live. (Rosaldo 1984:144–145)

> I would suggest that [this] is not the case . . . To be sure, their anger seems to be much more intense than ours, and its expression is much more violent, but, these quantitative dimensions aside, their anger and ours seem to work in similar ways. They, like we, get angry when frustrated, and they, like we, usually repress their anger in culturally inappropriate contexts only to express it symbolically in culturally appropriate ones. This indicates, I would suggest, that human feelings and the ways in which they work are determined not so much by the characteristics of particularistic culture patterns but by the transcultural characteristics of a generic human mind. (Spiro 1984:334)

> There is no contradiction in the contention that anger may indeed be related to one or more biological systems, and that anger is nevertheless a social construction. (Averill 1982:41)

In her essay ''Toward an anthropology of self and feeling,'' Michelle Rosaldo (1984) relates an anecdote about an Ilongot who, frustrated by his ''brother's'' careless planning, got drunk and fought with him. ''To me, the deed stood as a clear expression of disruptive feelings hitherto repressed. To the Ilongots, however, the fight was seen as nothing more than an unfortunate consequence of drink, which 'dissolved' consciousness and in so doing led the fighter to forget bonds with his brother'' (1984:144). Noting the absence of any later ''symptoms'' of repression and conflict, Rosaldo asserts that this example illustrates the extent to which emotions are culturally constructed and the dangers of ethnocentric projection.

Melford Spiro (1984) reacts strongly against this type of "particularistic cultural determinism." Citing comments Rosaldo makes elsewhere in her essay, Spiro points out that the Ilongot live in a society in which conflict is feared as something that can quickly escalate to homicide, and in which people explicitly recognize that anger is disruptive of social relations. Not only do such conditions provide a perfect context for repression, but there is also a clear symptom of such repressed antagonism in Ilongot society – headhunting. Spiro suggests that "the headhunter's victim is an unconscious symbolic representation of his frustrating fellows" (1984:333), and thus that the decapitation and "casting away" of the victim's head provides the Ilongot with a cathartic means of displacing their pent-up aggressions. Such actions are "entirely consistent with the 'Western' theory of emotions" (1984:334) and provide evidence for, rather than against, the universality of emotion.

As illustrated by the Rosaldo–Spiro debate, anthropological discussions of emotion tend to be cast in terms of a universalist-relativist dichotomy (Lutz and White 1986). The first section of this chapter will point out the problems associated with adopting an extreme, reductive form of universalism or constructionism. When cast in this manner, both of these perspectives have debilitating weaknesses, not the least of which is the tacit assumption of unidimensional determinism. Such problems are not, however, a necessary entailment of taking either a biological or a cultural point of view. The anthropology of the emotions needs new conceptual frameworks that can both accommodate and explore the interrelationships between such different levels of explanation. "Processualism" represents one possibility. In the second section I delineate this syncretic position more fully by showing how the emotions can be examined both synchronically (as emergent, hierarchically arranged systems) and diachronically (as dialectical systems that develop through ontogenetic time). The utility of this approach is then illustrated through an examination of attachment theory and of the process(es) by which the Ilongot brother's "anger" might have been generated. The chapter concludes by making suggestions as to how a processual approach can improve research in this domain of study.

Reductive approaches to the emotions

In order to understand what a processual approach to the emotions is, we need to discern what it is not. This section will describe the extreme, reductive forms of universalism and constructionism and then point out the problems associated with taking such unidimensional points of view. It is important to keep in mind that few people actually subscribe to such extreme perspectives; most scholars would agree that the emotions can best be explained by an approach that falls somewhere on the continuum that lies between these two poles. By identifying the problems with such “ideal-types,” however, we can discern the areas that need to be addressed by a more syncretic perspective.

Reductive universalism

Following evolutionary, biological, and/or psychodynamic perspectives, this extreme form of universalism tends to view emotions as intrapsychic states that are brought about by or that entail given physiological changes. If the researcher only looks beneath the epiphenomenal veneer of culture, she or he will discover reflections of this inner, biological essence.[1] Thus Spiro can point to the “symptoms” of Ilongot repression and assert that their feelings are part of “generic human mind.” Similarly, Paul Ekman (1980:83) sees facial expression as a direct index of neurologically hard-wired “affect programs” that are “set off.” While the “elicitors” and “display rules” associated with such emotions may vary from culture to culture, the phenomenon itself does not. Implicit within such universalistic views is the assumption that emotions are essentially innate, that is, “directed or facilitated by genetic programs” (Izard and Malatesta 1987:498–499).

While correct in noting that emotions have a biological basis, the universalist assumption of “innateness” and/or “hard-wiring” is both misleading and problematic. This type of “teleological determinism” (Hopkins and Butterworth 1990) intimates that emotion is under direct genetic control. Several theorists have pointed out (e.g., Gottlieb 1991; Greenough 1991; Hooker 1981), however, that it is a long way from the genotype to the phenotype.[2] As opposed to following the central dogma (i.e., a one-way flow of information from the gene outwards), organismic development is bidirectional. Since information flows both vertically between and horizontally within a number of different levels of organization (e.g. gene <-> cytoplasm <-> cell <-> organ <-> organ system <-> organism <-> environment), it would be inaccurate to speak of a phenotypic trait as if it were solely the product of genotypic properties (Gottlieb 1991). Moreover, the ontogeny of the central nervous system is “designed” to interact with the environment. During the process of early neuronal division, migration, and differentiation, for example, the dendritic connections that are eventually established are actively shaped by environmental cues (Changeux 1985; Edelman 1987). Similarly, during various “critical windows” (e.g., language acquisition), organismic development is predicated on interactions with the environment. Such a view of biology is in accordance with Clifford Geertz’ (1973) assertion that, with increasing complexity, the ontogeny of the central nervous system comes to rely more and more on environmental stimuli. This trend reaches its culmination in humans. As a result of our evolutionary history, human beings are ''naturally'' incomplete; we require culture to develop properly. In order to explain fully a phenomenon such as emotion, it is thus necessary to view culture as one of its formative ''ingredients'' (see Geertz 1973:76–77). When universalists assume that emotion is ''innate,'' their explanations do not adequately take culture into account and thus become flat and impoverished. As is evident from the above discussion, however, such an assumption is not an *a priori* requisite of an evolutionary, biological, and/or psychodynamic perspective.

Reductive constructionism

Drawing on ethnopsychological, linguistic, cognitive, and interpretive perspectives, this extreme form of constructionism asserts that emotions can be better conceptualized as ''feeling-thoughts'' (Lutz 1988; Wikan 1990). As opposed to being irrational inner states, emotions are viewed as culturally constructed judgments and appraisals that are negotiated in particular social contexts (Lynch 1990). Given that these interpretations are embedded in indigenous meaning structures (e.g., political relations, social organization, ethnopsychological beliefs, local symbols), it follows that emotions are relative and thus ''may vary from place to place as a matter of *kind*'' (Solomon 1984:252). Rosaldo's statements about Ilongot ''anger'' reflect the constructionist view that emotions ''are no less cultural and no more private than beliefs. They are instead cognitions – or, more aptly, perhaps, interpretations – always culturally informed'' (1984:141).

While providing rich insight into the ways in which the emotions are shaped by culture, the extreme form of constructionism, like that of universalism, can be criticized on a number of grounds. First, by asserting that emotions are ''essentially'' cultural constructs, constructionists usurp the very scepter of essentialism against which they inveigh. At the same time that they pay homage to the view that emotion is a context-bound form of ''social discourse'' (Lutz and Abu-Lughod 1990), constructionists often use abstract and reified emotion concepts to explain the emotional life of a given people. ''The move from enshrined noun/essence to narrative leitmotif, and the further move from motif to culture, fosters a kind of cultural naturalism in which a small set of Ur-principles lurk behind everything as first causes'' (Rosenberg 1991). This type of ''cultural naturalism'' directly parallels the genetic teleological determinism of the universalists. In order to avoid such symbolic reification, several theorists (Barth 1987; Bourdieu 1977; Keesing 1987) have urged anthropologists to refocus their attention on the situated practices within which meaning and action are generated. As we shall see, this type of processual perspective can help emotion theorists circumvent the dichotomous dead-ends into which they tread all too often.

Second, the ''top-down'' cultural determinism of constructionists perpetuates the same type of unidimensional explanation as does the ''bottom-up'' biological determinism of the universalists. To say that culture is a necessary ingredient in an ''emotional stew'' is to make a valid and important point. To assert that this ingredient constitutes the dish in and of itself is to foster an impoverished view of the phenomenon in question. A focus on one level of explanation is valid if the importance of other levels is acknowledged and properly bracketed. Constructionists, however, explicitly criticize physiological modes of explanation without paying adequate due to the current state of research in the field. Thus we find little mention of important biological findings concerning: limbic structures that mediate emotion (Papez 1937; MacLean 1973; LeDoux 1986, 1990), the reticular formation and the neurochemical secretions of its monoaminergic systems (Bloom and Lazerson 1988; Kandel *et al.* 1991; van Praag 1986), and/or neuroendocrinological regulators of emotion (Konner 1982; Kandel *et al.* 1991; Henry 1986). While there is evidence that some physiological arousal is more general and thus largely influenced by cognition (Cannon 1984 [1914]; Schachter and Singer 1962; Mandler 1984, 1990; and Lazarus 1984, 1990), there are also indications that emotional activation and processing takes place before the receipt of processed cortical inputs (Kandel *et al.* 1991; LeDoux 1986, 1990; Zajonc 1980) and can, in fact, prime given cortical structures (Tucker *et al.* 1990; Heath 1986 ''there are instances where emotional responses can occur without apparent cognitive involvement''). Moreover, data concerning the effects of psychoactive drugs, brain stimulation, and brain disease indicate that ''there are instances where emotional responses can occur without apparent cognitive involvement'' (Buck 1986:290). This evidence, when coupled with research showing that some emotions may be accompanied by more specific patterns of physiological activation (Buck 1986; Ekman 1980; Ekman *et al.* 1983; Henry 1986; LeDoux 1986; Papanicolaou 1989), supports the conclusion that biology must be acknowledged as an important part of emotional experience. It is surprising that within anthropology, a discipline that prides itself on representing disparate points of view, there is so much subdisciplinary myopia and caricaturing on the part of both universalists and constructionists. By implying that all physiological explanations of emotion are predicated on folk psychological assumptions,[3] constructionists essentialize biology into the type of ethnocentric category that is *a priori* anathema to cultural anthropologists. Just as the constructionists have criticized universalists for ''biologizing'' emotion into a form that obviates the need for a cultural analysis, so too can their ''culturalization'' of emotion be critiqued for relegating biology to the realm of epiphenomenon.

It is crucial to keep in mind that these criticisms are directed at the more extreme manifestations of universalism and constructionism. As illustrated by the work of people like Cairns, Gottlieb, and Changeux, biological aspects of the emotions can be studied in a manner that explicitly takes into account the important ways in which culture shapes such phenomena. Similarly, scholars have explored how the emotions are constructed in different societies while actively drawing on evolutionary, biological, and/or psychodynamic research (e.g., Averill 1982; Gerber 1985; Levy 1984; Shweder 1985). Instead of stereotyping and pointing fingers at the intellectual "other," anthropologists need to develop conceptual frameworks that can draw on the strength of both biological and cultural analyses. "Processualism" represents such a syncretic perspective, one that can not only accommodate both biological and cultural levels of analysis, but that can also examine how the dialectic between them generates those phenomena we call the emotions.

A processual approach to the emotions

Given the ambiguity and confusion that arise when disparate phenomena are lumped together into a category, it is not surprising that emotion typology, like species typology, has been plagued by dissension over what are its defining features (thus the essentialisms that polarize universalists and constructionists). A processual approach views this orientation as misguided. Before asserting what "emotion" is, researchers must examine the discrete processes and mechanisms by which the phenomena we throw into this category become manifest. Moreover, it is quite possible that as research in this area progresses, this folk category will need to be substantially revised and/or replaced by more refined typologies (see P. M. Churchland 1984; P. S. Churchland 1986).[4] In accordance with this perspective, *a processual approach can thus be said to examine the discrete process(es) by which the emotions are generated both synchronically and diachronically*. By asserting that its object of study is "the emotions," a process-oriented perspective highlights the fact that those phenomena we tend to indiscriminately label as an "emotion" are not homogeneous. By focusing on process and ontogeny, a processual approach emphasizes the emergent and multifactorial origin of these phenomena. Such an orientation stands in marked contrast to the unidimensional determinism of reductive perspectives.[5]

Jerome Kagan (1978, 1984) has nicely illustrated the processual approach by likening emotion to weather classification. As opposed to referring to a single thing, this superordinate category is used to describe certain "coherences" between wind velocity, humidity, temperature, barometric pressure, and type of precipitation. While weather is always present, we tend to only notice its particularly intense manifestations (e.g., a storm, tornado, blizzard, hurricane). In an analogous manner, Kagan encourages theorists to view emotion as a superordinate term that we use to categorize particularly salient coherences between external stimuli, physiological changes, and evaluations (e.g., anger, sadness, happiness, fear).

The processual approach follows a similar line of thought. As opposed to being either a cultural or physiological "thing," emotion is viewed as a general label we use to characterize phenomena that are generated from several sources (e.g., physiological, social, cultural, individual). As opposed to saying "that's an emotion," researchers need to delineate the specific coherences that give rise to those phenomena we place under this umbrella term. By focusing on the generative, multifactorial, and interrelational aspects of "emotion," researchers can begin to make meaningful distinctions in this domain of study.

This orientation also enables us to circumvent reductionism. Just as it is misleading to define a storm solely in terms of temperature, so it is erroneous to assert that an emotion is essentially a physiological state or a cognition. At particular times one factor may be particularly prominent to us (e.g., we can characterize a hot day largely in terms of the temperature), but others will also be playing a generative role (e.g., high humidity and a lack of wind on a hot day). While providing partial explanatory value, no one component can adequately describe an emotional "coherence" in and of itself. Moreover, the saliency of these components and their interrelationships will vary from emotion to emotion. In contrast to the essentialist biases of the extreme forms of universalism and constructionism, then, a processual approach views the emotions as phenomena that emerge from the interaction of both biological and cultural factors. While it is easy to pay lip service to this syncretic perspective, it is more difficult to delineate specific frameworks that will allow us to conceptualize the emotions in this manner. Systems theory (von Bertalanffy 1968; Laughlin and d'Aquili 1974) represents one attractive possibility.

Systems theory

While cybernetic incarnations of systems theory experienced an efflorescence in anthropological circles during the 1960s and 1970s (Bateson 1987; Rappaport 1984), its contemporary influence has diminished. Given the increasing popularity of this approach in biology and psychology (Fogel and Thelen 1987), however, perhaps it is time for anthropologists to reconsider how systems theory can contribute to their theoretical understanding in general, and to their study of the emotions in particular.

In contrast to the "flat" interactional framework of the Parsonian legacy (in which cultural, social, biological, and psychological factors serve as disparate pieces of the human pie), systems models are conceptualized in a much more dynamic form (Shore 1988). Given phenomena are viewed as arranged in hierarchical levels of organization which constrain and interact with one another through feedback. While lower levels serve in part as an underpinning for higher levels, the latter are emergent phenomena and thus are not reducible to the former.[6] Each level of organization thus operates in terms of principles that are internally generated yet embody properties of the systems as a whole (Polanyi 1975; Shore 1988).

As indicated earlier, we can look at organismic development in terms of a series of dialectical transactions that take place between different levels of organization. Thus, while it is quite valid to examine genes in terms of the processes by which codons are transcribed and translated, this level of analysis does not unidirectionally guide development. Genetic activity is constrained and influenced by information coming from other levels of organization (Gottlieb 1991; Kandel *et al.* 1991). What is crucial to recognize is the fact that while given levels of analysis can be studied individually, feedback from other levels of organization must be at least recognized and bracketed if not actively taken into account.

Linguistics can be conceptualized in a similar manner. On the one hand, it is possible to examine the properties of phonemes. This level of analysis includes an investigation of the human vocal apparatus and the various physiological processes by which such sounds are produced. On another level, research focuses on the ways in which phonemes are combined to form words and the manner in which words are used to make sentences. While informed and constrained by the properties of phonemes, this emergent level of analysis is explicable in terms of its own organizational principles (e.g., syntax and semantics). Finally, a third level of analysis looks at the way in which words and sentences are meaningfully employed by individuals in communication with one another. Again, while this level emerges out of and is constrained by the other levels, it also operates in terms of a distinct set of properties (e.g., semiotics).[7]

Emotional coherence

We can cast the study of the emotions in an analogous manner. One level of an emotion system would deal with biogenetic aspects of the emotions. Research in this area would involve evolutionary considerations, as well as a focus on how various limbic, neuroendocrinological, cortical, visceral, and reticular mechanisms conspire to generate the somatic component of the emotions. The social and cultural levels of analysis would embody aspects of the biogenetic level, but would operate in terms of their own distinct properties.[8] Research in these domains would focus on the ways in which the emotions are shaped by kinship ties, social status, cultural models and scripts, meaningful symbols, political authority, power, history, gender, economics, and ecological factors, etc. Finally, the individual level of analysis would examine how a person's life-history, temperament, personality, goals, plans, strategizing, etc., influence his or her emotional experience. It is crucial to note that, like the other levels of organization, this domain would both influence and be informed by the properties of the system as a whole. Just as the weather arises out of distinct combinations of its systemic components, so too would an emotion be generated from a given coherence of biogenetic, social, cultural, and individual factors situated within the context of particular situations, interactions, and practices.

It is important to realize that the study of such emotional coherences involves both synchronic and diachronic dimensions. As just illustrated, synchronic analysis looks at how different levels of organization constrain and inform one another at a given moment in time. A diachronic perspective, in contrast, allows us to see how these levels dialectically interact and shape one another during the life-course.

In order to get a better understanding of this diachronic perspective, it will be useful to briefly examine C. W. Waddington's (1957) ideas about ontogeny (since he has served as somewhat of a strawperson for dynamic systems theorists). Waddington proposes that development proceeds along genetically predetermined pathways, or "chreods." While given exogenous events might temporarily disrupt ontogeny, buffering mechanisms exist to canalize development along its "proper" course. Waddington calls this scenario the "epigenetic landscape." Development is likened to a ball rolling down a valley slope. The direction of movement is firmly guided both by the general contours of this slope and by fixed micro-valleys within it. As noted earlier, the extreme forms of universalism and constructionism make similar assumptions about the teleological determinism of ontogeny. Like Waddington, universalists assume that our genetic heritage leads to the development of universal hard-wired emotions. Similarly, within the constructionist landscape the ontogeny of emotion is viewed as being predominantly guided by sociocultural factors.

Reacting against such "nature or nurture" dichotomies, dynamic systems theorists have proposed a more interactive view of development (Baltes 1987; Cairns 1991; Cairns *et al.* 1990; Gottlieb 1991; Lerner 1991). As opposed to being predetermined, ontogeny is viewed as probabilistic and emergent. At each phase of development, structure and function arise stochastically out of a context-bound nexus between past events and contemporaneous influences (i.e., coaction between different hierarchical levels). Systems are thus emergent not only hierarchically, but also across time. As given events (both endogenous and exogenous) occur, the properties of different levels and/or of the system as a whole may change.

In the more extreme forms of dynamic systems theory, ontogeny becomes totally defined by context (see Fogel and Thelen 1987; Hopkins and Butterworth 1990; Oyama 1985). The probabilistic trajectory of development is seen as being continually defined and redefined by a multifactorial dialectic that results in qualitatively different syntheses (which constitute the basis for the next dialectical phase of epigenesis). From this perspective, ontogenetic process is always being created anew. Because there are no "universal" (i.e., predetermined) developmental constraints, the contours of the epigenetic landscape are constantly changing.

More moderate forms of systems theory acknowledge the existence of general developmental constraints (Baltes 1987; Cairns 1991). Robert Cairns *et al.* (1990), for example, note that general "buffering mechanisms" sometimes "bias the organism toward species-typical trajectories" (1990:50). Ontogeny thus takes place on an epigenetic landscape, but one that is not dotted by deterministic chreods (or perhaps we can speak of "dialectical chreods" that emerge out of microlevel interaction). The notion that epigenesis unfolds within a set of general parameters parallels Changeux's view of selective stabilization. While environmental cues actively shape the form of synaptic connections, this selective force occurs within a "genetic envelope" that establishes the properties and boundaries within which cell division, migration, and differentiation take place. Similarly, while the process of language acquisition is strongly shaped by sociocultural factors, this formative influence takes place within a set of biological parameters (Changeux 1985; Ochs and Schieffelin 1984). Culture may select the phones that are recognized and given meaning by a person, but the phones themselves are directly linked to human physiology.

Dialectical landscape of the emotions

The study of the emotions can be conceptualized in a similar manner if we recast the epigenetic landscape metaphor in a more processual form. Within this "dialectical landscape," biological and sociocultural factors are seen to interact and to actively shape given emotions during the life course. Like the epigenetic landscape, the dialectical landscape would consist of a broad valley slope that represents the broad constraints of the genetic envelope. As opposed to containing genetically predetermined pathways, however, the terrain of the landscape would consist of what I earlier called "dialectical chreods." At each moment in time, the trajectory of these pathways would be stochastically defined by past events and a contemporaneous interaction between different levels of organization. In contrast to Waddington's epigenetic landscape (in which all development is characterized in a similar manner), each phenomenon must be examined separately as it develops through time in the dialectical landscape. Moreover, the characteristics of a landscape may vary both from emotion to emotion, as well as within an emotion system over time.

As Changeux notes, the degree of openness of the genetic envelope will vary. For some emotions, then, the genetic envelope may be extremely loose. In such cases, the development of dialectical chreods could significantly alter or transform the contours of the broad valley slope. This extreme form of dynamic systems theory might be characteristic of emotions that are associated with general arousal (and are thus largely influenced by cognitive factors). In other cases, the genetic envelope may be tighter. While still subject to influence from the action of dialectical chreods, the broad valley walls of the landscape would remain relatively constant (in all but extremely aberrant cases). Language acquisition would fit in this category. While sociocultural factors could dramatically influence this process (as illustrated by Elinor Ochs and Bambi Schieffelin's [1984] comparison of language socialization in three cultures), they would do so within the limits of various physiological properties that guide language acquisition throughout our species. Similarly, some emotions may be instantiated in very different ways in disparate cultures, but may still possess some species-typical properties. We might expect such emotions to display a prototypic clustering across cultures. Finally, a few emotions may have relatively closed genetic envelopes. In these, both the valley slope and microlevel pathways would be subject to a fair degree of genetic determinism. The fight–flight response would represent one candidate for this category. Nevertheless, it is important to realize that even within this landscape development involves a dialectic. Sociocultural factors will still shape the expression and experience of these more "instinctual" responses (e.g., through display rules and/or the interpretation of incoming stimuli). I would argue that there are relatively few human emotions that fit into this latter category.

It is crucial to keep in mind that given emotions may themselves change in significant ways during ontogeny. As noted earlier, endogenous and exogenous events can alter the properties of the system as a whole. The system that emerges out of this flux may be constrained by a relatively more open/closed genetic envelope, and thus should be characterized by a somewhat different dialectical landscape. In some cases the change may be so significant that the emergent emotion should be called by a new name.

Processualism applied

Attachment theory

Attachment theory (Bowlby 1969) rests on the presupposition that, as a result of our evolutionary history, human infants are biologically predisposed to form attachment bonds with their primary caretaker(s). By maintaining proximity to these significant others, an infant benefits from increased security (e.g., protection from predators). So important is the function of this species-typical behavior that it can be considered on par with activities such as eating, reproduction, and caretaking (Ainsworth 1989; Ainsworth and Bowlby 1991).

As opposed to being a pre-existing, ''hard-wired'' genetic trait, however, the attachment system develops over the first year of the infant's life (Bowlby 1969). At birth, a baby uses signaling and approach behaviors (e.g., crying, smiling, clinging, sucking, seeking, following) to attract and maintain proximity to others. These behaviors tend to be emitted in general, however, as opposed to being directed toward the caretaker in particular. Sometime around the age of six months, increased neurophysiological and cognitive development enable the infant to discriminate, to make representations of, and to visually and orally track the caretaker. Well before the end of the first year, this repertoire of initially disparate capacities, experiences, and behaviors becomes organized into an (emergent) attachment system that serves to maintain proximity to the caretaker.

While acknowledging how environmental factors can influence this process, attachment theorists tend to emphasize the biological, species-typical aspects of the attachment system (Ainsworth 1989; Ainsworth and Bowlby 1991). Like Waddington's epigenetic landscape (Bowlby 1973), attachment behavior is viewed as progressing (in all but extremely aberrant cases) within the confines of a stable valley slope. Environmental events may knock development into alternative micro-pathways, but these chreods are themselves fairly predetermined.

This perspective is evident in Mary Ainsworth's Strange Situation test. Building upon John Bowlby's ideas and her own observations of Ugandan babies, Ainsworth noted two distinct manifestations of the attachment relationships: first, infants use the caretaker as a secure base from which to explore the surrounding world; and second, babies actively seek contact with the caretaker when faced with fearful or distressful conditions (Ainsworth 1978; Ainsworth and Bowlby 1991). Ainsworth designed an eight-stage test (that included conditions when the infant was separated/reunited with the mother and exposed to strangers) to assess this proposition. Based upon how babies reacted upon being reunited with their mothers, Ainsworth classified the infants as either insecure-avoidant (Type A), responsive-secure (Type B), or insecure-ambivalent (Type C).[9] As indicated by the designation, Type B behavior was assumed to reflect a ''secure'' mother–infant relationship (largely influenced by maternal responsiveness), while Type A and Type C behaviors were ''assumed to reflect poor mother–infant interaction and 'insecurity' of attachment'' (Miyake *et al.* 1986:250). Like Waddington's epigenetic landscape, this scenario assumes a species-typical trajectory that can be canalized into one of a few (predetermined) microlevel pathways. Cross-cultural data, however, have raised interesting questions about the universality of this framework.

In particular, an unusually large number of infants in other countries deviate from the Type B (i.e., the "adaptive" and "normal" middle-class American) patterns of behavior (Takahashi 1990; Sagi 1990; Grossmann and Grossmann 1990). Japanese infants, for example, display disproportionate amounts of Type C activity (and evince Type A behavior). As several investigators have pointed out (Miyake *et al.* 1985; Miyake *et al.* 1986; Takahashi 1990), this "aberrant" attachment behavior may be the result of a variety of culture-specific norms and practices. In contrast to emphasis placed on independence and autonomy in the United States, Japanese mothers tend to value dependence and interrelatedness in their infants. Takeo Doi (1973) has illustrated how the Japanese conceptualize the first half year of life as a time when the infant and mother are united in a sense of oneness. After this time, the child begins to become aware of him or herself as a separate individual and comes "to seek after the mother" (Doi 1973:74). This desire to be dependently bound to another, or *amae*, is not only a sought-after goal in the parent–child relationship, but also serves as an ideal for later relationships. These values permeate the mother–child relationship.

Child-rearing practices, for example, are geared toward maintaining a positive interdependence. In contrast to the more distal types of interaction that characterize middle-class American caretaking, Japanese mother–infant relations involve much more proximal contact (Miyake *et al.* 1985; Miyake *et al.* 1986). Thus we find: co-bathing, prolonged breast-feeding, co-sleeping, manual toilet-training, more tactile (*vs.* verbal) forms of communication, and the practice of carrying the infant on the back. Japanese caretakers also tend not to leave their babies alone or with baby-sitters. In order to maintain a close and positive bond, Japanese mothers rarely express negative emotions and/or make negative comments toward their child. Compliance is achieved more through appeals for empathy and the maintenance of good relations than through active disciplinary measures. Finally, from an early age mothers tend to instill a fear of the outside world (especially strangers) in their offspring, thus "encouraging the children to remain close and dependent" (Miyake *et al.* 1986:242). Given this set of child-rearing practices and cultural norms, it is not surprising that the Strange Situation test would prove more stressful to a Japanese infant than to one raised in middle-class America or in Germany. In fact, "it is quite possible that an interactive relationship characterized primarily by close physical contact and infrequent separation may lead to the establishment of an attachment that is qualitatively different from one that involves less physical contact and a great deal of distal interaction" (Miyake *et al.* 1985:280).

This latter conclusion would be in accordance with a processual stance. As opposed to viewing attachment in terms of an epigenetic landscape, we can cast it in a more dialectical light. On the one hand, it is important to realize that the attachment bond does not spring full-born into the world with the neonate. This behavioral system emerges from the organization and coalescing of a number of cognitive, neurophysiological, and individual factors, each of which will have already been informed by a dialectic with the environment. While few would disagree that attachment has a biogenetic basis, it is more questionable whether such predispositions can do more than generally constrain the ontogeny of this behavior.

I would argue that we should view attachment as an emergent system that develops through a dialectical landscape. While a genetic envelope may establish the broad valley walls of the terrain, it does not contain predetermined pathways (e.g., Type A, Type B, and Type C chreods). Instead, a variety of physiological, sociocultural, and experiential factors conspire to generate distinct trajectories through the dialectical landscape of development. Attachment will thus arise in both Japan and the United States, but its experiential quality and meaning will vary considerably (within the macrolevel constraints of the genetic envelope) in accordance with the dialectical activity of microlevel chreods.[10] In each case, a distinct emotional coherence will be generated as species-typical predispositions interact with culture-specific concepts, scripts, norms, and social relationships. To judge the ''adaptiveness'' of one of these emotion systems in terms of another is to perpetuate ethnocentric parochialism. The existence of such a bias also suggests that the Ainsworth test is predicated upon a culture-bound typology.

Finally, it is important to note that, just as the attachment system emerged from a repertoire of disparate components, so too will it be transformed as its various levels of organization change. Within our folk psychology, there is a tendency to assume that the attachment behavior of an infant is a rudimentary form of ''love.'' From a processual perspective, such assumptions are precarious. There are, for example, many types of ''love'' in our own society – romantic, caretaker, sibling, friendships (Ainsworth 1989). Moreover, by the time an infant has reached adulthood she or he has undergone a variety of changes associated with puberty, rites of passage, neurophysiological and cognitive development, adolescence, and socialization in general. Researchers must examine each emotional phenomenon separately to discover the processes by which it is generated. While it is probable that some of the cognitive models, cultural norms, and physiological mechanisms associated with early attachment behavior influence these later ''love'' systems (see Ainsworth 1989), most likely each phenomenon can be characterized by a distinct coherence of factors.

As illustrated by the contrast of *amae* (with its stress on relationships of dependence and hierarchy) and "Love, American Style" (which tends to emphasize autonomy, equality, and a social contract), ontogeny is a dialectical process that can lead to extremely different emotional outcomes. In the former case, the feelings of dependence characteristic of the parent–child relationship serve as a prototype not only for domestic institutions like marriage (in which the wife adopts the role of mother toward the husband), but for the vertical structure of Japanese social organization in general (Doi 1973; Nakane 1970). As opposed to idealizing such feelings of dependence, people in the United States actively strive for autonomy and independence. Thus marriage tends to be viewed as a type of social contract into which two autonomous and equal individuals enter. In each case, the emotion in question is mediated by a set of distinct social institutions and cultural values that shape it in culturally specific ways. Instead of lumping disparate phenomena under one folk label, we must begin to refine our understanding of the systemic properties (in both their synchronic and diachronic dimensions) of each of the emotions.

The emotional coherence of an Ilongot

Because attachment behavior is a fairly well-studied phenomenon, it can be recast in such a manner as to illustrate both the synchronic and diachronic dimensions of the processual approach. To be of practical value to ethnographers, however, it is necessary to illustrate how a processual approach can be applied to phenomena such as the Ilongot brother's "anger." This last section will attempt to determine how this emotional coherence might have been generated.

Before doing so, it is necessary to point out that these conjectures are by necessity speculative. On the one hand, we are not provided with much background information about the brothers themselves (e.g., age, marital status, past experiences) or about the larger context in which their dispute took place. On the other hand, there is not enough data to situate this manifestation of Ilongot "anger," or *liget*, within the context of a dialectical landscape. A truly processual approach attempts to set a given emotional phenomenon in ontogenetic perspective (as was done for attachment in the previous section). Despite these problems, it is still possible to use Rosaldo's other work (1980, 1983) to speculate about the process(es) by which the brother's "anger" might have been generated.

While *liget* is by no means isomorphic with aggression, the potentially violent nature of the emotion is explicitly recognized in Ilongot society (Rosaldo 1980). Moreover, the particular instantiation of *liget* with which we are concerned involved aggression. Physiological findings about aggression are thus relevant to our discussion. K. E. Moyer (1976), for example, has distinguished several types of aggression in animals (cf. note 4), each of which manifests a distinct pattern of physiological and environmental correlates. While it would be erroneous to assume that human beings have homologous neural systems, data concerning brain lesions, psychosurgery, and brain stimulation experiments suggests that there are neural analogues in humans (Averill 1982; Konner 1982; Moyer 1976). Of particular note for our purposes is ''irritable aggression'' (since the Ilongot was frustrated with his brother) and ''inter-male aggression'' (since the fight took place between two males).

In almost every species, males tend to engage in more aggressive behaviors than females, particularly towards one another (Moyer 1976). This aggression often takes the form of ritualistic threats and posturing, as different males attempt to establish dominance over one another. While mediated to a much greater degree by complex cognitive inputs, humans seem to fit this general pattern of inter-male aggression (Daly and Wilson 1988; Knauft 1987b; Konner 1993). Thus, in virtually every society we find higher levels of male aggression, much of which is related to status concerns (especially among younger men).

Such data support the view that, as a result of their evolutionary heritage (e.g., the demands of individual survival, the need to gain access to females and to resources), males are physiologically predisposed toward certain types of aggressivity. During a critical window in early life, for example, the brains of males are androgenized through the action of the sex hormones.[11] A variety of studies suggest that the organizational effects of this ''fetal androgenization'' are partly responsible for a number of sex differences in mammals, including those relating to an increased propensity for males to engage in aggressive behavior (Arnold and Gorski 1984; Ellis 1986; Konner 1982, 1993; Olweus 1988). One important consequence of this process relates to the activational effects of the male sex hormones. In addition to catalyzing a number of morphological changes in males, higher androgen levels (particularly testosterone) seem to facilitate aggression in males, particularly young ones (Katchadourian 1977; Kendrik and Drewett 1979; Konner 1982, 1993; Mazur and Lamb 1980; Moyer 1976; Olweus 1986, 1988; van Oortmerssen *et al.* 1987). These biological correlates do not ''cause'' males to aggress, but they do help potentiate such behaviors.

While dependent on contextual cues, pain, irritation, deprivation, and frustration have also been shown to increase the probability of aggression in both animals and human beings (Averill 1982; Konner 1982; Moyer 1976). If, for example, two rats are placed on an electrified grid, they will not normally attack each other. When shocked, however, they will often fight, especially if they are both males (Hinde 1966; Konner 1982). Such findings provide strong support for the ''frustration-aggression hypothesis'' (Dollard *et al.*

1939), which posits a correlation (not causation) between frustration and aggression. ''Complex organisms – the point is best made for mammals – appear to be designed to react to frustration with [aggression]'' (Konner 1993:179).

It would, however, be a mistake to assume that such predispositions are ''hard-wired'' or determine an emotion in and of themselves. As illustrated in the earlier discussion of attachment, an emotion system represents an amalgam of various components. During the lifespan, the particular combinations of these components will change and be modified (through feedback) by the properties of the emotion system as a whole. Just as attachment is distinct from, yet related to, the development of emotions like *amae* and love, so too do predispositions to aggress become incorporated into emotions like anger and *liget*.[12] In order to describe adequately the biogenetic component of such emotional coherences, it is necessary to examine how the overall organization of various biological subsystems (e.g., inter-male and irritable aggression) and processes (e.g., the organizational and activational activity of the neuroendocrine system; the hormonal and autonomic arousal associated with the fight–flight response; the action of physiological facilitators like allergens, alcohol, drugs, hypoglycemia; reticular and neurochemical activity) influence the phenomenon in question. This complex constellation of biogenetic factors, always shaped and informed through a dialectic (both synchronic and diachronic) with the other levels of the emotional system, serves to generate the somatic component of emotions like *liget*.

Rosaldo herself seems to recognize implicitly that emotions have such a biogenetic basis. She defines emotions as ''embodied thoughts'' that are ''somehow felt'' (1984:143) and notes that the Ilongot have a somewhat similar view. While *liget* is integrally embedded in social context, it is also conceptualized as springing from the ''heart,'' or *rinawa*, a physical organ that is the source of vitality and action (Rosaldo 1980:36–38). Given this physiological association, it is not surprising that the Ilongot use various embodied metaphors to describe their ''anger.'' Thus we find *liget* employed as a noun that suggests ''potency, energy, intensity, the irritating heat of chili peppers,[13] the rush of rapids, or force of wind'' (Rosaldo 1980:45). Moreover, ''anger'' provides a means to ''cast off'' feelings of ''weight'' that ''link physical sensation to the experience of shame and its release'' (Rosaldo 1983:139). While the ''energy'' of *liget* provides a source of strength and vitality for the Ilongot, they need ''knowledge,'' or *beya*, to give these ''affective impulses intelligible, social form'' (Rosaldo 1980:44). In addition to representing an ethnopsychological view of ontogeny that is dialectical (i.e., the interaction between *beya* and *liget*), this conceptualization of *liget* as an impulse that springs from ''interior experience'' (Rosaldo 1980:38) serves to highlight the fact that this emotion has a physiological component.

Given Rosaldo's focus, it is easier to discern the sociocultural aspects of *liget*. Within Ilongot society, there is both an absence of formal structure and class distinctions, and a strong stress on the social bonds that engender cooperation and reciprocity (Rosaldo 1980, 1984). While valued for the "energy" and "passion" it provides, *liget* also constitutes a violent force that can potentially undermine this egalitarian social order. In order to stem this threat, Ilongot children are taught from a young age to "cast off" their anger in disruptive situations and to acquire *beya*, or "a deep respect for others as 'equal-to-us-humans' and potentially cooperating friends and kin" (Rosaldo 1980:90). At the same time, Ilongot male youths are also taught to value *liget* as a means to taking heads, status, and marriage. In addition to being an attractive spouse, a young man with an "angry" reputation is admired for his self-confidence, independence, strength, and social standing. Once married, however, the young man takes on a new set of social obligations and duties that require his *liget* to be increasingly mediated by *beya*.

Liget also provides a means of redressing social imbalances (Rosaldo 1980, 1983, 1984). Living in a society that emphasizes "sameness," the Ilongot are concerned with maintaining their status as "equivalent" and autonomous beings. When this balance is upset through insult, confrontation, slights, and/or other occasions that give rise to the "shame" of inequality, *liget* provides a means to "cast off" this "weight." Through such displays of "anger," an actor is able to overcome such unacceptable imbalances, to make a statement about his/her "sameness" to disrespectful others. There is, however, another side to "shame." As noted above, children are taught from an early age to forget their "anger" in situations that can potentially disrupt all-important social bonds. A proper understanding of these kinship ties "means that one does not argue with one's kin, for fear that 'someone else' will mock or 'shame' [him/her] . . . 'shame' is accepted as a necessary constraint in order to avoid acknowledgment of conflict-breeding inequalities" (Rosaldo 1983:144). Individual Ilongot negotiate their daily interactions within the context of such sociocultural scripts, norms, values, and constraints.

Lacking detailed information about the Ilongot brother's life history, it is difficult to make statements about how his actions were informed by his personal experience and temperament. Given the preceding analysis of the biogenetic and sociocultural aspect of *liget*, however, we can speculate about how this emotional coherence was generated. To do so it is crucial to situate his *liget* in context. Rosaldo (1983, 1984) tells us that the two brothers had a history of tension and that their dissension had been growing acute in the days leading up to the incident. Moreover, we know that the Ilongot was frustrated about his brother's careless planning and that he had been drinking, an activity associated with "anger" (Rosaldo 1980). Whereas normally it would be considered "shameful" for two brothers to fight, drinking provided a context in which it was possible to forget these bonds (because consciousness had been ''dissolved'') and to become ''angry.''[14] Given the Ilongot emphasis on equality, it seems likely that the fighter felt slighted by his brother's carelessness. By becoming *liget*, he would have been able to rectify this imbalance and thus throw off the weight of his ''shame.'' Whatever his specific goals, purposes, and/or intrapsychic motivations, Ilongot norms required the brothers to forget their ''anger'' the next day in order to preserve the kinship ties that are so important in Ilongot culture. Because they had been drinking they could ''declare that they were 'ashamed' that the alcohol (and it alone!) had led them to forget their bonds'' (Rosaldo 1983:144).

What is crucial to note is that such ''anger'' cannot be adequately explained in terms of an extreme form of universalism or constructionism alone. As we saw earlier, *liget* seems to have a strong biogenetic component. In this case it seems likely that physiological processes related to inter-male aggression, to frustration aggression, and to the facilitative effects of testosterone and alcohol were involved. While these biogenetic factors are strongly shaped by social and cultural factors throughout the life-course, they still seem to bear a resemblance to our own anger. Thus we find Rosaldo acknowledging that Ilongot ''anger'' both ''overlaps with, yet is different from, our own'' (1984:145). Such a statement suggests that the activity taking place within the dialectical landscape of *liget* is subject to species-typical constraints, and thus shows a prototypic resemblance to that phenomenon (or one of those phenomena) we call anger.[15]

Regardless of what the dialectical landscape of *liget* looks like, it is crucial to keep in mind that what is ''somehow felt'' both influences an Ilongot's experience of the emotion and is construed through a set of sociocultural practices and norms. As we have seen, the egalitarian and cooperative nature of Ilongot society both shapes and constrains individual action. Similarly, there exists a rich repertoire of cultural symbols, norms, and scripts through which an Ilongot interprets emotions like *liget*. Just as the biogenetic level of organization is mediated by sociocultural factors, so too are the social and cultural levels informed by physiological factors. In this case the Ilongot seem to have built an elaborate symbolic cosmology around aggression (thus their headhunting, displays of ''anger,'' ideas about of the violent nature of *liget*, expectations about the effects of alcohol, etc.), one that has shaped these biogenetic predispositions in distinct, yet recognizable ways.

When we get to the level of situated individual practice, we find given actors attempting to succeed in accomplishing given goals and plans (which are, in turn, informed by the other levels of the emotion system). All of these factors conspire to give rise to an emergent emotional coherence. Thus the *liget* of the Ilongot fighter might have been generated out of: his somatic feelings (i.e., physiological sensations that are like the irritating heat of chilies and/or the intense rush of the rapids), feelings that were quite likely reinforced by the effects of, and/or his expectations about, drinking (cf. note 14); sociocultural norms, constraints, and scripts (i.e., the emphasis on "sameness" and the importance of social bonds, cultural models of "shame" and "anger"); and his own goals (i.e., to redress a perceived imbalance through a display of "anger" in a situation that would not "shame" him, to "cast off" his frustration about his "brother's" carelessness, to gain the benefits that come with a reputation as an "angry" young man). All of this, in turn, is set in and must be understood in terms of a given context (i.e., a history of tension, the brother's carelessness, drinking).

Regardless of whether or not such conjectures are correct, this analysis illustrates how a processual approach can proceed. As opposed to being forced to assert that *liget* is "either" the product of a generic human mind "or" a culturally relative construct, processualism is able to examine the ways in which biology and culture conspire to generate such emotions. While it is possible to legitimately examine each level of an emotion system separately, this must be done with an understanding of how the given level embodies properties of the others.[16] Ultimately, an emotion constitutes a coherence that emerges out of the dialectical interaction of biological, social, cultural, individual, and contextual factors.

Conclusion

This chapter has illustrated how researchers can take a more syncretic approach to their study of the emotions. In particular, processualism holds that we should examine the discrete processes by which the emotions are generated over time. This stance has direct repercussions on the emotion debate.

It allows us to escape reductionism. As opposed to asserting that the emotions are either "essentially" biological universals (nature) or cultural constructs (nurture), processualism maintains that the emotions should be conceptualized in terms of hierarchical levels of organization (e.g., biogenetic, social, cultural, and individual). While each level can be legitimately studied alone, researchers must recognize that each domain embodies aspects of the other levels of organization. A synchronic analysis of the properties of this emotion system should be augmented by (at least) a recognition of its diachronic nature. By examining how the biological, social, cultural, and individual levels of a given emotion system interact over time, researchers can escape the unidimensional determinism of the extreme forms of universalism and constructionism. Instead of being agonists, biology and culture define one another along a dialectical landscape that is itself subject to change.

Such a perspective provides us with a new way of approaching the definition and classification of the emotions. In the past, scholars have too often defined the emotions in a reductive manner (e.g., by asserting that they are essentially physiological states or cultural constructs). This type of "intellectual metonymy" (i.e., taking one part of an emotional system for the whole) stands in strong contrast to the dynamic, multifactorial orientation of processualism. From a processual stance, emotion can be defined as an emergent coherence that is generated out of the interaction between the different levels of an emotion system. Just as it snows when temperature, barometric pressure, humidity, and wind velocity coalesce in a certain manner, so too does an emotion like *liget* arise out of the nexus between given individual, sociocultural, and physiological factors.

These systemic relations are liable to change over time. As opposed to taking a term like "love" and looking for all of its instances throughout the life-course, processualism examines each emotion system in terms of its ontogenetic development. Thus the system that gives rise to attachment behavior is seen to develop in distinct ways into emotions like *amae*. It would be erroneous, however, to equate these two emotion systems – a variety of factors conspire to make them qualitatively different. Such findings suggest that the classification of the emotions should proceed in a more inductive fashion. Emotion researchers need to examine how physiological, sociocultural, and individual factors cohere in distinct ways at different points in the life-course. Anthropologists are in a unique position to make observations about these systems as they develop in different cultures. Such inductive research can help us escape the problems that arise when scholars assume *a priori* that a folk terminology constitutes an accurate index of a people's emotional life. While such terms provide indispensable clues about the emotions, they may also mask their complexity.

The power of the processual approach lies precisely in its ability to stay grounded in the everyday practice of individuals without losing sight of how such activities are shaped and constrained by physiological, social, cultural, and individual factors. Thus it is possible to study how Bedouin love poetry (Abu-Lughod 1990) serves as a form of defiance within a given sociopolitical context while simultaneously acknowledging the ways in which the hormonal changes of puberty may actively influence a Bedouin youth's feelings of "love." Similarly, we can see how the "anger" of an Ilongot is tied to his or her strategies and goals without denying the ways in which such feelings are physiologically grounded. Anthropologists must begin to realize that biological and cultural modes of explanation are not mutually exclusive. With regard to emotion *per se*, both levels of analysis are important to an understanding of how given emotional coherences are generated in time and within particular contexts.

The processual approach also suggests some research strategies. First, as opposed to using ''emotion'' as a grab-bag category, researchers should examine how disparate emotions are generated over time. Anthropologists in particular have the opportunity to make interesting comparative, developmental, and intracultural analyses of such generative processes. Such studies of ''the emotions'' may entail a significant revision of our understanding of ''emotion.'' Second, researchers need to develop syncretic frameworks which can enrich our understanding of such phenomena. Processualism represents one alternative. Others are certainly possible. Third, researchers should delimit the level of analysis upon which their work is taking place. Such a qualification would necessitate at least an understanding of how the given level of analysis embodies aspects of other levels of organization. Finally, theorists should think more carefully about what they mean when they employ the term ''emotion.'' As illustrated by the Spiro–Rosaldo debate, researchers often end up talking past one another because they fail to adequately define, reflect on, and/or bracket the phenomena about which they are drawing conclusions.

Acknowledgements

This essay was previously published in the December 1993 issue (volume 21, issue 4) of *Ethos*, under the title ''Prolegomenon to a processual approach to the emotions.''

This material is based upon work supported under a National Science Foundation Graduate Fellowship. I am grateful to Bradd Shore, Carol Worthman, Owen Lynch, and the anonymous reviewers at *Ethos* for their thought-provoking comments on earlier drafts of this essay. I would also like to thank Robert Paul, Fredrik Barth, W. L. Hinton, Iain Edgewater, Nicole Cooley, and the participants in Emory's biocultural seminar on emotion for their helpful suggestions. The ideas expressed remain the responsibility of the author alone.

NOTES

1. Constructionists have also pointed out that this type of ''scientific'' discourse is pervaded by the Euro-American view that emotions are precultural (or ''natural''), physical events that are privately and passively experienced by a person (Lutz 1988). Such a perspective ignores the important ways in which emotional experience is constituted within given interpersonal contexts and symbolic cosmologies. Moreover, because emotion and thought are dichotomized, the former is relegated to the realm of the ''irrational'' and uncontrollable. Thus we find Spiro (1984:343) asserting that the ''emotionally driven irrational'' leads not only to headhunting, but also to events such as the sack of Alexandria and the student riots of the 1960s.
2. ''Instead of a hypothetical partially ordered set of unit causes (genes) and an

unanalyzed causal relation between these and phenotypic characteristics, molecular (vs. classical Mendelian) genetics has a set of complex molecules (DNA), a fantastically complex set of biochemical processes by which specific proteins (roughly amino acid chains) are synthesized from these (the biosynthetic pathways) and finally a further relation between ordered sets of proteins and ordered sets of macroscopically observable characteristics'' (Hooker 1981:512–3).

3. It is somewhat ironic that constructionists place such a high value on culture while simultaneously assuming that because a cultural ideology rests on folk presuppositions it must be erroneous. In fact, an increasingly large body of evidence suggests that folk beliefs are often subject to real-world constraints (Johnson 1987; Lakoff 1987; Lakoff and Johnson 1980).
4. Moyer (1976) illustrates how this type of revision can proceed. He notes that different researchers often use the word ''aggression'' to refer to a number of disparate phenomena. Drawing on animal studies, Moyer distinguishes several types of behavior that are thrown under this umbrella term (e.g., predatory aggression, inter-male aggression, fear-induced aggression, irritable aggression, and maternal aggression), each of which is characterized by a distinct pattern of internal, external, experiential factors. Such work can serve as a model for future emotion research (see also Kagan 1978, 1984).
5. I use the word ''processual'' to highlight the contrast with reductive approaches to the emotions. ''Reductive'' is etymologically derived from the Latin word *reducere*, which means ''to bring back'' (*Oxford English Dictionary* 1971:316). Thus we find the verb ''reduce'' defined as: ''to bring down, diminish . . . to a single thing'' (*ibid.*) and/or ''to lessen in extent, amount, number, degree, price, or other quality'' (*American Heritage Dictionary* 1976:1092). This emphasis on diminished quality and singularity contrasts sharply with the meaning of process. The latter term is defined as ''a system of operations in the production of something'' (*AHD* 1976:1043); it involves ''continuous and regular action'' that is carried out ''in the course of time'' (*OED* 1971:2311). As opposed to viewing the emotions in a reductive manner (i.e., as diminished, unidimensional phenomena), a processual approach recognizes that each emotion is dynamically generated from a ''system of operations'' that is itself subject to change through time.
6. It is crucial to note that what are heuristically conceptualized as ''higher'' levels of organization are just as important as lower ones and often exert a formative impact on them. Thus, while it is legitimate to study each of these levels of analysis alone, none should be given explanatory hegemony over the others. Because each level explains given aspects of the system in question, the explanatory value of the others must be taken into account. ''Emergence'' is used here to emphasize that the phenomenon in question has distinct properties which are not reducible to those of its component parts. ''Most scholars in the life sciences accept the doctrine that a particular combination of component events creates an emergent synthetic phenomenon different from and not amenable to prediction by examination of each of the individual parts. The mitosis and differentiation of the zygote from the union of male and female gametes is as classic an illustration as any. This principle implies that it is often difficult or impossible to infer the

emergent state from any one index that is a participant in that state'' (Kagan 1984:51).

7. It is crucial to keep in mind that such ''higher'' levels of organization actively inform the ''lower'' levels. Thus, just as the level of semiotics is constrained by the properties of phonemes, so too does it influence the selection and use of given phonemes (see Changeux 1985).
8. See Johnson (1987), Lakoff (1987), and Lakoff and Johnson (1980) for an illustration of how our conceptual categories are ''embodied'' or grounded in human physiology and experience. As illustrated by Lakoff and Kovesces' (1987) analysis of cognitive models of anger in American English, this framework can be easily applied to the emotions (see also Lynch 1990:13–15).
9. Type A babies would avoid interacting with the caretaker (e.g., not seeking proximity, resisting being picked up) upon reunion; type B infants would seek proximity and contact with the mother during both distressful situations and upon reunion; and type C babies would behave ambivalently, seeking proximity sometimes, avoiding the caretaker on other occasions.
10. It is also important to see that, within a culture, the experiences of individuals can lead them along very different dialectical chreods. I emphasize the dialectic between culture and biology because the emotion debate has been torn along these lines. Nevertheless, intracultural variation is easily accommodated within the dialectical landscape.
11. The organizational process during which this ''fetal androgenization'' takes place is interesting insofar as the hormone that ''masculinizes'' the brain is aromatized estradiol, the ''female'' sex hormone. During fetal development, the body synthesizes a protein, alpha-fetoprotein (or AFP), that cannot penetrate the blood–brain barrier. Because AFP bonds to estradiol but not to testosterone, only the latter hormone is able to cross into the brain during its critical period of sexual differentiation. Ironically, ''once inside the brain, testosterone is aromatized to estradiol, and the estradiol thereby largely serves to masculinize the brain. Thus, while estradiol tends to have largely feminizing effects outside the brain, especially during the organizational phase of sexual differentiation, the effects are of a masculinizing nature'' (Ellis 1986:521).
12. It is crucial to keep in mind that these predispositions can be ignored or elaborated (see Robert Levy's [1984] distinction between hypo- and hyper-cognition), just as certain phones are incorporated, used minimally, and/or lost through disuse during the process of language acquisition.
13. This metaphor is consistent with George Lakoff's (1987) prediction that emotions bearing a prototypical resemblance to anger will commonly be described in terms of embodied metaphors of heat. While this prediction (based on Ekman *et al's* [1983] finding that certain emotions have specific physiological correlates – i.e., anger, for example, is associated with an increase in skin temperature) is speculative, it remains to be tested. The Ilongot data is merely suggestive in this regard.
14. Although there is no direct causal relationship between alcohol and aggression (Brain 1986), ethanol can serve as a reinforcer of such behaviors (Moyer 1976; Cox 1990). As Craig MacAndrew and Robert Edgerton (1969) illustrate, behaviors associated with drinking vary both across cultures and between contexts. While alcohol can decrease inhibition, reduce tension, and enhance mood, such physiological effects are mediated by a person's expectations about and

understandings of drinking (Cox 1990; Knauft 1987a). The Ilongot in particular seem to have a specific ethnotheory about alcohol. On the one hand, it is viewed as causing "anger" and violence. On the other hand, a person is not held responsible for his or her actions because alcohol "dissolves" consciousness. It thus seems likely that alcohol was able to serve both a facilitative and an excusatory role in the Ilongot fighter's behavior.

15. In general we should be just as wary of given ethnopsychological terms as we are of our own folk psychological categories. I would argue that not only Euro-Americans, but also the Ilongot, probably throw a number of disparate phenomena under such folk labels. A processual approach would attempt to distinguish between these phenomena. As opposed to finding a similarity between our "anger" and that of the Ilongot, we would most likely discern parallels between some of the phenomena lumped together under these terms.
16. On the individual level of analysis, for example, a researcher might examine the specific goals and practices that inform an actor's emotional experience. To do so, however, it would be necessary to take somatic, social, and cultural factors into account since they shape and constrain a person's actions. Similarly, the biogenetic level of analysis might look at the genetic envelope associated with an emotion, but this would have to be done with an eye to how a person's physiology embodies properties of the sociocultural and individual levels of organization. Problems arise when researchers assume that the level of analysis which they are investigating provides an all-encompassing explanation. Because it leads scholars to argue past each other, such intellectual metonymy represents a source of much confusion in this domain of study.

References

Abu-Lughod, Lila. 1990. Shifting politics in Bedouin love poetry. In *Language and the politics of emotion*, ed. Catherine A. Lutz and Lila Abu-Lughod, 24–45. New York: Cambridge University Press.

Ainsworth, Mary, D. S. 1978. *Patterns of attachment: A psychological study of the strange situation*. Hillsdale: Lawrence Erlbaum.

1989. Attachments beyond infancy. *American Psychologist* 44(4):709–716.

Ainsworth, Mary, D. S., and John Bowlby. 1991. An ethological approach to personality development. *American Psychologist* 46(4):333–341.

The American heritage dictionary of the English language. 1976. New college edition. Boston: Houghton Mifflin.

Arnold, A. P. and R. A. Gorski. 1984. Gonadal steroid induction of structural sex differences in the central nervous system. *Annual Review of Neuroscience* 7:413–442.

Averill, James R. 1982. *Anger and aggression: An essay on emotion*. New York: Springer-Verlag.

Baltes, Paul B. 1987. Theoretical propositions of life-span developmental psychology: On the dynamics between growth and decline. *Developmental Psychology* 23(5):611–626.

Barth, Fredrik. 1987. *Cosmologies in the making: A generative approach to cultural variation in inner New Guinea*. New York: Cambridge University Press.

Bateson, Gregory. 1987. *Steps to an ecology of mind*. Northvale, NJ: Jason Aronson.

Bertalanffy, Ludwig von. 1968. *General systems theory*. New York: George Braziller.

Bloom, Floyd E. and Arlyne Lazerson. 1988. *Brain, mind, and behavior*. New York: W. H. Freeman.

Bourdieu, Pierre. 1977. *Outline of a theory of practice*. New York: Cambridge University Press.

Bowlby, John. 1969. *Attachment and loss, Volume 1, Attachment*. New York: Basic Books.

1973. *Attachment and loss, Volume 2, Separation*. New York: Basic Books.

Brain, Paul F., ed. 1986. *Alcohol and aggression*. London: Croom Helm.

Buck, Ross. 1986. The psychology of emotion. In *Mind and brain: Dialogues in cognitive neuroscience*, ed. Joseph E. LeDoux and William Hirst, 275–300. New York: Cambridge University Press.

Cairns, Robert B. 1991. Multiple metaphors for a singular idea. *Developmental Psychology* 27(1):23–26.

Cairns, Robert B., Jean-Louis Gariepy, and Kathryn E. Hood. 1990. Development, microevolution, and social behavior. *Psychological Review* 97(1):49–65.

Cannon, Walter B. 1984 [1914]. Bodily changes in pain, hunger, fear and rage. In *What is an emotion?: Classic readings in philosophical psychology*, ed. Cheshire Calhoun and Robert C. Solomon, 142–151. New York: Oxford University Press.

Changeux, Jean-Pierre. 1985. *Neuronal man: The biology of mind*. New York: Oxford University Press.

Churchland, Patricia S. 1986. *Neurophilosophy: Toward a unified science of the mind/brain*. New York: Cambridge University Press.

Churchland, Paul M. 1984. *Matter and consciousness*. Cambridge, MA: MIT Press.

Cox, W. Miles, ed. 1990. *Why people drink: Parameters of alcohol as a reinforcer*. New York: Gardner Press.

Daly, Martin and Margo Wilson. 1988. *Homicide*. New York: Aldine De Gruyter.

Doi, Takeo. 1973. *The anatomy of dependence*, trans. John Bester. Tokyo: Kodansha International.

Dollard, John, Leonard W. Dobb, Neal E. Miller, O. H. Mowrer, and Robert R. Sears. 1939. *Frustration and aggression*. New Haven CT: Yale University Press.

Edelman, Gerald M. 1987. *Neural Darwinism: The theory of group selection*. New York: Basic Books.

Ekman, Paul. 1980. Biological and cultural contributions to body and facial movements in the expression of emotions. In *Explaining emotions*, ed. Amelie O. Rorty, 73–101. Berkeley: University of California Press.

Ekman, Paul, R. W. Levenson, and W. V. Friesen. 1983. Autonomic nervous system activity distinguishes among emotions. *Science* 221:1208–1210.

Ellis, Lee. 1986. Evidence of neuroandrogenic etiology of sex roles from a combined analysis of human, nonhuman primate and nonprimate mammalian studies. *Personality and Individual Differences* 7(4):519–552.

Fogel, Alan and Esther Thelen. 1987. Development of early expressive and communicative action: Reinterpreting the evidence from a dynamic systems perspective. *Developmental Psychology* 23(6):747–761.

Geertz, Clifford. 1973. *The interpretation of cultures*. New York: Basic Books.

Gerber, Eleanor R. 1985. Rage and obligation: Samoan emotion in conflict. In *Person, self, and experience: Exploring Pacific ethnopsychologies*, ed. Geoffrey M.

White and John Kirkpatrick, 121–167. Berkeley: University of California Press.

Gottlieb, Gilbert. 1991. Experiential canalization of behavioral development: Theory. *Developmental Psychology* 27(1):4–13.

Greenough, William T. 1991. Experience as a component of normal development: Evolutionary considerations. *Developmental Psychology* 27(1):14–17.

Grossmann, Klaus E., and Karin Grossmann. 1990. The wider concept of attachment in cross-cultural research. *Human Development* 33:31–47.

Heath, Robert G. 1986. The neural substrate of emotion. In *Emotion: Theory, research, and experience, Volume 3*, ed. Robert Plutchik and Henry Kellerman, 3–35. Orlando: Academic Press.

Henry, James P. 1986. Neuroendocrine patterns of emotional response. In *Emotion: Theory, research, and experience, Volume 3*, ed. Robert Plutchik and Henry Kellerman, 37–60. Orlando: Academic Press.

Hinde, Robert A. 1966. *Animal behavior: A synthesis of ethological and comparative psychology*. New York: McGraw-Hill.

Hooker, C. A. 1981. Towards a general theory of reduction. *Dialogue* 20:496–529.

Hopkins, Brian and George Butterworth. 1990. Concepts of causality in explanations of development. In *Causes of development: Interdisciplinary perspectives*, ed. George Butterworth and Peter Bryant, 3–32. New York: Harvester Wheatsheaf.

Izard, Carroll E. and Carol Z. Malatesta. 1987. *Perspective on emotional development I: Differential emotions theory of early emotional development. Handbook of Infant development*, 2nd edition, ed. Joy D. Osofsky, 494–554. New York: John Wiley & Sons.

Johnson, Mark. 1987. *The body in the mind: The bodily basis of meaning, imagination, and reason*. Chicago: University of Chicago Press.

Kagan, Jerome. 1978. On emotion and its development: A working paper. In *The development of affect*, ed. Michael Lewis and Leonard A. Rosenblum, 11–41. New York: Plenum Press.

1984. The idea of emotion in human development. In *Emotions, Cognition, & Behavior*, ed. Caroll E. Izard, Jerome Kagan, and Robert B. Zajonc, 38–72. New York: Cambridge University Press.

Kandel, Eric R., James H. Schwartz, and Thomas M. Jessell, eds. 1991. *Principles of neural science*, 3rd edition. New York: Elsevier.

Katchadourian, Herant. 1977. *The biology of adolescence*. San Francisco: Freeman.

Keesing, Roger M. 1987. Anthropology as interpretive quest. *Current Anthropology* 28(2):161–176.

Kendrik, K. M. and R. F. Drewett. 1979. Testosterone reduces refractory period of stria terminalis neurons in the rat brain. *Science* 204:887–879.

Knauft, Bruce M. 1987a. Managing sex and anger: Tobacco and kava use among the Gebusi of Papua New Guinea. In *Drugs in Western Pacific societies: Relations of substance*, ed. Lamont Lindstrom, 73–98. Lanham, MD: University Press of America.

1987b. Reconsidering violence in simple human societies: Homicide among the Gebusi of New Guinea. *Current Anthropology* 28:457–500.

Konner, Melvin J. 1982. *The tangled wing: Biological constraints on the human spirit*. New York: Holt, Rinehart and Winston.

1993. Do we need enemies? The origins and consequences of rage. In *Rage, power, and aggression*, ed. Robert A. Glick and Steven P. Roose, 173–193. New Haven: Yale University Press.

Lakoff, George. 1987. *Women, fire, and dangerous things: What categories reveal about the mind*. Chicago: University of Chicago Press.

Lakoff, George and Mark Johnson. 1980. *Metaphors we live by*. Chicago: University of Chicago Press.

Lakoff, George and Zoltan Kövesces. 1987. The cognitive model of anger inherent in American English. In *Cultural models in language and thought*, ed. Dorothy Holland and Naomi Quinn, 195–221. New York: Cambridge University Press.

Laughlin, Charles D. and Eugene G. D'Aquili. 1974. *Biogenetic structuralism*. New York: Columbia University Press.

Lazarus, Richard S. 1984. On the primacy of cognition. *American Psychologist* 39(2):124–129.

1990. Constructs of the mind in adaptation. In *Psychological and biological approaches to emotion*, ed. Nancy L. Stein, Bennett Leventhal, and Tom Trabasso, 3–19. Hillsdale: Lawrence Erlbaum.

LeDoux, Joseph E. 1986. The neurobiology of emotion. In *Mind and brain: Dialogues in cognitive neuroscience*, ed. Joseph E. LeDoux and William Hirst, 301–354. Cambridge: Cambridge University Press.

1990. Cognitive-emotional interactions in the brain. *Cognition and Emotion* 3(4):267–289.

Lerner, Richard M. 1991. Changing organism-context relations as the basic process of development: A developmental contextual perspective. *Developmental Psychology* 27(1):27–32.

Levy, Robert I. 1984. Emotion, knowing, and culture. In *Culture theory: Essays on mind, self, and emotion*, ed. Richard A. Shweder and Robert A. Levine, 214–237. New York: Cambridge University Press.

Lutz, Catherine A. 1988. *Unnatural emotions: Everyday sentiments on a Micronesian atoll & their challenge to Western theory*. Chicago: University of Chicago Press.

Lutz, Catherine A. and Lila Abu-Lughod. 1990. Introduction: Emotion, discourse, and the politics of everyday life. In *Language and the politics of emotion*, ed. Catherine A. Lutz and Lila Abu-Lughod, 1–23. New York: Cambridge University Press.

Lutz, Catherine A. and Geoffrey M. White. 1986. The anthropology of emotions. *Annual Review of Anthropology* 15:405–436.

Lynch, Owen M. 1990. The social construction of emotion in India. In *Divine passions: The social construction of emotion in India*, ed. Owen M. Lynch, 3–34. Berkeley: University of California Press.

MacAndrew, Craig and Robert B. Edgerton. 1969. *Drunken comportment: A social explanation*. Chicago: Aldine.

MacLean, Paul D. 1973. *A triune concept of the brain and behavior*. Toronto: Toronto University Press.

Mandler, George. 1984. *Mind and body: Psychology of emotion and stress*. New York: W. W. Norton.

1990. A constructivist theory of emotion. In *Psychological and biological approaches to emotion*, ed. Nancy L. Stein, Bennett Leventhal, and Tom Trabasso, 21–43. Hillsdale: Lawrence Erlbaum.

Mazur, Allen and Theodore A. Lamb. 1980. Testosterone, status, and mood in human males. *Hormones and Behavior* 14:236–246.

Miyake, Kazuo, Shing-Jen Chen, and Joseph J. Campos. 1985. Infant temperament, mother's mode of interaction, and attachment in Japan: An interim report. In *Growing points of attachment theory and research*, ed. Inge Bretherton and Everett Waters, 276–297. Monographs of the Society for Research in Child Development 50 (1–2, Serial No. 209).

Miyake, Kazuo, Joseph J. Campos, Jerome Kagan, and Donna L. Bradshaw. 1986. Issues in socioemotional development. In *Child development and education in Japan*, ed. Harold W. Stevenson, Hakuta Azuma, and Kenji Hakuta, 239–261. San Francisco: Freeman.

Moyer, K. E. 1976. *The psychobiology of aggression*. New York: Harper & Row.

Nakane, Chie. 1970. *Japanese society*. Berkeley: University of California Press.

Ochs, Elinor and Bambi B. Schieffelin. 1984. Language acquisition and socialization: Three developmental stories and their implications. In *Culture theory: Essays on mind, self, and emotion*, ed. Richard A. Shweder and Robert A. LeVine, 276–320. New York: Cambridge University Press.

Olweus, Dan. 1986. Aggression and hormones: Behavioral relationships with testosterone and adrenaline. In *Development of antisocial and prosocial behavior*, ed. Dan Olweus, Jack Block, and Marian Radke-Yarrow, 51–72. New York: Academic.

1988. Circulating testosterone levels and aggression in adolescent males: A causal analysis. *Psychosomatic Medicine* 50:261–272.

Oortmerssen, G. A. van, D. J. Dijk, and T. Schuurman. 1987. Studies in wild house mice: II. Testosterone and aggression. *Hormones and Behavior* 21:139–152.

Oxford English Dictionary (compact edition). 1971. New York: Oxford University Press.

Oyama, Susan. 1985. *The ontogeny of information*. New York: Cambridge University Press.

Papanicolaou, A. C. 1989. *Emotion: A reconsideration of somatic theory*. New York: Gordon and Breach Science Publishers.

Papez, James W. 1937. A proposed mechanism of emotion. *Archives of Neurology and Psychiatry* 38:725–743.

Polanyi, Michael. 1975. *Meaning*. Chicago: University of Chicago Press.

Praag, Herman M. van. 1986. Monoamines and depression: The present state of the art. In *Emotion: Theory, research, and experience, Volume 3*, ed. Robert Plutchik and Henry Kellerman, 335–61. Orlando: Academic Press.

Rappaport, Roy A. 1984. *Pigs for the ancestors: Ritual in the ecology of a New Guinea people*. New Haven: Yale University Press.

Rosaldo, Michelle Z. 1980. *Knowledge and passion: Ilongot notions of self and social life*. Cambridge: Cambridge University Press.

1983. The shame of headhunters and the autonomy of self. *Ethos* 11(3):135–151.

1984. Towards an anthropology of self and feeling. In *Culture theory: Essays on mind, self, and emotion*, ed. Richard A. Shweder and Robert A. LeVine, 137–157. New York: Cambridge University Press.

Rosenberg, Daniel V. 1991. *Language in the discourse of the emotions. Language and the politics of emotion*. Catherine A. Lutz and Lila Abu-Lughod, 162–185. New York: Cambridge University Press.

Sagi, Abraham. 1990. Attachment theory and research from a cross-cultural perspective. *Human Development* 33:10–22.

Schachter, Stanley and J. E. Singer. 1962. Cognition, social and physiological determinants of emotional state. *Psychological Review* 69:379–399.

Shweder, Richard A. 1985. Menstrual pollution, soul loss, and the comparative study of emotions. In *Culture and depression: Studies in the anthropology and cross-cultural psychiatry of affect and disorder*, ed. Arthur Kleinman and Byron Good, 182–215. Berkeley: University of California Press.

Shore, Bradd. 1988. Interpretation under fire. *Anthropological Quarterly* 61(4):161–176.

Solomon, Robert C. 1984. Getting angry: The Jamesian theory of emotion in anthropology. In *Culture theory: Essays on mind, self, and emotion*, ed. Richard A. Shweder and Robert A. LeVine, 238–254. New York: Cambridge University Press.

Spiro, Melford E. 1984. Some reflections on cultural determinism and relativism with special reference to emotion and reason. In *Culture theory: Essays on mind, self, and emotion*, ed. Richard A. Shweder and R. A. LeVine, 323–346. New York: Cambridge University Press.

Takahashi, Keiko. 1990. Are the key assumptions of the ''strange situation'' procedure universal? A view from Japanese research. *Human Development* 33:22–30.

Tucker, Don M., Kathryn Vannatta, and Johannes Rothlind. 1990. Arousal and activation systems and primitive adaptive controls on cognitive priming. In *Psychological and biological approaches to emotion*, ed. Nancy L. Stein, Bennett Leventhal, and Tom Trabasso, 145–166. Hillsdale: Lawrence Erlbaum.

Waddington, C. H. 1957. *The strategy of the genes*. London: George Allen & Unwin.

Wikan, Unni. 1990. *Managing turbulent hearts: A Balinese formula for living*. Chicago: University of Chicago Press.

Zajonc, R. B. 1980. Feeling and thinking: Preferences need no inferences. *American Psychologist* 35:151–175.

10 Emotion: A view from biogenetic structuralism

Charles D. Laughlin and Jason Throop

Introduction

The controversy between the universalist and constructionist accounts of emotion is a long-standing one in anthropology, one that is likely to be with us for a long time to come. The reason for the perdurability of this debate lies in the fact that much of anthropology reflects in its theories and in its research strategies a tacit Euro-American cultural bias toward mind–body dualism (see Bunge 1980 on this issue). This Cartesian bias is a fundamental attitude that holds that minds and bodies are different "substances" or domains of existence. Scientists reflecting this polarization will tend to fall into one of two camps, the universalists who see phenomena as being determined by the genome and the constructivists who conceive of no physical constraints to mental phenomena at all. In the anthropological study of emotion this polemic has resulted in universalist views where emotion is understood to be psychophysiological essences or processes for which culturally specific interpretations/models serve merely as rough markers and labels, and constructivist views in which emotion is understood to be inextricably tied to linguistically based conceptual models and schemas that are embedded within particularized indigenous knowledge systems (see Lutz and White 1986:408; Mesquita and Frijda 1992:179, Spiro 1984, 1993)

Of course, there will always be people who transcend this tacit dualism and who will develop a more unified mode of thinking. The trouble is that very few people can be persuaded to another point of view because the attitude to which they have been conditioned makes perfect sense to them within the context of their own experience – as Edmund Husserl might well have put it, their universalist or constructivist view of emotion is part of their "natural attitude" toward their private world of experience.

Henry A. Murray said somewhere, "in some ways all human beings are alike, in some ways some human beings are alike, and in some ways no human beings are alike." But many anthropologists, perhaps because of their own personal histories or training, narrowly focus on one of those perspectives – the particular, the communal, or the universal – to the exclusion of the other perspectives. They may focus their energies on the ways all humans are alike to the exclusion of intercultural and interpersonal variance (the universalists), or they may focus on the ways some humans are alike to the exclusion of universal patterns of similarity and structure (the constructionists, cultural relativists, postmodernists, etc.). It seems to be very difficult to persuade some anthropologists to take a position from which all perspectives may be considered as lying on a gradient from particular to universal.

Nevertheless, in this chapter we wish to summarize one possible theoretical perspective that does meet Murray's criteria for a mature science of humanity, and the requirements set out by Alexander Hinton (1993, and elsewhere in this volume) for a "process approach" to emotion. In outlining this perspective we will make no effort to review the literature on the constructionist-universalist debate because this has already been done by Hinton in the introduction to this volume, as well as by Besnier (1990), Leavitt (1996), Levy and Wellenkamp (1989), Lutz and White (1986), Lyon (1995), Mesquita *et al.* (1997), Russell (1991), and Shweder and LeVine (1984). We will first offer a brief description of our theoretical approach for those not already familiar with the work of our group, and then will proceed to use these notions to model the phenomena classed as "emotion." We will then introduce both Ernst Gellhorn's model of autonomic-somatic integration and Paul MacLean's idea of the triune brain, and then will combine these into a single perspective that may better account for the different phylogenetic and architectonic levels contributing to our experience of emotion in consciousness.

Biogenetic structuralism

Biogenetic structuralism presents a theoretical approach to the study of humanity that requires the embodiment of consciousness (Laughlin and d'Aquili 1974; Laughlin *et al.* 1990). The approach is grounded upon the axiom that "mind" and "brain" are two windows upon the same scope of inquiry. "Mind"[1] refers to a kind of inside-out view of consciousness and "brain" to a kind of outside-in view of the same scope. What this means is that, whether observable at the moment or not, for every mental event there is an activity within the nervous system mediating that event. As far as we can ascertain, there exists no such thing as a mental phenomenon that is not mediated by neural activity. Of course, all sorts of neural activity goes on which does not result in our experience of phenomena (e.g., regulation of heart rate, blood pressure, muscle tonus, hormone levels, etc.).

Because biogenetic structuralism requires the embodiment of consciousness, it is an interdisciplinary project that necessitates the merger of, at a minimum, anthropology, psychology, and the neurosciences. We have developed the view that the universal structures of consciousness, including structures subserving language, cognition about time and space, certain psychopathologies, as well as affect and emotion, are due to the genetically predisposed organization of the nervous system. It seems to us preposterous that the invariant patterns of behavior, consciousness, and culture being discussed in various structuralist theories could be located anywhere other than in the nervous system. After all, every thought, every image, every emotion, and every action is demonstrably mediated by the nervous system.

Moreover, it seems important to anthropology to develop a theoretical perspective that: (1) is non-dualistic in modelling mind and body; (2) is not reductionist in the positivist sense (i.e., that the physical sciences can give a complete account of all things mental and cultural, or visa versa); (3) is informed by all reasonable sources of data about human consciousness and culture; and (4) keeps in mind that our bodies are the products of an ongoing process of evolution.

The lifeworld

An individual's everyday, lived experience, or *lifeworld*,[2] is mediated by the individual's nervous system. A principal function of the cerebral cortex of the human brain is the growth of models of the world that are comprised of networks of living neurons. These models, and the cells that comprise them, are *entrained* (i.e., become interconnected via dendritic, axonic, synaptic, and endocrine pathways and processes) into momentary, dynamic patterns of organization that act to mediate the flow of the lifeworld. The total system of models entrained to mediate each moment of the lifeworld are called the *conscious network*, while the total set of neural models that may be potentially entrained to conscious network is the *cognized environment*.

Virtually all models making up the cognized environment develop from nascent neural structures already mediating the lifeworld of the fetus and infant. We call these nascent structures *neurognostic structures*, or simply *neurognosis* (Laughlin 1991, 1996; Laughlin and d'Aquili 1974:83; Laughlin *et al.* 1990:44–75). The term also applies to the genetically conditioned development of these structures. In other words, neurognosis refers to both the initial organization and function of neural models, and to the lawful processes of their growth, interconnection, and development (see Changeux 1985; Edelman 1987; Edelman and Mountcastle 1982; Varela 1979).

Let us emphasize this point, for it will become integral to our view of emotion. Neurognostic development is exquisitely ordered by processes inherent to the ontogenesis of the organism. There is no such thing as the development of neural tissues that is not constrained and guided to some extent by genetically constrained processes. Thus, there can be no such thing as "pure" cultural relativity in either the structure or function of emotion.

There is indeed interpersonal and cross-cultural variance in the experience, conception, and expression of emotion, but this variance should be understood as transformations upon universal structural properties operating in human ontogenesis, rather than as culturally relative patterns influenced solely by history, enculturation, or linguistic tradition.

An example of neurognosis that is germane to our discussion of feeling and emotion is the phenomenon of the phantom limb. As everyone knows by now, people who lose a limb from an accident, surgery, or in battle may experience sensations as if the limb were still there. Particularly serious is the experience of chronic pain in the absent limb experienced by some people.[3] An obvious explanation for this distortion of the lifeworld is that what is being experienced by the unfortunate person is the cognized limb – that is, the internal neuropsychological model of the limb, a part of their cognized body, which remains largely intact in cortical and subcortical tissue. But there is an added dimension to this story. Ronald Melzack (1992), one of the researchers who have worked out the gating theory of pain, has also shown that some people *who are born without limbs* may still experience pain in a phantom limb. Our explanation for this seemingly anomalous fact is that the cognized body – the internal system of neural models of one's body – is neurognostic, and according to the neurognostic body image, the person has all of their limbs. And the pain that is felt is in relation to the neurognostically perfect body image, not the actual body.

Reality

The cognized environment – the total assemblage of neural models that, when entrained within the conscious network, mediate an individual's lifeworld – may be contrasted with the individual's *operational environment* which includes both the real nature of that individual as an organism and the individual's external environment.[4] The primordial, biological function of the cognized environment is the adaptation of the individual to its operational environment. The emphasis upon adaptation is important, for we make the fundamental assumption that the operational environment exists in a reality forever beyond (is *transcendental* relative to) the capacity of any individual or social group to fully comprehend it. That is, the cognized environment is a point of view, a system of knowledge about the operational environment, and there is always more to know about the operational environment, or any aspect of it, than can be known by any particular individual or group.

What we said above about the phantom limb phenomenon offers a good illustration. Our view is that the ''phantom'' limb is in reality the person's cognized limb (part of their cognized environment), although their real limb (part of their operational environment) is missing. We are experiencing our cognized bodies most of the time, not our actual, operational bodies. Our own body exits in a reality that transcends our limited capacity to know or experience it in any total way. In other words, our real body is transcendental relative to our knowledge and experience of it. What is real to most of us is the body we experience as part of our lifeworld. The potential discrepancies between our "real" and "cognized" bodies can be attributed to the fact that our ability to acquire knowledge about our "real" body is circumscribed by: (1) the limits of spatial discernment and discrimination; (2) the capacity to apprehend and anticipate temporal and causal relations; (3) the ability to reveal and model the hidden forces operating in the operational environment (see Elster 1984: ch. 4); and (4) the tendency of the cognized environment to seek closure of knowledge relative to the transcendental enormity of reality and in the interests of producing meaning in the lifeworld (see Laughlin 1992, 1994).

Intentionality

As we have known since at least the nineteenth century, the moment-by-moment organization of the lifeworld is essentially *intentional* in its organization (Searle 1983; Gurwitsch 1940). This phenomenological fact is very important to our understanding of the role of emotion in the organization of the lifeworld. Intentionality means that neural networks tend to organize themselves, both spatially and temporally, around an object. The focal object, be it a precept, category, feeling, sensation, image, thought, etc., is also mediated by a neural network and constitutes, for the moment, the nexus of cognitive, affective, metabolic, and motor operations for the organism (Neisser 1976:20; Biederman 1987).

Intentionality in humans and other big-brained mammals derives from an intense interaction of the *prefrontal cortex* with the sensory association cortex and subcortical tissues. This intentional interaction is both neurognostic and ubiquitous to human consciousness, regardless of an individual's cultural background (Laughlin *et al.* 1990:105). Subsidiary structures entrained as a consequence of the dialogue between prefrontal and sensory cortical and subcortical processes may be located over a wide expanse of neuroendocrine tissues. And the functions they perform while mediating the lifeworld, including emotion, often occur non-serially. This simultaneous activity of many systems producing unitary experience has been called *parallel distributed processing* (see Rumelhart and McClelland 1986; McClelland and Rumelhart 1986). The point is that while we experience our lifeworld as a totality, there are actually hundreds, and even thousands of neural networks operating in parallel fashion to mediate that experience whose products "come together" in dialogue with prefrontal intentional processes. We are rarely aware of the myriad structures mediating the experience of our self and our world – only that our embodied self and our world are ''already there'' in consciousness.

It is also important to understand that intentionality is not a passive response to stimuli in the external or internal operational environment, but is literally a dialogue between patterns of sensory activity and models already dwelling within the vast society of cells that is the nervous system. That is why we emphasize that the conscious network is a feed-forward process. The brain is always anticipating what it will experience and is acting in concert with the rest of the body so as to produce the experience it desires (Skarda and Freeman 1987; Pribram 1981; Pribram and McGuinness 1975; Laughlin *et al.* 1990:107). And part of the anticipatory package, as it were, involves emotion (Gray 1982). We will often cognitively and perceptually operate and act in the world in order to produce a desired emotional effect; i.e., to experience love, excitement, anger, lust, surprise, etc., or to avoid experiencing anxiety, pain, anger, unhappiness, etc.).

Emotion

The term ''emotion'' refers to phenomena that everyone on the planet experiences, and yet it is notoriously difficult to define and research (Izard 1993:71; Parkinson 1995:8; Scherer 1988:1, 5; Stuss and Benson 1983: 113–115). Emotional phenomena are internal states which can only be accessed directly by introspection, and indirectly by self-reports, technological devices (e.g., electroencephalography), or by inference from facial expressions, body postures, or behavior (see Ekman 1982, 1994; Izard 1980; Scherer 1988; Plutchik and Kellerman 1986; Ohman and Birbaumer 1993). And as may be obvious from an entrainment model of consciousness, what an individual means by ''emotion'' depends upon which aspects of experience are being adumbrated and conceptualized. For instance, as Izard (1990:627) has pointed out, while William James' early and influential theory of emotion[5] recognized expressive, neurophysiological, and experiential dimensions, James focused most of his attention on the experiential component, which meant for him ''feeling.'' It is thus imperative that in our use of the term ''emotion'' we clearly outline those aspects of experience that we as anthropologists are focusing upon in the context of our research. Are we referring to sensations alone, or are there perceptual and cognitive associations included? Are we referring only to the raw interoceptive elements of ''feelings'' of, say, anxiety or arousal, or are the object of the feelings and the cognitive associations with the object being included, as in ''angry at. . .'' or ''anxious about . . .''? Clearly, the question of emotion cannot simply be reduced to biology when there are aspects of socialization and cultural meaning involved. Moreover, attempts to define emotion based solely upon either linguistic, behavioral, or physiological attributes are of little use to science (Ohman and Birbaumer 1993:4–5), especially to a naturalistic science like anthropology which has to account for the phenomenon as it spontaneously arises among people in their daily lives, and not merely under contrived experimental conditions.

Emotional intentionality in the lifeworld of humans and other big-brained mammals is mediated by a complex interaction among prefrontal cortex, sensory and association cortex, and subcortical tissues, the latter including the limbic system (which mediates certain affects like anger, fear, depression, etc.), the thalamus (which accomplishes the gating of information between cortical and subcortical areas), the hypothalamus (involved in arousal, regulation of endocrine and autonomic nervous system activities and information about internal states) and, via the inferior temporal lobe, the hippocampus (involved in perceptual recognition and memory; see Gray 1982; Fuster 1980; Stuss and Benson 1983, 1986).

The most important area of the brain in terms of understanding the integration of the parallel distributed systems that mediate an emotional state is the prefrontal cortex. If a human sustains severe prefrontal damage, especially if their frontal-limbic connections are injured, they may manifest lengthy periods of flat affect and apathy, punctuated by bouts of intense, uncontrolled emotion (Stuss and Benson 1983, 1986:121ff.). Much of this disruption of affect probably is due to a deficit in intentional processing. It is as though the patient can no longer pay enough attention to care about anything or invest a continuity of affect in it (Fuster 1980:121). Many of the areas of the nervous system integrated by the prefrontal cortex are represented by association areas in the prefrontal poles. For example, the limbic system which mediates many of the affective components of emotional states is fully represented by areas in the prefrontal cortex (Nauta 1973).

It was once thought that emotion was very much a simple matter of top-down control from the associative cortex to subcortical tissues. It was believed that there were essentially two emotions, negative and positive, and that the complex variation of emotion experienced and expressed by human beings was the result of cognitive attribution of these bipolar affects to specific objects (e.g., see Schacter and Singer 1962). But we now know that stimuli from the sensory systems are sent directly to the limbic structures, and that, under certain circumstances, emotional responses remain unimpaired even when higher cortical functions have been (see LeDoux 1986, 1989).

MacLean's model

One way to make this complexity more understandable is to realize that the organization of the thousands of parallel networks making up the different parts of the central nervous system evolved during different periods of phylogenesis. Neuroscientist Paul MacLean (1973) speaks of the human central nervous system as a *triune brain;* that is, the brain is made up of three parts, the *reptilian* (including the brain stem and hypothalamus), the *old mammalian* (primarily the limbic system) and the *new mammalian* (the cerebral cortex) brains, each carrying out one or more of the processes that may be entrained to an ''emotional'' state. If the semantic field labeled by an emotional label is fairly extensive – say, incorporating somatic, arousal, autonomic, affective, perceptual, and cognitive aspects of experience – the range of neurophysiological entrainments may include structures from all three of MacLean's ''brains.'' These entrainments might include the phylogenetically ''reptilian'' autonomic, proprioceptive, interoceptive, reticular activating, and endocrine systems, as well as ''old mammalian'' midbrain and limbic structures such as the cingulum and external capsule (which are connected to virtually all areas of neocortex), and ''new mammalian'' higher cortical systems (prefrontal poles, inferior temporal lobe, etc.) mediating the experience of sensory objects, expression, memory, and intentionality (see Heath 1986:7–8).

It appears to be true that the more phylogenetically archaic the neurophysiological system – say, in the ''reptilian'' brain – the less varied will be its development across individuals and across cultures. By the same token, the more phylogenetically recent the system – say, in the ''old'' or ''new mammalian'' brains – the more variation may occur during development. This means that how cross-culturally variant an emotion appears will depend in part upon which level of neurocognitive functioning one is referring to as ''emotion'' (see Wierzbicka 1986 on cultural variation). The somatic, autonomic, arousal, and endocrine functions mediating the mood element of ''depression,'' for example, will vary little other than in intensity of sensation cross-culturally,[6] whereas the cognitive and perceptual associations entrained to these lower functions that are associated with the interpretive aspects of ''depression'' may vary greatly (i.e., what one is ''depressed about''; see Kleinman and Good 1989).

Gellhorn's model

We have found that the most useful neuropsychological model of emotion from an anthropological point of view is Ernst Gellhorn's theory of autonomic-somatic integration (Gellhorn 1967; Gellhorn and Loofbourrow 1963; see Lex 1979 for a summary).[7] According to Gellhorn's model, the somatic system that controls emotion is comprised of two complementary (sometimes antagonistic) systems, each of which entrains functions located at every level of the nervous system. In other words, each of Gellhorn's two energy systems cross-cuts each of MacLean's three "brains." One system is called the *ergotropic system* and the other the *trophotropic system*. Let us briefly describe each system.

The ergotropic system

The ergotropic system subserves our so-called fight or flight responses. That is, the ergotropic system is comprised of all the neural networks at every level of our nervous system (from the cortex on down) that mediate our adaptation strategies relative to desirable or noxious stimuli in the environment. Anatomically, the ergotropic system incorporates the functions of the sympathetic nervous system (one half of the autonomic nervous system), certain of the endocrine glands, portions of the reticular activating system in the brain stem, the posterior hypothalamus, and portions of the limbic system and frontal cortex. The principal function of the ergotropic system is the control of short-range, moment-by-moment adaptation to events in the environment. The system is designed to come into play when the possibility of responding to stimuli arises. It is so constructed as to shunt the body's metabolic energy away from long-range developmental activities (like tissue reconstruction, digestion, etc.) and into carrying out action in the world directed either at acquisition or avoidance of stimuli of interest to the organism.

Under generalized ergotropic arousal a number of organic responses may be experienced, including shivering, constriction of the surface veins and capillaries (paling of the skin), dilation of the pupil of the eye, increased heart rate and blood pressure, increased muscle tension, decreased salivation ("dry mouthed"), constriction of the throat, increased rate of respiration, erection of body hair ("hair standing on end"), and desynchronization of cortical EEG patterns (indicating disordered or disharmonic cortical functioning). These responses, all of which subserve adaptation in one way or another, are commonly associated in experience with positive (say, lust or excitement) or negative (say, fear or revulsion) affect. Objects or events associated with responses will typically be perceived as desirable or undesirable, attractive or repulsive, friendly or hostile, beautiful or ugly. The ergotropic system prepares the organism to obtain objects (like food, water, or a mate) required for the continued survival of the organism or species, and to avoid objects (like poisons, dicey situations, and predators) dangerous to survival. A fundamental problem in nature is how to eat without being eaten. The ergotropic system in humans is the product of millions of years of selection for neurognosis that solves that problem.

The trophotropic system

The trophotropic system is far less dramatic in its activities, but is none the less the system responsible for regulating the vegetative functions, such as reconstruction and growth of cells, digestion, relaxation, sleep, and so on. Again, the trophotropic system includes structures at every level of the nervous system from the neocortex on down. More specifically, the trophotropic system incorporates the functions of the parasympathetic system (the other half of the autonomic nervous system), various endocrine glands, portions of the reticular activating system, the anterior hypothalamus, and portions of the limbic system and frontal cortex. It is the trophotropic system that controls the somatic functions responsible for the long-term well-being, growth, and longevity of the organism. This system operates to maintain the optimal internal balance of bodily functions for continued health and development, both of the body and consequently of the mind.

Under the influence of the trophotropic system, a variety of physical and mental responses may be experienced, like warmth and ''blushing'' at the surface of the body due to release of sympathetic constriction of veins and capillaries, constriction of the pupil of the eye, decreased heart rate and blood pressure, relaxation of tension in the muscles, increased salivation, relaxation of the throat, slowing and deepening of respiration, erection of the penis and clitoris, and synchronization of cortical EEG patterns (indicating harmonized higher cortical functions). Relaxation (reduced arousal) and its concomitants are commonly associated with disinterest in events in the environment, with dispassionate concentration upon some object, or peaceful enjoyment of being. Judgments as to desirability or undesirability of the object are suspended. The relaxed person is typically experiencing a clarity of consciousness, lack of discursive thought and fantasy, and a comfortable, warm, acceptant relationship with the environment. The fundamental function of relaxation is perhaps less obvious than that of ergotropic arousal, but is nonetheless crucial to the survival of the organism. It is mainly during relaxation, and particularly during undisturbed sleep, that the body processes nutrients and resources required by the immune system, and uses these to repair and grow. In other words, when the body is not finding food and avoiding becoming food (ergotropic reactivity), it is reconstructing and developing itself (trophotropic reactivity).

Complementary

The ergotropic and trophotropic systems have often been described as ''antagonistic'' to each other. This means that the increased activity of the one tends to produce a decreased activity in the other. This is the case because

Table 10.1 *A summary of some functions of the trophotropic and ergotropic systems*

Trophotropic System	Ergotropic System
Storage of vital resources	Expenditure of vital resources
Digestion and distribution of nutriments	Digestion stopped
Bronchi leading to lungs constricted and coated with mucus	Bronchi opened
Heart rate and blood pressure reduced	Heart rate and blood pressure increased
Collection of waste by-products	Endocrine system releases chemicals that increase efficiency of muscles
Constricts pupils	Dilates pupils
None	Erection of body hair
Synchronized EEG	Desynchronized EEG
Erection of penis and clitoris	Ejaculation
Increased salivation	Decreased salivation
Respiration slower and deeper	Respiration faster and shallower

each system is physically designed to inhibit the functioning of the other under most circumstances. If a person gets excited about something (angry, anxious, afraid, strongly desirous, etc.) the ergotropic system not only produces the requisite physiological, emotional, and behavioral responses, it also puts a damper on the trophotropic system which was previously subserving digestion and other metabolic activities. Likewise, when a person relaxes (say, after a heavy meal), the trophotropic system actively dampens the activity of the ergotropic system. A summary of the reciprocal functions of the two systems may be studied in Table 10.1.

The relationship between the two systems would be better described as complementary, rather than antagonistic, for each serves the short and long-range well-being of the organism. It is really a matter of balance of functions, the trophotropic system maintaining the homeostatic balance so necessary for health and growth while the ergotropic system facilitates the moment-to-moment adaptation of the organism to its environment. As such, they are not anatomical mirror images of each other. The ''wiring'' of the ergotropic system is designed to arouse the entire body for potential response to threat. Under normal conditions, when the ergotropic system is activated, the entire body/mind becomes aroused. Properly functioning, it is a turned on/turned off kind of system. By comparison, the trophotropic system is ''wired'' for the fine tuning of organs in relation to each other as the demands of internal maintenance shift and change. Its resources can be activated for one organ or body part, or it can turn on globally as during sleep when the entire skeletal musculature is ''turned off.''

The point to emphasize is that whereas the trophotropic system is designed for continuous activity, the ergotropic system is designed for sporadic activity. We are ''wired'' for short, infrequent bursts of adaptive activity interspersed with relatively longer durations of rest, recuperation, and growth. Prolonged ergotropic reactivity may cause depletion of vital resources stored up by the trophotropic system in various organs, and may cause fatigue, shock, body damage, decline in immune system functions, and, in extreme cases, death (Selye 1956; Antonovsky 1979).

Tuning

The particular balance of ergotropic and trophotropic activities under particular environmental circumstances is susceptible to learning (Thomas 1968; Hofer 1974; L. E. Roberts in Schwartz and Shapiro 1978), and there is evidence that their characteristic balance under stress is established as early as pre- and perinatal life (Grof 1976; Richmond and Lustman 1955; Wenger 1941; Thomas 1968; Chamberlain 1983; Verny 1981). The learned ergotropic–trophotropic balance relative to any environmental stimulus is called *tuning* (Gellhorn 1967: 110ff.). When we say that someone ''gets uptight around authority figures,'' we are referring to a discrete ergotropic–trophotropic tuning relative to people perceived to be in authority. Or when we say that someone ''calmed-out when he got a back-rub,'' we are referring to a different discrete tuning relative to being stroked.

A learned change in the characteristic ergotropic–trophotropic balance relative to a stimulus is called *retuning* (Gellhorn 1967; see also Miller 1969). Events like football games, rock concerts, and combat patrols that previously elicited excitement (ergotropic reactivity) may after retuning be met with a relaxed response (trophotropic reactivity). Some researchers have argued that ritual control of ergotropic–trophotropic balance forms a basis for primitive healing techniques and for evoking alternative phases of consciousness (Gellhorn and Kiely 1972; Lex 1979).

Combining Gellhorn's and MacLean's models

Gellhorn's theory of emotion effectively integrates the human nervous system into a simple, bipolar network of complementary functions subserving the interests of adaptation and internal coordination. MacLean's notion of the triune brain also provides a holistic view of the nervous system, but recognizes the evolutionary emergence of different neural organizations at different levels of processing. Thus it seems to us that it would be interesting to consider emotional states in relation to a model that combines Gellhorn's and MacLean's work within the current understanding of parallel distributed processing leading to unitary consciousness of the lifeworld.

Table 10.2 *Combining Gellhorn's theory of autonomic–somatic integration with MacLean's model of the triune brain*

MacLean's *Triune Brain*	Gellhorn's model: *Trophotropic system*	*Ergotropic system*
New mammalian	Clear consciousness, rumination	Adaptational meaning, planning, conceptualization
Old mammalian	Neutral affect, bliss	Affects, core emotions, facial expressions
Reptilian	Relaxation	Arousal, proclivity to act

In Table 10.2 we show how the two models may be usefully combined, and suggest some of the neurocognitive operations that may be carried out by distributed networks comprising the ergotropic and trophotropic systems at each of the three levels of evolutionary development. Each of the cells could be much elaborated, but this is sufficient we think to give the gist of the idea. An individual or culture may focus on and conceptualize an ''emotion'' that connotes operations in one or more of these cells. But one must keep in mind that these cells are not intended to represent exclusive categories of operation, particularly since most emotional states will be a tuning of more or less ergotropic and more or less trophotropic reactivity. And, of course, there is no really clear-cut division between the levels of the triune brain.

The combined model should be used as a heuristic for evaluating just what neural processes may be indicated in any particular native category of emotion. For example, an individual can refer very specifically to the experience of sympathetic reactivity on the surface of his/her skin as ''bliss'' without inferring anything about what he/she is feeling blissful about.[8] The meaning of ''bliss'' in this instance would refer quite narrowly to activities at the lowest, or ''reptilian'' level of processing. On the other hand, if an individual is asked how they are feeling today, they might answer ''I'm in bliss!'' It is doubtful that they are referring to sensations of bliss on their skin. Instead, they would be using the word ''bliss'' to refer to being very happy, a more global state than the former, and one that involves operations at all three levels of processing. The paramount role of both personal history and culture in determining the meaning of emotional categories and labels relative to the various operations modeled here should be obvious.

Culture, meaning, and emotion

For our present purposes, ''culture'' may be defined as recursively enacted patterns of socially controlled conditioning of ergotropic–trophotropic tuning relative to the demands of environmental circumstances and tradition. The evolutionary roots of culture are to be found, of course, in the flexibility of adaptational entrainments in the early hominid species, a flexibility also evident in the adaptations of living primates and other non-human animals (see Bonner 1980). The part of the brain most responsible for this flexibility is the ''new mammalian'' brain; that is, the neocortex. The natural operation of the nervous system in higher species of mammals is to construct systems of ergotropic–trophotropic entrainment adaptively appropriate to varying environmental situations. Where these situations recur, the patterns of entrainment are reinforced and become relatively static patterns of ''meaning'' produced primarily by neocortical models (see Ogden and Richards 1923:56–57). Using C. H. Waddington's term, neural models become relatively fixed in organization and structure, and thus produce *creodes*; i.e., become regularized, recursive, and predictable in organization, content, function, response, and interaction relative to the object of consciousness (Waddington 1957; see also Piaget 1971, 1985). This is why it is accurate to say that the natural motivation of the human brain is toward an ''effort after meaning,'' rather than an ''effort after truth.''[9] Thus, each moment of consciousness is a unitary field within which sensory form and meaning merge in an exquisitely ordered process of pattern recognition and signification (Gibson 1969; Grossman 1987). This field is renewed in each subsequent moment of consciousness in a fluid stream of form and meaning.[10] And each creode may entrain emotional operations at any or all levels of evolutionary origin.

Culture, in the guise of attitudes, responses, social expectations, meanings, perceptions, images, and interpretations – all mediated by neocortical models – may exercise a tremendous control over the experience of all forms of feeling and emotion. It is well to re-emphasize that enculturation has its greatest influence upon the formation of neocortical models. For example, one might naively presume that the one feeling state that enculturation might not influence would be the experience of pain. Yet numerous studies have demonstrated that one of the best predictors of the experience and response to both acute and chronic pain is cultural identity (Zborowski 1952; Bates 1987; Bates *et al.* 1993, Pugh 1991). So even with this seemingly most ''kneejerk'' of feelings, enculturation has an influence upon the intensity, response, and interpretation of pain, as well as its causes and appropriate responses, including emotional responses to pain. Indeed, programs for reducing the intensity of chronic pain require that cultural variables be understood and addressed in order to maximize success (Bates *et al.* 1993:110). Again, the experience of pain depends upon the totality of conscious network entrainments, and not just the raw signals from nociceptors interpreted as ''pain.''

We must resist the common temptation to conceive of the object of intention and emotional attribution as being ''out there'' in any objective sense.

Remember, the object of these intentional operations is also provided by the activity of the nervous system and mediated by models that have developed in tandem with the entrained "meanings" that are associated with the object.[11] The focal object is, for the moment, the nexus of cognitive, affective, metabolic, and motor operations for the organism (Neisser 1976: 20ff.).

This intentional coordination of associations with any object of consciousness will always involve ergotropic–trophotropic tuning, regardless of the cultural background of the subject. For instance, there will always be a characteristic level of arousal and of sympathetic–parasympathetic tuning associated with emotional facial expressions (Ekman *et al.* 1983). But whether or not an "emotional" state is recognized by the subject depends upon the cultural tradition involved. For instance, Buddhist psychology considers "feeling" (*vedaṅa*: see Bodhi 1993:80) to be a universal property of all states of consciousness, but the Buddhist system recognizes "neutral" affect, as well as positive and negative affect, as feeling. In other words, when there is neither positive nor negative affect present to consciousness, the Buddhist system still interprets a feeling state to be present. By contrast, Euro-American cultures tend to recognize emotion only when there is a positive or a negative affect discernable to consciousness.

Simple and complex entrainments

There appears to be a handful of core emotions, like anger, fear, happiness, surprise, and sadness, that are more or less recognizable from facial expressions and body language across cultures (Ekman *et al.* 1983; Levenson *et al.* 1990; Izard *et al.* 1996), and even across species, as Charles Darwin (1965) recognized in the nineteenth century. But as Heider (1991 and in this volume) has pointed out, mapping different languages onto even these core emotions can prove difficult. A number of cultural factors can intervene to confound the already complex relationship between affect and language.[12]

First, if a culture routinely does not discuss the emotional aspect of experiences, they may fail to have words for some emotions, even though they experience them. Levy (1973, 1984a) has explored this factor in his influential work on emotions in Tahiti where he designated those emotions that are highly elaborated conceptually within any particular culture as "hypercognized" and those on which little or no such emphasis is placed as "hypocognized." Second, natural categories in perception tend to have fuzzy semantic boundaries (see Laughlin 1993a, 1993b on this issue). Thus, in our own culture, the meaning of "love" in the three different semantic contexts, "I love this painting," "I love my son," and "I love my wife," usually refers to three different systems of affective entrainment. Moreover, different cultures may manifest different semantic boundaries for essentially the same emotion, depending upon what perceptual, cognitive and situational contents are associated with the concept (see Fridja *et al.* 1995). And third, the expression of certain negative emotions may be treated as taboo in any specific culture. For instance, among some Inuit groups, the emphasis in interpersonal communication is upon maintaining peace at all costs. People will usually dissemble in order to de-escalate negative confrontations (see Briggs 1970 on the Inupiaq). Here the cultural proscription against the *expression* of negative emotion does not mean that these emotions are not experienced by individuals within a particular culture. As Hollan (1988:58) discovered in his work among the Toraja of Indonesia, where the emotion of anger is also conceptualized in very negative terms and where there is a strict prohibition against any overt display of this feeling, ''the relatively successful [cultural] control of overt hostility and aggression do not mean that the Toraja never become angry.'' In fact, Hollan points out that the Toraja do indeed experience anger but the discrepancy between the feeling of anger and the culturally mediated negative interpretation is mitigated by an individual's ability to perform strategies of emotional management similar to those methods that were described by the sociologist Arlie Hochschild as ''emotion work''[13] (Hollan 1992:59).

There also seem to be other emotions that involve a much more complex system of entrainment – that is, a more complex linkage among cognitive, affective, and somatic functions – and may thus appear to be even more culturally variant. An example of a complex emotion having great cultural variation is humiliation. The complex affective associations attending humiliation may range from anger to despair, depending upon cultural conditions and personal development (Miller 1993:159–161), and thus manifest tremendous variation in experience, expression, and language cross-culturally.

To give a more culturally specific example, among the Navajo with whom Laughlin has lived, the ''core'' emotions are expressed in fairly straightforward terms; e.g. ''to become fearful,'' *násdzid*, ''to become angry,'' *bá háchi*, ''sadness,'' *ch'íínáíí*, etc. But the closest one can get to expressing ''ecstasy'' is the word *adiniitła*, which also may be used to connote ''hysteria,'' ''convulsion,'' and ''fit'' in various contexts. And even with words connoting the ''core'' emotions, other connotations may be dragged into the gloss. The word usually used by Navajo to express ''joy,'' or ''happiness,'' *ił hózhǫ́* has an enormous range of connotations. The root meaning of *hózhǫ́* is ''harmony'' or ''beauty'' and is the most important and profoundly ramified concept in the cosmology and the healing system of the Navajo people. Entire books have been written about the concept and its philosophical associations (see e.g., Farella 1984).

Moreover, as mental health workers in Navajo will attest,[14] there is no term that clearly glosses ''depression'' in the Navajo language. Health workers have had to work up a series of questions from which they infer the presence of depression. Phrases like *táadoole'é ho'diił'a* may be used to describe the syndrome, but they only approximate certain aspects of the syndrome – in this case the phrase refers to "something is bothering you." Or there may be recourse to such terms as *ch'íínáí*, "sadness, dejection," which come as close affectively as one can get in the language. In any event, mental health workers have had to be creative in selecting a range of terms that monolingual Navajo clients can apply to describing what they are experiencing.

It is important in terms of a pan-human theory of emotion that we realize that just because the Navajo lack a traditional term that precisely labels a semantic field similar to the English term "depression" does not mean that they do not experience depression (see Kleinman and Good 1989 for various positions relative to this issue). They do indeed experience depression, as well as the sequelae of depression – alcohol abuse and suicide. They simply do not categorize the various aspects of the syndrome in the way we do in English, and they are traditionally reticent when speaking about emotional aspects of their experience, especially negative emotions associated with unhappiness.

It may be helpful to thus understand human emotions as ranging experientially along a spectrum in which there are focal points of "discrete emotions" that are separated from one another by "fuzzy boundaries." As the developmental psychologist Paul Harris has noted, by envisioning emotional experience as a spectrum "we can reasonably conclude that the terms of different languages do pick out the same focal points of landmarks within that spectrum, and [that] they vary in the extent to which they differentiate some local area of the spectrum" (1995:353). Support for the notion of a spectrum of emotional experience can further be found in the work of Levy (1984b:409) who has drawn some important comparisons to Berlin and Kay's (1969) work on the color spectrum, and similarly in the much earlier work of Hildred Geertz who has expressed an analogous idea in her assertion that, "In the course of the growth of a given person, this potential range of [universal] emotional experience becomes narrowed, and out of it certain qualitative aspects are socially selected, elaborated, and emphasized" (1959:225).

Emotion, ritual, and facial feedback theory

It seems to us to be commonsense to think of emotional expression as internally generated and externally expressed (through posture, body language, and facial expressions). And this is the case when the emotional expression is being initiated from internal affective processes that are eventually entrained to, and expressed by, somatic systems. However, it is important to understand that neural pathways are now known to be reciprocal in the nervous system, and the causation of emotion may be upon occasion in the opposite direction.

That is, somatic systems may in certain circumstances evoke affective systems. This is an important consideration with respect to the question of how ritual activities may produce the emotional aspects of intended states of consciousness – a question that came to interest Gellhorn toward the end of his life (Gellhorn and Kiely 1972).

One of the more intriguing and controversial theories relating affect and facial expression is the so-called facial feedback hypothesis (see Ekman *et al.* 1972; Tomkins 1982). According to this view, responses of the facial musculature to stimuli in the world may actually penetrate to and evoke the systems controlling affect, rather than affect as an initial visceral response being a bit later expressed by the face. If true, the facial feedback hypothesis could account for a number of ritual phenomena of interest to those studying performance, especially those performances involving the wearing of masks (see Young-Laughlin and Laughlin 1988; Webber *et al* 1983). Elements in ritual such as wearing masks, dancing, undergoing ordeals, ingesting psychotropic substances, and the like, may operate as drivers that eventually produce the socially desired emotional state in the participant.

This also may help us to understand the emphasis placed in many cultures upon developing proper posture, facial expression, and behavioral repertoire preparatory to realizing the extraordinary states of consciousness – including affect – with which the postures, etc., are culturally associated. For instance, this emphasis upon body posture and facial expression is common to both Hindu and Buddhist Tantric yoga techniques. Other examples can be found in the exaggerated facial expressions practised in Western clowning and Japanese Kabuki theater, practices requiring the painting of the face into a mask in such a way that expressions are controlled by facial musculature.

We are not endorsing the more extreme forms of the facial feedback hypothesis (see Buck 1980), but rather are suggesting that affective, as well as perceptual, cognitive, and other neuroendocrine systems may be entrained from both the "inside-out" and the "outside-in." We suspect that, in some situations, affect is evoked by facial musculature, and in other situations, facial expression is an expression of affective systems.

Development and emotions

As we have seen, neurognosis develops. There are undoubtedly core emotions in the neurognostic repertoire of the human brain. But, as we have also seen, the conscious network may consist of relatively simple or relatively complex systems of entrainment. Just how complex a particular pattern of entrainment may be depends upon many factors influencing the development of the individual, including early pre- and perinatal factors (Laughlin 1991), enculturation, routinization of emotionally laden circumstances, conditioning relative to particular objects, spiritual motivation, etc.

The development of the cognized environment is usually uneven[15] and patchy with some systems remaining relatively open and growing while other systems become creodes and closed to further development. Emotionally traumatized creodes are the classic example of arrested development where certain objects become associated with intense negative affect and arousal early in childhood and remain so thereafter, unless reopened by some kind of therapeutic experience. Phobic reactions to certain objects or experiences provide another example of arrested development.

But these are merely extreme examples of arrested development. Most emotional development becomes "arrested" after some point in development and relatively closed to further growth. Most of our emotions become bound up in creodes. We thus become fairly predictable in our emotional responses to particular objects and events (i.e., our emotional reaction to loved ones, a Wagnerian leitmotif, domestic disorder, red sports cars, etc.). Yet there is always the possibility of opening up emotional creodes to growth and change. Traumas and phobias can be "cured" and new emotional entrainments may become established under a new developmental regimen. After all, our neural networks are living tissues, not mechanical microchips, and new entrainments may be established under the right therapeutic conditions.

Development of higher emotion

Many of the world's spiritual traditions explicitly target emotional creodes for further development. Some clearly distinguish between "lower" and "higher" emotion – that is, between mundane emotional states and emotional states associated with, or conducive to, higher knowledge. For example, Buddhist psychology teaches that maturing self-awareness is a process that begins with awareness of the body (*kāyanusati*; *kāya* = "body" and *sati* = "awareness"), progresses through awareness of feeling or emotion (*vedanānusati*; *vedanā* = "feeling"), and on to more advanced levels of awareness (Bhikkhu Bodhi 1993:80). "Feeling" is considered to be an attribute (*cetasika*) universal to all states of consciousness. But, as was pointed out above, this is because "neutral" feeling is included as an emotional state.

More mature states of awareness in Buddhist contemplation require that the practitioner cultivate a quality of consciousness termed "equanimity" or "one-pointedness" (*ekaggatā*), a state that may be learned through the practice of loving-kindness (*mettā*; see Bhikkhu Bodhi 1993:89; Laughlin 1985).[16] The state of consciousness characterized by equanimity is one in which both positive and negative emotional reactions to objects of consciousness have been transcended. One learns to simply "watch" whatever arises before the mind without emotionally reacting to things. This is considered the requisite state of mind from which to access still more mature states of consciousness, as well as the eventual realization of *nirvāna*.

Creative activity and insights of all kinds are often, if not always, accompanied by positive affect (Hadamard 1945; Ommaya 1993). In Laughlin's own personal experience, the attainment of intuitive insights, whether they be realized during meditation or during the pursuit of intellectual problems, are often accompanied by bliss states of various intensity (sometimes with the intensity of full-blown ecstasy). In this regard, Ayub Ommaya (1993:15) notes the importance of the research done by Marcus Raichle (1992) using PET scans and showing that novel speech acts are accompanied by limbic system activity, while redundant speech acts are not. This demonstrates the intimate involvement of limbic-affective components in creative operations and activities. Those who are in touch with their creative faculties know that, no matter what their field of endeavor, there is an aesthetic-emotional quality that permeates the creative act, or the apprehension of a creative solution.

What we mean to suggest here is that, because the limbic system so thoroughly and reciprocally connects with virtually the entire neocortex of the human brain, the range of entrainments of "emotional" states is virtually unlimited. Affective qualities will often permeate the conscious network, and how these affects are experienced, and perhaps expressed, will be shaped by the pattern of entrainment in which they arise. And as the conscious network develops – that is, as the set of possible entrainments comprising conscious network develop – so too will the limbic and other systems mediating the emotions develop. The more mature the consciousness, the more mature will be the emotions experienced by that consciousness. Thus, linguistic categories of emotion in any language will typically have very fuzzy semantic boundaries indeed.

And in societies in which advanced states of consciousness are sought, a considerable range of affects may be labeled by a single term. For instance, in the Navajo quest for the realization of "beauty" (*hózhǫ́*), one person using the term may simply mean they are feeling happy while another person may be reporting that they are feeling well after a bout of sickness, and yet another person may be expressing their realization of an advanced state of totality and flow (see Csikskentmihalyi 1975; Turner 1979:154; Laughlin *et al.* 1990: 299–300). Indeed, unless the culture specifically provides distinct labels for advanced states of emotional maturity, as is the case for Buddhist psychology, in all likelihood the native terms will carry a considerable semantic load, perhaps connoting a range of emotional entrainments from the most immature to the most mature known to that culture. Consider the fact that in English the term "love" can connote a range of feeling states from infantile infatuation, through "unconditional positive regard," to saintly compassion.

Discussion

What we have done in this chapter is sketch the outlines of an entrainment model of emotion which allows us to move past the simplistic formulations of the universalist–constructivist polarity. While acknowledging the universality of certain core emotions, we nonetheless have shown that from a neuropsychological point of view there can be no such thing as an emotion that does not involve developmentally flexible structures of the nervous system. We have also suggested that emotions are not always expressible in any particular natural language, and that there exists a range of maturity in the development of emotional states that may or may not be clearly distinguished by a culture's semantic categories.

We have emphasized the importance of the fact that all emotions are ultimately rooted in the neurognostic structure of the nervous system. The models of Ernst Gellhorn and Paul MacLean have been combined to form a matrix for distinguishing the various parallel distributed processes that may be mediating states we call "emotion." It is perhaps easier to see from this matrix that emotional neurognosis is the reason why we anthropologists feel that we are able to so easily comprehend and share most of the emotional experiences had by our hosts in other cultures. Neurognosis is also the reason why we can empathize with what other animals are feeling, and why animals of different species can correctly interpret the emotional content of each other's body posture, facial expressions, and communications (see Masson and McCarthy 1995 on this issue). And the more the emotion involves older mammalian and reptilian level processing, the more easily may these affects and their expressions be interpreted. As any clinician knows, if a client is video-taped during a psychotherapy session, and the tape is later played with the sound turned off, the clinician may more accurately determine what the underlying emotional state of the client is, than if the clinician only pays attention to what the client is saying.

Where our interpretation of other peoples' emotions may be significantly erroneous is in situations in which entrainment of new mammalian, higher cortical modeling provides a major component of the experience. These are the processes that are associated primarily with the meaning content of emotion.[17] Processes at this level – especially those involving prefrontal cortical processing – are the most susceptible to enculturative influence. Those at the phylogenetically older, or "reptilian" and "old mammalian" (limbic, midbrain, autonomic, endocrinological, and metabolic) levels are involved in the more primitive, non-cognitive aspects of emotion and are much less susceptible to cultural variation. We have suggested that how universal or culturally relative an emotion appears to be in any particular culture depends upon how ramified are the processes included within the semantic field of the cultural label.

This biogenetic structural perspective also has a lot to offer the debate over the existence of so-called "culture-bound syndromes" (Simons and Hughes 1985). These are forms of psychopathology that occasionally appear to be culture-specific. These syndromes include such exotic behaviors as the running *amok* and killing people in Malaysia and other South Pacific cultures, or the *pibloktoq*, or "arctic hysteria," among the peoples living in the far north. And, of course, these syndromes include emotional attributes in both their cultural and their psychiatric definitions.

But as Hughes (1990:142) has noted, just how unique a syndrome appears depends upon the level of abstraction at which the concept of the disorder is considered. It is clear from a study of these disorders that there are no affects that are unique to the particular cultures involved. Rather, it is the details of the behavioral complex and the meaning associated with the behaviors that appear so exotic. For example, Malay people seem to suffer from an anxiety-related syndrome they term *latah* (Kenny 1978). The *latahs* are usually older females known to become very agitated when repeatedly startled, and appear to go into a trance-like state. The *latah* is a recognized social role in Malay society[18] and on the surface seems to be quite unique. But on closer scrutiny we find that people in other societies vary in their susceptibility to the startle response (Grillon *et al.* 1993) and the only thing that is unique about the Malay *latah* is the cultural coding of susceptible individuals, and perhaps the acting out of cultural expectations (Simons 1985).

Another example may be found in the *malgri* syndrome of the Lardil peoples who inhabit Mornington Island off Queensland, Australia (Cawte 1974). The Lardil make a clear distinction between things having to do with the sea and things having to do with the land. They exhibit intense anxiety – a virtual paranoia – about being attacked by spirits called *malgri.* The spirits will attack if a person enters the sea with something on their bodies associated with land, and vice versa. All considered, this is a classic culture-bound syndrome, for no one other than Lardil are afraid of *malgri* spirits. Most of us would feel no anxiety about dipping our hands into a pool of fresh water without first making sure no salt water was on our hands. Yet the anxiety the Lardil feel is presumably the same affect as one of us might feel about touching a snake or getting too close to a precipice. What is "culture-bound" is the whole bundle of entrainments mediating the total experience of the syndrome.

Our entrainment view of emotion is also in keeping with current evidence regarding the physiology of anxiety and fear. Joseph E. LeDoux of New York University (1986, 1989) has shown that the network producing fear and anxiety involves the lateral nucleus of the amygdala, a body of tissue lying near each of the poles of the temporal lobes that are connected by large tracts to other areas of the limbic system and to the sensory and prefrontal cortex, and that have long been known to be associated with fear and rage. These areas receive stimulation from the sensory areas directly, and interact with many other areas of the cortex and subcortical centers. But they do not require higher cortical inputs in order to initiate emotion-related responses. Michael Davis of Yale University School of Medicine (1992, 1993; Kim and Davis 1993) has shown that the amygdala is connected directly to the brain stem and may initiate startle and other anxiety related actions independent of cortical inputs. Moreover, damage to relevant amygdaloid nuclei will suppress anxiety and related responses.

Conclusion

In conclusion, one of the major methodological problems facing the ethnology of emotion is the lack of self-awareness of many ethnographers. Ethnographers are often unable to discern the various nuances and combinations of arousal, affect, body activity, imagination, and cognition that make up their own emotional experiences. They may thus be poorly prepared to comprehend the emotional experiences of their hosts and informants. We believe that the very best grounding for understanding the complexity of emotion is a neurophenomenological approach;[19] that is, an approach that combines mature self-awareness with an understanding of how the nervous system works. The problem with ethnological treatments of emotion cross-culturally is that ethnographers often have no direct access to the native's experience of emotion, and thus they tend to overinflate the importance of the semantic analysis of language. And of course this strategy biases the results of research to the products of higher cortical activity.

We can think of no better example of this exaggeration of affective distinction than the decades-long debate, begun originally by Margaret Mead and Ruth Benedict, over whether cultures may be clearly distinguished into shame or guilt cultures (see Creighton 1990). And of course the Navajo have been construed as a textbook example of a ''shame culture'' (Leighton and Kluckhohn 1948). According to the shame *vs.* guilt theory claim, negative feelings about doing something wrong only arise for the Navajo relative to social relations, and only if other people find out what they have done – this as opposed to people in a ''guilt culture'' where the focus of negative feeling is supposedly on the individual identity, so that one feels one has failed one's own internalized expectations, whether or not other people know about the wrong doing.

Shame and guilt of course are Euro-American concepts that have been neatly dichotomized and projected onto other cultures whole cloth. The fact of the matter is, if Laughlin's friends in Navajoland are any evidence, Navajos are indeed a very socially oriented people and will feel intense shame if they have been publicly caught-out doing something wrong. If they speak about it, they might say something like *baa yá nísin*, ''I feel ashamed (or humiliated)'' (shame = *yá,* feel = *nísin*). But this does not mean that Navajos do not also experience an internalized self-blame corresponding to Mead and Benedict's definition of guilt.[20] They certainly do. There is no Navajo term that cleanly glosses as ''guilt,'' but they may speak in terms of something that is lodged in their minds and weighs them down, perhaps even making them sick. For example, one may say *baa shíni' dah si'ą́,* which approximately means ''it's about something that is sitting (or positioned) like a solid object on (or in) my mind'' (Johnson Dennison, personal communication).[21] Moreover, healing in Navajo understanding commonly involves the patient becoming aware of their ''guilt'' – of the weighty blame, memory, and associated negative feelings in their mind – and transforming the ''guilt'' into something akin to Mead and Benedict's view of shame. With the acknowledgment of the wrong doing in a more public way, say between the patient and the medicine man, the guilty feelings can be alleviated and healed, perhaps in conjunction with a healing ceremony.

Our hunch is that those theorists who insist upon an extreme dichotomy between pure shame and guilt cultural types are trapped by what might be called ''etic-itis'' – the temptation to let our theoretical constructs run away with us and dominate our empirical exploration of complex human nature. They also appear to have an inability to parse the various levels of neuropsychological structures that are mediating the complex experiences that become conceptualized as an emotion. This is why our group has long advocated training ethnographers in phenomenological methods. An ethnographer who has attained mature self-awareness will be capable of the kind of phenomenological parsing[22] required to realize the various levels of experience grouped within concepts of emotion. He or she will know from direct experience the actual role that higher cortical imagery, conceptual, and linguistic operations play in their experience of emotion. They will not be fooled by theories that, for example, naively claim that emotions are the byproducts of language – views incidentally that also tend to deny that pre-linguistic infants, or fetuses, as well as non-human animals have emotional experiences (see Laughlin 1991; Laughlin and Spack 1994; Masson and McCarthy 1995 on this issue).

In any event, we hope that we have successfully made the case for an entrainment model of emotion. Emotional states may be initiated from any of a number of sites – from expression and posture, from generalized arousal, from deep limbic nuclei, from perceptual or cognitive cortex, and from the environment via the senses. Moreover, because consciousness is essentially intentional, the affective aspects of emotion can combine with sensory and cognitive-interpretive processing such that states of consciousness are experienced in which affect and meaning merge in a field of experiential totality.

An adequate anthropology of emotion should be sufficiently versed in the relevant fields of developmental psychology and neuroscience, as well as show some cognizance of the transpersonal aspects of emotion. Failure to recognize the developmental dimension of emotion can lead to simplistic, ''hard-wired,'' universalistic notions of emotion, while failure to appreciate the intricate complexity of the neurophysiology of emotion may lead to the unrealistically extreme, cultural-relativistic views of constructivism. And inclusion of a transpersonal perspective allows us to form a picture of the full range of human emotion from the most infantile to the most enlightened of human beings, and the reflection of this range of emotion in various cultural traditions.

NOTES

1. ''Consciousness'' and its constituent processes are considered a subset of ''mind.'' There are mental faculties that operate unconsciously, but all conscious operations are also mental operations
2. The concept of the lifeworld, or *Lebenswelt*, originated with the last major work of Edmund Husserl (1970: 103–189), and was later developed in works by Merleau-Ponty (1964), and Schutz (Schutz and Luckmann 1473, 1989; see Spiegelberg 1982: 144). It means the ''reality that is lived,'' including knowledge about the world that is pregiven in experience.
3. In this chapter we are treating pain as an emotion, even though some people in Euro-American culture would exclude pain. This exclusion is more cultural than real, and it makes both biological and cross-cultural sense to include pain in our deliberations.
4. We are indebted to Roy Rappaport (1968) for the concepts of cognized and operational environments. It is clear from Rappaport's (1979:97–144, 1984:337–352) later writings that the meanings we have constructed for these terms are even closer to his thinking than we initially thought. We originally interpreted him as simply equating cognized environment with the native worldview and the operational environment with the world as viewed by science. And, of course, we consider scientific views of the world as also being cognized environments. Rappaport's (personal communication, May, 1993) thinking, does not differ from this view. For our own development of these crucial concepts, see Laughlin and Brady (1978:6), d'Aguili *et al.* (1979:12ff.), Rubinstein *et al.* (1984:21ff.), and Laughlin *et al.* (1990:82–90). An important link can also be made between the concept of cognized environment and Irving Hallowell's (1955) much earlier notion of a ''behavioral environment'' which he described as that environment the individual actually experiences (i.e., perceives, feels, and acts in) as distinguished from the physical or geographical environment which according to some Western thought exists as a separate reality distinct from human perception, feeling, and action. For Hallowell, the behavioral environment is thus ''the world of the individual as experienced by him [her] and in terms of which he [she] thinks, is motivated to act, and satisfies his [her] needs'' (1955:88).

5. James' theory of emotion is based on the view that it is the *feeling* of bodily changes as they occur in the viscera that contributes most significantly to the experienced emotion (Ellsworth 1994; Myers 1986:331–332). As Gerald Myers points out, for James "an emotion is identical not with bodily changes but with the *feeling* of such changes [as they occur]" (1986:235; emphasis added).
6. This point may well underlie the observations of such scholars as Levy (1984a:223) who assert that while aspects of "emotional feeling" such as intensity certainly vary to some degree from one culture to the next, the "*qualitative* character of the emotional feeling [however] probably has the same shape, the same initial stimulus characteristics [cross-culturally]" (emphasis in original).
7. Gellhorn and his associates worked within the theoretical formulations first outlined by W. R. Hess (1925).
8. Indeed, insight meditators in the Buddhist tradition are taught to isolate such sensations and explore them.
9. We are indebted to Earl W. Count (personal communication) for this distinction which he attributes to I. A. Richards.
10. In the interests of clarity, let us be more explicit about the relationship between "meaning" and "information." Meaning is information that participates in organizing the life-world. Information is the lateral "in-forming" (*à la* Varela 1979), or entrainment of neural networks mediating any regulatory or control function of the nervous system, whether that function participates as meaning or not.
11. Ours is not a solipsistic theory. The object of consciousness may well be "out there" in the environment as a noumenon in the operational environment. We may be interacting with a real object in the world, but that object is still being constituted before consciousness by neural structures.
12. As Fridja *et al.* (1995:126) note, the complex relationship between language and emotion can be at least partially accounted for by the fact that the emotion words of any one particular culture can refer to any combination of a number of different elements of an emotion, including: (1) the eliciting event; (2) individual appraisal – perception of personal or cultural meaning; (3) ensuing affective evaluation; (4) resulting changes in action readiness and body involvement; (5) behaviour; (6) subjective experience – the emotional feeling; and/or (7) individual evaluation of the total reaction.
13. Hochschild's concept of "emotion work" describes the processes by which an individual can consciously shape their feelings to coincide with culturally and socially constructed norms, judgments, and values – what she calls "feeling rules" (1975:287, 1983, 1990). In Hochschild's view then, "emotion work" consists of a conscious process of trying to evoke, shape, as well as suppress, feelings which are experienced as discrepant when compared to the "feeling rules" established in any particular culture (1979:561). In our model "emotion work" can thus be viewed as a conscious process of "retuning."
14. We are indebted to Dr. Phil Summerville and Ms. Linda Torres of the Indian Health Service in Shiprock, New Mexico, for this insight.
15. Jean Piaget (Piaget and Inhelder 1969) referred to this unevenness of development as the presence of *décalages*.
16. This is the Theravadin teaching of the Four Divine Abodes (*Brahma vihāra*). The realization of each abode is sequential, beginning with the full activation of

undifferentiated beneficence (*mettā*), followed by the realization of compassion for the suffering of all beings everywhere (*karuṇā*), then the realization of sympathetic joy for the growth and well-being of all beings everywhere (*muditā*), and then the balance of both compassion and joy producing the state of equanimity (*ekeggatā*). It is said that without realization of these states, the realization of liberation is impossible. Note that this entire practice involves learning new and more mature emotional states.

17. There may indeed be culturally labelled ''emotions'' that are so heavily mediated by higher cortical processes that lower level processes are very attenuated. This is what William James might have been getting at when he referred to the ''subtler emotions''; i.e., aesthetic feelings, and some types of bliss. This is an interesting hypothesis, but as far as we are aware, there are as yet no neuropsychological data to support the idea.
18. Ronald Simons has produced a movie of this syndrome entitled ''Latah: A Culture-Specific Elaboration of the Startle Reflex.''
19. See Laughlin *et al.* (1990:24–33) for a discussion of ''mature contemplation'' and its possible role in ethnography.
20. While Mead and Benedict distinguished between shame and guilt as external and internal sanctions respectively, an important theoretical shift took place in the early 1950s in redefining shame and guilt toward a psychoanalytic perspective that directly contradicted and later effectively replaced Mead and Benedict's earlier views (see Lebra 1971:242; Caims 1993; Creighton 1990). Engineered by Piers and Singer (1953), this ''new'' theoretical shift understood both shame and guilt as equally internalized forms of self-blame. For Piers and Singer, guilt was thought to be tied to transgressions caused by ''id'' impulses resulting in a dissonance between the ego and the functioning super-ego, while shame was seen as connected to personal shortcomings and the failure to reach goals presented by the ego-ideal (1953:23–24). In the discipline of psychology, Piers and Singer's revolutionary formulation was expanded upon in a much heralded work by Helen Block Lewis (1971) who argued that shame and guilt can not only be distinguished structurally but also phenomenologically. According to Lewis, even though both shame and guilt are ultimately registered as experiences of the self, a major phenomenological difference between the two emotions is that in shame it is the ''whole self'' that is the primary focus of evaluation while in guilt it is not the ''self itself'' but the acts or behaviors attributed to the self that are focused upon (1971:30, 40). More recently this theoretical position is perhaps best viewed in the work of Michael Lewis who, building on both Piers and Singer and Helen Block Lewis, understands guilt to be a perceived failure resulting from the violation of standards and ensuing ''self-blame'' that is focused on specific actions of the self, while shame is in contrast a perceived failure resulting from the violation of standards and ensuing ''itself-blame'' that is focused on the ''whole self'' (1992:65–72).
21. *Baa shíni' dah si'ą́* literally means ''concerning an elevated solid object sitting (or hanging, or positioned) in my mind'' where *baa* means ''about'' or ''concerning,'' *shíni'* means ''my mind,'' *dah* means ''up, at an elevation above the surface of the ground,'' and *si ą́* means ''it (a rock, hat, mountain, house, or other solid object) sits, lies, or is in position'' (Johnson Dennison, personal communication). Hence, the connotation of the phrase is approximately ''it's

about something weighing heavily on (or in) my mind.'' The Navajo concept of mind is one of an experiential space which is located in the body, and which is dynamic and associated with the concept of ''wind'' (see McNeley 1981). Thus, ''guilt'' is the experience of negative feelings weighing down the mind over a significant period of time.

22. Edmund Husserl used the term ''reduction'' for this kind of parsing.

References

Antonovsky, A. 1979. *Health, stress, and coping*. San Francisco: Jossey-Bass.

Bates, Maryann S. 1987. Ethnicity and pain: a biocultural model. *Social Science and Medicine* 24(1):47–50.

Bates, Maryann S., W. Thomas Edwards, and Karen O. Anderson. 1993. Ethnocultural influences on variation in chronic pain perception. *Pain* 52:101–112.

Berlin, B. and P. Kay. 1969. *Basic color terms: Their universality and evolution.* Berkeley: University of California Press.

Besnier, Niko. 1990. Language and affect. In Berbard J. Siegle, Alan R. Beals, and Stephen A. Tyler, eds., *Annual Review of Anthropology* 19:419–451. Palo Alto, CA: Annual Review Inc.

Biederman, Irving. 1987. Recognition-by-components: a theory of human image understanding. *Psychological Review* 94(2):115–147.

Bodhi, Bhikkhu. 1993. *A comprehensive manual of Abhidhamma (The Abhidhammattha Sangaha of Acariya Anuruddha).* Kandy, Sri Lanka: Buddhist Publication Society.

Bonner, J. T. 1980. *The evolution of culture in animals.* Princeton, NJ: Princeton University Press.

Briggs, J. 1970. *Never in anger*. Cambridge, MA: Harvard University Press.

Buck, R. 1980. Nonverbal behavior and the theory of emotion: The facial feedback hypothesis. *Journal of Personality and Social Psychology* 38:811–824.

Bunge, M. 1980. *The mind–body problem: A psychobiological approach.* Oxford: Pergamon.

Cairns, Douglas L. 1993. *Aidos*. New York: Clarendon Press.

Cawte, John. 1974. *Medicine is the law*. Honolulu: University Press of Hawaii.

Chamberlain, David B. 1983. Consciousness at birth. A review of the literature obtainable from Chamberlain Communication, 5164 35th Street, San Diego, CA 92116.

Changeux, Jean-Pierre. 1985. *Neuronal man: The biology of mind.* Oxford: Oxford University Press.

Creighton, Millie. 1990. Revisiting shame and guilt cultures. *Ethos* 18:279–307.

Csikskentmihalyi, M. 1975. *Beyond boredom and anxiety*. San Francisco: Jossey-Bass.

D'Aquili, Eugene G., Charles D. Laughlin, and John McManus, eds. 1979. *The spectrum of ritual.* New York: Columbia University Press.

Darwin, Charles. 1965. *The expression of the emotions in man and animals.* Chicago: University of Chicago Press.

Davis, Michael. 1992. The role of the amygdala in fear and anxiety. *Annual Review of Neuroscience* 15:353–375.

1993. Fear-potentiated startle: A neural and pharmacological analysis. *Behavioral Brain Research* 58(1–2):175–198.

Eccles, John C. 1989. *Evolution of the brain: Creation of the self.* New York: Routledge.

Edelman, Gerald M. 1987. *Neural Darwinism: The theory of neuronal group selection.* New York: Basic Books.

Edelman, Gerald M. and Vernon B. Mountcastle. 1982. *The mindful brain: Cortical organization and the group selective theory of higher brain function.* Cambridge, MA: MIT Press.

Ekman, Paul. 1994. *The nature of emotion: Fundamental questions.* New York: Oxford.

Ekman, Paul, ed. 1982. *Emotion in the human face.* 2nd ed. Cambridge: Cambridge University Press.

Ekman, Paul, Wallace V. Friesen, and P. O. Ellsworth. 1972. *Emotion in the human face.* New York: Pergamon.

Ekman, Paul, Robert W. Levenson, and Wallace V. Friesen. 1983. Autonomic nervous system activity distinguishes among emotions. *Science* 221:1208–1210.

Ellsworth, Phoebe C. 1994. William James and emotion: Is a century of fame worth a century of misunderstanding? *Psychological Review* 101(2):222–229.

Elster, Jon. 1984. *Ulysses and the sirens.* Cambridge: Cambridge University Press.

Farella, John R. 1984. *The main stalk: A synthesis of Navajo philosophy.* Tucson, AZ: University of Arizona Press.

Frijda, N. H., S. Markam, K. Sato, and W. Reinout. 1995. Emotions and emotion words, 121–143. In J. A. Russell *et al*, eds., *Everyday conceptions of emotion: An introduction to the psychology, anthropology, and linguistics of emotion.* Boston: Kluwer Academic Publishers.

Fuster, J. M. 1980. *The prefrontal cortex: Anatomy, physiology, and neuropsychology of the frontal lobe.* New York: Raven.

Geertz, H. 1959. The vocabulary of emotions: A study of Javanese socialization processes. *Psychiatry* 22:225–236.

Gellhorn, Ernst 1967. *Principles of autonomic-somatic integrations.* Minneapolis: University of Minnesota Press.

Gellhorn, Ernst and W. F. Kiely. 1972. Mystical states of consciousness: Neurophysiological and clinical aspects. *Journal of Nervous and Mental Diseases* 154:399–405.

Gellhorn, Ernst and G. N. Loofbourrow. 1963. *Emotions and emotional disorders.* New York: Harper and Row.

Gibson, E. J. 1969. *Principles of perceptual learning and development.* New York: Appleton-Century-Crafts.

Gray, Jeffrey A. 1982. *The neuropsychology of anxiety: An enquiry into the functions of the septo-hippocampal system.* Oxford: Clarendon Press.

Grillon, Christian, Rezvan Ameli, Michael Foot, and Michael Davis. 1993. Fear-potentiated startle: Relationship to the level of state/trait anxiety in healthy subjects. *Biological Psychiatry* 33(8–9):566–574.

Grof, Stanislov. 1976. *Realms of the human unconscious.* New York: Viking Press.

Grossman, H. 1980. A central processor for hierarchically structured material: Evidence from Broca's aphasia. *Neuropsychologia* 18:299–308.

Gurwitsch, Aron. 1940. On the intentionality of consciousness. In Martin Farber, ed., *Philosophical essays in memory of Edmund Husserl.* Cambridge, MA: Harvard University Press, 65–83.

Hadamard, J. 1945. *The psychology of invention in the mathematical field.* New York: Dover.

Hallowell, A. I. 1955. The self and its behavioral environment. In *Culture and experience.* Philadelphia: University of Pennsylvania Press.

Harris, P. 1995. Developmental constraints on emotion categories. In J. A. Russell *et al.* eds., *Everyday conceptions of emotion: An introduction to the psychology, anthropology, and linguistics of emotion.* Boston: Kluwer Academic Publishers, 353–372.

Heath, Robert G. 1986. The neural substrate for emotion. In Robert Plutchik and Henry Kellerman, eds., *Emotion: Theory, research, and experience.* New York: Academic Press.

Heider, Karl G. 1991. *Landscapes of emotion: Mapping three cultures of emotion in Indonesia.* New York: Cambridge University Press.

Hess, W. R. 1925. *On the relations between psychic and vegetative functions.* Zurich: Schwabe.

Hinton, Alexander Laban. 1993. Prolegomenon to a processual approach to the emotions. *Ethos* 21(3):417–451.

Hochschild, Arlie. 1975. The sociology of feeling and emotion. In Marcial Millman and Rosabeth Moss Kanter, eds., *Another voice: Feminist perspectives on social life and social structure.* Garden City: Doubleday/Anchor, 280–307.

1979. Emotion work, feeling rules, and social structure. *American Journal of Sociology* 85:551–575.

1983. *The managed heart: Commercialization of human feeling.* Berkeley: University of California Press.

1990. Ideology and emotion management: A perspective and path for future research. In Theodore D. Kemper, ed., *Research agendas in the sociology of emotion.* Albany: SUNY Press, 117–142.

Hofer, M. A. 1974. The role of early experience in the development of autonomic regulation. In L. V. DiCara ed., *Limbic and autonomic nervous systems research.* New York: Plenum.

Hollan, Douglas. 1988. Staying "Cool" in Toraja: informal strategies for the management of anger and hostility in a nonviolent society. *Ethos* 16:52–72.

1992. Emotion work and the value of equanimity among the Toraja. *Ethnology* 31:45–56.

Hughes, Charles C. 1990. Ethnopsychiatry. In *Medical anthropology: A handbook of theory and method.* New York: Greenwood, 132–148.

Husserl, Edmund. 1931. *Ideas: General introduction to pure phenomenology.* New York: The Macmillan Company.

1970. *The crisis of European sciences and transcendental phenomenology.* Evanston: Northwestern University Press.

Izard, C. 1980. Cross-cultural perspectives on emotion and emotion communication. In H. Triandis, ed., *Handbook of cross-cultural psychology.* Boston: Allyn and Bacon, 95–126.

1990. The substrates of emotion feelings: William James and current emotion theory. *Personality and Social Psychology Bulletin* 16(4):626–635.

1993. Four systems for emotion activation: Cognitive and noncognitive processes. *Psychological Review* 100:68–90.

Izard, C., L. M. Dougherty, and J. Abe. 1996. Differential emotions theory and emotional development in adulthood and later life. In Carol Magai and Susan H. McFadden, eds., *Handbook of emotion, adult development, and aging*, 27–41. San Diego: Academic Press.

James, William. 1967[1884]. What is an emotion? In Knight Dunlap. ed., *The emotions*. New York: Hafner Publishing Company.

1950[1890]. *The principles of psychology*. New York: Dover Publications.

Kenny, Michael. 1978. Latah: The symbolism of a putative mental disorder. *Culture, Medicine, and Psychiatry* 2:209–223.

Kim, Munsoo and Michael Davis. 1993. Electrolytic lesions of the amygdala block acquisition and expression of fear-potentiated startle even with extensive training but do not prevent reacquisition. *Behavioral Neuroscience* 107(4):580–595.

Kleinman, A. and B. Good. 1989. *Culture and depression: Studies in the anthropology and cross-cultural psychiatry of affect and disorder.* Berkeley: University of California Press.

Laughlin, Charles D. 1985. On the spirit of the gift. *Anthropologica* 27(1–2):137–159.

1991. Pre- and perinatal brain development and enculturation: A biogenetic structural approach. *Human Nature* 2(3):171–213.

1992. *Scientific explanation and the life-world: A biogenetic structural theory of meaning and causation*, Report No. CP-2. Sausalito, CA: Institute of Noetic Sciences.

1993a. Fuzziness and phenomenology in ethnological research: Insights from fuzzy set theory. *Journal of Anthropological Research* 49(1):17–37.

1993b. The fuzzy brain. *Social Neuroscience Bulletin* 6(2):20–21.

1994. Apodicticity: The problem of absolute certainty in transpersonal anthropology. *Anthropology & Humanism* 19(2):1–15.

1996. The properties of neurognosis. *Journal of Social and Evolutionary Systems* 19(4):375–400.

Laughlin, Charles D. and Eugene G. d'Aquili. 1974. *Biogenetic structuralism.* New York: Columbia University Press.

Laughlin, Charles D. and Ivan A. Brady. 1978. *Extinction and survival in human populations.* New York: Columbia University Press.

Laughlin, Charles D. and Tracey Spack. 1994. Animal consciousness: The view from biogenetic structuralism. Paper presented before the Society for the Anthropology of Consciousness, Tempe, AZ.

Laughlin, Charles D., John McManus, and Eugene G. d'Aquili. 1990. *Brain, symbol and experience*. New York: Columbia University Press.

Leavitt, John. 1996. Meaning and feeling in the anthropology of emotions. *American Ethnologist* 23(3):514–539.

Lebra, Takie. 1971. The social mechanism of guilt and shame: The Japanese case. *Anthropological Quarterly* 44:241–255.

LeDoux, Joseph E. 1986. Sensory systems and emotion: a model of affective processing. *Integrative Psychiatry* 4(4):237–243.

1989. Cognitive–emotional interactions in the brain. Special Issue: development of emotion–cognition relations. *Cognition and Emotion* 3(4):267–289.

Leighton, D. and C. Kluckhohn. 1948. *Children of the people: The Navajo individual and his development.* Cambridge: Harvard University Press.

Levensen, Robert W., Paul Ekman, and Wallace V. Friesen. 1990. Voluntary facial action generates emotion-specific autonomic nervous system activity. *Psychophysiology* 27(4):363–384.

Levy, R. I. 1973. *Tahitians: Mind and experience in the Society Island*. Chicago: University of Chicago Press.

1984a. Emotion, knowing, and culture. Pp. 214–237 in R. A Schweder and R. A. LeVine, eds., *Culture theory: Issues on mind, self, and emotion*. Cambridge: Cambridge University Press.

1984b. The emotions in comparative perspective. Pp. 397–412 in K. Scherer and P. Ekman, eds., *Approaches to emotion*. Hillsdale: Erlbaum.

Levy, R. I. and J. C. Wellenkamp, 1989. Methodology in the anthropological study of emotion. In Å. R. Plutchik and H. Kellerman, eds., *Emotion: Theory, research, and experience*. Vol. IV. New York: Academic Press, 205–232.

Lewis, H. B. 1971. *Shame and guilt in neurosis*. New York: International University Press.

Lewis, M. 1992. *Shame: The exposed self*. New York: The Free Press.

Lex, Barbara. 1979. The neurobiology of ritual trance. In E. G. d'Aquili, C. D. Laughlin, and J. McManus, eds., *The Spectrum of Ritual*. New York: Columbia University Press.

Lutz, Catherine and Geoffrey M. White. 1986. The anthropology of emotions. In Bernard J. Siegle, Alan R. Beals, and Stephen A. Tyler, eds., *Annual Review of Anthropology*, Vol. 15. Palo Alto, CA: Annual Review Inc.

Lyon, M. L. 1995. Missing emotion: The limitations of cultural constructionism in the study of emotion. *Cultural Anthropology* 10(2):244–263.

McClelland, J. L. and D. E. Rumelhart, eds. 1986. *Parallel distributed processing, Vol 2: Psychological and biological models*. Cambridge, MA: MIT Press.

MacLean, Paul D. 1973. *A triune concept of the brain and behavior*. Toronto: University of Toronto Press.

McNeley, James K. 1981. *Holy wind in Navajo philosophy*. Tucson, AR: University of Arizona Press.

Masson, Jeffrey Moussaieff and Susan McCarthy. 1995. *When elephants weep: The emotional lives of animals*. New York: Dell Publishing.

Melzack, Ronald. 1992. Phantom limb. *Scientific American* 266(4):120–126.

Merleau-Ponty, Maurice. 1964. *The primacy of perception*. Evanston, IL: Northwestem University Press.

Mesquita, B. and N. H. Frijda. 1992. Cultural variations in emotions: a review. *Psychological Bulletin* 112(2):179–204.

1997. Culture and emotion. In J. W. Berry, P. R. Dasen and T. S. Saraswathi, eds., *Handbook of cross-cultural psychology: Volume 2 – Basic processes and human development*. Boston: Allyn and Bacon, 257–297.

Mesquita, B., N. Frijda, and K. Scherer. 1997. Culture and emotion. In *Handbook of cross-cultural psychology*. Vol II. Boston: Allyn and Bacon.

Miller, N. 1969. Learning of visceral and glandular responses. *Science* 163:439–445.

Miller, William Ian. 1993. *Humiliation*. Ithaca: Cornell University Press.

Myers, G. E. 1986. *William James: His life and thought*. New Haven: Yale University Press.

Nauta, W. J. H. 1973. Neural associations of the frontal cortex. *Acta Neurobiologiae Experimentalis* 32:125–140.

Neisser, Ulric. 1976. *Cognition and reality: Principles and implications of cognitive psychology*. San Francisco: Freeman.

Ogden, C. K. and I. A. Richards. 1923. *The meaning of meaning*, 8th ed. New York: Harcourt Brace Jovanovich.

Ohman, Arne and Niels Birbaumer. 1993. Psychophysiological and cognitive-clinical perspectives on emotion: introduction and overview. In N. Birbaumer and A. Ohman, eds., *The structure of emotion: Psychophysiological, cognitive and clinical aspects*. Seattle: Hogreffe and Huber.

Ommaya, Ayub K. 1993. Emotion and the evolution of neural complexity, Part 2. *WESScom: The Journal of the Washington Evolutionary Systems Society* 31(1):8–17.

Parkinson, B. 1995. *Ideas and realities of emotion.* New York: Routledge.

Piaget, Jean. 1971. *The biology of knowledge.* Chicago: University of Chicago Press.

1985. *The equilibration of cognitive structures.* Chicago: The University of Chicago Press.

Piaget, Jean and B. Inhelder. 1969. *The psychology of the child.* New York: Basic Books.

Piers, G. and M. B. Singer. 1953. *Shame and guilt: A psychoanalytic and a cultural study*. New York: W. W. Norton.

Plutchik, Robert and Henry Kellerman. 1986. *Biological foundations of emotion.* Vol. 3 of *Emotion: Theory, research, and experience*. New York: Academic Press.

Pribram, Karl H. 1981. Emotions, in *Handbook of clinical neuropsychology*, ed. S. K. Filskov and T. J. Boll. New York: Wiley.

Pribram, Karl H. and D. McGuinness. 1975. Arousal, activation, and effort in the control of attention. *Psychological Review* 82:116–149.

Pugh, Judy F. 1991. The semantics of pain. *Culture, medicine and psychiatry* 15:19–43.

Raichle, M. A. 1992. Cortical information processing in the normal human brain. In A. A. Asbury, G. M. McKhan, and I. W. McDonald, eds., *Diseases of the nervous system: Clinical neurobiology*. New York: Saunders.

Rappaport, Roy A. 1968. *Pigs for the ancestors.* New Haven, CT: Yale University Press.

1979. *Ecology, meaning, and religion*. Richmond, CA: North Atlantic Books.

1984. *Pigs for the ancestors*. 2nd ed. New Haven, CT: Yale University Press.

Richmond, J. B. and S. L. Lustman. 1955. Autonomic function in the neonate: I. Implications for psychosomatic theory. *Psychosomatic Medicine* 17: 269ff.

Rubinstein, Robert A., Charles D. Laughlin, and John McManus. 1984. *Science as cognitive process*. Philadelphia: University of Pennsylvania Press.

Rumelhart, D. E. and J. L. McClelland, eds. 1986. *Parallel distributed processing, Vol. 1: Foundations*. Cambridge, MA: MIT Press.

Russell, J.A. 1991. Culture and the categorization of emotions. *Psychological Bulletin* 110(3):426–450.

Schacter, S. and T. E. Singer. 1962. Cognitive, social and physiological determinants of emotional states. *Psychological Review* 69:379–397.

Scherer, Klaus R., ed. 1988 *Facets of emotion: Recent research.* Hillsdale, NJ: Lawrence Erlbaum.

Schutz, Alfred and Thomas Luckmann. 1973. *The structures of the life-world*. Evanston, IL: Northwestern University Press.

1989. *The structures of the life-world:* Vol. II. Evanston, IL: Northwestern University Press.

Schwartz, G. E. and D. Shapiro. 1978. *Consciousness and self-regulation*, Vol. 2. New York: Plenum.

Searle, John R. 1983. *Intentionality: An essay in the philosophy of mind.* Cambridge: Cambridge University Press.

Selye, H. 1956. *The stress of life.* New York: McGraw-Hill.

Shear, Jonathan. 1990. Mystical experience, hermeneutics, and rationality. *International Philosophical Quarterly* 30(4):391–401.

1994. On mystical experience as support for the perennial philosophy. *Journal of the American Academy of Religion.* 62(2):319–42.

Shweder, Richard A. and Robert A. LeVine, eds. 1984. *Culture theory: essays on mind, self, and emotion.* Cambridge: Cambridge University Press.

Simons, Ronald C. 1985. The resolution of the Latah Paradox. In R. Simons and C. Hughes, eds., *The culture-bound syndromes: Folk illnesses of psychiatric and anthropological interest.* Dordrecht: D. Reidel.

Simons, Ronald C. and Charles C. Hughes. 1985. *The culture-bound syndromes: Folk illnesses of psychiatric and anthropological interest.* Dordrecht: D. Reidel.

Skarda, C. A. and W. J. Freeman. 1987. How brains make chaos in order to make sense of the world. *Behavior and Brain Sciences* 10:161–195.

Spiegelberg, Herbert. 1982. *The phenomenological movement: A historical introduction* 3rd ed. The Hague: Martinus Nijhoff.

Spiro, Melford. 1984. Some reflections on cultural determinism and relativism with special reference to emotion and reason. In R. Shweder and R. LeVine, eds., *Culture theory.* Cambridge: Cambridge University Press, 323–346.

1993. On a feminist/constructivist view of emotion. Unpublished manuscript.

Stuss, D. T. and D. F. Benson. 1983. The emotional concomitants of psychosurgery. In Kenneth M. Heilman and Paul Satz, eds., *Neuropsychology of human emotion.* New York: Guilford Press.

1986. *The frontal lobes.* New York: Raven.

Thomas, C. C. 1968. *Early experience and behavior*, Springfield: IL.

Tomkins, S. 1982. Affect theory. In *Emotion in the human face* 2nd ed. by Paul Ekman. Cambridge: Cambridge University Press.

Turner, V. 1979. *Process, performance and pilgrimage.* New Delhi: Concept Publishing 63 House.

Varela, Francisco J. 1979. *Principles of biological autonomy.* New York: Elsevier North Holland.

Verny, T. 1981. *The secret life of the unborn child.* New York: Dell.

Waddington, C. H. 1957. *The strategy of the genes.* London: George Allen and Unwin.

Webber, Mark, Christopher D. Stephens, and Charles D. Laughlin. 1983. Masks: A reexamination, or Masks? You mean they affect the brain? In N. Ross Crumrine and Margorie Halpin, eds., *The Power of symbols.* Vancouver: University of British Columbia Press.

Wenger, M. A. 1941. The measurement of individual differences in autonomic balance. *Psychosomatic Medicine* 3: 427.

Wierzbicka, Anna. 1986. Human emotions: universal or culture-specific? *American Anthropologist* 88:584–594.

Young-Laughlin, Judi and Charles D. Laughlin. 1988. How masks work, or masks work how? *Joumal of Ritual Studies* 2(1):59–86.

Zborowski, M. 1952. Cultural components in response to pain. *Journal of Social Issues* 8:16–30.

Index